DIVERSITIES ESSAYS IN ECONOMCIS SOCILOGY AND OTHER SOCIAL PROBLEMS (1958)

D1880124

Owing to the antiquity and rarity of this book, certain pages are regrettably absent, and readability is compromised due to the blurring of the original text. If you possess any insights regarding the availability of these missing sections, kindly inform us. Your assistance is crucial in ensuring the completion of this significant work for the benefit of future generations.

DIVERSITIES ESSAYS IN ECONOMCIS SOCILOGY AND OTHER SOCIAL PROBLEMS (1958)

D. P. MUKERJI

GYAN

Published by

Gyan Publishing House
5, Ansari Road
Daryaganj, New Delhi-110002
Phone: 011-47034999, 9811692060
E-mail: books@gyanbooks.com

Distribution Network
gyanbooks.com
India, USA, Canada, UK, Australia

© Publisher

All rights reserved. No part of this work may be reproduced, stored, adapted, or transmitted in any form or by any means, electronic, mechanical, photocopying, micro-filming, recording or otherwise, or translated in any language, without the prior written permission of the copyright owner and the publisher.

ISBN: 978-93-7447-845-5 (PB)

First Published, 1958

2nd Impression 2026

Printed at: Gyan Press, Delhi.

The book is sold subject to the condition that it shall not, by way of trade or otherwise, be lent, resold, hired out, or otherwise circulated without the prior publisher's written consent.

DIVERSITIES ESSAYS IN ECONOMCIS SOCILOGY AND OTHER SOCIAL PROBLEMS (1958)

Author: D. P. MUKERJI

Diversities

Diversities

Essays in Economcis
Sociology and Other
Social Problems

D. P. Mukerji

PROFESSOR AND CHAIRMAN, DEPARTMENT OF ECONOMICS
MUSLIM UNIVERSITY, ALIGARH

People's Publishing House

CONTENTS

PART FOUR SOCIAL PROBLEMS OF LITERATURE

PREFACE

A NUMBER OF ARTICLES HAVE BEEN COLLECTED HERE TO FORM *Diversities*. They have been written at various times, but not always on odd occasions. Such continuity as there may be in these articles arises out of our experiences of national struggle and independence and out of my own experience as a student of social sciences.

The articles are classified under four heads. The economic ones are not, however, purely economic. They are a-piece with the wider problems of sociology and include those I had to deal with during the short time of my office as a government servant. I have connected planning with human issues and economics with the study of humanities. The second relates to the philosophy of Indian history, but, as usual, I could not just be a historian in the narrow academic manner. Culture was a wider process than 'historical' scholarship, I had to complete a series of lectures for the Bharatiya Vidya Bhavan, Bombay, on that topic, but it still remains incomplete. The three sections, however, can give a picture of my general view on history and culture. The third is essentially sociological. It tackles a large number of subjects, but they again form one social pattern. Am I wrong to suggest that the overall idea is that of personality in the context of socialism? The ultimate goal of socialism is the association of persons, that is, of free individuals functioning collectively in society and coming out of it as persons. My emphasis on traditions is to be taken in that context. The fourth, and the last, section deals with the social problems of literature. They are in a sense live issues. The article on the sociology of Indian literature was first written at the instance of a friend of Rockefeller Foundation and given shape at the instance of an American professor at the Fisk University, U.S.A. It was lost in transit. I have rescued it with difficulty from the notes of a friend.

Nineteen books of mine, including *Diversities*, have been published, ten in Bengali and nine in English. Bengali friends of mine have ignored the English ones, and non-Bengali friends have not read the Bengali ones. In Bengali, I am taken as one interested in literature and music: in other parts of India, I am treated as a sociologist and an economist. So I have paid the penalty of double allegiance. But I shall like to say that my living has been more or less integral. First books, then ideas, and lastly, experience—that has been my way. It is that of many others, but it is mine also.

There is one more point I want to make. My readers think that my interests are more than one sided, that they are lost in their manifoldness, and that it would have been better if they were limited to one or two. But that is exactly my difficulty. I was trained to think in large terms. It made me look closely into details, but it made me search for the wood behind the trees. My professors, friends and people I have met, made me feel that largeness of the canvas. I could not take anything but a synoptic view. Right from the start I had accepted the synthesis of the social sciences, and it has followed me ever since. Perhaps, my generation is over by now. But if it is not, it may also be that in the following generations specialisations will also go the way of all flesh and they will come to appreciate the way of the unity of all knowing.

I am grateful to the People's Publishing House (Private) Ltd. for bringing together a few of my diverse articles. The publishers have selected the desirable ones among them. But for them they would have lain in the box. I am also grateful to the parties concerned for the opportunities they have given me for the publication of the articles sponsored by them.

6 September 1958 D. P. Mukerji

to kumar

and

saugata

PART ONE

ECONOMICS

An Economic and Social Service : Its Premises and Implications

THE PUBLIC IN INDIA HAS BEEN TRAINED FOR LONG AGAINST bureaucracy. One of the main planks of our national movement has been the opposition to officialdom. Phirozeshah Mehta and Surendranath Banerji had thundered against it, and C. Y. Chintamani was pouring vials of heavy wrath on its head till the other day. The new leadership's anathema was no less strong. In a sense, the impetus behind the silent progress of the voluntary services, so generously reinforced by the Congress under the guidance of Gandhiji, was a positive reaction against bureaucracy. And then the war-controls came with all their corruption, costs, incompetence, incoherence and inconveniences blazing a trail of bitterness. In such a background a plea for the establishment of a new bureaucracy, viz., an economic and social service, is likely to be dismissed without a hearing. Yet individuals and nations have been known to overcome their resistance to institutions and ideas under the pressure of new situations. Nothing was more repugnant to India's history than division; but we have accepted it and are turning it to our purpose by consolidating the States. The so-called imperial services have not been dispensed with: only their immobilities have been reduced and their privileges curtailed. Even the intelligence branch of the police, the hidden hand, retains its usefulness and will probably increase it with public approval if war is declared or witch-hunting begins on a larger scale. Thus does society bow to emergent circumstances. It is not ashamed to create means and instruments that look like old ones to serve fresh and complex ends. In fact, with the acquisition of international status, India is already developing a foreign service.

Eminent authorities have fully discussed the origins and

functions, the pros and cons of bureaucracy. We can do worse than take a leaf out of their knowledge. Their findings are as follows: Bureaucracy is an administrative means to the end of a policy. If properly selected, trained and built up with healthy traditions it becomes a precision instrument. It provides expert information, if not knowledge, through fixed and official jurisdictional areas governed by administrative regulations; it assures stability and regularity of activities recognised as duties to be continuously fulfilled; it is effective by stable and defined distribution of authority to command and to see that command obeyed; and above all, by virtue of its conception of office as 'vocation,' i.e., not as exchange of services for equivalents, it succeeds in regulating affairs in a non-personal, non-specific, objective fashion. The importance of the last point will be apparent if we note that democratic administration is a course of social training in impersonal exercises as constrasted with the autocratic, but human, specific, case-method of the *kazi*. Modern democracy, which has helped the growth of bureaucracy, and often been hindered by it, does not permit a bureaucrat to have personal predilections and loyalties. A modern bureaucrat's allegiance is purely functional; he is neither a vassal nor a disciple. Thereby he makes the caravan move. In return, but not in exchange, for precision, expertness, 'rational,' impersonal and stable discharge of duties delegated by policy-makers, the bureaucrat enjoys a type of social status, claims a 'right to office,' a 'right to security' in and out of office and a certain amount of independence in advice. These are usually granted by all civilised governments.

Be it noted that the bureaucrat does not directly frame the end, though he contributes to it by his information and expert ability. As on him devolves the duty of executing and defending the policy, it is but natural that he should have a clear understanding of most of the reasons behind the policy. Besides, as it is also presumed that understanding comes from a comprehensive grasp of essentials and far-reaching incidences of the policy on particular situations, bureaucracy is made up of grades the highest occupants of which are expected to look to over-all impersonal principles and the lower ones to care for individual bases and detailed application to cases. Bureaucratic hierarchy is dependent on the length of passage from the general to the particular, and *vice versa*. To sum up in the language of Max Weber:

> Bureaucratization offers above all the optimum possibility for carrying through the principle of specializing the administrative function according to purely objective considerations. Individual performances are allocated to functionaries who have specialized training and who by constant practice learn more and more. The "objective" discharge of business primarily means a discharge of business according to *calculable means and without regard for persons.*

The defects of bureaucracy are so well known that they need no reiteration. Its habituation to routine breeds laziness and conservatism; its indispensability makes the political master look like a dilettante *vis-a-vis* the expert; its secretiveness enhances the distance between the government and the governed; its method of recruitment and regulated certainty of prospects and status tend to create a caste, or a closed guild; and its preoccupation with its own interests is often a school for anti-social, almost biological, self-multiplication. And yet these well-known features of bureaucracy are not qualities of its own nature. A study of various bureaucratic forms and their evolution down the ages shows that there is nothing inherently wrong in bureaucracy as such. Thus, for example, the defects of the honorific type, the earliest in history, were cured by the collegiate and those of the collegiate by the vocational, until the monocratic type, that with which we are most familiar, is reached in the interest of greater economy, consistency, permanence and efficiency. In other words, it is not beyond the ingenuity of a democratic government to devise methods by which the reactionary aspects of bureaucratic inertia can be controlled. It is well to remember that while bureaucratization was a positive step in the democratic process, in so far as it checked the course of an honorific nobility and held up the idea of equality of law against privilege, it is the same democracy, but far richer in content and effectiveness than ever, that is ever willing to counteract the bureaucratic concentration of power, open up the closed status by universal accessiblity of office through competitive examinations under the highest authority and provide genuine opportunities for the exercise of public opinion through more liberal rights of recall. Thus it is that increasing democratization, (and not socialization as it is often alleged to be), helps in the increase of the number and power of bureaucrats and simultaneously controls them. Such is one aspect of the dynamic relation between bureaucracy and democracy.

There is another equally relevant process in the evolution of bureaucracy. 'The development of the money economy, in so far as a pecuniary compensation of the officials is concerned, is a presupposition of bureaucracy.' As subsistence economy began to yield place, the patrimonial and feudal elements with their 'farming' income in kind, fixed or residual, and 'prebends,' i.e., rent payments for life, became the rule, until the age of commerce and chartered corporations was reached to produce the salaried personnel without personal obligations. This personnel was further expanded in the period of industrial capitalism. An interesting lesson of European economic history is the fact that it was industrial capitalism that first developed the pure form of bureaucracy and that it was this capitalist bureaucracy which opposed interference in business by the state through its honorific bureaucrats. Since then, industrial capitalism has passed through a phase or two with increasing complexities and hierarchies implicit in monopolistic combinations. The modern state, partly in self-defence, had to become more bureaucratized. And not merely the state, but also every institution working in that context, in voluntary and involuntary collaboration with it, e.g., the universities which had to depend upon trusts or endowments, or in opposition to it, like trade unions and labour parties, had to be officialised. Professor Hayek's *Road to Serfdom* was paved by capitalistic 'planning'; and the way had to be traversed by those who lived under or wanted to control capitalism by the same magical word 'planning.'

They walked with a different purpose, however, and the purpose transformed the state's humble functions of securing the minimum of life, liberty and prosperity into something more positive. No more was the state going to live an apologetic existence in a corner by the grace and pressure of capitalism, it was forced into the unenviable position of keeping the ring between a seasoned fighter and an untrained pugilist suspected to have reserves of strength yet untouched, viz., labour. The present position of all modern states barring one, is that they seek to balance these two parties. Nearly all the well-known evils of officialdom spring from the modern state's hesitancies as the umpire between two unequal contestants. Independent India is no exception to the rule. The Indian bureaucrat is no more busy with keeping the balance between communities, but he still continues to equilibrate the conflicting unequal economic interests in the names of harmony, identity, unity, national emergency, etc. If and when the modern state, the Indian state as well, becomes genuinely positive, then the word planning will have another significance and the evils of bureaucracy will tend to disappear allowing the vestiges of the old order to remain here and there. Bureaucracy will then be truly creative, shedding its routine-conservatism and apparent arbitrariness in the passage.

The foregoing analysis was called for in view of the ambivalent attitude of a growing democracy like India's towards such further extension of officialdom as is implicit in the plea for a new economic and social service. Increasing democratization endorses it. The new capitalism of India forces, even when it opposes, it. And the rising tide of interests either set at naught by capitalism or not covered by it is fast breaking the resistances to state operations. Nobody will suggest that Indian governments are in any sense socialistic, yet their appreciation of common interests has increased, the quantity as well as the intensity of the work of administration have developed, and the sphere of collective action is no more lost in the shameless expanse of *laissez faire*. This is a golden opportunity for giving a little push to history.

Certain conditions precedent exist in India. Among the psychological ones the chief is the desire of the people to be administered. The attitude is qualitatively different from the filial piety to which an insulting paternalism had driven the people. Now that independence has generated a sense of the community of stock, Indians are less anxious about politics and more concerned with what lies behind politics, viz., material existence. Thus it is that the idea of 'control' of all that affects material living has come to stay. Prices, wages, profits, production, business, trade, industry, education, marriage, civil liberties, entertainments, there is no sector of life which is not considered to be within the purview of a national state's operations. Not only that, there is an increasing feeling that economic considerations should now become prior to every other. The secular religion of patriotism is fast becoming 'materialistic.' Many dedicated servants of the country are now willing to join the services of the state. Institutions are growing up to support the above psychological attitudes. Advisory boards have been established in nearly all of the important spheres of industrial life. Their existence is more relevant than the inexperienced performances thereof. Price control of essentials and rationing, rent control, fixing the issue of capital, management of currency, import and export licenses, tariff regulations, cotton, coal, sugar, and steel boards, employment, labour, health, and multipurpose associations sponsored by the state: these and many more are supposed to look after production, distribution and exchange; and the citizens have recognised their relevance even when they have opposed them. The cry for the reimposition of control is as insistent as that for decontrol a few months ago. Labour always wants the state to implement the findings of its committees and to order the employer to effectuate the awards of its officers. Such attitudes are reflected in the directive principles of state policy incorporated in the draft constitution, even though the corresponding supporting institutions are not explicit in its operative part.

To remind ourselves of the economic implications of the Indian Constitution, we will quote its section 31. 'The state shall, in particular, direct its policy towards securing:

(i) that the citizens, men and women equally, have the right to an adequate means of livelihood;

(ii) that the ownership and control of the material resources of the community are so distributed as best to subserve the common good;

(iii) that the operation of the economic system does not result in the concentration of wealth and means of production to the common detriment;

(iv) that there is equal pay for equal work for both men and women;

(v) that the strength and health of workers, men and women, and the tender age of children, are not abused and that citizens are not forced by economic necessity to enter a vocation unsuited to their age and strength;

(vi) that childhood and youth are protected against exploitation and against moral and material abandonment.'

This section alone requires a special trained service. If we add to it the implications of the industrial policy of mixed economy, labour welfare, multi-purpose works, projects and cooperatives, higher agricultural production, rehabilitation of refugees, to mention a few of the accepted programmes in progress, the increase in the quantity and intensity of new administration demanding a new type of personnel in addition to the existing ones, and replacing them whenever necessary, will be apparent.

How to institutionalise the satisfaction of our national need which has been reflected in the directive principles of our draft constitution? Surely, we cannot leave them hanging in the air. At the same time, for reasons stated above, it is obvious that no one of the older types of bureaucracy is equal to the task. The honorific type, a revival of which is unconsciously sought in the idea of services as missionary bodies, has been definitely proved to be uneconomic. In fact, we have had no counter-part of the English nobility or squirearchy performing civic duties in the countryside. The average Congressman, who could be the counterpart, is developing urban interests. The monocratic type has proved its superior advantages in its economy and in the due discharge of impersonal, objective, calculable rules. Without minimising the modern monocratic bureaucrat's training in general ability, for which the scope will never diminish, one can still note its creaking inflexibilities and certain foci of confusion in its apparent adaptability and plead for the special training that facilitates expert knowledge and generates mutual confidence.

People have attributed the failure of controls to corruption, and criticised their high and multiplying costs. As the data of corruption belong to the realm of private discourse, a part of the sources of corruption as well as some of the reasons for the high expenditure on controls can be publicly traced and attributed to an inefficiency that springs from lack of training, describable as incompetence. The greater the ignorance of the economics of a given material situation, the greater become the chances of bribery and the needs of expenditure for defensive cover. In short, corruption is oftener an intellectual deficiency than a moral dereliction; and governments are always more generous in hiding the former than in condoning the latter. Similar troubles for similar causes have been noticed in the workings of the agriculture, cooperative and labour departments in every provincial government. The number of officers who are conversant with the economic principles of farm management, cooperatives, wages, profits and prices, and yet deputed to take charge of their operations, is very small indeed. One can quote many instances of the effects of ignorance in such matters.[1] We will not refer

[1] And not merely the bureaucrat's ignorance but of the alleged practical men in business as well. Their ignorance is surprising. Few have reliable data; and fewer still know how to collate them and make them yield significance. The knowledge of many is limited to the ability to distort.

to the neglect of sociology. We have not yet realised the importance of training in social service,[2] which posits social statistics, social economy, social psychology and social biology. Yet we are legislating on industrial relations, children, marriage, inheritance, i.e., on family life, on social security and welfare! The confusion of opinion in regard to the Hindu Code, the failure of a true adjustment within a factory and of reasonable relations outside, the crude notions about population and the absence of any policy in this regard, these are only a few cases in which better and probably, less costly solutions could have been thought of with the help of a permanent body of civil servants trained in economics and sociology.

The nucleus of such a body actually exists in every provincial administration. We start with the province for various reasons, e.g., convenience, more intimate knowledge, greater desirability of building from the base than imposing a prefabricated structure on it, the reality of unequal development, different socio-economic conditions and positive existence of important sectors of socio-economic life yet untouched, or not directly touched, by all-India or extra-Indian factors.[3] In the UP, the nucleus consists of the department of economics and statistics with its staff at headquarters and in the forty-nine districts. One may call it the neutronic core in more senses than one. Round about it move the statistical branches of the labour commissioner's office collecting prices and materials for cost of living indices, the offices of the director of industries, agricultural marketing officer, registrar of cooperatives and the cane commissioner, each with a personnel primarily concerned with matters economic. The degree of relationship with the nuclear department varies with personal equations and physical distance.[4] Other departments like revenue, finance, agriculture are

[2] The Kashi Vidyapith is the only oasis in the UP. The Lucknow university has been giving theoretical training and making field investigations so far.

[3] This is without prejudice to the larger question of linking up a provincial service with an all-India service. It is the author's sad experience that waiting upon an all-India lead often springs from a desire to evade responsibility.

[4] It is also well-known that the senior staff in the various offices who should be doing economic work and thinking are compelled to spend most of their time in the disposal of files. A little adjustment, say the appointment of a couple of clerks, can easily rescue them from such mechanical duties and give them time for self-education, although one does not expect much from that process at their age.

essentially economic departments. Heaps of most valuable economic materials have been lying in stacks there without being properly or fully used for economic purposes. It was natural in those circumstances where revenue was an integral part of the magistracy, taxation a means of paying for foreign rule and a graveyard's peace, and agriculture an instrument to bolster up the loyal rent-receiving class. Today one can presume that revenue, finance and agriculture have shed their connection with politics, and one can also see them standing out in their economic, uninhibited nakedness.

Yet, and this is the tragedy of the situation, the liaison of these departments with the department of economics and statistics is tenuous. Each has trained (or untrained, but experienced) statisticians, but they do not combine, either in grades or in functions. In any case, they are there. Remoter examples are the irrigation and forest departments. They retain statisticians who must be good in mathematics or botany; but one wonders if knowledge of economics is at all considered necessary for such appointments. We suppose the civil supplies, rehabilitation and development boards, etc., are all staffed with excellent arithmeticians; but we are not speaking either of arithmetic or its higher designation, elementary statistics. Our idea is to pool these scattered individuals (trained or experienced) wherever they are in order that they may subsequently form one coordinated atomic pile from which the various departments may draw that very necessary canalised energy. At present, the staff have not the chance of enhancing their knowledge; but the best of them may still act as the nucleus of the new service.

The question of status is the least difficult to answer. An economic and social service should not in any case be inferior either to the provincial, judicial or the executive, the police or the educational services. Therefore, the same grade is recommended. One who looks after the export and import of consumer's and producer's goods from one big moffusil area in a district to another, who watches the economic implications of flood and drought, prices, wages, and profits, recruitment and movement of labour, the replacement of food crops by cash crops, rent remissions, *taqavi* loans and agricultural credits, rationing, the organic life of villages, etc., discharges functions as important as those of the headmaster or the deputy superintendent of police, the deputy collector or the munsif. The days of Ram Raj are gone beyond recall; and status, which is as much a gift of esteem from the people as a condition of freedom from worries for the purpose of dedication to the people is now, unfortunately for the government, otherwise not addicted to austerity either, a function of economics. The plight of the economic intelligence officers to keep their face before such sources of their intelligence as petty shopkeepers is really sad. No reference need be made about the possible grades of the provincial economic and social service. There is no room for caste system in the non-technical services of a democratic state.

On two points, however, namely, (a) conditions of betterment, and (b) functions, this service, for certain inherent reasons, will have to be somewhat different from other provincial cadres. The laws of economics partake much less of the generality and permanence of natural laws than, say, those of administration or civil and criminal laws. There is no economic or social code like the Indian Penal Code. Here the economc and social service will be analogous to the educational service in which there is greater elasticity and relativity than in the other two. To put it in another way, a greater disservice to the country can be perpetrated by an economic and social service if it sticks to old economic and social doctrines than what the magistrate, the policeman, or the judge, even the school and college teachers can do in the name of outworn methods of administration, adjudication and instruction. Hence the urgency for refresher courses, say, as in the medical services. Concretely, the efficiency bar of the economic and social service will be crossed only by those who have acquired up-to-date knowledge. Hence also the greater need for foreign study, leave opportunities and a staff college.

The functions of the economic and social service can be classified under three heads:

(a) *Information*: which may be collected from existing records, now stored in godowns, blue books and reports, and by undertaking a perennial census of wages, income, investment, rent, prices, production, man-power and the like. Obviously, much of this information will be of a statistical nature. Economic statistics are more useful here than mathematical statistics.

(b) *Advisory*: on the basis of the information gathered in the above fashion the economic and social service can discharge the advisory functions only if its officers meet and discuss at frequent intervals.[5] An amendment to the purely monocratic type of bureaucracy is suggested here. In fact, it is not new. The modern tendency is for frequent consultations between officials. Whatever may be the tendency and its effects elsewhere, the need for a common coordinated advice is urgent in economic affairs. When there is no economic code, no labour code, no code of investment, no code for agricultural marketing, except the perfunctory administrative rules thereupon, a collegiate method of tendering economic and social advice is clearly indicated.

(c) The provincial economic and social service is expected to discharge certain executive functions. Separation of functions is always difficult. It has been particularly so in view of the subordination of all other functions to the one, single, primary, remnant function of keeping law and order and collecting revenue. But in view of the major social developments mentioned earlier, namely, the increasing domination of economic over other interests and the consequences flowing therefrom in the shape of sharper differentiation of issues, the problem of the separation of functions need not be insoluble. As this is not the place to go into detail only a few guiding principles may be enunciated: (i) The economic policy which is reached by the executive after due collegiate advice of the economic and social service should be operated by the economic and social services, wherever possible. (ii) The final sanction alone should be with the chief executive of the district, as it happens in all other branches of district administration. (iii) Intermediate process will always bear the signs of overlapping.

While it is true that economic and social policy cannot be cordoned off the political, yet one could think in terms of greater or less dominance and urgency. Thus, for example, the economics and sociology of rehabilitation is of greater weight and immediacy than its politics, which is now a dead issue. If, therefore, the economic and social service plans for the settlement of refugees in certain areas, for their occupational training or employment, the executive head should give effect to the plan, say, in passing orders for the acquisition of land, etc., by adding only

[5] Travelling allowances will no doubt increase further, but they will fetch better returns in the way of avoiding the wastes of uncoordination.

the fruits of his experience in legal and police matters. In such cases his function becomes advisory and that of the economic and social service the truly executive. The matter of signature on orders is one of minor adjustment. Nothing beyond the guiding principles of the dominance of interest and urgencies in specific cases can be suggested here. We do not expect a 'debacle' in administration on the ground of a possible conflict of functions. Such conflict will always be there so long as life is an organic whole. On the contrary, we expect the executive head to welcome a sharing of the burden of his responsibilities.

The economic service has to be expanded beyond the nucleus to meet the growing needs of economic and social legislation. Obviously, the recruitment has to be done by the public service commission with or without assessors. No direct nomination is desirable. Political sufferers, if otherwise unqualified, are apt to bring about economic suffering by sheer good will and enthusiasm. New methods of selection, particularly through closer study of the candidates in camps by experts and psychologists, if the latter have devised or can devise a technique for testing ability in this direction, will have to be adopted to supplement written and oral examinations. After selection, rigorous training will be given for at least six months in a staff college attached to the public service commission, to be followed by another probationary period of the same duration in which practical problems will be tackled in conjunction with senior officers and outside experts in a camp or an office. These are only the minimum requirements. Conditions of employment are to be the same as those of any other service barring the two qualifications mentioned before. Both our centre and Pakistan have started staff colleges with the best men available. If cadet schools are a fixture in defence services, we fail to see how they are an impossibility for defence against ignorance, want, poverty and exploitation.

Space forbids discussion of curricular training in the staff college. Any hidebound course will be controversial. On certain matters, however, common agreements are possible. A gentlemen's understanding between the universities, the Kashi Vidyapith, and the proposed staff college under the auspices of the PSC is perfectly feasible. Thus, for example, if a sound analytical training in modern economic and social theories—we stress the world 'modern' for obvious reasons[6]—is already provided in the universities, the extent of their applicability to local, regional and national consideration may be undertaken by the staff college for the necessary orientation. Two instances should suffice: modern economists have analysed at least half a dozen types of inflation with which senior students at the universities should be familiar. The present inflationary gap in India shows the dominance of a type or two over others, plus certain special features of its own. One of these latter may as well be due to the disbalance between a fast developing urban economy—the sole occupation of academic economic theory—and a comparatively static rural economy. This lack of equilibrium may be studied either in terms of general equilibrium theory, or in those of imperfect competition and temporary, local or retail monopolies. The theories popular in university circles may or may not explain the disbalance. If they do, the university training is almost adequate; almost, because to the author's knowledge, no study of the variations of the prices of city goods and country goods in these years seems to have been an integral part of the course of economics in any university in the United Provinces. If they do not, then the staff college may utilise the figures accumulating in the government departments for no known purpose of good or evil, and tell the candidates their practical significance for price control and rationing as an instrument of fighting inflation. A training in this manner will certainly obviate the necessity of passing numerous amendments to a measure of economic legislation like the sales tax. Ignorant gyrations of governmental policy are as undignified as genuflexions before powerful groups.

One more instance from the labour front: Though there is plenty of economics behind industrial unrest, there is very little of plausible known academic economic theory of industrial unrest. Even the marginal productivity theory of wages has shown deep cracks. It does not explain the dynamics of the labour movement in any manner. The only sensible conclusion about wages is that it is a matter of collective bargaining strengths of the two parties. This does not mean an abdication

[6] Who does not know that both governmental and business economic policies betray symptoms of crude and dated doctrines, e.g., quantity theory of money, the mercantilist fear of goods, Ricardian rent, residual profit and subsistence wages? Even an open mind, as Keynes used to say, is often a storehouse of discarded theories.

of analysis. Economics will always remain an apparatus of thought, a logical explanation of certain behaviours. It only suggests that a socio-economic theory should supplement the academic economic theories. By socio-economic theory is meant a body of generalisations on the economic behaviour of certain social groups; e.g., the rural migrant and the urban factory unit, age and sex division, family, caste, community and classes. Attempts are being made elsewhere to study these behaviour patterns; but very few universities in India even recognise this approach. A staff college may easily adopt it, say, at first for the rehabilitation staff and the labour welfare and conciliation officers. We hope that the Kashi Vidyapith is doing this work in the right spirit. If need arises, as it is bound to arise, study leave to foreign universities, or the importation of foreign scholars, may be in the programme of staff training.

No mention need be made at this stage about the nature of policy to be pursued by the ministry. We are concerned here only with the aspect of implementation. Besides a staff of civil servants with the special functions and training discussed above, such a ministry should have at its elbow an economic general staff for the due discharge of certain duties. Two views seem to obtain in regard to this institution which has become quite popular of late: (i) that the economic general staff should enjoy the status of an independent research bureau financed out of public funds fully free to enquire into and appraise the policy followed not only by a particular department of the government but of the government as a whole; and (ii) that each government department should have an economist who would act as the personal adviser to the minister concerned on the economic aspects of his departmental activities: and the different departmental personal advisers are then expected to meet and exchange confidences with each other. In the latter case the procedure is informal while in the former it should be open in the shape of published memorandums. Recently there have been many examples of both types of economic advising.[7]

We should now examine each type. An independent research

[7] *Vide* (i) M. A. Copeland, 'Economic research in the government' in *American Economic Review*, September, 1941.

(ii) J. Viner, 'Short and Long View in Economic Policy,' *American Economic Review*, March 1940.

(iii) E. R. Walker, 'From economic theory to policy' in *Economic Advising in Practice*.

bureau can have only limited influence. Its findings cannot be mandatory nor can they be reached with the speed which politicians demand for the urgencies of the hour. In the absence of crucial data, no scientific certainty can be attained by it. It is quite likely that its conclusions may not be palatable to certain interests. This actually happened in the state of Queensland in Australia where its bureau of economics and statistics ran up against the trade unions and the labour opposition when its director recommended a wage-cut as a remedy for depression. The truth of the matter is that the modern tendency of all governments is to treat all types of information including the economic, as a political instrument. So unless there is a strong democratic tradition in the government as well as outside it to assure toleration of differing conclusions every government will try its best to influence, subtly or openly, the topics of research, the scope of the enquiry and above all, the slant in the conclusions of an economic general staff which is financed out of government funds. Such traditions exist in Australia, New Zealand and Great Britain. Professor Copeland who has had great experience as an economic adviser says with regard to research in the USA government that 'with a fair amount of ingenuity in form of expression, the research worker can find a way to say almost any thing without violating the canons of governmental propriety.' It has been said that if you want to attack the United States government all that you have to do is to write to Washington for ammunitions. The reports of the president's committees are unsparing in their criticisms of the misdeeds of the American state departments.

On the other hand, the process of personal advice is fraught with dangerous possibilities. To some extent the role of personal advice will always be there. But it is also always hard to draw the line betwen benign and malign influences. One can even make a concession to the part that personal intuition plays in the study of economic affairs. Even then, the personal advisers must have their data collected and analysed by a permanent body. The English practice seems to be a synthesis of the two views and types discussed above. In 1928, the liberal party's industrial enquiry report known as *Britain's Industrial Future* stressed the need for a general economic staff to advise the cabinet. Some sort of an economic advisory council was set up two years later but no appreciable success was achieved mainly on account of the inveterate habit of Mr. Ramsay Macdonald and

Mr. Baldwin to depend upon private friendly advice. In 1939, the British cabinet set up an economic policy committee which established another committee of economic survey under the presidentship of Lord Stamp. This latter committee ultimately developed into an economic and statistical secretariat which proved very handy when the war cabinet established a co-ordinating committee on economic and financial policy. According to one who knows, the secretariat consisting of academic economists and other officials trained in economics have become an 'effective organ of thought, stimulation, admonitory comment and initiative.'

It is not possible to discuss all implications of a possible conflict between the theory and practice of economics and sociology within the limits of this paper.[8] Generally speaking, the duties of the economic general staff for the ministry of economic and social affairs should be those as were envisaged by the liberal industrial enquiry committee's report of Great Britain:

(1) To engage in continuous study of current economic problems affecting national policy and the development of industry.

(2) To coordinate and, where necessary, to complete statistical and other information required by the government and by parliament.

(3) To act on its own initiative in calling the attention of the cabinet to important tendencies and changes at home and abroad.

(4) To suggest to the government plans for solving fundamental economic difficulties, such, for instance, as measures for stabilising trade conditions, avoiding unemployment, and developing national resources.

It is obvious that these proposals are tentative. The point about the economic general staff is that it should have high status to enable its conclusions to be listened to seriously, which is inconceivable without a permanent secretariat at the apex of a different type of service. Between the danger of its decisions being frozen out by lip-sympathies and its reports running to academic waste of ponderous memoranda, the economic general staff has to steer a middle way. Herein lies the final need of an economic and social service whose senior officers must

[8] Walker, *ibid.*

needs be included in the secretariat of the economic general staff to give the ballast of reality to possible abstraction as also to facilitate a smooth execution of the policy formulated by the ministry of economic and social affairs in the light of the conclusions reached by the economic general staff.[9]

Fuller treatment is not possible now. An economic and social service is an urgent necessity. And so is its corollary, a staff college. Both are productive, nation-building expenditure. They are economic in every sense. The possible bureaucratic defects are curable under democratic stresses. Once this service is started in the provinces round their own nucleus, it can easily be linked up with an all-India economic and social service whose functions can be empirically demarcated along well known lines like customs, railways, banking, currency and international trade. The cone of the pyramid is naturally the *ministry of economic and social affairs,* in the provinces and in the centre. Our province can easily take the lead, particularly when it knows that it has to make much leeway in the matter of socio-economic information and development. One with a large teaching

[9] The position of the India government in regard to this matter was thus stated by Premier Nehru before the constituent assembly (legislature) on 19 March 1949. The government did not contemplate a separate ministry of economics and planning. This question had been previously considered. 'The report of the advisory planning board, presided over by Mr. K. C. Neogy, had recommended the establishment of a planning authority. The report was generally approved by the government and it had been their intention to have some organisation for overall planning. The government felt, however that before such an organisation and authority was set up, certain preliminary steps should be taken to that end. They have, therefore, constituted an economic committee of the cabinet, and also an economic coordination committee and a separate statistical unit of the cabinet.' Such an arrangement seems to be based on the British model, but without a Cripps. Each major department meanwhile has a number of economists and statisticians on its staff, besides an advisory board. As one is not in a position to assess the achievements of the 'back room boys,' one can only point out that the establishment of a provincial and central economic and social service is one of the important preliminary steps towards the policy of overall planning to which Premier Nehru as well as Pandit Jawaharlal Nehru, the former president of the national planning committee, are committed in principle. At present, the general impression is that the dozen economists and the hundred statisticians at the centre are for reasons subjective and objective not being as effective as they could be. At any rate, neither the staff economists nor the invited ones at stray committees are a substitute for a regular economic and social service; at best, they are complementary.

experience in the province can assure the government that the young graduates, men and women, if they are given the additional training by a staff college and other opportunities, will not lower the standard of this service. Both supply and need are present: only they are not meeting. This service will bring them together.

2. *On The Present State of Economic Theory*

THE ANNUAL NUMBER OF AN ECONOMIC JOURNAL, IN THE MAINtenance and betterment of which I am interested, should be an opportunity for putting before its readers some of the doubts and difficulties that have assailed me in course of my readings of the year or so. The reason for this is the expectation that men of my tribe will come to my help in order that some constructive economic thinking may emerge out of a comparison of notes. Our country and our countrymen want a lot of it, now that the honeymoon of political independence is over and the lady of the household has to look to the price of wheat and rice, napkins and aspirin.

Lest it be misunderstood, I shall not cite the number of books on economics I have been reading round about 1949. (Some of them were published earlier, but that should not matter). They mount up to a fairly large figure and they are by the leading economists of England and America, old and young. A few volumes of European authorities have reached me in English translation. The latest and the best journals in English have also been by my side. Certain books and articles have thrilled me, others have bored me, while quite a number have been useful for delivering 'impressive' lectures to innocent graduates. Two volumes declared by the cognoscenti to be fundamental have beaten me completely by their mathematical treatment.[1] I am still after them, but I have a feeling that I shall never be able to master them.

Mathematics seems to have an ambition of becoming the

[1] Samuelson, *Foundations of Economic Analysis* (his *Introduction to Economics* belongs to a different category) and Neumann and Morgenstern, *Theory of Games and Economic Behaviour.*

new mysticism of the social sciences, economics in particular. I have sought defence of my weakness in Marshall's view that mathematical economics is but a passing phase marking the transition towards biological economics. A number of methodologists have also given me self-respect with their logical criticisms of the limitations of 'quantification,' Northrop, Cohen and Stigler,[2] for example, but how can I be consoled when the world seems to think that mathematics is the science of precision and prediction? Scientific knowledge, in so far as it claims to annex the *whole* of knowledge as against the point of view of *an aspect* of knowledge, must have its magical formula, its *mantrams,* its incantations and rituals, not only to assure its rightness but also to prove to the people that rightness has been or is going to be achieved in *all* spheres of knowledge. Professors Samuelson, Morgenstern and Neumann are brilliant mathematicians and economists, and Keynes was not. Yet Keynes, despite his tautological and 'fuzzy' equations (the word is Stigler's *re* the multiplier), knew how to write for the lesser breed. A touch of the literary hand seems to be still needed in order that ordinary students like me may not lose heart and sense of self-respect. After all, economics is related to the behaviour of men and women in their ordinary activities. It is becoming all too esoteric, like English poetry, continental painting and music of 'thirties. When one looks for light one is naturally disappointed to find mist. I sometimes wonder if all this unintelligibility and mystification were the result of alienation of knowledge from life in the name of specialisation.

Keynesian economics, as I have hinted, is more congenial to my level of understanding. In the four volumes on it that I have gone through recently there is only a limited sector for mathematics, the rest being logic, and more or less a plain one at that. Not that all the intricacies of interpretations have been clear to me, but they do not always arise from the subtleties of argument. Somehow or other, I feel that Indian intellect, and particularly that of a Brahmin who comes from the home of Nabyanyaya, is not incapable of following up an argument to its end. But I confess that some of the implications of Keyne-

[2] Northrop, *The Logic of the Sciences and the Humanities;* Cohen, *The Meaning of Human History,* and *A Preface to Logic;* Stigler, *Lectures on Political Economic Problems* (LSE). For the opposite view, Lundberg, *The Foundations of Society* and Dodd, *Dimensions of Sociology.*

sian economics do not quite enter into my skull. For example, this question of full employment; I have grave doubts about the applicability of this concept, if it be at all a concept fulfilling all the logical conditions of a concept to the conditions of an undeveloped country like India. It is at best a highly significant hypothesis with the help of which we Indians can rectify some of the hastily drawn conclusions from our study of classical economics. But there again we can think only of *higher* or *fuller* employment, that is, over and above the under-employment, covert and overt, prevailing in India. On the other hand, that 'er' takes away the sting and reduces the concept to a wish for development. A very human wish indeed, but hardly a theory to satisfy the needs of India.

Probably, I am doing an injustice to Keynes himself, which is the farthest from my wish. He was a psychologist; at least, he found himself on the brink of human nature through the narrow bridle path of 'expectations' and 'propensities.' If only he had lived to read Noyes,[3] one of Roosevelt's men, he would have been right into the valley where men feel and behave economically. Probably he would have written a devastating review of that impossible book where economic behaviour is tracked down to the cortex, yet he would have profited by it. Keynes was not above incorporating ideas from men he felt himself superior to and from books he disliked in the famous Bloomsbury fashion. However, there's no use crying over what cannot be undone. Let us not forget that he could not reply to Mantoux (Jr)[4], either.

Keynes is enjoyable by virtue of his brilliance and intuitive intelligence. His interpreters usually lack these human qualities and stray into academic consistency, the virtue of derivative minds. The result is not often fortunate. In collections of essays centering in Keynesian economics,[5] even if estimates of Keynes' contributions sometimes agree, conclusions differ. In a sense it is natural, but it is not always helpful. Full dress volumes by single authors stem out from Keynesian postulates in all direc-

[3] Noyes, *Economic Man.*

[4] E. Mantoux, *Carthaginian Peace (Economic Consequences of Mr. Keynes).*

[5] S. Harris, *New Economics.*

Lerner and Graham, *Planning and Paying for Full Employment,* and Oxford Institute of Statistics, *The Economics of Full Employment.*

tions. Dillard and Klein contradict each other.[6] Perhaps the sin is original, that is, social. Economic thought seems to have got itself entangled in the meshes which crisis, and worse still, the fear of crisis, has cast on a part of the world that thinks itself to be its leader. As a result, that part wants a hero, a hope a port in storm; and Keynes is the *avatar* and his economics is the gospel of crisis-averters. He and his economics can alone save the world from ruin, which is nationalisation, socialism, Communism, in a crescendo of meaning according to taste. Some would fondly quote Keynes in favour of state action while others on behalf of socialism. The publishers of Mises' *Human Action* class Keynes with Marx! But Keynes was just not interested in changing the world. He was never a socialist. He was only careful to preserve 'a good state of mind' and secure the absence of that annoying friction which makes such a state impossible in this world of fools. Keynes hated stupidity more than poverty. As he himself says in his credo, his whole approach was conditioned by Moore's ethics, which, sociologically, looks like a code of decent manners for Cambridge dons. Be that as it may, Keynesian economics is one long exercise in the disutility of any attempt to change the present economic system with the help of a brilliant theory. At least, that is my view after the third reading of *General Theory*. In contrast, I find Pigou's small volume refreshing. The *Veil of Money* is the English way of calling it a fetish. Pigou retains his discriminating dullness in the revised edition of his analysis of *Employment and Equilibrium*, which in parts is also too stiff for me.

Some economic literature on socialism has come my way this year. Hoff, a Norwegian economist, has lost his faith in socialism. I have yet to find any reason other than what is furnished by the phrase 'culture-compulsion' for the translation and publication of this supreme example of academic futility, viz., *Economic Calculation in the Socialist Society*. Mises' old essay was enough to show that planned, socialist economy 'is a logical impossibility in the absence of a pricing system.'[7] This line of

[6] L. R. Klein, *The Keynesian Revolution*, D. Dillard, *The Economics of J. M. Keynes.*

[7] His *Human Action* has just reached me. Is he the one to change? From whatever little I have read of this book it is fantastic to claim, as as the blurb does, that it is a counterweight to Marx and Keynes on any level.

argument only convinces those who are already convinced. It does not satisfy one who wants to understand. Dr. Hoff is determined to overawe his readers by learning. On the other hand, Beckwith, an American army officer, is clearer and more direct in the *Economic Theory of Socialist Economy*. I am afraid, he is having a bad time in his country with a certain section of the intelligentsia. Anyhow, the issue is joined now. Lange and Taylor, whose essays have been reprinted in a booklet,[8] and a few others, are of the opinion that socialist accounting and socialist allocation of resources are not contradictions in terms. I prefer Sweezy's *Socialism* for its clear statement of a position that goes ahead of the previous writers' and falls short of extreme versions. Of course, it does not compete with Strachey's earlier volumes.

In this connection I would like to point out that one bright focus of attention this year has been the problem of national accounting,[9] socialist or otherwise. This is a good sign, because it really means that the old unformulated distinction between non-politically pure economics and business economics is being extinguished in favour of the latter. It makes one see things in their proper perspective, which is nothing more than the fact that the rope which business has so long given to theory is being shortened. From now on it will be business economy all through. We will finally bid adieu to economics as a tool, an apparatus of thought, and be made to hail economics as the book keeping of business, private or state. It shocks one to know of the economic system as primarily a set of accounts and see economic behaviour reduced to a system of 'accounting entities' and 'sectors.' Yet, without a system of national accounting planning cannot work; without solving the problem of allocation of resources, human mostly in India, socialism is wish fulfilment. Stone and Kuznetz are the new masters, and not Keynes. Shoup[10] I found to be useful. For planners their volumes are essential. I however, sometimes wonder if our social accountants ever cared for Lenin's views on the matter. Like many other topics Lenin discussed this question in the context of socialist planning. It were better if we looked into his views, otherwise at some date or the other we may have to regret much in the same manner as

[8] Lange and Taylor, *On the Economic Theory of Socialism*.

[9] *Measurement of National Income*, etc., with an appendix on definition and measurement.

[10] Shoup, *Principles of National Income Analysis*.

Mrs. Robinson has done in regard to Marx's analysis. We had better concede soon that Lenin was at least as intelligent as any professor of economics in London, Cambridge, Oxford and Stockholm, or Harvard and Chicago, or even any government economist.

Speaking about planning there is Professor Samuel Harris' book[11] dealing with the planning of fourteen countries, and with analysis too. Harris is diluted Hansen, who is diluted Keynes. The point about this tome is that you do not get the thing you want and get all the things you do not want. The analytical part is not particularly revealing. I very much preferred E. F. M. Durbin[12] and J. E. Meade.[13] I was looking forward to Durbin's *Economics of Democratic Socialism*, but this good man was cut off in the prime of life. It was a pleasure to read his lucid essays once again in this handy volume. Meade, as usual, is penetrating without being pompous. But I was pleasantly surprised to meet a new economist, Professor Lewis. His *Economic Survey of 1919-39*, is a little masterpiece of economic history. My only trouble with Lewis's writing is that they are so compact that I cannot summarise them for students and pass them as my own. He seems to be a Fabian; so there will be no harm in recommending his other book, that on planning,[14] to the young. It is safe and sound. By the way, Carl Landauer[15] on the theory of planning is becoming my favourite for his reasonableness, and Lerner and Graham's book of essays[16] for its insights into concrete problems.

But A. Rothstein, a lecturer in the London University, has produced a small volume[17] which has given me the shock of my life. On finishing it I had to change my views about so many things I was hearing about Soviet economy, e.g., that all its plans were imposed from the top, that collective farms were engines of repression of the poor, freedom loving *moujhik*, that the whole system is totalitarian, undemocratic, etc. Not that I gulped it ever; in fact, I considered my Hindu system of society to be the extreme perfection of totalitarianism in which

[11] S. E. Harris, *Economic Planning*.
[12] E. F. M. Durbin, *Problems of Economic Planning*.
[13] J. E. Meade, *Planning and the Price Mechanism*.
[14] W. E. Lewis, *The Principles of Economic Planning*.
[15] Carl Landauer, *Theory of Economic Planning*.
[16] Lerner and Graham, *Planning and Paying for Full Employment*.
[17] A. Rothstein, *Man and Plan in Soviet Economy*.

the life of an individual is regimented right from pre-natal to postmortem stages, from three generations up to three generations below, and that therefore it is infinitely superior to what the cossack of a Stalin can ever conceive and produce. At the same time, being human I could not quite resist that flood of propaganda, known as activities of free press. I thought there must be something in it. Rothstein, who is paid out of the British funds and teaches in London, has shown how plans in the USSR are made by the people, how production is increased by people's efforts, how farms are run by cooperative methods, how currency is an aid to development, how capital is formed, and various other interesting items. Isn't it news that a lakh of amendments make up the 'totalitarian' plan? So this book should be read by those who believe that India is neither in this bloc nor that. If academic objectivity is not possible, let us deduce it from our political neutrality. Rothstein's figures are of course Russian: which may mean that they are lies to those who have heard of Colin Clark's Russian statistics without reading it, or knowing either the same statistician's slight departure from his original position or the controversy that followed. For me, however, quoting Russian figures about Russian life is on the same level as quoting American figures about American life. I cannot check up on either. Haven't the Americans quite a reputation for tall talk? All that I know is that one should not use statistics as a drunk uses the lamp post, viz., for support. Andrew Rothstein uses Russian figures for light. Therefore, his criticisms of Soviet economy also appear to be sensible. This discussion of planning versus democracy is getting boring and senseless, except when it is a deliberate throwing of red-herring across the scent, in which case it is to be judged on other grounds. To my mind, the issue should be either socialism or barbarism.

I really do not know what to say about the American books on economics. Most of them are weariness of the flesh. Devaluation has done one good, at least to the Indian youth in India, they will not purchase them. I shall have to, otherwise I shall fall back in the race. Scholarship in India has become very competitive. Adam Smith, Malthus, Ricardo, Marx, Mill, Marshall–don't you know they are ancient? Haven't you seen the latest American ones on oligopoly, price leadership, economic maturity, the cobweb theorem, and last month's journals from Chicago and the north western, and also from Amsterdam,

Tokyo, Toronto, and Cape Town? So I have to see them all even when I remember Turgeniev's *Critic*, even when I am bankrupt and there is dollar shortage.

Yet, this must be due to my age and upbringing—I derive great pleasure in re-reading the classics, which are mostly non-American. With a little adjustment here and there I find them very stimulating. These non-American master minds had a vision and method; because they stuck to man and his behaviour, they were not yet alienated from life, hence their knowledge was fuller and understanding deeper. (I make an exception for Veblen who I remember, could not get a permanent job at a university in the States.) Leading American economists look rather small by their side. It is not always wise to swear by Haeberler, Knight, Hansen, Samuelson, and all the rest of them, when our knowledge of the classics is obtainable in fairly cheap editions, Everyman's for example. I am not minimising the American significance. But to take their names in the same breath with the masters is a token of some loss of values.

I have read Heimann's *History of Economic Doctrines* and Gruchy's *Modern Economic Thought—The American Contribution*. The former is defective in many ways, but the latter only supports my prejudice in favour of the European classics. So does Leder's admirable *Studies in the Theory of Welfare Economics*. I still prefer Adam Smith's *Theory of Moral Sentiments* as an introduction to the study of weal and woe to Bergson, Lerner or Hicks. Thus it is that I am grateful to Hla Myint's treatment of calssical economics.[18] He has left the taste in my head unimpaired. Stigler's third lecture at the London School is very much after my heart. The immediate stimulus to my classicism has been offered by Vol 3 of *Capital*[19] and the *Critique of Political Economy*[20], both published in India, which I have been reading patiently. I have trusted Messrs. Blakiston's *Readings*[21] and survey of contemporary economics[22] for keeping me modern. In a sense, their classicism is their academic

[18] Hla Myint, *Theories of Welfare Economics.*

[19] Saraswati Library, Calcutta.

[20] Bharati Library, Calcutta.

[21] *Readings in Business Cycle Theory, Readings in the Theory of Income Distribution*

[22] *A Survey of Contemporary Economic Doctrines,* all published by Blakiston.

strength and their modernism a measure of their inability to size up reality.

My purpose is not to write an impressionistic survey or to offer a complete picture of the state of economics as it has appeared to me. It is a partial and a very personal picture. In this year, more than in any of the previous years that I had been spending to catch up with economics after a period of partiality towards sociology, a doubt has been haunting me. Keynes is reported to have said in some other connection that after five years' study of economics one should change over. When Marx wrote that he was getting bored with economics Engels sympathised with him. I really do not know. I have a suspicion that just when economics is in the greatest demand for lighting the way, it has entered into a blind alley; or as Walker says,[23] 'there is a blight on economic theory.' I do not like this phrase. If there be a blight on theory there must be a blight on intellect. And I cannot be an anti-intellectual social worker, or a businessman, or an administrator dismissing theory as an occupational disease of professors and thereby seeking cover under outmoded theories (Keynes again). So is it the economist who is failing, or economic theory?

The only conclusion seems to be that either there must be something radically wrong with our premises and methodology, or that this indecision, this mystification, this Babel of opinions, this lack of courage, has some relation to the world crisis. The latter view is borne out by developments in the theory of social knowledge. Leaving sociology and premises aside, I feel that the need has arisen for questioning our method. Economists start with abstraction, proceed by approximation and then die 'in the long run' without bringing the abstraction down to earth, or taking the next step. It is natural, because life is short and art is long and science is longer. My doubt begins when economists behave as if the model were the reality, as if the second or the third step in approximation were a dead end.

A dynamic approach, one would think, would have corrected it. It is certainly a better approach, more realistic and all that. But will this solve my problem? Though there is a science called dynamics and though modern mathematical economics is doing its best to analyse changes in economic patterns (e.g.,

[23] E. R. Walker, *From Economic Theory to Policy*. (of Tasmania University)

population-studies), yet, strictly speaking, there can be no 'logic,' and therefore, no 'science' of dynamic economic behaviour *as such,* that is, *of economic movements.* Dunlop has tried it with the theory of wages and the theory of trade unionism.[24] He has not succeeded. By movements I do not mean socialism, Communism, and all those things which are now discussed as comparative economic institutions. Movements should mean movement of capital, labour, etc., that is, the social impulse behind what economists describe as allocation (structure of relations?), as distinguished from employment. By logic is meant Aristotellian logic; and science is grounded on Aristotle's system. Now, such logic and such science as we have adopted so far have been pre-occupied with *aspects,* or *cross-sections* of reality, which, however, is the totality of human behaviour. They have been concerned with this aspect of phenomena or that. Naturally, the transition of one class of phenomena into another is an extension of the first class; the variety of aspects is a quantitative expression of the initial aspect. Naturally, also, reality becomes an inflated model. The existence of a qualitatively different class, that is, a *kind* of behaviour, is dismissed on the model of 'there ain't such an animal,' e.g., so there can be no planning, Soviet economy cannot succeed, etc.

But movement means growth, development, progress, recession, gradual or *per saltum,* propelled by changes in the structure of relations, proportions, functions. All this is a different kind of reality. Which means history; and history cannot be clamped into the procrustean bed of syllogisms. All social sciences are essentially historical. Economics is a science, most closely related to the natural sciences, yet a human, social science of group behaviour. I would be the last person to denigrate the marvellous analysis of marginalists and mathematicians. I respect them as I do the impressionists and the symbolists. At the same time, honesty demands an expression of doubt, a query about the nature of any further utility of that type of analysis in view of today's *social,* and *hence theoretical* needs. Why not give historical method, that is, the logic of process a chance? I know that this method is not what is pursued even by most historians. Still it must be tried in India, because the basic fact about India

[24] J. T. Dunlop, '*The Development of Labour Organiastion: a theoretical framework,*' in Lester and Shister's *Insights into Labour Issues.*

is neither food nor devaluation, neither Pakistan nor the reported fall or rise in productivity, but simply the fact that *it is changing.*

I know the implications of my suggestion, viz., the sacrifices of precision, even of economic theory, as most of us have come to know it. But after all, in what are we vitally interested, precision that has proved to be imprecise because of its unreality —and nobody but the professor pins his faith on economic analysis today—or, reality, which, by definition, is imprecise and indeterminate, but from which we have to wrest a few large generalisations and working hypotheses? Let us be clear on this issue. I vote for reality as a process. I also want Indian economists to do the same. Dr. Zakir Husain in his excellent lectures on *Capitalism* has done it, but along Sombart's lines of cultural understanding. Will Rangnekar and Krishnamurti pay heed to my humble request to question the method they have followed in writing the two, alas, the only two to my knowledge, significant attempts at theoretical analysis made in India this year or so?[25] They may lose caste, but it is worth the chase of what the ancients called truth and moderns like Whitehead call reality.

I find that I have omitted to mention about half a dozen other books on economics, particularly on labour and international economics. They are usually descriptive. I should have mentioned the various reports of the UNO, the ILO, and our central government. My impression is that usually the UNO publications are inferior in quality to those of the old League of Nations. Probably inexperience is the reason. Reserve Bank reports and bulletins have a standard of their own. But India government publications have little or nothing. Poor printing, late publication, avoidance of theoretical discussion and unavailability continue as before. There are a dozen of our best economists at the centre and more than a hundred research scholars. I wonder what has happened to them. Are they being forced to hide their light under the bushel?

[25] S. B. Rangnekar, *Imperfect Competition in International Trade;* B. V. Krishnamurti, *Pricing in Planned Economy.*

3. *Man and Plan in India*

I

Two questions vex thinking men at the time of major social changes: what is the new society, and what is the new man? The time of questioning is seldom fixed; it may be before, during and after the change has occurred, acquired speed and impressed itself on the life-habits on all or most concerned. Sometimes the two questions arise separately. The intensity of anxiety to raise them and answer them varies, in the first instance, with the quality of the change. If the change is drastic, basic and comprehensive, that is, when 'the material conditions for their (higher relations of production) existence have matured in the womb of old society,' one would expect a common concern with such questions. Marx wrote that 'mankind always takes up only such problems as it is in a position to solve; for when we look at the matter more closely, we shall always discover that the problem itself arises only when the material conditions, needed for its solution are also present, or at the least are in the process of formation.'

Marx's 'always' refers to revolutionary situations. But even when such situations are not at hand, problems about the nature of the new society and the new man disturb a few souls who formulate them under the pressure of personal responsibility towards the present and the future, and/or of acute disgust with the present. In these cases the popularity of the issues would depend upon the prestige and the number of such souls, no less than upon the extent of discontent and the means of communication.

When these conditions conspire, there grows the envelope of the great debate in which defeat or victory is a matter of serious concern. Questions are sharpened though the answers are not necessarily so, because they are often the replies to other questions which have not been solved. A revolutionary change, in the Marxist sense, poses sharper issues and offers clearer aswers than a 'natural,' evolutionary change. In the usual Marxist interpretation of revolutionary change, there is, however, a tendency towards simplification in the attempt to focus the problems with all that it means in the way of serving a broad line of action, a certain narrowing of vision and the operation of a peculiar type of the sense of rightness and finality which is often akin to a puritanism of the spirit and hostile to the philosophical temper and inquiry necessary for adequate solutions.

Clarity and simplicity can be synonymous, but simplification is neither simplicity nor clarity. Thus it is that revolutionary solutions may throw up problems in very sharp relief but answer them in a manner that is partial. More or less clear views of the nature of society desired may emerge, but the men who formulate them are seldom full men. Probably, such is the fate of all systematic, rational and conscious change. The impersonality of the process tends to diminish human personality in the interest of realism, action and situation, even when the mere tempo of change and the adequate ideology would inflate it. Even utopian thinking, which has a reasoning of its own though it be not historical and which has a consciousness that is quite often undifferentiated from the awareness of traditional values, ultimately makes for a restricted society and a closed personality. Actual utopian experiments would bear witness to it.

India's social change, which is both a fact and an act, has not had the benefit of a clear or a systematic theory or design of new society behind it. Nor was the outline of the new man which could be filled in by the movement towards the new society ever firmly sketched. Apart from various religious, sectarian *ashrams,* which could be interpreted as a sort of blueprints of a desired state of society offering models of new men in the making, no pattern as such either of the new society or of the new man was envisaged by Indians before India came in contact with the west. Yet, sociologically, an 'ideal type' of man in the Weberian sense could be spotted. The characteristics of such a man were the performance of customary functions and duties fixed at birth, their working out through the four defined stages to a possible state of complete non-attachment, and the resultant development of personality in the pursuit of *dharma. Moksha,* or salvation, being the goal, the 'ideal type' of man could not but be a potentially religious person with his eyes beyond the world. It might have led to greater integration of personality, more poise and peace than are given to the modern man; but the problems it had to face did not spring from the dynamics of social change for the simple reason that no social change was drastic enough in the absence of any change in the modes of production.

The impact of Islam was no doubt strong, but the resultant Hindu-Muslim culture, ideologies and ways of life were not materially different from those of the pre-Muslim period. No marked change seems to have occurred in the nature of the 'ideal type.' If anything, renunciation became a more marked trait than ever. Anti-Muslim, or anti-foreign rebels like Rana Pratap or Shivaji were not quite the new ideal types. The former was the hero of an age of chivalry and the latter was probably one of an earlier age. Both were idealised by nationalist historians, but it is debatable if they were or could be identified with the ideal Kshatriya, say, like Bhishma, Arjuna or Karna. Bhakti-cult generally centred in the perfect man-god, Krishna or his *avatar*, or the founder of the sect. But in so far as he was a deity or deified, the pull of approximation which the 'ideal' type connotes could only mean a merging, an immersion, in other words, renunciation. The glimpses of a 'new' society in the literature of this period are faint. Ordinary men and women pursued their usual tenor of existence, and extraordinary men wanted a little toleration to do the same according to the traditional light. It is not strange that no utopias were built in India. (*Satya Yuga* was no utopia. It was the golden age of the past.). The social urges were not strong.

The west came with a different and a disturbing message. It shook Indian society out of its torpor. Raja Ram Mohan Roy was the first historic man to absorb it. He was steeped equally in Hindu and Muslim lore, and he studied Christianity with the same zeal. Probably he had no clear vision either of the new man or the new society. But his emphasis on rationality was not quite the rationality of Hindu logic or of Budhist disputations. It was more akin to the western rationality of the eighteenth and early nineteenth century in its faith in natural laws, in reform and the greatest good of the greatest number, and in progress to be achieved perpetually through human effort. At the same time, it was different from the rationality which was the essence of capitalism, that is, its emphasis on accounting and technology. The old Indian logic, before it became the new logic (*navya nyaya*), had always been linked with the pursuit of the absolute or the divine (*anvikshiki vidya*), and even with the Bengal logicians it did not become secularised.

Ram Mohan's rationality was definitely human reason, though he never cut himself adrift from religion which he could accept only in its rationalised form. In his view, Hindu religion had acquired many excrescences which had to be removed by the application of human reason, e.g., by higher criticism, scientific scholarship, etc. This he did with marvellous learning and efficiency. There is hardly any major intellectual trait in modern India, be it in its attitude towards language or social reform, democracy and internationalism, which cannot be traced in his writings. Above all, he was himself a full man, and not a renouncer of life. He took modern civilisation in both hands and made it the vital impulse of the cultural development of modern India. He did not envision a new man or a new society as such, but he introduced the new strains of rationality, of an openness of attitude, and of a certain amount of courage to face the new order, attitudes which proved to be invaluable dynamic elements in the social change that followed. No more can it be said of India that she specialises only in the production of *sanyasis* and mystics whose eyes are always inturned to soul or upturned to heaven. India's self-consciousness and world-consciousness in the secular sense have gone together since the days of the Raja.

A number of reformers and reform movements followed. Barring one, the tendency was of synthesis with a tilt towards Indian traditions. The exception was the Nava Bidhan Samaj of Kesub Chandra Sen, which leaned towards western Christianity and eclecticism. It made less headway than the Arya Samaj, the Sadharan Brahmo Samaj and the Prarthana Samaj. The founders of each were dynamic personalities and well acquainted with the main currents of western thought and action. Their main effort was to make them run through the Indian bed to remove its choking weeds in order that the ancient stream might flow. The Arya Samaj would have the Vedas back and the Adi Brahmo Samaj the Upanishads instead of the Puranas and the later rituals. Yet none of them was a revivalist and the Prarthana Samaj and the Sadharan Brahmo Samaj the least so. Each movement used Samaja (society) for its title, though in course of time it shrank into a small community or sect. On the other hand, there was some sort of Hindu resurgence through the spread of Arya Samaj and the Theosophical Society. It was more of a general awakening than a movement. Rama Krishna cannot be said to be founder of a counter-reformist Hindu movement nor Swami Vivekananda its Loyola or Xavier. If anything, the Swami was more a Buddhist than a Hindu revivalist. His monachism and rationality, his emphasis on service and missionary zeal are more Buddhist than Hindu. Philosophically, he was a Vedantist and actively, he followed the Geeta and the Tripitaka. His devastating criticisms of the Hindu Samaj and his missionary efforts equally appealed to the educated Indian who was unwilling to cut away from his social roots and yet felt that Hinduism needed revitalisation.

Through his teachings and personality the Indian gained self-confidence. From now on the average Hindu ceased to feel that his only duty was to conform to the type of the 'gentle Hindoo' whom the west had discovered. His pride would now come from the dynamic principles of Hinduism itself. Beyond this, there is no trace of Hindu revivalism in the movement of voluntary social reform and service which the Swami initiated. Other examples of Hindu resurgence are not significant from the point of view taken here. Their importance was derivative in so far as Hindu resurgence was absorbed in the larger national movement. The Muslims had always a suspicion of this element and never felt easy about it. If the British could take advantage of it to drive a wedge between the Hindus and Muslims, none can wholly blame them. The most that can, therefore, be said about the conceptions of society and man vaguely current in this period is this: it would be a reformed society and he would be a reformed nationalist Hindu. No social or human transmutation was necessary, and thus not conceived; it was almost inconceivable.

The next important man was Tagore. He was untouched both by the fighting Hindu nationalism of Dayanand and Tilak and the anti-westernism of revivalists. He could not also subscribe to the westernisation that had captured the imagination of a few 'England-returned' Indians. Neither the strain of ratonality once noticed in Ranade or Gokhale, nor the legalism of the brilliant liberal intellectuals of Madras was prominent in his attitudes. He was too much of a poet for all that. Though he was the product of a reformed family, he was not a reformer in the usual sense. His analysis was essentially sociological. One might say that he was more interested in society than in the urban roots, and more in the invigoration of the rural roots than in the grafting of the foreign notion of nationalism on the branches or the trunk. His new society was basically rural, self-growing, decentralised and cooperative. He believed that in the process of self-growth India would easily take in all the communities that lived in India, and the universe (*visva*) too. He saw no basic difficulty in a liberated and dynamic India's assimilating western culture. For him neither science nor technology, neither secularism nor democracy was an indigestible substance. He wanted all of them to come, but not in the protean shapes of power. His politics were social. People called his ideas utopian, but he built no literary utopia. (Neither the origin nor the history of Santiniketan betrays a utopian spirit.) Sociologically, he was a realist.

It is this which abolishes all other distinctions between him and Gandhiji. Both knew that India lives in the villages, both wanted villages to be the growth-cones of India, both believed in decentralised economy, and both wanted self-mastery, 'self-kingdom' (Swaraj) before exchange took place. Negatively, too, they were similar—they both failed to point out the way of absorbing the new social forces which the west had released through science and its application to large-scale production. Tagore saw them as power uncontrolled by social sense and morality, while Gandhiji saw them as evil, even when he considered some machines as necessary. To the sociologist the mutual admiration of the two is not strange; nor is the fact that Tagore uncannily forecast the character and technique of Gandhiji in *Vairagee Dhananjaya* amazing.

This does not mean, however, that Gandhiji's conception of the future social order was identical with Tagore's conception of Swadeshi Samaj. For one, Gandhiji's conception as formulated in his *Hind Swaraj* had a clearer outline; for another, by virtue of the later use of the words Rama-rajya, it lost its clarity but gained a wider appeal; for a third, its blurred outline became a cloak for the social content. Today, many reactionaries have rallied under that nomenclature. But the basic difference was in ideas of the new man who would build and reside in the new society. For Gandhiji, he would be a moral man, ready to sacrifice his all for truth, simple, direct and pulsating with the lowliest of the lowly. Truth, nón-violence and participation would be his nature. Tagore's new man was not the renouncer. He thought of renunciation as a means of higher enjoyment, as the Upanishad has it. Sacrifice he admired, not for its own sake, but as an excellent means of discipline. In fact, he had renounced renunciation quite early in his poetic career, and he could not recommend it to the new man or as social policy. Being the son of the Maharshi he could not minimise the importance of truth. He would want every young man to pursue truth in every way but preferably through rationality and science whose spirit he understood better than Gandhiji. Truth or *satyam,* in his view, was one of the three eternal values of Indian thought, (the other two being *advaitam* and *anantam,* that is unity and infinity, and not beauty and joy); but it was not identical with God, in the personal nature of whom he did not quite believe, say as the Christians, the Vaishnavas, or the common Hindus do, or as Gandhi did. Yet for him, truth, in a sense, was personal, almost human.

Many characters of his stories and novels object to traditional values (and party discipline) on human considerations, and Tagore sympathised with them. The strong note of dissent in the Brahmo movement, (which can be traced to earlier reformist ones, and even to the Upanishads), was evident in his treatment of human themes in prose and poetry. In regard to non-violence his position was not clear. Apart from the fact that every Hindu loves peace and is averse to conflict and hears *shanti* (peace) muttered on every important occasion, he had faith in the laws of harmony. This did not prevent him from admiring the terrorists whose courage of conviction, however misplaced, always appealed to him. His objection to them was on the score of their blind obedience to impersonal, and hence inhuman, discipline. It can, therefore, be said that the new type of man he liked and conjured up was an honest dissenter, emotionally rich, rational and tough enough to die for a cause. Such a man was a fuller man than either the puritan or the one who merely accepted. He was essentially the affirmative-creative type. Unfortunately, however, the type that was immediately produced by his influence was the literary-romantic one believing more in the spontaneity of talent than in discipline, a soft and tender type, in fact, effeminate.

Gandhiji produced a different type altogether. The new man, viz., the Congressman, was basically the moral type. His test was courage that was implied in and born out of the manner of abandonment of bourgeois caution. He was to sacrifice himself at the altar of the country in a non-violent, truthful and simple manner. He was to be the common man (and not merely to be the one with him), self-dependent, living simply in self-sufficient villages. He would have no wants which he could not satisfy with simple, home-made implements. He need not be a thinker; simple faith in God would do. He need not be of studious habit either; the Geeta, the Ramayana, the Bible, or the Quran would suffice. But he had to be pure, physically primarily, and clean, truthful and efficient in whatever he undertook. Poetry, music, science, learning were not relevant unless they sang the praise of God. What was wanted was moral strength, and not aesthetic or intellectual sensibility.

This morality was connected with will. Modern India has not produced a leader with greater will that was less divorced from love of power than Gandhiji. It attracted Sardar Patel to him. Gandhiji connected it with faith in God. He would want the new man to be prayerful in the first instance, to be transformed into the blessed man in the next. Like aesthetic sense, rationality was secondary. The impulse of creativity, which was a vital ingredient of Tagore's new man, was to merge in the creative love of God and service to his fellow-beings. Joy as such, the joy that comes from contemplation, from creation of new art-forms, or from the disinterested pursuit of knowledge, was, if anything, a by-product of service or its hand-maid.

In short, the new man was to be built round the two concepts of praxis, the facts of Indian life, and truth which was equivalent to God who was personal. The relevant question is how many were true to the type made and contemplated by Gandhiji. They were more than what we imagine. All sorts of people were gathered by him in the national movement. They were not of equal merit. But they were uplifted and occasionally transmuted by the moral fervour of the open movement and the moral genius of the man. In some cases the transformation was genuine, in others it was not. The strain was too much, few men could be angels, and fewer still truthful and moral, prayerful and wilful without caring for power; that is the usual explanation of the amazing fact, as a wag put it, that the white Gandhi cap has so soon become the symbol of the black-market. But, probably, more plausible explanations are possible. Ramarajya, as a concept, was wonderful, it did not demand the rigour of the society of the *Hind Swaraj*; it was based on plenty, though references to famine, war, untouchability and other social crimes in the reign of Rama are not rare in the Ramayana.

Business cycles, fluctuations of employment, war contracts, economic exploitation of men, women and children, utter dependence of Indians on foreign imports, sharp contrasts of wealth, belching factories and stinking slums were not known in Ayodhya. They were known to Indians when Gandhiji ruled their hearts. They were the basic realities of the day. So Rama-rajya only excited nostalgia. It was not a projection of the present into the future. It was not even the millennium; it was a throw-back into the pre-*kali yuga.* For most Indians a vacuum intervened between the present realities and the past dreams; and no wonder that they soon ceased to dream.

In other words, the type of the new society enveloped in the vulgarised notion of Rama-rajya was not only non-historical but anti-historical. But when society is what it is in India the only hope and treasure of Indians become the historical sense, the acute feeling for social forces and their human direction according to laws, which may not be the laws of nature but are none the less the laws for all practical purposes, that is, sound hypotheses for social action In the absence of that sense and feeling among large sections of Gandhiji's followers Rama-rajya remained an election slogan. Gandhiji intuitively realised the implications of political success. In his last testament he advised the dissolution of the Congress and wanted Congressmen to diffuse themselves in the villages for concentrated social work. The deliquescence of the hard core of the *Hind Swaraj* in the moist, simple notion of Ram-rajya as a political slogan is the history of the rise and fall of the Congress movement.

The new man, the Congressman, who was going to be the 'ideal' type, was thus not the full man. Though it is true that some men of fine intellect plunged into the movement initiated and impelled by Gandhiji, it is equally true that neither they, nor the artists and scientists did so without caveat. The usual charge usually levelled against them is that they stood out. If they did, they did so because they felt that they had no place in the movement, that they could not find any intellectual system in it, that they could not make it fit in with any theory they knew or had read about.

The movement was certainly anti-intellectual—most movements are; at the same time, the Indian intellectuals were as full of foreign ideas as they were blissfully, and often, contemptuously ignorant of Indian culture or Indian realities. Still the fact survives that the middle class had long been the most articulate class and had enjoyed social prestige by virtue of their contacts with the west, its knowledge and ways of living, in addition to what was attached to the services and professions, which the foreign administration had fixed and done its best to limit. The hard historical core of middle class prestige and domination was their knowledge of the modern social forces, that is, science, technology, democracy and sense of historical development, which the west stood for. This knowledge the political movement which was to usher in the new society was not expected to possess as its first requisite of success and the new man, that is, the Congressman, who was to be the ideal type of the new society, was not expected to utilise it. The result was a partial man, a smaller man, a shrunken man. Modern times demand a fuller person. Hence shrunken men have shrunk further when the moral fervour, unredeemed by the sense of history and rationality, has lost its power of breath to inflate and uplift. This seems to be the basic reason of moral degradation in the ranks of the Congress.

It is here that Pandit Jawaharlal comes. As he is the frankest statesman in the world, nothing more than what he has written or talked about himself can be written on him. But here his influence on the conception and making of the new society and the new man is the issue, and very little has been written on that. So what follows is tentative. He has quite a few years to go, but it is not likely that he will change his commitments. A few facts about his influence are basic. He is of the Congress and yet out of it. He does not belong to the crowd, and he does not conform to the 'type,' then or now. He loves the crowd whom he calls the people, and the crowd is fascinated by him. For the crowd he is the charismatic person. But he is also the idol of the middle class educated man who knows that the world is not exhausted by India, that India must make confident strides towards the future, that willy-nilly, modern forces, like nationalism for the colonies, democracy, science, and technology, have come to stay, that civilisation belongs to the city, that culture is man-made, that history halts unless it is pushed, that there is no marching back like frogs to the well, that the blind forces of nature or of social systems have to be harnessed, and that the universe has to be faced openly and squarely, without fear or favour. A part of Nehru's fascination for the middles class is snobbishness, but the rest is the conviction that he is the man of that present which enters into the future. It is this courage to recognise modern social forces, to build on them and face the future, which attracts him to the educated community. He has no 'party' to follow him, but he has a whole community of educated people to follow him with awakened intelligence. Where he goes they would like to go. If he moves towards a planned society, they would move as social engineers.

A long, lasting social order possible to attain has been conceived and men and women are exercising themselves to achieve it. The best of Nehru is in the Plan, however vague and unsatisfactory it may be to the perfectionist. And the Plan will work India even though some Indians may not work it excitedly. Those who would do it would make up the ideal type of man for India. It is an achievement of the highest order—this transference of allegiance from Rama-rajya to a planned social order, this shifting of the axis of morality from sacrifice to planned endeavour.

Gandhiji's constructive programme also demanded the highest effort and the highest sacrifice. But the programme of the Plan is for another type of society, and the typical man wanted for it is naturally also different; he should have more knowledge, more technical ability, more historical sense than his counterpart of the Sarvodaya programme; probably, he too sacrifices, but he is expected to sacrifice less. The Plan means both a change of the axis of the ideal type of man and society as well as a change of gear. Thus it is that Gandhiji's influence is reported to have disappeared. It is true in direct proportion to the reverence with which his name is held. But gone with it is his view of morality—a view which, though partial, was a genuine binder through its linkage with faith in God; and gone with it also is the faith in the spontaneity of people's creative love, however crudely it might have been held.

From now on the ordering has to come from the engineers, social and technical, who have faith in organisation, knowledge of exact and less exact sciences, and who are rational in their outlook. So they will make the ideal type for the next generation: the technocrat with imagination, the bureaucrat with the democratic touch and flexibility; in fact, a middle class know-how type. This type is going to be the norm. Voluntary village workers as envisaged in the Plan and community projects, etc., cannot but gravitate to that type. Will it be different from the modern western counterpart? Probably not. Will it be fuller than its predecessors? In secular knowledge, yes; but in religious ethics, no. Aesthetically, it will be poor, because the cult of science and technology betrays this hatred of 'literary' education, this mistrust of knowledge for its own sake. The work of hired experts, technocrats and bureaucrats, can be very cramping indeed. An amount of ruthlessness is also inevitable in all planning; individuals have to be sacrificed for the aggregate. So the ideal type will not always be very human either. Scope may be said to have been given to humanity and aesthetic sense in and through cottage industries and decentralised economy. But only a fool will believe that they will maintain their exclusive beauty against the vulgar invasion of large-scale state or private enterprise. The river valley projects, the science laboratories, the state factories and services, the norms of economic pattern and knowledge, will draw them unto themselves in one mighty embrace of Hercules.

There is a vague fear of it in the country; it is deeper than the fear of the unknown and more uncomfortable than the loss of the habitual. It is spiritual nervousness before the possibilities of dehumanisation. One wonders if this be not at the back of the so-called frustration of the country. Nehru and the Plan have changed the axis and the gear; they are changing the pattern of habits; they would make young men face the unknown with courage; they would seek to modernise on the basis of knowledge of technology and historical forces. No wonder that some of them feel, with their ancient parents, that all is lost. The fact is that something is lost, and something else and more has been gained, at least, can be gained. Only the concepts of the new man and new society have not yet been clarified. For this the Indian intellectuals are to be blamed. The fault of modern Indian education does not lie in its literary, non-vocational, non-useful bias; it lies in the lack of clarity in the concept, if it has any, of the new social order and the new man. It has so long left the ideal types to be fixed by blind forces and allowed them to slither into the average, the common and the temporary. In fact, it has not thought clearly about them at all. The function of universities is to fix the 'ideal' types, and only incidentally and indirectly, to build charater.

II

We have seen in the preceding section how the views about the new order and the new man held by some of the leading men of India of the last century and the first half of this were defective and how they could not materialise. From the *sannyasi*, or the *mukta purush,* who was more the perfect man than the 'ideal' type in the Weberian sense, to the middle-class successful professional, who was becoming the typical man far away from the perfect one, the transition was effected by forces released by contact with the west and foreign administration. Attempts were made to control these forces; in fact, that is the sociological significance of the national movement; but they were not wholly successful due to the absence in it of an adequate appreciation of the historical and social nature of the new forces and of a planned rational utilisation of that knowledge in terms of a comprehensive national endeavour. Such endeavour could come in the Indian circumstances only through a state which was popular and democratic, that is, a state which sprang from the loins of the people. India had no state, not to speak of such a state, before 1947. So the failure can be easily explained on political grounds alone.

This is not to suggest that the present state is a social one. Far from it. What is meant is that in committing itself wholeheartedly to the Plan, the present state may be expected to help in stimulating social conditions for a new type of social order and a new type of man, and in enabling India to face the possible implications of their imposition upon the old types and their remnants. (For reasons mentioned earlier the new types do not grow out of the old types; hence imposition.) The expectation is that in the large sphere of voluntary social action it will be successful mainly through the Bharat Sewak Samaj, an unofficial body working with the blessings of the state, central and provincial. A number of people, however, feel that this Samaj is in reality a party organisation, that its ultimate purpose is to strengthen the party in power though its declared purpose is 'to strengthen the foundations of the state.'

Some honest men who were close to Gandhiji and trained in his school of service also think that the Bharat Sewak Samaj is basically different from Gandhiji's conception of Lok Sewak Sangh, the rules of which were suggested by him in the last days of his life. This, however, is no serious objection. We have already accepted it when we stated that the Plan would work Indians even if some Indians did not work it. The Plan works on a different axis, call it distorted if you like, and with a different, a faster tempo. So the objections will in any case be overruled by events. The real point is to find out if the functions of the Bharat Sewak Samaj have been well thought out, if they contradict each other, if they are likely to serve the new order of society in the course of their operations, if they will produce a different order not conceived, and also if the new type of man to be trained by the Bharat Sewak Samaj will be suitable for the conceived order of society, or create, consciously or unconsciously, another order altogether inconsistent with it.

A sympathetic study of the stated functions of the Samaj leads to the following conclusions. No distinction has been made between its aims and functions. And it was necessary unless the old concept of Rama-rajya was accepted as an aim. This is quite likely, because the Samaj comes, as it were, as Gandhiji's legacy, and also because it is intellectually difficult, or utopian. At best, it is an exercise of humility before evolving situations. It may also be politically inexpedient. Yet intellectual difficulties have to be faced; yet some utopianism is uplifting; yet all humilities are not pieties, some of which are concessions or indifferent to emerging forces which are more often blind than not.

In short, the functions may destroy the aims. Thus, for example, it is stated that one of the functions of the Samaj is 'to create social awareness among the people with regard to prevailing conditions and problems, and their own obligations.' The word rights is not mentioned here, presumably on the supposition that all people have already got all the rights, and therefore they should not any more worry about them and would do well to concentrate on the discharge of obligations instead. But, unfortunately, 'social awareness among the people with regard to prevailing conditions and problems' can only arise from an acute sense of rights. Prevailing conditions being not always satisfactory, the economic situation being what it is, mere discharge of obligations cannot create 'social awareness,' even if the stupendous shift from fifty years' agitational conditioning in the sense of (political and social) rights to the sense of constructive obligation could be effected overnight. Peaceful, ungrudging discharge of obligations is possible in the midst of plenty, security and equality, or under the total sway of religion.

In either case, it is a mechanical performance of rituals. An awareness of obligations will certainly 'restore and improve the social health of the community,' which is another function of the Samaj; it will improve manners, no doubt, but what does restoration mean? Of Rama-rajya? Was Indian society ever healthy, at least, in the last two hundred years? What does improvement connote? With open or disguised unemployment stalking the land, can improvement of social health be brought about by sweet words of obligations? And what is social health? Is it the absence of disease as a static condition, or is it a state of social action which a dynamic society takes in its stride without bothering much about the cost? Another function is 'to train and equip those who offer themselves for work in the organisation, in order to enable them to render official and useful services.'

The noteworthy fact is again the omission of any reference to the right to work (and employment) at a comfortable standard of living. We will not refer to equipment and training. Whatever training is largely available is political training. American experts in social service are seldom useful; they all seem to end up in the study of caste tensions and local factions. The only Indian expert voluntary social service organisation known to the author is the Ramakrishna-Vivekananda Mission. There may be others, but this Mission at least does not conduct itself on sectarian or communal levels. It has no politics either. One wonders if that be the reason for its being neglected. Then why only those 'who offer themselves for work in the organisation' are to be equipped and trained? 'In the organisation' is likely to be inside the organisation, the declared purpose of which is 'to strengthen the foundations of the state,' that is, for all practical purposes, the party in power.

And lastly, the conjunction of 'official and useful services'; it is quite possible that some official services, despite intentions, are completely useless, and some useful services are, and had better remain, unofficial. Examples of official (and party) frownings at useful services are quite common, e.g., the peace movement.

One more remark about the voluntary workers in the organisation. The intention is that they will have the initiative in many matters. In actual practice, they will have to implement the policy of the 'keymen' in the village-level, or they will come into conflict with them. Those who know Indian villages need not be told that the keymen are the minor government servants or their nominees. These latter are usually party men. Village factions, when they are not based on caste, kinship and family loyalties, can be traced to partisan selection. Factionalism cannot but creep into the relation between 'workers' who belong to the ruling party and 'voluntary' workers. If this happens on a large scale, as is not unlikely, then the contribution of the Bharat Sewak Samaj towards the concept of the new order or the creation of the 'ideal' type will be small. It is true that the Samaj has been declared to be non-partisan, but in the absence of urgent, overpowering social incentives it may become a pawn in the game of power-politics.

Thus it is that the non-distinction of aims and functions of the Bharat Sewak Samaj is likely to limit its own functions and thus handicap it in the formation of the outline of a new *samaj*, a new society. In intention, the Bharat Sewak Samaj is the popular instrument of the Plan, which will operate on the existing *samaj* to produce the new type of *samaj*, or social order. It almost seems that a people's instrument had to be devised, if not for anything else, at least, for expiating the original sin of formulating the Plan mainly with the help of bureaucrats and with the last-minute suggestions of a few hand-picked leaders of other parties, and presenting it to the people as an accomplished fact. (It is said with regret that with the best efforts not even a professor of social sciences deeply interested in planning could secure from the market a printed copy of the report eight weeks after its publication. He managed to secure it at last from an MP who apparently had no use for it.) The Bharat Sewak Samaj is thus obviously an expression of that feeling of original guilt. Psychologically, it looks like an act of meritorious expiation. It is indeed difficult to see how a fabricated *samaj* can bring a new *samaj* into being when incentives are admittedly not there and the prospects of an increase in the standard of living with its help are not dramatically vivid. It could be done by undemocratic means, which, of course, we have rightly abjured.

The preceding account deals with the mechanism of general public cooperation, or what may be called a general schooling of the people in the creation of a sort of climate of social conditions for the success of the Plan. But specific spheres of voluntary action, the third sector, have also been indicated, in which more intensive participation is expected. As many as five sectors, or fronts have emerged out of the Plan:

(1) The National Extension Service and Community Projects have a target of covering about 25 per cent of rural population by 1955-56. By Oct 2, 1954 about 44,000 villages with a population of nearly 30 millions will come under the network. Certain blocks will at once be intensively developed by the Community Projects and the remainder will come under the Extension Programme. Apart from the fact that much leeway has to be made to include 270 millions of the rural population, that the process of amortisation of foreign and central aid by higher rates of saving and investment in the countryside remains dark or has not yet begun to operate, and also that this 100-crore programme appears to be expensive in one way and a mere drop in the ocean in another, the matter of rural cooperation is still an open question so long as disguised employment and unemployment are not linked up with the idea of the next social order through an altogether different set of incentives. Some incentives may be whipped up, as they have been to some extent, by the administration; but not all of them are stable, sound and sufficient for maintaining and stimulating the higher tempo that is necessary for the *continuous ascent* (or passage) of the Plan from even one state of equilibrium to another. The sociological distinction between the community of the Community Projects and the Indian village community is sought to be abolished by the implementation of the former. That had to be done. But the point to note is the implications of that change of meaning; on the one hand, resistance, and on the other, the time taken for substitute institutions to grow. Still, a new leadership seems to be in the offing. At present, it still comes from the top where power resides.

(2) A Local Works Programme sector (with a provision of Rs. 15 crores) has started working. The local contribution is to be about half of the cost of each work made up of contributions of the state, local bodies and local people in cash, kind or voluntary labour. The government pays the same amount as the local contribution. Out of 3 crores of this year's budget for the purpose 2½ crores go to the States on population basis and 50 lakhs have been set apart for direct allotment with Rs. 10,000 maximum for each work. The works are necessarily small-scale, which is an important point in their favour in so far

as they are in a better position to serve the local needs in a decentralised manner than the big schemes, the value of which cannot be immediately seized by the people within their customary horizons of experience. The LWP seems to be an effective agency for creating local group incentives in terms of immediate, realised results and perspectives. Its danger is dispersion. Too many projects may be wasteful.

From the broader point of view, another source of possible conflict may be indicated. The type of incentives for small programmes is different from that for large-scale ones. The attitudes are also different. In the former, the economic order assumed and envisaged is of self-sufficiency with agriculture, cottage-industries and processing industries working on a higher level with electricity, etc. Their market is limited to town-economy. On the other hand, the assumption and the vision of large-scale programmes are not self-sufficiency but export, both internal and external. Their market is the city in the main. So the attitudes are of urban economy and all that it means. India needs both. But 'both' is a vague word that covers many conflicts. First, it has been found that when both flourish together, it is at the expense of the former. Economic history is full of examples where the former has become the parasite of the latter. In the modern world, the dynamic is of the large-scale programme. It is inconceivable that 75 per cent of the people will remain content while the dynamic element furnished by 15 per cent will forge ahead in the mad rush for higher and higher production and standard of living. Tomorrow is more often the enemy of today than its friend. And tomorrow has the largeness of adventure.

(3) Then there are the provisions for students' participation in the shape of helping in the Community Projects either as cadets, or as voluntary groups. *Sramadan* for a limited period has been prescribed. One crore of rupees has been set apart for the youth front. So far nothing material has been achieved in this sphere. The vagueness of it is covered by wild talks about the necessity of changing the whole basis of education indulged by all manner of people, educated and uneducated. Unfortunately, however, this is the weakest portion in the Plan. Much of the labour of youngmen's *sramadan* is being wasted by lack of coordination in the schemes of voluntary manual work, by the confused objectives and the impermanent, if not the inconsequential, nature of the work assigned, etc. It

is not encouraging to see so much enthusiasm wasted. Besides, there is not much sense in making school and college boys do work which under-employed or unemployed workers could do better. Manual work is good on many counts, but not because of that abstract, puritanic concept of the dignity of labour. When the total number of occupations is so small—it was about a hundred only in the 1931 census as compared to about four thousand in the UK—diversification of occupations should precede undiversified *sramadan*.

(4) Voluntary participation of women is at present chiefly confined to the inculcation of (small) savings habit among women. In March 1953, 42 lakhs of rupees were collected by women in the Savings Week. A permanent organisation has started functioning. It is too early to say how it will work in the countryside. A number of educated women from the cities are interesting themselves in family-planning. Their efforts have not yet been reflected in the birth-rate and death-rate as such. One can hardly forbear from feeling, as in the case of the youth front, that the available energies are not yet being fully tapped and utilised. Women leaders who are not politicians are yet to come. It is a big jump from the home to the outside. But if Indian women can take it the Plan becomes a success.

(5) A Social Welfare Board with a provision of Rs. 4 crores has just been constituted. Pandit Jawaharlal, in his inaugural address, very relevantly pointed out the limitations of welfare work. In his opinion (he had said it earlier too), welfare touched only the fringe of the problem while its heart was the removal of poverty, the creation of higher levels of employment, standards of living, etc.

A few remarks are necessary here in view of the popularity of the word 'welfare' in connection with welfare state, and welfare schemes of a voluntary nature. The concept of welfare arose out of British life and thought. Its basis was the philosophy of utilitarianism or philosophical radicalism. The postulates of utilitarianism still cling to modern economics of welfare, or welfare economics. The impulse of voluntary welfare, or services, had an even earlier origin in the moral idealism of puritanism. Towards the end of the nineteenth century another impulse came in the shape of the state as the benevolent aspect of power. And in the twentieth this power has been simultaneously humanised and bureaucratised in planning. Negatively, welfare is a defence-system against the vagaries of capitalism in the outlying world and its operations inside. Now, India has caught up only with the last two, but is without the traditions of utilitarianism, philosophical radicalism and the moral fervour of puritanism and non-conformist dissent. In fact, Indian traditions are their opposite.

If this analysis be true, then the Welfare Board has to meet certain unconscious resistances in odd sectors and work in vacuum elsewhere. To that extent the activities of the Welfare Board will be hampered. Obviously, the welfare workers cannot at once be the 'natural' leaders. That inner deficiency implicit in the temporal lag is likely to be covered by more bureaucracy. In any case, a welfare board cannot bring about a new social order. It will be said that it is not expected to do so. Unfortunately, institutions under government auspices soon acquire the habit of feeling more important than what they are, that is, of trying to fulfil expectations which were not there and failing in those which were. Humility is seldom the virtue of fabricated organisations, organisations without roots and traditions.

III

We can now pass on to the real active element, viz, the Plan. Its study reveals the following assumptions of a new social order, though no outline as such is firmly sketched anywhere.

(1) The order is to be harmonious. Harmony, negatively, means exclusion of class conflict, exploitation, unequal rights and privileges, and gentle regulation of unbalanced development of parts and sources of wealth on the socio-economic plane. Positively, on the social plane, it means class collaboration, trusteeship, education in mutual obligations, and immediate recognition of the superior claims of the whole as interpreted by the central government. The idea of slow tempo is implicit in harmony. A torrent cannot be a harmonious flow. Harmony of interests dis-assumes force and violence in form.

(2) The social order will be a moving order, of course, slow in the interests of harmony. Movement, negatively, means getting away from old habits, customs, traditions, etc., and positively, getting on towards some equilibrium, on whatever level

that may be at the conclusion of every five years or so. The assumption is of comparative static equilibrium. It is to be noted that the movement is not to a point, a state, or a goal, but towards the fluid state reached after the lapse of scheduled years. Targets, in this conceptual context, are merely pointer-readings indicative of the passage in space over a number of years rather than of the thrill of reaching a prescribed goal in time. (Note that the two passages are different. The one in time is a one-way traffic; and while its movement forward can be counted in hours and years to move backward is to be lost in the eternity behind the present. There is no *tendency* as such in space; either you are there or you are not there. As it has been said, time helps you with space, but space does not help you with time). In short, any social state may be equilibrium-state for the purpose of the corresponding stage of the planning series. Historically, therefore, dynamic processes are not assumed except as (a) growth of technology and applied science, and (b) growth of population.

(3) Technology cannot but enter into the social order: but it should be gently introduced so that the delicate balance (equilibrium?) of various parts be not upset at once. Similarly, population should be controlled by family planning.

(4) As a result, the standard of living will begin to grow higher and higher after a certain period. A raised standard is not only inevitable but desirable. So wantlessness or reduction of wants involving simplicity, renunciation and self-sufficiency, is discarded. The evil effects of technology are to be controlled by rural bias, decentralised economy, state control, and certain countervailing effects of river valley projects, among other agencies.

(5) A general dichotomisation of economy into free and state enterprise, with a mixed type acting as the model and regulator, is the desirable variety of economic organisation. That type of organisation is expected to save India from ruthless exploitation, on the one hand, and regimentation, on the other. It is not assumed that economic conditions ultimately govern the social order, though the expressions of the 'fundamental urges' mentioned are all material, e.g., 'the right to work, the right to adequate income, the right to education and to a measure of insurance against old age, sickness and other disabilities.'

(6) Opportunities should be provided to as many possible, and also equalised. The means are education of different

types organised by state devices. Needs and abilities are not proportionately related but are allowed to grow leaving their adjustment to work itself out.

(7) The development, according to the Plan, is to be comprehensive. But little or no assumption is made in regard to the organisation of patterns of values in the process of their evolution through the implementation of the Plan. Beyond 'communities,' which are neither defined nor distinguished from the familiar Indian types of communities, no reference is made to the institutional framework of emergent values or to the modification of the existing framework in the light of the Plan's working on economic life. Only common obligations are emphasised.

(8) The new social order is to be brought by democratic processes on the assumption of a basic unity of purpose in the community, which is described as constituting the ultimate sanction behind the Plan and its driving force, and is also held to be evocative of the necessary sacrifice and effort on the part of members of the community. Democratic processes include 'effective power, based on the active cooperation of citizens, in the hands of the state, an 'earnest and determined exercise of that power in furtherance of the ends' and 'an efficient administrative set-up, with personnel of requisite capacity and quality.' The expectation is that 'the democratic process will energise the entire community' and 'call forth all its latent creative urges' by the Plan's placing 'a goal of endeavour' before it. The goal is not stated. But the democratic process is again expected to work through the Bharat Sewak Samaj and the five fronts mentioned before. Freedom in the expression of opinion is assumed. Toleration of other possible plans, the natural growth of a second plan out of the first, adaptation and re-adaptation, freedom of organisation, are some of the implications of democratic processes. As the relation between democratic processes and effective power and the earnest and determined exercise thereof is not discussed, the inference is that a process (state?) of no-conflict is assumed. This follows from the very first assumption, viz, harmony of interests.

(9) A band of honest, efficient, knowledgeable administrators with social imagination should be made available. The Plan devotes much attention to their training. One implicit assumption is that government service will not require loyalty to the party in power as the only test of merit and will not suc-

cumb to bureaucratic rigidity. The actual ways of assuming flexibility, securing heightened awareness of issuing problems, and creating habits of initiative and inventiveness are not analysed and discussed. Only words of appeal are used. The idea seems to be that between the old ideals of sacrifice, which will continue, and the new ones of national unity, patriotism and democratic participation, which will grow, the deed will be done. This, however, does not carry the self-evidence of an axiom, or a basic assumption. At best, it is a presumption.

(10) The state is a welfare state. Its dynamic is to be primarily supplied by the growth of community feeling, cooperative habits of action and social education, on the one hand, and simultaneous economic and social development under central direction, guidance and control, on the other. It assures freedom in spheres where it can be trusted, but the state retains the commanding strategic heights. The negative implication is that the dynamic of welfare is not that of history, which is blind or partially blind; and the positive implication is that welfare, when it cannot be measured in terms of inter-personal marginal utilities, can be felt and achieved only in the aggregate. In short, welfare is a way of life ruled by the inter-play of interests, general and sectional, and therefore, non-personal. To put it in another way, it is possible to have welfare increased by the state even if unemployment spreads.

Such are the assumptions of the social design which is seeking to come out of the sincere and laborious six hundred and fifty nine pages of the First Five Year Plan, of which this is the third year. Its vagueness would be a disqualification, if humility before the future were not a virtue and paucity of statistics were not a fact. But, psychologically, finality, sharpness and downrightness in the formation and statement of ends are sometimes more evocative of latent creative urges than the humility of intellectual planners and earnest administrators. Men fight better when they are certain of victory; and to the common mind clarity is the glow of certainty. Well-defined aims may also be indicative of cowardly acquiescence, and even avoidance of action, but only when they are conceived mechanistically. But plans can eschew any mechanistic philosophy of history. In fact, the Indian plan appears to have none of any kind. It seems to believe that history can have no philosophy, which again may be its qualification. But if some philosophy of history is at all needed for the planned development of a country which has been thrown into the vortex of history and which wants to contribute to the evolution of world peace by its own example and ideology, then its absence can only end in eclectic or empirical endeavours, *sans* guidance, *sans* direction, *sans* enthusiasm. Naturally, the psychology of building the new social order is weak in the Plan, not merely because of the poverty of incentives and the lack of tempo but also because no psychology is strong without philosophy. And philosophy without a philosophy of history is metaphysics, which is a highly intellectual pursuit indeed, but is a little academic in the context of the immediate objective of changing the physical world of India. After the Plan none need blame only the academicians for being academic, for being distant, both psychologically and sociologically, from the mighty rush of reality that is India's history today.

Few can take exception to the basic assumptions of the Plan if the actualities of the Indian conditions are considered in the manner as they have been done. One cannot still escape a feeling of coldness in the description of the actualities, of a certain nervousness in pushing their analysis to its logical conclusion, a sort of vague fear of unknown forces. Being a teacher, this author is acquainted with such feelings; he is used to calling them symptoms of intellectual detachment, *sraddha*, that is, humility and scientific attitude; and naturally, he has learnt to appreciate them. But bigger things than knowledge are involved in the Plan, namely, the life and death of a whole people who have plunged or been dragged into the maelstrom of world forces. For that a little bolder analysis was probably necessary. Bold analysis does not mean reckless generalisations; it signifies an umbilical contact with the life of the people, the resultant appreciation of the forces that move them, and the analysis of these forces, both endogenous and exogenous, in the light of local actualities, including traditions, institutions, myths, beliefs, ideas and symbols. Only the people can offer the springs of courage, and only the rational understanding of social forces can furnish the impulse and the certainty of the analysis. People's will, desires, hopes and aspirations do not seem to well up through these pages: no analysis merges its cautious subtleties in the depths of historical understanding: no idea soars up with facts in its talons.

Those who composed the Plan are highly educated people, competent, knowledgeable, scrupulously honest and industrious —everybody recognises their merits; still they do not seem to be of their Indian earth, earthy; nor do they create the impression of being the agents of mighty social forces. Those who once conceived it had some touch with the soil: they too were not firmly planted on it, as Gandhiji was; but the Plan is even further away from them. Pandit Nehru, who was once the chairman of the planning body, conveys the impression on the people of being an agent of history. But it is a romantic feeling on both sides. If in the implementation the Plan moves out of the orbit on its own without conscious direction and loses Nehru's feeling of historical urgency in the meantime, then it will be like the sorcerer's apprentice who is unable to get rid of the spirit he has raised, and the plight of the planned, that is, the Indians, will be like that of creatures haunted and possessed, full of fear and uncertainty. This has to be avoided. The Plan is a beneficent social force, an endogenous one; but its implementation may make it maleficent, even if we exclude the ugly possibilities of its being tied up so early in its career with foreign aid.

The reported basis of this fear and uncertainty is our bureaucratic inefficiency, corruption and unimaginativeness. Without minimising their effects, it may be said that the real mischief lies elsewhere. The present writer has had the fortune of knowing intimately some of the finest, sea-green incorruptible men in the country among its officers. They love their country deeply. They are flexible and human. They are rooted in the Indian traditions. They are efficient and intelligent. But their efficiency falls below their 'installed capacity' for two reasons; (*a*) the manner in which they are made to behave and act kills their self-respect. When it is easier to rise, or even to keep a job, by flattery or saying ditto to the men in power, dignity suffers and efficiency remains 'unutilised,' to put it mildly; (*b*) their time is so grossly wasted over trifles and routine, in talking piffle with visitors, in pleasing the bosses that nothing is left for study, thinking and leisure. The present writer has also been told that there are bureaucrats the breath of whose nostrils is intrigue, whose sole occupation is sycophancy, men with closed minds and mean hearts, men whose patriotism is limited to their caste, men who would exploit their subordinates and stab them in their back. The author is not in a position to check on the vague charges. At the worst, it can be held that there is as much intrigue in the government offices and circles as in boards of school management and university bodies.

The bureaucracy, at any rate, is no more good or bad than an average sample of the best of middle-class Indians. It is what the set-up makes of it. The real defect of bureaucracy is that it feeds on itself, it grows by itself, and thereby it removes itself from reality the more it wants to come closer to the actualities. It reminds one of the love-making of porcupines who throw quills at each other when they would congress. (The finest description of bureaucracy is in Kaffka's *Castle*, a book which along with the Plan should be in every planner's hand). Bureaucracy, as such, however, is the chief instrument of planning; it would have more planning if it could; only it has no ideology. The Congress organisation could supply it. Now it cannot. The Plan itself could be expected to do it; it will probably do it; but it is cold, distant from reality to the same degree as it is near to the so-called actuality. So the Plan's implementation is very likely to be cold and impersonal. The enthusiasm that is reported in the press is not yet genuine though it looks that the period of deadening frustration is over. The Indian people are between the flow and the ebb tides. A faster tempo, a little more of fervour, a little more of faith in the people, a little more of historical knowledge, a little more of the philosophy of social movement, and a little less of partisanship, would make all the difference.

How to give that push to the Plan? It has come to stay; it is the framework; it cannot be, must not be, scrapped; it will work us even if we do not work it. The Plan is the datum. It lays the necessary, if not the sufficient, conditions. Whatever can be built will be built on it. But who will build on it? In other words, new men are wanted. They are the raw materials of the 'ideal type.' It will be argued that only the prospects of a new society will generate stakes in it, which in their turn will produce the new type of men. As the present writer noticed in Russia, men can be trained to have a patriotism of the future in which all or most can be made to invest their comforts and even their little freedoms. Russia may be far away; but a social system may well be devised for India by which a little adventure may well be undertaken with some profit.

The real difficulty lies in the historical fact that these principles issued out of the incentives of private enterprise and private profit. But there are elements in the Plan, and they will grow in the process of implementation, which presuppose other motives and incentives. In the unformulated psychology of the Plan, these two sets of incentives are sometimes held to co-exist, as in mixed economy, to grow each on their own and supplement one another. At other times, still less obviously, it is expected that the incentives of private profit and property will be (somehow) transmuted into social profit, welfare, etc. (This has actually happened in one case, viz, the nationalisation of air-trasport in which the transition has been smooth. But one swallow does not make summer). Looked at in this way, there is a confusion of incentives. But the real problem can be stated in another manner. Motives, incentives, drives, impulses are not transmuted in a split second; nor do they change on their own steam. They are changed, and changed in a time which may be short or long. The impulse behind this change is known as revolutionary ardour—a full tide in the affairs of men. In individual life, it is known as faith, a faith that moves mountains in the path. If the word 'faith' is too medieval for our taste, we can use the word 'historical understanding' for social matters. That a particular phase is not eternal is its first article.

Now the fact is that the Plan is an earnest of the new order. It may be a poor earnest, but earnest it is all the same. It is neither the social order of the Brahmins nor the Sarvodaya of Gandhiji, nor even the Rama-rajya of politics. It does not say that there was history and there is none now. Only it does not tell you clearly how to make history. Its eyes look ahead though they do not clearly see anything. In short, it spells the doom of the old order and mutters the runes of the new. It posits a partial historicity. The problem is to make it full. How to do it will no doubt depend on the implementation of the Plan; but it will have to be an implementation instinct with knowledgeable faith in the full historicity of Indian life. The old order is passing and the new knocking at the door. Once that is believed to the point of conviction, the rest should follow. One wonders if any system other than Marxism could generate this type of historical conviction. If there is, let us have it by all means. If there is none, and we cannot build a substitute-system and make it acceptable to those whose lives are involved, then Marx should be read by the planners, along with Kaffka. Besides the historical sense, there is a healthy activism in that system. Faith, after all, belongs to men who hold it and enrich it by action, but there is also the climate of faith.

Therefore, in any event, the first requisite of utilising the Plan to produce a new order is an understanding faith in the historical fact that the era of the incentives of private profit based on private property is over. The psychological counterpart is recognition of the historical fact that human nature can change. The Plan has to be modified in that direction. The bureaucrats have first to be educated in that belief. Their education should be easy. There is one aspect of their training which makes them lean towards a planned, socialistic order. (More of them later on.) In the mixed economy, however, that faith cannot be easily acquired, because it is a divided faith, which is no faith. Such faith will enhance the capacity of innovators to wait and undertake risks for social profit, liberate people's creative energies and draw sustenance from the growing pains and pleasures of the life of the people. This cardinal faith solves the purely intellectual difficulty about what should come first, the new man or the new Plan. It abolishes the distinction of means and ends of building on the Plan. In a certain type of movement and at a certain stage, man is the Plan and the Plan is the man. The peculiarity of such type and stage is faith in the historicity of the social order. It is lacking in the Plan.

The Five Year Plan recognises a period of time, that is, its passage in the course of implementation. This, in its turn, is expected to create conditions, let us say, for another plan, which, at present, is not supposed to be envisagable. The momentum of the first Plan is there, but its nature is not unfolded. Here lies the second source of the distinction between the mechanistic dynamics of the Plan and the historical dynamics we are referring to. While the former notes the passage of the Plan in time and even makes adjustments with new situations as they unfold (e.g., unemployment), as if without notice, the latter presupposes that the nature of the next phase, mostly created by the implementation of the Plan, is foldable with the help of certain general principles, if one does not like the use of the word 'laws,' of social development in, at least, the last few years or so. So the next emergent phase, in this view of dynamics, comes under human deliberation and under human control. The faith in the historicity of the present phase is thus rational. When leaders ask young men and women to execute the Plan with missionary zeal, that is, without historical understanding, they are making irrational appeals to those who would, could, and should understand.

IV

Now a few indications of the probable state of affairs after the next two or three Plans have been implemented without external disturbance are to be noted. (This is necessary to show that the implementation of the Plan without historical understanding may defeat even the limited purposes of the Plan.) The river valley projects will have started working in full blast; production in the private sector will have enjoyed a boom; the average standard of living will have been (slightly) uplifted; new townships will have grown, etc. The river valley projects are conceived integrally; let us concede that for the present. But so was the Tennessee Valley Administration. What is happening there today should, therefore, be an eye-opener. Out of eighteen projected dams sixteen have been completed and the remaining will operate in a year. According to a reliable observer, the emphasis has already been shifted from agriculture to industry, so much so that agricultural labour is no longer available in the Smoky Mountain region because, displaced by machines and fertilisers, he has run away to the Atomic Energy plants at Paducah and Oak Ridge.

> To be precise: in 1929 agriculture produced 23 per cent of the region's total income, and industry only 15 per cent. But, despite this shift of emphasis, agriculture in the seven states bound up in TVA has not suffered but has greatly increased its prosperity. In order to do this, it had to alter its character.

The whole region has been so thoroughly industrialised that the TVA finds it difficult to cope with the increased demand of power and light. The alteration of the character despite the shift of emphasis is the pointer. Some such alteration in the long run will surely take place in the river valley regions of India. That may be good or bad by itself. But it is good to remember that the 'conceived' integration of agriculture and industry has been disrupted and agriculture itself has been industrialised in the Tennessee Valley. Simultaneously, the ideas of balanced economy, decentralised economy, rural bias, etc., have ceased to obtain notwithstanding the best of wishes and efforts. It is not known how far the TV has been made dependent on the growing industry roundabout. If the dependence has increased, as it is likely, the idea of public corporation, which was the pride of the New Deal and the panacea of both capitalism and socialism, may also go the way of all flesh. These are more than probabilities: they are acute possibilities revealing the historical fact that industrialisation sucks up agriculture and upsets the 'conceived' balance. The concrete implication is that mixed economy has every chance of becoming one-sided economy. On which side will Ghatotkacha fall? On the side of the Kauravas or the Pandavas? Will the disbalance be that of capitalism with its developing market and crisis, its higher production, higher standard of living and unemployment 'once the brackets of authority which hold it together are removed,' or will it be the guided instability of a controlling Plan which knows the inevitability of the process, believes it to be a historical phase, and consciously leads the industrialisation (and the corporation) to the next historical phase, the nature of which is not a mystery to it?

Major indications are of the suction of large segments of India's rural life into urban industrial life. It is hardly worthwhile to remind ourselves of the history of the early phases of capitalism in other countries. Here, nearly all the phases are present, including free enterprise, monopolistic concentration, public corporation and state capitalism. (Public corporations already seem to have lost ground in India.) The associational counterparts are also present: they are recognised and fostered by the Plan as private and public sectors. Within the public sectors there is a socialised area. As it is, the socialised area is not held by the people suffering from patent or latent shortage of goods to be of striking importance. When an agricultural people with a long history of adjustment to poverty awakes to growing needs, they prefer goods to services. The socialised area, therefore, cannot but turn to the production of goods in purely democratic interests, for otherwise, under the influence of mere social services the people fall back to the slumber of ages, have nightmares, or walk like somnambulists. In order that this may not happen—and this cannot happen when the state and society grow from the same roots and draw their sap from the same soil—the socialised area of production must be consciously and deliberately extended. Social welfare is not enough for democracy, because, to repeat, at a certain stage of political, non-economic democracy, goods are more serviceable to the human materials it has to deal with than social services in the way they are usually comprehended by the term welfare in the context of a welfare state. In the era of private enterprise goods and services are mixed up by money-values; in that of a socialist enterprise they are first separated by social urgencies allowing goods to take precedence over services; but in that of mixed economy they are again confused in the name of welfare.

The trend towards industrialisation involves urbanisation and the rule of technology. Both are unmistakable tendencies. Transport facilities alone have almost disrupted the character of the hinterland of the important Indian cities. For miles around people's habits have changed, mores have been shaken and folkways disturbed. No such countryside is self-sufficient. Its economy is not decentralised; it is only parasitical. Its society is not a community either in the sense of Baden-Powell or Tonnies or that of the Community Projects. It is neither 'closed' nor 'open'; it looks to have been opened by bad surgery, and the wound has gone septic. The unregulated transition from 'community' to 'society' is an ugly phenomenon. Ram-rajya cannot flourish in the Indian city-slums; nor can the attitudes of slum-dwellers and daily passengers of petty clerks be suitable to it. And suburbs can only have suburbania.

The Plan has sensed the position and recommended legislation for town and country planning and slum-clearance. But the angle is that of the 'housing problem,' and not of home-building. That rural attitudes have shifted is not actively considered. If 60,000 labourers have made the long trek from Madhya Pradesh to Delhi, if lakhs of people are sucked and spat out every day from Calcutta, if five hundred Bombay suburban trains a day bulge out with workers and clerks, milkmen and foodcarriers, and if on top of that, the refugees remain without habitation and settled rural occupation, then even the best of Acts and provisions are not strong enough to counter the tendency towards urbanisation and growth of metropolitan culture. Before that finally happens all the institutions which rural society had built up as an integrated pattern of living will have completely disappeared and a floating population with mobile attitudes will have been created. That population will be the new masses, and their uncertainties will be the powder of 'mass revolt.'

What we are witnessing today in cities like Calcutta, Madras, Bombay or Delhi is just this 'mass-culture.' India cannot afford to ignore this aspect of urbanisation. No amount of 'rural bias' in education, as postulated in the Plan, can check this upsurge when urban income *per capita* even in a non-industrial state like UP is nearly two and half times more than the rural income *per capita*, and that in spite of definite increase in the latter in recent years.

The solution is not to send people back to the villages. Villages are a geographical fiction kept going by the myth-making, nostalgic propensities of romantics. They do not exist today as nuclei of power or foci of self-sufficient freedom, because the villagers have no active influence on the state (except for voting —and we know how it is manipulated by urban politicians), because the prices of the goods they produce are fixed and manipulated by urban markets and urban interests, because nearly all of the older attitudes, customs, habits, etc., are being modified, and the new vital attitudes are being set, by the urban ones. Like industrialisation, urbanisation has come to stay.

If more urbansation is brought about in the course of the Plan's operations—as it is most likely to be—then the solution of the problem of unregulated growth of cities is more than the regulation of real estate; it lies in the creation of cities which their citizens can humanly conceive, seize in their understanding, and use as means of developing their personality in the imaginable context of their living. Such cities require the background of a socialist state to be created if only because their civic life cannot be integrated in any other context. Theirs will be the 'ideal' pattern of life in the industrial society that is on us. But that pattern is not the next 'natural' pattern of cities, which is megalopolitan. To convert with the least social costs the next 'natural' pattern into the pattern suitable for the next 'historical' phase of social development will be the positive function of the state. A mere welfare state is curative and regulative: a socialist state is preventive and directive. Freedom in this context means flexibility in the margin of manœuvring. A non-socialist state may flounder in the gap between fixity and flexibility.

Between industrialisation and urbanisation, on the one

hand, and a welfare state involved in the implementation of its plan of social services, on the other, the importance of bureaucracy will naturally grow. Here we come again to the question of who will give a push to the Plan. We have said before that bureaucracy is not dangerous by itself; its growth too is not dangerous so long the state it consciously (not just conscientiously) serves, grows into the next historical stage. What has happened in these years is that under the pressure of the welfare state and the exhortations of its trustees, the Indian bureaucracy has become cynical in private and sentimental in public. Besides impairing efficiency, it splits the personality of those who bid fair to set the 'ideal' type of man in planned India in so far as most young men aspire to become government servants. The exceptions are the sons and very near relations of very important persons who can fix them up in foreign firms. In fact, these firms would not appoint anybody else. Such young men are supposed to be the prospective managers. At present, they are mostly snobs who acquire business experience in their off-time from cocktail and canasta parties. But the number of VIP's being very limited, that of prospective trained managers in private firms will also be limited. They will not be able to upset the 'ideal' pattern set by government bureaucracy.

Technocracy is another story. At present the bureaucrats know or learn the technique of administration within the limits of the larger technique of pleasing the boss and the party; they are thus in a position to handle human materials, more or less in the raw, (they are somewhat out of depth with refined criminals), but they are not experts in manipulating impersonal materials, like values, social forces, social dispositions set by technology, etc. For the latter, a special type of technocrats is necessary. There is a great shortage of such personnel. At the same time, quite a number of them, including scholars sent abroad by the government for purely technical training, remain unemployed. Probably, theirs is a case of 'frictional unemployment.' Whatever it is, in the long run, that is, with increasing industrialisation, urbanisation and planning, technocrats will come into their own. There may be some conflict between technocrats and government bureaucrats so long as government administrative service enjoys greater prestige, and so long as administration issues orders. But when the next historical phase begins, technocrats will push out the old bureaucrats and set the 'ideal' type of man. It may take a long time, but the tendency has to be noted. India cannot remain content with Keynes' hedonistic dictum, 'In the long run we shall be dead.' Oh, how difficult it is to exorcise the spirit of Keynes from the mind of India's planners!

The technocrats will obviously be of as many types as technology is. Technology can be conveniently classified into that of power and goods. Each has its own sub-divisions, some of which overlap. But the essence of technology remains the same whether power is social, that is, political, economic, legal or religious, or goods are consumers' or producers'. In between comes the technology of services and distribution. That essence, or common quality, consists in (1) rationality based on the exact sciences, which at present are the physical ones (with the social sciences lagging behind), and on accounting principles, which are also conventionally exact; (2) inventiveness, mostly on the physical plane; (3) concentration of power, inclusive of organisation. Organisation involves ownership of the means of control over all types of power and goods. So technology is not a thing-in-itself; it has social roots in classes in the Marxist sense.

Now each sub-type of technology creates its own technicians. A non-Marxist sociological classification may re-arrange them in a different manner, e.g., (A) the scientist and the inventor; (B) the organiser who may be an innovator or a labour leader. As technology is inconceivable without a large labour force, ownership and conditions of employment are what they are, and the impulse of applied science remains profit, the labour leader is as much an organiser as an innovator and (C) the bureaucrat who is the manager, the manipulator within the unit, the administrator. Each creates its own type of personality.

(A) is that of the back-room boys, shy, unobtrusive, efficient within his narrow circle of duties and interests and detached from life. When these ferrets come out in the sun, they blink or are blinded, e.g., the atomic scientists who gave away top secrets. They are known to be cases of undeveloped personality. A truer statement would be that their personality had been warped by the non-social, and often the anti-social, forces of socially uncontrolled technology. The inventor's type, when invention is not of mechanical readjustment but one of the application of exact and pure sciences, is not much different from the back-room boys of laboratories. In any case, that type is unknown to India. It is not known how the 'creative urges' to be released by the Plan will lead to invention and produce inventors (not to speak of artists and philosophers). So this type of personality is not on the cards, which is a singularly unfortunate thing, because industrialisation without a band of inventors and a series of inventions would only mean payment of royalty on other people's patents and a slavish following of their order of development.

(B) The organiser's personality-pattern is different from that of (A). It is built on enterprise, impatience with the traditional, love of experiment, gift of combining the known with the unknown, capacity of taking calculated risks, a certain ruthlessness in the pursuit of intermediate ends, and vast self-confidence. It is also a disengaged personality tending to become inhuman but seeking compensation in various human ways ranging from the patronage of fine arts and science to that of chorus girls, from conspicuous charities to furtive oddities. The sole measure is success, which is competitive. Schumpeter's innovator is a tired creature before the race is over. The organiser who is a labour-leader, or a party-boss, develops more or less the same personality in essentials. He must succeed, or he dissolves. (The inner vacuum of the type has been described in modern American literature. In India, as the vacuum is filled by the absolute, or by devotion, Indian litterateurs have not yet been able to spot it. Yet it is there. Bombay money-makers and Calcutta money-changers are hollow men. They cry for literary treatment.)

(C) The bureaucratic type of personality is well-known. An ideal bureaucrat can have no life apart. But being human, the average one leads two lives. Gradually, personal life recedes, and public life is personalised back till at last the second nature becomes the only nature. Here, again, the Indian escape is through devotion. Indian bureaucrats' diaries after retirement should be most revealing. The one which this author has seen is 'notes to the absolute for orders.' Be that as it may, to have double face is bad enough, but 'double-think' is devastating. One face-one mind makes up the confident one. The bureaucrat must feel and make others feel as if he were the government, the *sarkar*, but of policies he is only the instrument. A separation of ends, which is the purview of popular cabinet, from means, which belongs to the executive, is implicit in democracy. What is not implicit is the resultant dehumanisation, which is a continuous process, a degrading process, a process of disintegration on both sides.

Natural dignity is drained off the bureaucrat, the manipulator, the manager, the business executive, in varying degrees, in the various stages and forms of democracy. Yet democracy's aim is human dignity. Individuals are not born dignified or undignified. When status, by the definition of democracy, is mobile, that is, not fixed by birth or congealed by traditions of elite-groups, dignity is the by-product of a social process in which the non-dignified of today can acquire dignity tomorrow. So dignity could be 'saved' only if it is faithfully, understandingly, known that a new era, a new stage can be and must be brought in. The so-called ruling class, the managerial class and the administrative cadres, are no more 'dignified' than workers with no rights over the machine they run. Those who know it and accept it are the successful bureaucrats: rather narrow, a bit ignorant, not quite willing to take or capable of initiative, yet solid and useful. In the present disposition it is they who form that 'ideal pattern' which is congenial to the average and conducive to conformity. But can they form the 'ideal' society? They appear to be drags on it.

V

There is one aspect of bureaucracy which merits attention. It is faint yet, but it is likely to develop under propitious conditions. At the extreme periphery of the Plan's operations (on the village level), the nature of bureaucracy seems to be changing without much publicity. Those who are operating the Community Projects, the Extension Services, and various other schemes, seem to have somewhat different outlook. The reasons are varied. They are no longer concerned with the problems of law and order. The materials of operation being novel, they are less hampered by precedence. Being local men, they are familiar with the local actualities. With less 'education' of the usual type the psychological distance from the people is also less. The absence of official paraphernalia also is an advantage. Probably, the official interference being less, they have more scope for experiment. So, in a sense, they are bidding fair to be a new type of rural bureaucracy, as distinct from the village hierarchs of old, from the kanungos to the patwaris, from the officials in the secretariat to the offices in the village, from the centre to the district. So far as this writer has heard, the immediate difficulties they are facing are village-factions and party-politics. The work, being vague, indeterminate and spread over a large area, the energy is naturally dispersed. This may be an advantage; the seed of the matter is that in such efforts and in such areas, there is no such thing as a mistake; every first mistake is an experiment, and only the second or third experiment which has failed is a mistake.

But, unfortunately, from the financial point of view, every failure is a mistake and has to be avoided at all costs. The result is a loss of initiative. It may undo the possibilities of the emergence of a new type of bureaucrats from the village level. Another danger of an early submergence comes from the lack of analysis of the reasons of failure, or of a low degree of success. Till now, no mechanism exists for what may be called a creative evaluation of the process. An evaluation programme, we are informed, is being set up. Much will depend on the way in which it works. If it succeeds, and it can ill afford to fail, it will still have to face the problems of incentives and impulses (the two are different), of rural leadership, tensions and factions, and of political partisanship. The last is very important, because the general feeling is (as it was when primary schools were being established everywhere before 1950) that these village projects may be used for the consolidation of power of a political party. Multi-purpose projects may be used as party-cells, instead of radiating centres of creative energy. These are not imaginary dangers; they should be guarded against, otherwise the rural bureaucrats will only be bureaucrats in the villages.

Technicians who are just technicians would always isolate themselves from the rest. The big designers and engineers apart, this isolation tends to create a new type of personality. There are bureaucratic grades here too, but because the result of efforts is sooner perceived and can be more precisely measured here than elsewhere, efficiency and work are more closely related. In other words, success is more visual and concrete here with the result that the corresponding personality is more directly engaged in work and competition. A fitter is lower than a foreman, a taxi or bus-driver is lower than a motor-mechanic, but the mechanistic-competitive attitude towards men and things is common. Those who have watched the behaviour-pattern of these technicians are more or less convinced that a 'new species' of Indians has been born, reckless in almost every action barring the mechanical, a little a-moral, competent, quick and alert in competition, and not always conformist in their social relations. Keyserling once described the chauffeur as the ideal type of the modern age. It is too early to say the same about India. But the mould is there. The social prestige of mechanics and mere technicians is yet too low for the bus-driver to oust the organiser or the bureaucrat in their possibilities to become the ideal type. A middle-class father still thinks twice before marrying his daughter to a technician or a foreman drawing four hundred a month in preference to a poor clerk in a government office getting a hundred.

The types described above are the probable ones in the social order that is likely to emerge after two or three such plans. Their common point is this: all the types are partial personalities. Both Gandhiji and Tagore would not recognise them as those they wanted. Nehru, or any other cultured person, would not feel at home with them. And an Indian who is steeped in the traditional values, if any such is left outside the villages, would shy at them. That would not be a serious loss as such; but warped, disrupted or fragmented personalities create social problems on their own. Planning is too serious a business to be trusted to such planners.

So the reason for the emergence of none but divided personality-types (not of personality), should be known first. There are many reasons, but the basic educational reason seems to this author to be the creeping paralysis of alienation. A scientist, or an expert knows only one aspect of a thing by alienating it from other things and calling it a 'subject'; the subject itself is detached from its history and marked off from other 'subjects.' We know how production, consumption and distribution are sealed off from one another. Similarly, things are plucked out of the complex of reality and fished out of its flow, and facts are sterilised from the contamination of values for the sake of 'purity.' But history is the process of growth; other 'subjects' are the only indices of relations; facts are the bare bones of values; and reality is the stream of knowing and living. When knowledge is separated from knowing and knowing is quarantined from living—Marxists would call it 'action'—then the process of paralysing abstraction begins. Organisers, scientists, designers, innovators, experts, professors, bureaucrats, manipulators, technicians are the creatures of abstraction; the more they abstract the 'better' they are; and the 'better' they are the more partial are their personalities. If this general analysis of the reasons for the peculiarity of the personality-types of this age of Euro-America and the next in India be accepted, then broad suggestions for the cure of the types may be ventured. The general line of treatment is already indicated. It is de-alienation. But are de-alienation and alienation reversible? We do not think so. The direction itself is irreversible, because it is in time, and not in space. The backwash, of course, is always there, but the forward push is on the whole stronger in nature and man.

Writing as a university teacher, at least one matter relating to the production of the type of men to be trusted with the Plan may be discussed at this stage. The broad presumption is that educational policies and programmes also mould personality-types. It is, however, generally assumed by the public that education is the chief agency for moulding personalities. This is a myth. In the course of more than thirty years of teaching experience the author has realised in his bones that the Indian universities, at least, do, and can do, nothing of the kind. They have functioned to produce materials out of which only one or two types of personalities could be, and have been, made, viz., the bureaucratic and the liberal-professional. Out of the second, some social and political dissenters, that is, reformers and agitators, have emerged.

No painter, no sculptor, no architect, no literary artist of any rank has come out of the portals of Indian universities in the sense that university training as such was alone responsible for his creative urges. Some scientists have; but after the very brief period of their creativity is over they become bureaucrats or administrators in the universities, or outside. No inventors or innovators have been produced. Religious leaders of note too are not university products. But with the exception of Gandhiji, all important political and social reformers, and all bureaucrats, are so. (Pandit Jawaharlal is Cambridge: more Harrow than Cambridge.) All honour to our university men for what they have done and been; in the main, they have created a general awareness of the world, which has been of the highest value. But these are different times demanding different types. The days of liberal-professionalism can be counted. Lawyers' rule is over. Constitutional lawyers will certainly remain and flourish, but with the executive gradually encroaching upon the legislature and the judiciary they cannot dominate any more. Similarly, the doctors will have to turn to prevention and amelioration, which are the very lines of action to push them away from prescription and service in the cities to measures of public health, sanitary, engineering, dietetics, etc.

These measures mean a different type of training; they involve fuller contacts with men and women who are more than patients. They necessitate a social vision; their measure is not success in practice, but the achievement of improvement in that intangible thing, health and well-being. One can go on taking other examples of liberal-professions and yet come to the same conclusion, viz., that the type of personality they fostered among university products was useful for dissent and general awareness, but is no more so when creation should replace both dissent and consent and awareness is to be converted into positive, concrete, historical consciousness. One wonders if the universities, the bureaucratic bodies as they are today, can at all do it.

The teaching profession demands a little more notice, because its position is pivotal and at the same time more tragic than that of any other. On the one hand, the vocal popular expectation remains the same; on the other, its real, functional position has altered. People continue to express the old belief that teachers by their personal examples and precepts mould youthful character. Meanwhile, however, family-life, which is the genuine nursery of personality (not of types) has been more or less disrupted. In short, school-life and family-life are no longer complementary units. Guardians are either indifferent or hostile to teachers. For most guardians sending children to schools is an escape from the drudgery of looking after them at home. The only contact between guardians and teachers in the majority of cases is during and after the examinations. That all primary school teachers are ill-paid is well-known. Teachers of higher schools and colleges supplement their income in odd ways. Their sole test is to get the students through the examinations. That by itself would not be bad if the examinations helped to test the growth of personality-types other than the clerk's. It is said that good clerks are not being produced.

At the university stage, which may last four years, the same obsession with examinations persists. Research, for whatever it is worth, cannot re-cast the already formed pattern. This writer has been directly and indirectly concerned with many research projects, theses and degrees, but he is still waiting for a piece of research which is an adventure of the spirit, for exactitudes which are winged with intuition, for scholarship that breaks new paths. The scholars alone are not to be blamed for this degrading spiritual timidity—it is nothing else than that. It is the system that prevents the guide or the director from launching the scholar on new, venturesome ways of thinking. Doctoral dissertations too are examined on set rules, which are no better than government rules. There is too much direction in these rules, whereas in any creative work there should be *indirection* in all matters but the social purpose. And it is this sense of social direction which our teachers do not possess. They make up for it by technical direction, by 'selecting' the 'subjects' for the scholars, none of whom seems to have lost a single night's rest over them as personal problems, not to speak of their being seized as national problems. The reasons are various. Sometimes it is inertia or force of habit. How many young men merely adjust themselves to the routine work of academic life through frustrated idealism is not known to outsiders, but it is a fact that should be known to honest educationists.

Though 'dangerous thoughts' as such are not taboo in the universities, the life which their statutes, rules and ordinances indirectly prescribe and directly condition offers many a bar sinister to even provocative thinking. University life makes teachers play safe, think safe, and act safe. Too much safety is bad for creation. But the chief reason has so long been the absence of social direction in the state and the society. Universities do not flourish in a vacuum. They are not, cannot be, perfectly autonomous. At best they can only formulate the social direction, impart its sense to young minds and train them accordingly. Training without social direction is the mechanical repetitiveness of factory work. If teachers still dictate old notes they are only underlining the process of a soulless mechanisation which is the academic order of the day. And the pity is that you cannot blame them. For how many people can it be said that they can rise above the system? Can the bureaucrats do it? Can factory labourers do it? Can the members of parliament do it? Yet teachers alone are exhorted to over-ride the system. They are asked to '*give social direction*,' which neither the society nor the state knows, gives or demands with firm voice.

The Plan comes in here. For the first time, some direction can be deduced. So universities can come to their own only when they are first seized by the spirit of the Plan and push on with it. That spirit by itself is not enough. The direction which the movement of the Plan posits and involves is not inspired by a vision of the new social order, its inevitability and superiority. All that it does is to indicate an interim order, a half-way house. As such, the educational institutions which are to work according to the Plan and do nothing more, can only produce 'interim' personalities, and not the dynamically integrated ones. Even that is not possible unless the schools, colleges and universities get rid of the system under which they have run or been run. Whatever people may say or think, they have been run or driven by the Invisible Hand with the whip of hunger and insecurity. So the teachers, by themselves, can do very little in the way of producing personality-types other than the usual ones. They can only spread frustration whereas they should spread divine discontent with the existing order. The merit of the Plan consists in its non-acceptance of such a single finality; its defect lies in the rejection of a known and historically conceivable series of finalities. Not that the Plan should have had faith in the absolute; but it ignores the search for the absolute, which is the only absolute in historical life.

It is the chief function of higher education to disprove the finality of any historical stage of development. The old Upanishadic motto, *'Charaibeti, Charaibeti,'* 'Forward, Forward,' is a sound motto for universities operating in an unplanned, or a semi-planned social order. In any case, a spiritual restlessness seems to be the only immediate guarantee against the warped personality-types which the next 'natural' technological, urbanised, bureaucratised social order is going to throw up. But that guarantee is not likely to be forthcoming. Mistrust of intellect, excepting what is necessary for prescribed standards of efficiency, is growing apace. India too has been invited to the feast of unreason. It will require tremendous courage for the universities to ask India to refuse to attend.

Where will this courage come from? When 'military courage' has ceased to be individual courage, when anarchist activities have lost their usefulness, when open mass-movement has yielded better results than personal acts of bravery, it is idle to expect university, college or school teachers to derive the strength to resist from their inner, personal resources. In the present organised social order that is not possible. The forces making for inertia (*tamas*) are not airy nothings; they too are organised. Unreason is an institution: it bids fair to be the supreme vested interest on the strength of its close association with power. Personality-types are already being moulded by it, *vide* the student-politicians, teacher-politicians, bureaucrat-politicians, business-politicians. In this situation, only organised courage can yield results. Fortunately, intellectual workers are forming associations of their own on the vague but correct supposition, and a partial realisation through hunger and loss of prestige, that they are not a class apart, that they too are workers. At the same time, the evils of trade-unionism are there for all to profit by. Trade unions lose their perspective in their day to day fight and transform themselves into huge bureaucracies. It is they who have formed the Welfare State in England and have not been able to prevent Malaya and Kenya 'incidents.' Associations of teachers, clerks, journalists and civil servants will only be too happy if their conditions of service are improved. But deeper issues than provident funds, family allowances and leave for pension-rules are involved. The idea of historical phases has to be introduced into the living of the people first; and then the planned march from the starting point of the Plan to the next phase has to be organised and undertaken. For this type of issues, teachers' or intellectual workers' associations of the union type are not enough, though necessary.

In so far as at no conceivable time the intelligentsia, the teachers in particular, are likely to be participants of power, they will meanwhile have to remain content with acquiring influence on the powers that be and establishing prestige with the people. At present, the influence is nil, if not negative, for a variety of reasons; and the social prestige is dwindling. India's case may be a little different, but dispassionate studies of the role of intellectuals in countries where they have had a place reveals a connection between prestige and some reasonable income. Thirty or forty rupees a month do not build up prestige even in Indian villages of today. Yet on the village level, some planners think, the schoolmaster is a useful nucleus of constructive activities. The state governments too have issued orders to treat them with respect, e.g., inviting them to occasions and parties. It is not strange that many teachers take it as worse than insult. So the government's direct contribution to the building up of teachers' prestige is not going to be considerable. 'Missionary zeal' alone remains. That phrase, too, could have a meaning in other contexts; with forty rupees a month for the missionaries it is mean and hypocritical. One should not be surprised if in the heart of any man who has seen how those who mouth the phrase live there should arise the same feeling as 'culture' raised in the heart of Goering.

So when there is no zeal forthcoming on the asking, the only way left is to fall back on traditional values. The writer is not unacquainted with at least one of them, viz., the Brahmin's pride. He has seen it in action in a place famous for Brahminical culture; he has felt it in his family life, in the behaviour of his relations; and he has sought to live on that pride in his academic career. He knows how extremely difficult it is to remain proud as a Brahmin. At best, Brahminism today can mean a negative code of conduct: certain things are not done. But these are new things; and Brahminism does not throw any light on them. Disinterested service? The old story is back again, missionary spirit and all that. Today's problem is not disinterestedness, but deep involvement. For that Brahminism is no help. Besides, it is questionable how far the Brahmins as a class ever practised high thinking and simple living in the spirit of *nishkama*. With kings and common people at their feet, with their command over the after-life, with their magical hold over every detail of living and death, they probably could afford to approximate to the ideal Brahmin of nationalist phantasy. But that magic is gone. He who wants to recapture that spirit is either a fake or a fool.

Everywhere the old elite-groups have disappeared; here too they are going; and no new ones, barring the professional politician and the bureaucrat, are to be seen. To keep Brahminism as a going social concern in this universe is an old maid's dream. The historical category of neo-Brahmins is made up of other personality-patterns, other groups. Ten presidents can wash the feet of ten thousand Brahmins, but the Brahmin's prestige in this field cannot be restored. Any individual attempt to do so is an exercise in self-pity, and not in self-confidence. (Here we are not speaking of the caste system as such. For aught we know, the caste feeling in the country is as strong as, if not stronger, than ever.)

Many ardent patriots speak about India's genius and its capacity to adjust itself to new situations. They are right in one way and wrong in another. If 'genius' signifies 'daemon,' then it is Teutonic mysticism with its cult of Kultur-imperialism. If it means Indian traditions as they are, then the Indianness is a superfluity, because all traditions *are*; in which case, the specificity of Indian culture remains undefined. If again, it suggests that traditions *have been,* that is, if traditions mean what has happened to India and in India, then Indian culture is merely a record of happenings. This is the way in which Indian historians understand Indian genius, if and when they refer to it by implication. But genius has overtones of reference in the manner in which the happenings are recorded in the mind, crystallised in the life-habits of men and women, and emotionally held by them. Such records, crystallisations and complexes have great value as conserving forces. And India has certainly conserved a great many values, some good and others bad. The point, however, if that is possible, is that of utilizing the forces which are foreign to Indian traditions, e.g., technology, democracy, urbanisation, bureaucratic rule, etc.

Adjustments there will certainly be. It is almost guaranteed that Indians will not vanish, as primitive tribes have done, at the touch of western culture. They have sufficient flexibility for that. Indian culture had assimilated tribal cultures and many of its endogenous dissents; it had developed a Hindu-Muslim culture; and modern Indian culture is a curious blending, *varnasankara.* Traditionally, therefore, living in adjustment is in India's blood, so to speak.

VI

The present problem, however, is more of the phase *after* the adjustment. And here doubt begins. Tagore and Gandhi were creators in the genuine sense, and they were not the only ones. In fact, one is surprised at the number of men, probably not of the same rank, thrown up by India in the last century or so of her contact with the west. Yet it is not possible to dogmatise on the question as to how far these creators drew their inspiration solely from Indian traditions and Indian values *per se.* Tagore had the Upanishadic base, but those who have been influenced by him have had no such base. For them Tagore's appeal lies in his western values covered in the outer Indian garb. It is generally held that Gandhiji's strength lay in his firm hold on the Indian masses. This is true. No other leader knew the needs of the people better than he did; and naturally, no other leader has been more successful than he was. It is also held that he was steeped in the Indian traditions and values, e.g., his dress, his looks—he looked like a peasant, and above all, his techniques, satyagraha, non-violence and exploitation of Indian mores, folk-ways, myths and symbols. This is also true, but not wholly true. As people who knew him intimately have said, his will power was his supreme quality of attraction. There are stories of his 'ruthlessness.' Will power, except for personal salvation, is not quite an Indian trait; nor have many traditions been collected by it; (*Shakti* of Tantrikism is a different thing); and resignation, renunciation, fatalism, India's practised values, are negations of will power, unless not to will is the supreme example of willing.

In certain matters, Gandhiji was more Christian, Buddhist and Jain, than Hindu, more Protestant than Catholic, and more English than Indian. His ethics is more reminiscent of Christ's than any Indian saint's. These aspects of his personality and doctrines or faith have been noted; and so have been his amendments to certain Hindu traditions. (Orthodox Brahmins were opposed to him.) Some people have also averred that not being a Sanskrit scholar, some of his interpretations of Hinduism were not always correct. One is not quite sure if non-violence as a social concept is implicit in Hindu ethics. For the matter of that, there can be two opinions on his view that the Gita preaches non-violence as truth. In any case, his puritanism was very English. He, himself, has expressed his gratitude to some western thinkers and to the Bible. A man of such tremendous will power trained his supreme quality to the task of broad-basing a movement, which, to his following, was essentially a national movement.

Nationalism as such, however, is a western value of recent times. Gandhiji invested it with Indianness. So it cannot be confidently stated that his creative urges came only from Indian values and traditions. If it were so, then the wholesale prescription of western values in the post-Gandhian era would not have been possible. To a sociologist, the failure of Gandhiji's constructive programme so soon after his death, (only remember the military funeral to the prophet of non-violence), is as noteworthy a phenomenon as his tremendous personal success in his life-time. His technique of creation could not be very Indian if it could be forgotten and abandoned by Indians so soon. His birthday celebrations, the Gandhi *margs* in every city, his name on every lip, his ubiquitous pictures, do not prove that he was driven by the Indian daemon, or inspired by the Indian genius. It only proves how good the Indians are at the remembrance of things past. Gandhiji's creativity has been transformed into a tradition. This is the real Indian technique, which is more powerful than non-violence and satyagraha. India made of the Buddha a God in her populous pantheon and broke the back of Buddhism. Her capacity for absorbing anything, including poison, is superb. India's genius lies in her liver.

Thus it is that two systems of data are to be worked out. One is the Plan with its basic western values in experimentalism, rationalism, social accounting and in further western values centering in, or emerging out, of bureaucratisation, industrialisation, technology and increasing urbanisation. The other is not so much the Indian traditions as India's forces of conservation and powers of assimilation. At present, they are not sharply opposed. If anything, the first datum is gradually becoming ascendant. This is a bare historical fact. To transmute that fact into a value the first requisite is to have active faith in the historicity of that fact, just as it is necessary to actively know that individual life has an end in order to convert the personal facts of living into social and higher values. The second requisite is social action to push on with the Plan and to push it, consciously, deliberately, collectively, into the next historical phase. The value of Indian traditions lies in the ability of their conserving forces to put a brake on hasty passage. Adjustment is the end-product of the dialectical connection between the two. Meanwhile is tension. And tension is not merely interesting as a subject of research; if it leads up to a higher stage, it is also desirable. That higher stage is where personality is integrated through a planned, a socially directed, collective endeavour for historically understood ends, which means, as the author understands it, a socialist order. Tensions will not cease there. It is not the peace of the grave. Only alienation from nature, work and man will stop in the arduous course of such high and strenuous endeavours.

4. *An Economic Theory for India*

'In any case, the establishment sooner or later of economics as an exact science is no longer in our hands and need not concern us. It is already perfectly clear that economics, like astronomy and mechanics, is both an empirical and a rational science. And no one can reproach our science with having taken an unduly long time in becoming rational as well as empirical. It took from a hundred to a hundred and fifty or two hundred years for the astronomy of Kepler to become the astronomy of Newton and Laplace, and for the mechanics of Galileo to become the mechanics of d'Alembert and Lagrange. On the other hand, less than a century has elapsed between the publication of Adam Smith's work and the contributions of Cournot, Gossen, Jevons, and myself. We were, therefore, at our post, and have performed our duty. If nineteenth century France, which was the cradle of the new science, has completely ignored it, the fault lies in the idea, so bourgeois in its narrowness, of dividing education into two separate compartments: one turning out calculators with no knowledge whatsoever of sociology, philosophy, history, or economics; and the other cultivating men of letters devoid of any notion of mathematics. The twentieth century, which is not far off, will feel the need, even in France, of entrusting the social sciences to men of general culture who are accustomed to thinking both inductively and deductively and who are familiar with reason as well as experience. Then mathematical economics will rank with the mathematical sciences of astronomy and mechanics; and on that day justice will be done to our work.'

(Leon Walras, Preface to the fourth edition of the *Elements of Pure Economics*, Lausanne, June 1900.)

I MAY at once confess that my knowledge of the mathematical manifestations of modern economic analysis is extremely circumscribed by my predilections for classical economics and training in history and sociology. But I am also aware that where academic and intellectual values are involved, trust helps one to overcome limitations, aye, to transmute them into sources of strength. I hope and pray that I shall respond to this psychological truth of human behaviour and render my account to the university and to its economics department to the best of my ability. After all, academic values are an integral part of human values; and if the human values are a piece with psychological truths, the academic values secure an order of assurance which otherwise they would not receive or earn.

I have a feeling that the older seats of learning and the older methods of instruction worked on this principle of integration. Scholars who are not in the habit of glamorising the past have described in detail the human relations between the master and the pupil, the methods and subjects of instruction which centred in what was later known as the humanities. Be it Padua or Paris, Al-Azhar or Nalanda and Vikramshila, learning was personal behaviour. Thus knowledge was imbibed in the climate of human relation which facilitated instruction through personal discussion. The emphasis on personality humanised knowledge. Even such abstruse subjects as rhetoric, grammar and metaphysics, were rendered concrete and human by the method of disputation.

It is said that philosophy, till the sixteenth century, was existential in the true sense of the term; that is to say, it was bound up with the real and live problems of personal existence. Dogmas were real and urgent issues of life. The material branches of knowledge were undeveloped, crude and empirical in the main. But their very empiricism kept them close to the conditions of living. Ultimately, both types of knowledge, the sacred and the profane, the transcendental and the mundane, (*bijnãn* and *gnañ, parã* and *aparã vidyã*) became dependent upon authority. It was against this authority, both divine and traditional, that the mind of the new man protested. Through various channels the fresh stream of energies flowed to produce a new humanism. It was new in the sense that while the older type of humanism was subordinated to and subserved the interests of the supra-human, the new type asserted the dignity of man by virtue of his being the noble creature that he was, full of infinite potentialities, realisable through the reason that was inherent in nature and through the spirit of adventure and enquiry into the secrets of nature which was man's calling. The shift from the supra-natural to the natural was not a clear severance. Traditions were not discarded; they were only subjected to human scrutiny. Yet it was a grand liberation of the mind. Reformation and Renaissance had their share in it, but the birth of modern science, with its methods of induction and spirit of experiment, was the great divide. It would not be unhistorical to say that the growth of scientific ideas and the emergence of the scientific spirit, which the material necessities of the period had fostered, created the temper of modern civilization.

I am delving into the past history of the west because I guess that the intellectual content of the culture of modern India is analogous to that of the well-known renaissance of the west. India has been entering into modern civilisation, which is essentially the western civilization, in the last hundred years or so, and the western man with his type of culture the 'ideal type' for the Indian. Let us make an attempt at striking some rough balance-sheet of this new transaction. It is in this background that the nature and method of social sciences, as we understand and follow them today, would be best revealed.

Who would deny the great gain that accrued to the western man? This upheaval of human reason brushed aside all the guild, the feudal and the mercantilist restrictions; and a new class was ready to ride the tide. Human rationality was extended to politics in the American and the French revolutions; it was responsible for the capitalist spirit; and it also made for its decay and the growth of scientific socialism. In short, it served with zeal every aspect of what is known as modern history. It is true that this type of rationality was yet confined to the west. It is equally true that irrationality, rather than rationality, was the impulse of imperialism. Even, today, irrationality is not dead; it is playing a rear-guard action against the forces of rationality. Racialism, war-mongering, mass-hysteria and waves of fear are, alas, too well-known to us. At the same time, one must admit that the forces of reason are putting up a grand fight in the name of peace and planning, negotiation, toleration, and co-existence. Speaking historically, it is more than a fight with the back to the wall. Socialist reconstruction, which is the supreme stake of peace, is a further dose of reason in the social process. All this is on the credit side of reason and science in the ledger of history.

But the debit side can be ignored only at our peril. Historical processes are seldom unilinear. They involve huge social costs some of which are permanent. He who has watched the course of history, not in a mood of contemplation but with his eyes and ears open, can no longer deceive himself with the new religion of progress, with the new cult of science and its dogma of value-free neutrality. Human nature has paid heavily for its marriage with reason. Surely, it has not shed the old orthodoxy to wed the new orthodoxy, the old mechanism of rituals and dogmas to adopt unquestioningly the new folkore of mechanical scientism. It would certainly be idle to blame the scientist for the atom bomb, or for unemployment, or for the technological forms of exploitation. Yet, these are the social costs of an ideology in which mechanical scientism is considered to be coterminous with human reason, its finest flower and consummation. When many misconceptions have gathered round this scientism, it should not be waste of time to look into its effects a little more closely.

To my mind, the social costs incurred in the process involved the gradual dissociation of knowledge from the urgencies of living and, on the intellectual level, the replacement of norms by concepts. The process of dissociation, or alienation, was largely sociological in nature. We now know that the interest in science and experiments was to a very great extent conditioned by the interests of the class which was coming up, if not always on the ruins of the older ruling one, at least, to challenge the earlier social hierarchy. That challenge could be effective only if and when that class could be dominant in all spheres, including the intellectual. Although there is a great need of caution in the sociology of knowledge, it only stands to common sense that what is now known as scientific spirit should be cultivated and accepted by a special group of people of a certain stratum whose interests are identifiable with the uses of science in its applied forms. The material motives were certainly not personal. They were class motives and impulses. To put it in another form, the conditions for the spread of scientific attitude were the increasing weakness of a metaphysical view of life, the growth of a class, the bourgeoisie, and their functioning as the spearhead of the industrial and the technological re-

volution and as a separate order. Once these conditions were fulfilled, the scientific attitude became a special attitude, science a special pursuit of scientists in the laboratories, just as production became the special occupation of labourers in the factories, and investment the special vocation of some men in the stock exchanges.

These specialisms of social functions were, in my view, at the back of specialisation in knowledge. I am not saying that the relation was deterministically causal, but I do suggest that it is most unlikely that the extreme separation of science from life, as we notice today, could be achieved only by the autonomous movement of any disciplined knowledge towards refinement and perfection, and that the movement could hardly collect all the strength and prestige it commands today if it functioned in a social vacuum. It is true that a systematised body of knowledge creates its own momentum, its own ways and means of development through the drive for inner consistencies. At the same time, every such discipline becomes disengaged from life when it is entangled in its own cocoon of endogenous correspondences and autochthonous concepts. I am of the opinion that such fate has overtaken nearly all the natural sciences and is going to overtake some of the social disciplines, particularly, economics.

We have read stories of the personal disintegration of many nuclear physicists. But, in my view, the origin of their psychoses is neither the horror of wholesale destruction nor a matter of personal conscience: it is the terror of the vacuum that gapes between science and life, the vacuum which scientism and the class structure had conspired to produce. On the personal level, it looks like guilt; and the traitor-scientists are worried by it. In reality, I repeat, it is alienation. I suspect that this sense of guilt, this horror of the vacuum, is creeping into the mind of many honest economists and social scientists. They are beginning to question their methods of enquiry and analysis. But most academic economists still feel that their world of models would be the best of all possible worlds if only it could be mathematically conceived. In a situation like this, the only hope seems to lie in the capacity of the real world to burst the shell of self-complacency in order that knowledge may rush back to life's needs and urgencies and derive fresh strength from them.

Conceptualisation has always been a levitating force. It is in the very nature of intellect to use concepts as mental tools to get *its* work done. Introspection in its lower reaches might do without concepts, but intuition at least, cannot function without symbols. I have no time to go into the details of the decaying processes of symbols in the modern age but, I think, I can ask you to accept the general proposition that the processes are generally social and conditioned by the increasing prestige of the physical sciences due to their wide application in productive processes. Once introspection and intuition were rendered unfashionable, the way was open for conceptualisation to reign supreme in knowledge. I must declare that the rule was very necessary and extremely useful. How could knowledge grow without concepts? In fact, to a very large extent, the two went together. Concepts were necessary for precision. The finer the concepts the subtler was the understanding. And mathematics was there to ensure precision and subtlety. Once these qualities were collected, prediction could proceed with greater certainty, and prediction was necessary for man to control nature. At first, it was physical nature; recently, it has been human nature and social behaviour.

We all have heard of the application of field theory to psychology in the hands of Kurt Lewin and his disciples, of calculus and the higher manifestations of mathematics to economics in the hands of Walras, Pareto, Edgeworth, Ramsay, Schlutsky, Neumann, Morgenstern, to name only a few. Modern economic methodology is best seen in mathematical economics, econometrics, input-output analysis, national income analysis, and economic statistics. I do not suggest that valuable work in economic history or in realistic economics and surveys is not being published nowadays. But the weightage, at least, in the academic circles, is on the former. I greatly admire these developments in the only way I can, viz., by not fully understanding what they are all about. To be honest about it, I feel that they have, in a way, a snob-value. This snobbishness of an esoteric pursuit strictly confined to the elite of the initiate seems to be a common disease of modern culture. In the thirties, poetry was made unintelligible in the name of images and symbols having a life of their own, and hence was not obligated to observe all the rules of communication. The poets formed coteries, they enriched poetry in many ways, particularly by trying to make personal experience precise. But precision became an enemy of reality, and personalism that of communica-

tion. A similar degenerative process is observable in modern economics, which one would still like to call a social science.

The cult of unintelligibility is rampant among modern economists. It is fortunate that a leading economic journal has cavilled at it. Is it not a noteworthy sign that an Oxford professor writes on the concept of mind in a non-technical language? I hope therefore, that when the worm has begun to turn in philosophy, the paradise of concepts, the economic worm will also soon make bold to do the same. That will take a long time for the Indian worm, because of the culture-lag between the Indian thought and the western thought. There is however, no reason for the delay. Whatever the Indian professor of economics may say or do, the pull of Indian institutions against over-conceptualisation will be operative. Here our very backwardness may be a privilege.

There is one point in the over-conceptualisation of economics which requires immediate attention. From now I shall be speaking only of economics, not merely because it is going to monopolise me, but also because it is the most popular and the most well-developed of the social sciences. Over-conceptualisation in economics has led to the exclusion of certain concepts by one door and the inclusion of others by another. In other words, the process has been very selective. The interest behind over-conceptualisation in economics is held to be quantitative ascertainability. We all know the history of the theory of value. Originally, that is, with the classical economists, value was both use-value and exchange-value. But in course of time, the former began to be taken as datum and was thus politely dismissed, and market-value became the only value. The argument was that as labour in its embodied form could not be measured uniquely, its character of commanding value in the market, that is to say, as one commodity of exchange among other commodities, alone should be gauged. That too could not be sustained for long. With the tremendous increase in production in the heyday of capitalism, the emphasis was shifted from supply to demand, that is effective demand, because goods had to be sold at a price for a given level of profit. So utility, neither use, nor need, had to be raised into a concept. Its psychological law was found, and the marvellous tool of analysis, viz., the concept of the margin, was forged. Later on, when its own quantitative ascertainability began to be doubted, the concept of marginality was not discarded, but the cardinal analysis was changed into ordinal analysis. The way was thus paved for the establishment of the general equilibrium theory, with its mathematical symbols and equations, in the heart of economics.

Let us note what other things were involved in the shift. The first casualty was the labour theory of value. With it went the realistic background of evaluation, viz., the appreciation of a social relation. The classical economists would not separate their analysis of value, which for them was a relation and not an entity or a substance, from class relations. For them the social relations were real and the problems of factors of production were urgent and concrete in the context of social relations, that is, distribution. The historical school of economists, who were the progeny of the German school of history that sprang from the Romantic movement, objected to the deductive method of the classicists. Their criticism was just in so far as it related to the end products of the classicists' endeavour, viz., the Ricardian system. But it was unjust when it referred to the manner in which Ricardo understood the concrete problems of history.

The recent definitive edition of Ricardo's writings leaves this abiding impression on one's mind that his primary concern, like that of Adam Smith, Petty, and even the Physiocrats, was with the concrete, day to day problems as they rose in the mind of thinking men of the rising class, that is to say, as they operated in the context of class relations in a particular phase of English history. At least one reader got this impression from the Ricardo-Malthus controversy that though its terms were the so-called factors of production in an expanding market, its basic issue was the emerging conflict between the land-owning class and the industrial bourgeoisie, and the victory of the one over the other. The concepts of rent, wages, profit and their relation to price, the concepts of stock and glut, and even of the Malthusian devil, were the products of the concrete social conflict that was apparent to the discerning minds of those days. Only the attempt to solve the conflict led to the conceptualisation in which rent, wages, profit etc., shed their historicity and assumed the qualities of uniformity and recurrence to prove themselves eternally valid. So historicity had to be sacrificed, ostensibly for the sake of a scientific system, but really and truly, for solving the social conflict in the cool, dehydrated atmosphere of universality on behalf of a certain class. Marx, who was the last of the classicists, saw through this trick, and devoted his giant's energies to square the demands of history with the demands of reason. For this he had to give up the Aristotelian base of thinking and adopt the Heraclitean one. How far he succeeded is not my concern now. My immediate interest is to show the nature of the sacrifice.

I beg your leave to develop this point about sacrifice. Since the days of the classicists the dichotomy between the subjective and the objective interests has been widening. We know how in spite of the mathematical reasoning of welfare economics, the matter of measuring inter-personal marginal utilities remains the headache of economists while the objective interests are held to be more or less ascertainable. The same headache troubles the analysis of the pricing process, the absolute and the relative prices. In my view, one of the main concerns of modern economists is to devise methods to overcome this type of dichotomy. But, as has been aptly said:

> The dissolution of this dichotomy, the raising of the subjective appraisals of interests to the level of comprehensions of their objective contents, may be all the 'amplitude of freedom' that is left to rational argument in social and economic matters. That this 'amplitude of freedom' is very narrow and that it is *without rather than within* its confines where the causes of all important political and economic departures are to be sought, is perhaps the most important insight gained thus far by social science.[1]

I would like you to note that phrase, 'without rather than within,' and the word, 'departure.' In other words, no theory of economic development is possible without a study of the forces operating *outside* those narrow confines of the 'amplitude of freedom' which excessive conceptualisation had set to itself; and positively, such study is possible only with the help of those forces which are still stubbornly refusing to be mathematically ascertained. Forces generated by increasing or decreasing population, migration, mobility, quality or skill, etc., by technology and all that it means in the way of investments and their time lags and bottlenecks, by innovation, by invention, by class conflict, both in the metropolitan and in the colonial areas, are genuine, operative social forces; but though they have been

[1]Paul A. Baran, 'National Economic Planning' in *A Survey of Contemporary Economics,* Vol. 2, p. 367.

sought to be indirectly measured, they have not yet lent themselves, at least, not to my knowledge, to a precise mathematical treatment.

Whatever models have been constructed seem to have abjured the impulses behind, or outside, the reality of the abstract situation conceived in the model. Neat static models and some clumsy comparative static models have no doubt been devised. Probably, they have a theory of economic inertia or stagnation. Perhaps they have also a theory of endogenous growth by jumps and spurts. But, realistically speaking, are these enough? Some economists know that they are not, but in practice they behave as if they are. In consequence, they make us think that economic reality, which is a social process, is not their 'cup of tea,' that it is the intrusion of some impurity. This is the public meaning of the sacrifice involved in the scientification of economics, in its purification, in its over-conceptualisation. I would like you to note the change in the very nature of concepts undergone in the process. They started as tools of analysis; now they are acting as highly competent, efficient, and respectable, but extremely narrow, sieves.

One more sacrifice I would like to mention before I proceed. In our younger days the subject was called political economy. When we came to the college we had to do Marshall along with Mill. We remained content with Marshall's definition of economics, the centre of which was occupied by man. His grip of reality, both empirical-social and historical, never failed to engage our total attention. Along with Mill's *Political Economy* were read his other works, his *Liberty*, his *Representative Government*, his brilliant essays, and above all, his *Logic*. Continental thinkers had no part in our training. We never knew of what Walras and Pareto, Wicksell, Bohm-Bawerk, Sombart and a host of others were doing and thinking. Then came Keynes and Robbins.

The definition given by the latter of economics in terms of scarce means, alternative uses and varied ends, seemed to bring clarity in all that vagueness. It appeared so logical, so pure to us. We felt that we had received a charter of freedom. It was no doubt a charter, but it soon became a charter to organise a guild, a corporation, a free masonry of secret service. Lionel Robbins' definition still rules the academic world. His concept of scarcity seems to be holding the key to the purity of economics, a sort of cestus of Venus. But it does not require

a Boccaccio to show that this concept is extremely unrealistic. To mention one and only one instance of exclusion: the scarcity occasioned by private property, which is the law of the state. As the late Professor Commons put it: what is scarcity in economics is private property in jurisprudence. And jurisprudence is a matter of political theory. Professor Robbins, it is very interesting to observe, has since then been looking over his shoulder. It could be his own sense of guilt, or is it the ghost of the rejects and discards of pure thought haunting the fringe of reason? Professor Robbins' definition is only a symptom of the spiritual shrinkage that comes to all men whenever they equate logic with reason and reason with reality. His is a case of non-mathematical conceptualisation.

Mill too was a logician of note; Marshall too had training in mathematics. But one finds fresh air, the air of reality blowing through their pages. There is space, light and spirit, an architectural solidity in Mill and Marshall, as one gets, let us say, in Raphael's *School of Athens.* Modern definition of economics is closed, deliberately closed, because it avoids norms and values, all in the name of logical analysis. If equilibrium could be just equilibrium then there should have been no search for equilibrium. Like art for art's sake, this type of 'pure' thinking is really a mark of decadence though it looks like being prompted by the desire for the establishment of the autonomous science of economics.

No discussion of modern economic theory is possible today without bringing in Keynesian economics. Keynes was, if my information is correct, a moderate mathematician, and in the opinion of a knowledgable man like Bertrand Russell, a superb logician. If I am not mistaken again, he seldom used a mathematical formula. He was a realist, quite happy with the short period, though he had a hand in the building up of modern macro-economics, the economics of levels, aggregates and secular trends. In his earlier works he was not immediately concerned with concepts as such. There he was in the grand tradition of the economists of social behaviour, broad, humane, and close to the earth, close to man and his realities. His notable works on Indian currency, on the post-war peace, on monetary theory, and his brilliant essays make one feel that economics, in his hand, was still a branch of the humanities, a pursuit for a whole man, a cultivated, almost a sophisticated, man, and not merely the professional work of a professor. His *General Theory* still retains that flavour.

The three important concepts of the *General Theory,* marginal propensity to consume, liquidity preference and marginal efficiency of capital with its association with expectation, denote his recognition of the importance of impure psychological tendencies even in man's monetary behaviour. They at least show that things like propensities, preferences and expectations cannot be, must not be, in Keynes' view, thrown out of the economic counter. The stress on psychology is never overlaid, but it is there, peeping out of the economic reasons. And no wonder, because the economics of Keynes, if not all of his followers, is a state of mind, a certain way of life, mixed up with a special meaning of goodness which, by his own admission, he imbibed from Professor Moore's *Principia Ethica.* Philosophically, it may be a fall from the idealistic pitch of early economists, but the philosophy of good life and decency, which suffuses, like the light of an autumn evening, Keynes' writings, succeeds in maintaining the connection between economics and the humanities. That connection, however, was already tenuous, probably because of the tenousness of the relation between ethics and philosophy, but we are grateful to Keynes for not breaking away from it.

Keynes, it seems, has had two sets of followers, the right Keynesians and the left Keynesians. The latter are trying to use the Keynesian tools for the interpretation of old masters, particularly Marx; and the former are doing the same for the building up of a welfare state. Both schools believe in planning, although it is possible that they mean different things by planning. Whatever the difference, the processes of planning which use Keynesian tools meet with early difficulties. I am not merely referring to the gratings and the creakings of their application to what is loosely described as under-developed economy, though they may be revealing on their own right. My concern is with the dual problem of *attaining and maintaining* full employment within the capitalistic system.

We know that the capitalistic system has protean shapes; we also know that unless we are satisfied with less than full employment and choose to call it full employment in the name of realism, the question of *attaining and maintaining* full employment involves physical controls and other forms of state action. The state under the capitalistic system is at best an umpire; it must not interfere with the game. But the state that will be necessary for *attaining and maintaining* full employment with the help of Keynesian economic tools, it seems, will have to be more than an umpire. It will be a player on the field. Now all players are not clean players, and some play dirty games. Keynesian economics recommends state intervention without laying down the rules of the political game. For Keynes, as the game was a gentlemen's game, no Queensberry was necessary. But, unfortunately, where and when the state as such is not fully developed, or is no more than a bureaucracy, or again, when and where the state is under the influence of pressure-groups, or can ill afford to subordinate vested interests to social interests, then certain rules are necessary. I wonder if Keynesian economics, by itself, offers any such rules as will assure fair play. Which means that Keynesian economics posits state participation and intervention without a theory of the state.

We will now turn for a moment to planning and its economics. The economics of planning, be it Keynesian planning or socialist planning, the Soviet planning or the Chinese planning, is political economy, with norms and ideal types, in Weber's terms, of political and social behaviour and ends. There can be no escape from norms and values in planning. And in the social world, the source of mundane values is the relation between the state and the society. If the society is many societies, composed of many strata, many groups and classes, then the state cannot represent all of them. It must choose. That state which is the presumption of Keynesian economics does not choose. It is more or less content with what exists; that is to say, it has been chosen. Let us follow one of the implications.

Indian planning, on its organised economic side, is Keynesian. It has some theory of state connoted by the term welfare state. Welfare, as we know, is a value. It is an individual value and a social value. If the social value implicit in the concept of welfare is dependent upon the relation between the Indian state and the Indian society, further, if the Indian society is really homogeneous as the state is homogeneous, then the welfare state is nothing more than a new phrase for the old romantic notion of democracy by which the state is the people and the people's will is the will of the state. Apart from the fact that such a notion is redundant and can be mischievous, it is unrealistic. It is unrealistic because the Indian society is not as homogeneous as the state is. Though class consciousness is not there for all to see, being hidden by caste, the classes do exist, and class interests do operate. In case the conflict becomes sharper, then the gentlemanly assumption of good life led by decent men who need not be told the rules, may not obtain. And if gentlemen's democracy is not there, the state becomes a different state, choosing between the classes, determining the priorities in the light of the interests of the class chosen, and directing the flow of employment and effective demand in addition to raising their levels accordingly. This additional burden cannot always be carried by Keynesian economics. The realm of social values in a country like India posits a theory of state and a theory of society other than what is implicit in Keynesian economics. I have a suspicion that it is this logical deficiency which is sought to be remedied by a change in article 31 of the Constitution, our rules of the game, in regard to compensation.

It comes to this then: the search for making economics value-free with the help of refined conceptualisation, or of mathematics, does not enable one to choose between priorities, or to consciously direct economic policy. Once the theory of the state is discarded, or kept in the background of economic analysis, the matter of priorities is reduced to one of the inner forces generated within the system. In which case, whatever is, is rational, and therefore, is socially good. The method of fixing priorities then becomes a matter of hunches, which, alas, are often another name for falling in line with the status quo, or what the dominant class wants to be done. That will be planning of some sort, no doubt, but it will not be social planning. For that, certain impurities, I mean, political values and social values, have to be imported. Perhaps some historical values too will also be necessary. Because, if dynamic economic analysis is essential for the theory of economic priorities *and* direction, that is, if static analysis, or even comparative static analysis, is not adequate for the purpose, then we will have to take recourse to history. And, of course, to mathematics as well. In fact, these are the only two tools for dynamic economics. The historical tool is not a precise instrument, but it is realistic; the mathematical tool is very precise within its assumptions, but if the assumptions are different, then mathematics is a variety of mysticism. The philosophy of mathematics is the philosophy of order; that of history is the philosophy of change. So these two tools may not be satisfactorily used for the same purpose at the same stage. I shall not refer here to the basic conflict between certainty and actuality and the choice between precision of measurement and the comprehension of reality it ultimately involves for every seeker of truth.

If you agree with me thus far, you will have agreed that economic studies should be integrated with the studies of politics, history, psychology, jurisprudence, and other social disciplines, even at the cost of being condemned as 'unscientific.' When we remember the original costs of scientism we should not be cheerless in standing up to the charge. In other words, at the universities, at least, economics should be treated as a cultural subject, one of the humanities, and not of the natural sciences, unless, of course, both humanities and the natural sciences are brought within the scope of philosophy. As that is a far cry, I content myself with entering a plea for 'impure' economics, the economics that would not part in spirit with history, politics, law, psychology, and philosophy.

I am fully aware of the fact that the different social disciplines are at different levels of development. It also cannot have remained unknown to one with the experience of more than three decades of university teaching that each discipline tends to become a vested interest and is jealous of its sister discipline. Yet I persist in entering my plea, not merely as a student of economics, or as an educationist, or even as a humanist, but also as an Indian. I have an idea that Indian culture is *not yet* so disintegrated that one aspect of life is completely severed from another, as it is reported to have happened in other cultures. Further, I have been told by people who are in the know that integration of personality is the supreme need of the age. If this is correct, then India has some advantage of survival value. So, would it be quite wise to so teach economics to the Indian student at an Indian university today as if it related to one, and only one, part of man in one and only one section of his activities? With that query I would have liked to end. But if you really want a plain assertion I shall then declare my faith in the indivisibility of values, of academic values and human values, in a sort of dialectical relation.

Even then my task is not done. The general tone of my feeling about the study of economics that I have tried to communicate to you should be made more specific. It is not enough to plead that economics is, and should be, treated as a cultural subject, as one of the humanities. That pleading should be related to our academic conditions to get the hearing of this distinguished academic audience I have just hinted at certain advantages which an Indian student of economics enjoys, or shall I say, should enjoy, by virtue of his being an Indian living in a certain pattern of values that has not *yet* been torn to shreds. For him, his intsitutions are still real, and certain non-economic values are also still real. I know how they are being shaken. It is also true that judged by other standards these institutions, values and attitudes, are feudal, if not primitive. But as I have said before, backwardness may be a privilege, but if, and only if, there is a pervasive sense of historical urgency.

We, in Indian universities, should be concerned with this sense of urgency. So our problem, primarily, as Indian students of economics, and secondly, as future Indian citizens, is to create this sense of urgency, if there is none, and hasten it, enrich it, give it a direction on the basis of our training, if it is already there. I think that on the whole India is changing perceptibly in recent years. The tempo is certainly not fast, at least, not so fast as one would like it to be. You have heard of the opinion-poll that was taken on the community projects and the extension schemes. Only a small portion of the five hundred thousand and odd villages has been covered. More than fifty per cent of our people have not yet heard of them, but nearly twenty-five per cent of those who live in these areas have said that they have materially profited by them. There is noticeable change in the attitude of those people. I would not implicitly trust the figures of voluntary work and its money-value. Yet some enthusiasm where none existed is a good sign. And if it is the Five Year Plan that has done it, we cannot but welcome it, from this angle, as well as from other angles. *The Plan, therefore, is the new social framework.* It could be, and will be, modified, but this Plan's operative processes have to be adopted as the spring board of urgency. *This is the first datum of dynamic economics for the Indian student to-day.*

The moment he accepts it, he is faced, if he is a genuine student, with some theoretical difficulties. Should he accept wholly, or partly, or reject entirely, the economic theory of the Plan? This is a serious intellectual dilemma. The student reads the Plan and the reports on its evaluation. He discovers the shadow of Keynesian economics over its postulation and analysis. He is not in a position to notice how in the day to day working of the Plan the postulates shift and the analysis is modified. He notices unemployment and wonders how its covert and overt types could be tackled with the help of Keynesian analysis. He vaguely feels the gaps in the analysis; and if he is intellectually disposed, he does not find satisfaction in the concept of the community's propensity to consume when he knows, as an individual, that the community has different layers, each with its consumption pattern. In the matter of investment, if he has read about the over-reaching of certain targets in industrial production, he is not sure if it were not a function of the degree of utilisation of the existing implict excess capacity, at least, in the short and the middle periods, rather than that of increased savings out of the small increase in income. Further, if he has a sense of social justice, which he usually has, he searches, as a student of economics, for a *theory* of distribution in the Keynesian framework of the Plan, and does not find it. He finds acute analysis of monetary phenomena there; he finds great play with the theory of savings; but of a theory of profit, which he knows to be still the most popular incentive of investment, or of a theory of wages, there seems to be no or little trace. So, he is uneasy. And if he has cared to break up the recent National Plan loan subscriptions, he must have noticed the high proportion of business and institutional savings therein. Naturally, he argues that these savings must have been at the instance of certain corporate decisions which are more at the mercy of how the board of directors choose to spend between depreciation, reserves and dividends than dependent upon the psychology of gentlemanly behaviour assumed in Keynesian economics.

If, on other hand, the student is just a common man, a realist, he expects to know from the 'theory' of Indian planning the answer to the elementary question, how exactly are prices determined; and more often than not, he does not get the answer, though he knows that inflation at least, could be, and has been, partly controlled with the help of that 'theory.'

These purely economic doubts of the Indian student are legion. They are reinforced by the typically Indian experience that most economic behaviours are linked up with customs, mores and folk-ways. The Indian student knows for certain that economic behaviour is one thread, though a very important thread, of the cultural pattern in which he moves and grows. Yet this cultural pattern is not recognised in the Keynesian system. Assailed by these doubts and conflicts the Indian student of economics either likes to give up all theory and theorising, or he turns to the alternative theory, viz., that of Marxian economics, which he has often heard, and sometimes read, to have been responsible for quicker changes from equally bad, if not worse, situations. In any case, the Plan suffers from the doubts of the Indian students of economics who are expected to carry its message to the people.

The extent of anti-theory prevalent in the country is much larger than what appears on the surface. It is not confined to those who come to Marxism in despair. I shall not refer to its source in the anti-intellectual character of our national movement to which those who control public opinion today are heirs. I am not minimising the pull of Indian politicians and businessmen in modifying and fixing academic opinion along non-theoretical, severely empirical, and practical routes. Under the influence of big business, economics is becoming business economics and administration, but I shall leave that fact aside. I am not even referring to the bureaucracy whose intimacy with the administration of the Plan is often in inverse ratio to its interest in theory. Not that these practical men have no theory; in fact, their theory is so old that it has become an instinct, a prejudice.

Be that as it may, only the type of academic research that is being made popular at present is in my mind. Our students and teachers have become very fact-minded. Every rift of a thesis is loaded with descriptions of Indian economic conditions, economic history, labour and agricultural situations. That facts are extremely valuable is a truism; that the Indian mind, if there be any such entity, is addicted to speculation and requires a ballast of facts, is also a fairly plausible statement. And who does not deplore the extreme paucity of Indian data? At the same time, as facts, like human beings, are born free and equal, but grow up in chains and inequality, the assembling of mere facts is mere weariness of flesh. Many doctoral dissertations it has been my fortune to guide and examine, but the extreme paucity of any theory and logical structure therein leads me to believe that our scholars are becoming allergic to theory.

The process has been precipitated in recent years under the influence of the type of American research-technique with which India is being acquainted. This is not merely a dangerous intellectual symptom; it spells disaster for the Plan itself, for our very economic growth. It means that with merely descriptive economics—it is sometimes called institutional economics, at other times, economic history, and at all times, economic research—we can at best produce ad hoc measures *sans* coordination, *sans* direction, *sans* enthusiasm, *sans* understanding. My experience tells me that the rejection of all theory, because of the inadequacy of one particular theory, in our case the Keynesian, for the purposes of under-developed economy, is not merely a counsel of despair but may make the despair breed a brood of economic monsters, like Fascist economy. That economy was anti-theory, anti-intellectual, a forced coordination of ad hoc plans; and it led to war because it flourished on armaments. I do not in the least suggest that descriptive economics drives straight to Fascist economy—that will be ridiculous—but I do assert that anti-theory is a dangerous state of mind. Please do not misunderstand me. I am not pooh-poohing surveys and factual researches. They are, I repeat, essential, but such researches should belong to a project, and a project posits a theory of growth. I also greatly admire American scholarship, but I am not sure if the theoretical poverty of many of the social research techniques it is sponsoring or popularising, however brilliant they may be otherwise, quite suits our need of a theory of economic development at this stage.

So Keynesian economics is unsatisfactory and inadequate, and purely empirical economic studies lead nowhere unless they are led by somebody somewhere. Two other systems remain for the Indian student, the Schumpeterian and the Marxist. It is a pity that the average Indian student of economics is not familiar with the Schumpeterian system. I am however convinced that he can profit by it. This is not the place for its estimate. Only a few broad hints can be given here on the basis of my own impressions. I find the Schumpeterian system more satisfying than the ruling system on these major counts:

(1) It gives a full view of the capitalistic processes of economic development in terms of their major endogenous impulse, viz., innovation, and in the context of the circular flow of economic activity. The model, though of a closed domain, is fairly comprehensive.

(2) It brings together the results of theoretical, historical and statistical analysis to bear upon the understanding of capi-

talistic development. It has thus a synoptic view of the theories of the firm, credit, profits, business-cycles, and economic growth.

(3) And so, it marshalls several disciplines, sociology, statistics, economics, and history, in particular. Schumpeter's posthumous work, *History of Economic Analysis*, would be the pride of historical scholarship. These marshalled forces are trained on specific problems. That, to my mind, is more fruitful than the search for purely methodological synthesis. The result is not so much the birth of a new discipline, viz., economic sociology, as has been claimed,[2] as its enrichment.

If my impressions are even partly right, the relevance of the study of the Schumpeterian system to my plea for the study of economics in the context of socio-cultural development, particularly at an Indian univeristy, is obvious. Our economic problems are social and historical, i.e., dynamic. Our economy is known as undeveloped economy. That phrase is unfortunate. I was told that it was used for the lack of any better term and that it was not meant to be an insult. But the misfortune lies elsewhere; it lies in the capacity of that phrase to mislead us as to the real nature of its content. Undeveloped economy, as I understand it, is only the *arrested* economy of a relatively static society. It is an economy that has been arrested by the superior needs of the expansion of a metropolitan economy, and which, mainly for that reason, needs a higher tempo of development and possibly, newer lines of development, than what the developed economies with their own special problems, arising out of fear of stagnation and depressions, need. This aspect of growth through innovations, in all the variety of meanings attached to them in the Schumpeterian system, suits our need, at least, that part of our needs which can be met by capitalism growing out feudalism.

The last clause is important in its indication of the strength and the limitation of the Schumpeterian system. Its strength lies in the fuller exposition of the capitalist system and its neutral development than is offered by the Keynesian. The limitation was noted by Schumpeter himself at least twice, once, in his famous essay, the '*Instability of Capitalism*'[3] and again, in his *Business Cycles*.[4] Lest we forget what he said, we

[2] Cf. Clemence and Doody, *The Schumpeterian System*, p. 99.
[3] *Economic Journal*, September 1928.
[4] p. 145.

may remind ourselves that his analysis relates to a certain historical epoch prior to 'trustified capitalism,' and as such, excludes the operations of huge organisations, like modern monopolies, modern labour unions and bureaucracies, both private and public. So I am not sure if the system would be very useful for the analysis of even the American and the British situations today, where the countervailing effects of three such powerful systems may necessitate the use of another scheme. But for the Indian situation in which capitalism of the pre-trust variety is still the rule in, at least, the private organised sector, the Schumpeterian system retains its superior usefulness.

Of course, no model as such can be a guide to policy. But the point is which schema is more useful for understanding the growing, or developing social economy of India? It is more likely to be the Schumpeterian than the Keynesian. The latter, however, scores over the former in the matter of policy formation within the same capitalistic ambit. To translate the Schumpeterian system into policy directives is a difficult job. The Keynesian system is more amenable in that way.

But there is another limitation to it. This 'innovation' is, to my mind, essentially, a sociological category. It means that innovations which cluster round about equilibrium points are generated through the instrumentality of a special elite group, once called the entrepreneurs, now called the innovators. How is this elite-group formed? How does it persist? How exactly does it function vis a vis other groups, and the largest of them, the state? The answers to these questions, in my opinion, lie outside the system. (Innovation is an endogenous factor in the business cycle analysis). Outside the Schumpeterian system does not mean outside the social order, the premises of which are historical and lie in the resultant relations of production, private property, for example. Now supposing a particular country wants to skip over that historical stage, or hasten its evolution to the next, if it wants, as India wants, to make the rate of development faster in order to catch up with the times, or to very rapidly improve the income per capita, then it may have to change the premises of fixed relations of production by appropriate state action, provided of course that the state is positively responsive to social needs and is capable of bold action and direction.

To expect the Indian entrepreneurs to act as they are expected to act in the Schumpeterian system would be a pious wish. Much of the virtue of innovation is wasted in speculation in India. So we in India cannot expect the cluster of innovators to grow out of the situation unless the state creates the situation; nor can we wisely permit them to grow like the banyan tree casting its shade all over. In the mixed economy, which is our policy, there is an important role for the state. Though we know that the Indian innovators—are they really innovators?—are mustering their strength, the role of the state is also becoming important. The future of the impending conflict cannot be ascertained in terms of the Schumpeterian system. In short, the system which is the reflection of a pre-trustified capitalistic order of 'free enterprise,' is likely to be impaled by the horns of mixed economy.

Thus the Indian student of economics, who is interested in the rapid and more rapid development of the country without incurring the huge social costs of progress via capitalism, may be forced to accept the Marxist system as the only alternative left. Personally, I do not find this compulsion objectionable, least of all, in any moral sense, so long as our facts, our situations, and our needs, do not throw up a theory. That, I must say, would be the ideal position. But as facts are, most young people come to Marxism through a short cut. Quite a few adopt it as a counsel of despair, in the spirit of religious conversion, or as the gospel of millenial hope. There is nothing unpsychological about it. In this world there are ample causes for despair, ample incentives for utopianism or millenialism, and ample needs for simplification. But I am referring to another set of motives and impulses for the study of the Marxist approach by the Indian student of economics. As far as I have been able to understand Marxism, its pattern of utility consists of three major strands:

1) The historicity of institutions and the relative nature of concepts. In Marxism each epoch is specific; and its specificity is responsible for its adequate concepts. Thus neither feudalism, nor capitalism, nor socialism is final. Nor are the concepts of rent, wages, profit, etc., nor are the ideologies. At the same time, this is not historical relativism. The universality is there: it consists in the search for the universally valid laws of social development. This perennial search for laws is strongly reminiscent of classical economics, the only difference lying in the fact that while in classicism the laws are prior to the search in Marxism they follow it. (The practice of 'vulgar'

Marxist economists is however, often different). This particular type of historical understanding is congenial to the dynamic point of view, which every good Indian student of economics I know, that is, good as an Indian and good as a student, feels that he should have. I consider this to be even essential.

(2) The realism of the analysis. It is evident in many ways but never more clearly than in the recognition of the class structure of society and the manner in which it enters into the social processes. In my view, this analysis is a challenge to the Indian historian and the economist, both of whom seem to have ignored it. Class is a sociological category which includes the economic concept of surplus value, the historical concept of movement through conflict, and the logical triad of dialectics. It is possible to separate them mechanistically, but the category of class is a bloc, and as such can be fruitfully used as one, whole tool of analysis for certain particular purposes. Unfortunately, little or no work has been done by Indian scholars with this tool. I feel that our understanding of the Indian social processes will gain thereby in depth. But so long as that is not done according to the highest standard of scholarship, one may turn to other aspects of Marxist realism, such as the analysis of the relations of production, the influence of technology on social relations, the working conditions of labourers and peasants and their relation to incentives, the conflict between village economy and urban economy, the growth of large scale organisations and monopolies, and the birth of ideologies and their growth Some of them are implicit in Marxism, while others are explicit. The implicit ones, in my opinion, are extremely suggestive. To bring them out into the open will be very useful academic exercise. But for that the method so far adopted by Marxists is insufficient. There is a wealth of analytical technique outside the Marxist system waiting to be utilised. The explicit ones, again in my view, are very often cliches. They hinder more often than help realistic analysis. Still the realism of Marxist analysis is very pertinent to the Indian student who feels that he has been deluded, if not deceived, by the concepts of what is called bourgeois economy.

(3) The Marxist approach has a sweep of its own. In a sense, Marxism is a study of the history of the entire process of alienation, and it prescribes certain processes for de-alienation. The alienation is all round, man from nature, distribution from consumption, production from both, class from society, and the

individual from the social process. As I understand it, the Marxian analysis of this universal alienation is eminently satisfying. I do not often subscribe to the Marxist prescriptions for de-alienation, but if the knowledge of a psychological complex helps its cure, then the Marxian approach to the malady of alienation is a contribution to the technique of social and personal integration. It may even be used as a course in preventive social hygiene.

The methodological corollary to all this is interesting. Negatively speaking, it means no compartmentalisation of knowledge, no static analysis, no confusion of a historical category with a universal concept; and positively speaking, it suggests an integral, synoptic view of the social process. So the study of the Marxian system enables one to look at economics as a cultural subject. Having said this of the Marxist system within the short time at my disposal, I hasten to add that unless the gaps in the Marxist theory are filled, its loose ends are tied up, unless its psychological and anthropological assumptions are scrutinised and brought up-to-date, unless its macro-economic analysis is checked up by the micro-economic analysis, as in the matter of price-theory, it is likely to be unrealistic, dogmatic, and derivative of other people's experiences in other contexts. These are the real dangers of intellectual foreign aid, and we should beware of them when we study the Marxian system. I use the word study, not apply. I am against the *application* of any intellectual system to conditions that may not hold it. Application per se is a risk. Does it not also hurt one's sense of dignity? May I add, one's sense of history too?

At the fag end of my lecture I realise that the systems I have mentioned are all non-Indian. This sense comes more out of sorrow than of any feeling of guilt. We Indians have no indigenous economic theory of our own yet. By that I mean that no economic theory has yet grown out of our objective situation. I need not go into the reasons now. It may be argued that Gandhian economics is native to our soil. There is no doubt about the fact that Gandhiji's views on economic matters, no less than those of men who are humbly, and nobly, practising them in the villages, are extremely realistic. But I am speaking here on theoretical economic systems and their study by the Indian student at the university level. One wonders if Gandhiji's views on Indian economic life and its regeneration, however pertinent they may be, could be reduced to a theoretical system. Elsewhere I have tried to describe their evolution and bring out their assumptions. Here, at this stage, I can only state that the norms and values implicit in Gandhiji's economic views and the corresponding practices do not fully square with the historical demands of the time. Gandhian values hinge upon traditionally fixed needs as the immediate, and *wantlessness* as the final goal, whereas everything which the Indian is doing or expecting, and which he is being made to expect by the Plan, by the state, by the market, by every agency acting on him, means *increase* of wants without limit.

Personally, I subscribe to this norm of final wantlessness, to this value of quiet and simple life, though I cannot practise it. And so I presume, cannot many others, particularly, the young people. What is more, the economic evolution of India is marching towards contrary norms. In view of this fact alone, the Gandhian views on economic life can be studied mainly for the purpose of correcting the risks of importing other theoretical systems. This is no mean function to make us constantly aware of 'a sense of existence, of action, of ambushed reality about us.' But beyond it are other functions the discharge of which no shame need haunt, because there is a good bit of imitation and derivation in every act of invention. India need not be afraid of any theory, any 'ism.' Her genius, as I have said, has always lain in her liver.

I have spoken of the alternative systems available to the Indian students of economics in some detail, and in that process I must have taxed your patience. But the case is urgent. We cannot do without a theory; and with the utmost respect to our leaders and thinkers I say that we have not yet produced an economic theory that fulfills the demands of a theory. We have one ready made academic theory, viz., the Keynesian. There is another, the Schumpeterian, which has not yet gained currency. And the third is Marxism, the wood of which is lost in its trees. So what is to be done at the university level of studies? I think I have indicated how my mind works on that problem. Whatever may be the virtues or defects of this system or that, it is clear that a synoptic, dynamic view of economics is imperative. And that view must be trained on a planned system of social order which is committed to living, better living and still better living. Which really means that the discipline known as economics is a part of the disciplines known as humanities. Economics is a cultural subject; and culture is a dynamic social process, and not another name for traditionalism. And this should be particularly true for the Indian student who is facing a big crisis of Indian culture. I do not want him to be lost between compartments of knowledge and waste his integrity which he still possesses in a large measure. I only want him to be dynamic with a richer, forward-looking culture.

PART TWO

HISTORY

5. *Philosophy of Indian History*

I

Those of us Indians who have taken up the academic profession in earnest seldom find the time and the opportunity for that mutual exchange of opinions which should be the very salt of our life. We also live inside sanitary cordons with the help of specialised subjects within which we form ourselves into narrow groups fighting over minor issues. On the other hand, anybody who has attended a sitting or two of the annual conferences of learned bodies will amusingly agree with the late Prof. R. G. Collingwood's description of them as debauches. 'Such gatherings,' he is referring to the annual meetings of philosophers in university towns, 'introduced one to people in one's own profession and they were useful as showing how delightful might be the society of men whose doctrines are disapproved, or how unnecessary it was to waste time over the works of some much advertised person who had only to stand up and speak in order to proclaim himself an impostor. But these discussions served no philosophical purpose.' There speaks the Oxford don, and though the dreaming minarets of Lucknow have been compared to the dreaming spires of Oxford, I have no intention to imitate such superior airs. In fact, we Indian scholars could not, even if we willed to, cultivate them because whatever intellectual life is available in the United Kingdom is not to be had here. It is regrettable from the larger point of view. But what concerns us here is that in reaction to this starvation we retreat further into our little vanities and take cover under specious arguments to 'keep face.' One such argument is that in the present state of knowledge we cannot but be selective in our field of study; or what comes to the same thing, a scientific study being based upon a patient accumulation of facts requires a division of labour between a number of scholars each of whom can only be mindful of the facts within his selected range of vision. In regard to the humanities the argument takes various shapes; one such is that history of economics can have no philosophy. It will be my unpleasant duty to expose this spurious logic and show that its fallacy arises not so much from the logic itself as from the person or the group using it.

In the official universities of India knowledge has been so compartmentalised that its unities are ignored. Faculties are divided; departments are split up; subjects are atomised until a situation arises in which a learned professor on the arts side privately asks about the distinction between botany and zoology, and a learned colleague from the faculty of science does not know that sociology is neither the preaching of birth control nor of socialism. Students also suffer from this atmosphere of ignorance. There is however no sense in blaming individuals who, as individuals, are worthy people. What is wrong is not general ignorance, but the ignoring of the fact, a fact which sociology has brought out very vividly through its sub-sciences like anthropology, history and ethnology, viz. that at a given time, in a certain context and in a spatial unit, the culture-pattern is one. This unity of culture is not unitary, but multiform. It may have a federal or a confederational character and structure. In short, the oneness may as well be a union of diverse organic patterns, and the diversity may turn the whole gamut from the contradictory to the identical. But the culture-pattern must have one or more singularities, specificities, homogeneities, and functional integrities, to distinguish it from any other. Now, our university instruction staggers this basic unity of culture-pattern by disbelieving in the basic unity of knowledge. I find from the curriculum and the pedagogics followed in the Bharatiya Vidya Bhavan that at least one aspect of Indian culture is being sought to be understood integrally.

If we go into this question of our ignoring the basic unity of culture-pattern deeper than the disbelief in the unity of knowledge we come to the root of our trouble. It is a mistrust of action which is a synonym for the fear of life. Fear or mistrust is not openly avowed. What appears is its rationalised form. We are scholars; what have we got to do with political, economical, social, legal, ethical practices except to contemplate them from some ivory tower? Life is a stream, and not being flotsam and jetsam in its current, we stand on the banks unruffled and dry with the desiccated peace of hard intellect. We believe in thought, its priority and its self-sufficiency; all action is illusion, delusion, hallucination; or all action is deduction, application, and therefore, subordinate to thought. And we are the thinkers, the idealists. Our latest nomenclature is 'the pure scientists.' Our inventions may be patented to rain bombs on defenceless people, we remain 'pure' scientists; a nation may be starved out of existence by economic exploitation, we remain 'pure' economists preaching the virtues of free trade and the vices of planning; we may be writing pornography, but we are 'pure' artists, practising art for art's sake. And so runs the mad career of purity, profit for the sake of profit, power for the sake of power, philosophy for the sake of philosophy, and history for the sake of history. The word 'sake' is not used; instead we use science, scientific spirit, scientific attitude. Its plain and simple connotation is sakes' sake. To put it mildly, it is arguing in a circle. When a panicky herd of sheep move in a circle the shepherds call it milling. When learned men do it they call it scholarship. And historical scholarship is a supreme offender.

No sooner do we seek to come to the subject of history than we meet at least three vital questions guarding the approach. The first question can be framed thus: a) What is the expectation from history which is not usually fulfilled and which philosophy alone can satisfy? The second question relates to a more concrete situation: b) What are the main defects of Indian history so far written which can be removed by philosophy, either Indian or Western? The third is a general one, viz.: c) Can there be any philosophy of history at all? Probably, the first and the third questions are aspects of the same problem. Strictly speaking however, there are a number of differences. The two questions which on discussion reveal at least one aspect of the relation between philosophy and history are posed by people trained to different disciplines, the first being by historians and the third by philosophers. Then they are raised at distinct periods. For example, when new life is bursting forth out of a moribund society, when a society is undergoing revolutionary change, the emphasis is on the side of history. Then all thinking men look to the past for guidance or glorification, for continuity or confidence, for support of the triumph of experiment over tradition. Such a stress has been noticed in all periods of Renaissance; in the Italy of the fifteenth and nineteenth centuries, in Germany at the beginning of the nineteenth, in the USA, in China, Japan and India. Even in Soviet Russia, which is generally supposed to have broken away with the past, the same phenomenon is observable today. During the second world war the Russians sought inspiration from Peter the Great and Suvarov, from many semi-mythical heroes who not only fought the enemy but also consolidated villages, tribes, cities, regions, and built up the country. In other words, some people in a certain period become dissatisfied with history hitherto written because they are dissatisfied with the history as it was being lived. Positively, they are prompted by the new modes of living or by their prospects, and so they want their past history to be rewritten in the light of their present and their future; or they want to write their contemporary history in the shape of pamphlets, articles, pictures, statues, public works, novels, poems and what not; in fine, they create and collect materials for the future history of their epoch and achievements.

I do not propose to crowd my lecture with unfamiliar names, but any student of Burckhardt on the Italian Renaissance will bear me out in the above proposition. Once the need of rewriting old history or composing new history arises it cannot but simultaneously generate some philosophy. I say some philosophy, but not necessarily a full-fledged system, because what we find is a combination of faith and attitude, a way of life, a world-view, a *weltanschauung* at the beginning. Men of renaissance behave for the time being as if they believed in something outside, behind, and all pervasive. It may be faith in themselves as human beings, faith in reason, progress, nation or science. Then the thing believed appears in a generalised form, in capital letters so to speak. Human beings become Men, then it is Humanism, intellect becomes science and reason, then it is Positivism, and when expansion becomes progress, then every attitude is coloured by Darwinism. Even then, no relevant philosophy as such is born. First the head comes out as the study of method. In history it is critical history, in the study of classics it is interpretation of texts, in theology it is higher criticism, in philosophy it is logic. Slowly or abruptly, philosophy comes out.

I do not suggest that the process is unilinear or continuous, or that the relation between the newly awakened sense of history and the formulation of any metaphysical system is one of an object before a mirror to the exact reflection of the image. The mirror of the human brain is never clean, and its surface is seldom plane. Objects too are infinite, they jostle one another, and they rarely occupy the same position in the same foreground for any length of time. Yet some correlation between history and philosophy is always there to prove that the urge for action and the sense of history are prior to the impulsion of a philosophical system. I shall mention only two cases: a) The urgent philosophy of Europe in the seventeenth century was intimately conditioned by the tremendous growth of natural sciences in that period; and this growth was almost at the direct instigation of a phenomenal development in trade, commerce, communications, and in knowledge of the non-European world. At the height of this upheavel, Edward Hyde, the Earl of Clarendon was writing his great work, *The True Historical Narrative of the Rebellion and the Civil Wars in England,* gathering materials from his own experience as a member of the Long Parliament, as a fighting Anglican and as an adviser to Charles II. Clarendon began to compose his history in his period of exile that began in 1641. His contemporary was Hobbes who planned out a systematic philosophy of matter, human nature and society in Latin between 1642 and 1658. One of them, '*De Corpore Politico,*' was subsequently worked up in the text of the *Leviathan* published in 1651. Hobbes was building up a materialist philosophy based upon induction the laws of which Sir Francis Bacon had formulated. We know how Hobbes in his continental tour had met the two Italian scientists Galileo and Gassendi, and the two French mathematicians Descartes and Mersenne. And Hobbes was not above writing an account of contemporary events. His story of the civil wars and the Long Parliament was entitled *Behemoth* which was suppressed. If Hobbes were the only representative of the seventeenth century's pattern of history, science, and a particular type of metaphysics and politics, one could have dismissed the relation I am seeking to establish as an accident, a freak. But there is a whole host of eminent writers to support my contention—Harrington, Milton, Algernon Sidney, the groups known as the Levellers and the Diggers, with Locke closing up the epoch of the revolution that culminated in 1688 with his *Essay Concerning Human Understanding* and the two Treatises of Government, published in 1690. As many as 20,000 pamphlets of this hectic period are reported to have been collected so far, and the important ones have been studied. Their main preoccupation has been described as the search for the bond of political principles and action in the conception of natural law. Thus it was that history in the making was referred to a dominant premise of social action and social philosophy and sought to be connected with it in the formative period of modern England.

From Hooker to Locke it is the same story running throughout seventeenth century England. The curious may pursue it in that very interesting book by Dr. Stark on the philosophical foundations of economics, called *The Ideal Foundations of Economic Thought,* in which the basis of classical economics is discovered in the manner in which Locke sought to resolve the great antithesis between Man and Nature, and subsequently by Leibniz who thought he had resolved it in the border between Adam Smith's Invisible Hand and Bastiat's harmonies. It may also be pertinent to mention here that modern researches into the life of Newton, the greatest scientific figure of the age, do not support Wordsworth's view of him, his 'mind for ever voyaging through strange seas of thought alone?' The seas were perilous but not strange, nor did he embark alone. Newton's mathematical ideas and cosmological beliefs were conditioned by the main cultural-compulsive of the age, which was the growth of mercantilism out of the bondage of feudal and clerical fetters on trade. It is a pity that I cannot dwell upon one whom I consider the tallest of them all, John Milton. Here was a life, if ever there was one, consciously dedicated to poetry, deliberately weaning himself away from his dedication and devoting his mighty talents and his orchestral voice to the cause of revolution and freedom, acting as a secretary and a pamphleteer, inventing a whole system of cosmogony and welding it into magnificent poetry, and thus behaving as the model for all genuine artists at the crisis of the history of their nations. If these makers of history were not averse to philosophy, what are we, the puny intellectuals of libraries and laboratories, to fight shy of it?

(B) My second example comes from the movement of a later period. It started in Europe from about the second quarter of the nineteenth century, and in a sense, it continues even today. The Industrial Revolution was completing its course in England and starting on its career on the continent. It affected every aspect of living. The agricultural pattern, the rural setting, the family complex were upset. People began to move to industrial areas, cities grew, women and children weer employed away from their home, the guilds were gone, handicrafts were disappearing, and a new class appeared wielding power and prestige by virtue of their wealth acquired partly by their skill as middlemen but eventually from their ownership of the machines and other means of production. Society was finally split up into two classes who found no more of the old bonds and failed to discover new ones. But the nation's wealth in terms of material goods, trade and industry, and in population, increased very rapidly. All these made for a new attitude towards life. It was no longer tied up with anything transcendental; it was directed towards this earth and better life in this earth; it believed in the ability of man to better his condition, for which certain minimum reforms were needed, but otherwise for which individuals could be trusted with their self-regarding motives. The idea was that if individuals were left to themselves social good would automatically secrete like hormones. But meanwhile society was becoming complex, and the problem of social good thrust itself forward. Some intellectuals wanted to solve it by what is known as the hedonistic calculus, the essence of which was simple, arithmetical addition and subtraction, viz., the greatest good of the greatest number. Be it noted that the problem was not an immediately aggressive one because the activities of the period were treated as symptoms of prosperity. Remember how David Ricardo sensed the inherent deficiencies of the system and yet concluded by defending it. Anyhow, the leaders of the philosophical radicals and the utilitarians, the progenitors of liberalism, men like Grote and James Mill, were considerable historians even if they were poor philosophers.

The story did not come to an end there. Slowly but inevitably were the social contradictions coming to the fore. The country was prosperous, no doubt; in fact, the forties and the fifties of the nineteenth century were the heyday of capitalism; but the labourers were restless practically all over Europe. The history of socialism dates from that period. In England, France and Germany, trade unions of various types, socialisms of different complexions ranging from pink to scarlet-red, and cooperative societies grew up fast. In 1848, the year of the third French Revolution, were published John Stuart Mill's *Principles of Political Economy* and the *Communist Manifesto*. It is very profitable to note the contrast between these two works. Mill's treatise is a gradual recession from pure Benthamism, its individualism, its dependence upon utility and its liberalism. The older utilitarians had objected to the combination laws on the ground that restriction by the state to the formation of trade unions was just not necessary; Mill, on the same principle of the *laissez faire,* argued that any such restriction was an interference with the freedom of contract and supported[1] the growth of trade unions. Not only this, he soon began to make exceptions to the Benthamite dogma in favour of reduction of hours of labour by legislation. We know how the number of exceptions included children, prostitutes, lunatics and others who could not think for themselves. He went further to say that the division of society into two hereditary classes, employers and employed, could not be permanently maintained,[2] and that the relation between the two would be superseded either by co-partnership or by labourers' associations. But the following passage looks the very antipodes of Benthamite radicalism and the utilitarianism of his father's group. It occurs in the third edition of the same book, *Principles,* a book which was considered until the other day as the bible of classical or Ricardian political economy. Mill writes:

> If, therefore, the choice were to be made between 'communism' (note that the word evoked no very great 'prejudice' in those days and was commonly accepted by the intellectuals of the period) with all its chances, and the present (1852) state of society with all its sufferings and injustices; if the institution of private property necessarily carried with it as a consequence, that the produce of labour should be appointed as we now see it, almost in an inverse ratio to the labour—the largest portions to those who have never worked at all, the next largest to those whose work is almost nominal, and so in a descending scale, the remuneration dwindling as the work grows harder and more disagreeable, until the most fatiguing and exhausting bodily labour cannot count with certainty on being able to earn even the necessaries of life; if this or communism were the alternative, all the difficulties, great or small, of communism would be but as dust in the balance.

[1] *Principles* (Ashley's edition), pp. 933-39.
[2] *Ibid.*, p. 761.

Obviously, John Stuart Mill seems to have travelled a long way from Bentham. To be very accurate, the critical attitude towards Bentham's doctrines which Mill imbibed from Coleridge's romantic philosophy was not yet extinguished; the influence of the French thinkers, like the Utopian Socialists and Comte, and of the British Chartists was becoming apparent. But listen to the folowing two sentences[3]: 'But to make the comparison applicable, we must have communism at its best, with the regime of individual property, not as it is, but as it might be made. The principle of private property has enver yet had any fair trial and less so, perhaps, in this country than in some others.' Mill goes on to distinguish between the laws of property and the principles by which private property can be justified, and concludes that there is no necessary connection between the principle of individual property and the many evils which socialist writers attribute to individual property. This is old Benthamism pulling Mill back from his own conclusions. We will not go into Mill's political philosophy. His famous essay, *On Liberty* (1859), made hay of consistent utilitrianism; in fact, 'the essay was morally persuasive precisely because Mill exceeded the limits of consistent utilitarianism,' and the urge to transgress came from his faith in the freedom to think, to enquire and to know as inherent in a human being. On the other hand, Mill was nervous about mass opinion and the capacity of the majority to repress. He therefore got himself entangled between the inherent right to think and certain practices which were emerging. He ended by pitting liberty against democracy.

Let us follow Mill's evolution in other spheres for finding out the root of the matter. The story of an honest man's mind, his approach and aversion to a conclusion at the rigorous dictation of understanding, is more interesting than the biography of a great man. It, ultimately, is to show that a certain critical historical situation should try to formulate a philosophy of history. Immediately, our enquiry is to trace out the reason of Mill's embarassment before philosophy. If we put gentler influence aside we notice how long, with the slow liberation from Benthamism, Mill was shedding his faith in natural law, a faith which he had acquired from Coleridge and which saturated all his earlier writings. It is hardly necessary for me to say how this idea of natural law had very often served and

[3] *Ibid.*, pp. 208-9.

continues to serve the cause of the oppressed of every nation and in every age, including India, where the word birthright has been on the lips of everybody since Tilak's days. .Natural law has always been behind the movements for equality and freedom. From the seventeenth century onward the phrase, natural law, began to assume new content. It became 'laws of nature.' In the hands of the English and the French thinkers these natural laws became one of the planks of the philosophy of deism. The scholastic compromise of two separate orders of laws, those of God and of Nature with the laws of God dominating, was substituted by other devices. The essence of the trick was to find a parallel to natural law; and it was found in the natural religious impulse which by definition was the reasonable, the moral and the useful ground, the blue-print and the structure of all religions. And the second, viz., the natural economy, was built upon a natural order by the physiocrats in particular, and guided by the invisible hand according to Adam Smith and his immediate predecessors. The result was interesting. God was sent up to a lofty place allowing the laws of nature to operate below. A very English solution indeed. As Kahler puts it,[4] 'In the realm of thought, God had assumed the position of an English monarch.' For the inner significance of this achievement we must however go to Voltaire who said that natural religion, as opposed to artificial religion, was 'a philosophical system rather than a religion,' a goal of enlightenment rather than a revealed beginning. This philosophy of enlightenment branched off in several directions, such as Holbach's materialism and Condorcet's philosophy of progress. In England, the deist trunk remained stocky and gnarled. Priestley was a Unitarian, Dalton and Quaker, Faraday a Sandemanian, (Eddington and Jeans Quakers again). Such was the philosophical climate of John Stuart Mill. He had believed in natural laws; but the laws of nature had supplanted them. Some consequences ensued:

1) Mill must find a substitute for natural laws which had served human history so long as a criticism of historical inertia. This he hoped to do first by using Coleridge's conservatism as a weapon of attack against the evils of society for reform; Mill was of the opinion (Dissertations and Disquisitions, essay on

[4] *Man, the Measure*, p. 472.

Coleridge) that Coleridge's conservatism was a valuable philosophy inasmuch as it marked the beginnings of a philosophy of history. The second manner was to adopt an institutional approach and assume human progress. Let Mill speak on his own behalf[5]

> That the human mind has a certain order of possible progress, in which some things must precede others, an order which governments and public instructors can modify to some extent, but not to an unlimited extent: that all questions of political institutions are relative, not absolute, and that different stages of human progress not only will have but *ought* to have, different institutions; that government is always either in the hands or passing into the hands, of whatever is the strongest power in society, and that what this power is, does not depend on institutions but institutions on it: that any general theory or philosophy of politics supposes a previous theory of human progress and that this is the same thing with a philosophy of history.

At long last, natural law is reduced to a theory of instutional progress. That is all that Mill could reach in his search for a philosophy of history. If you like John Stuart Mill you will say that the fact that he recognised the need for such a thing is as important as his failure to formulate it.

2) The second consequence of Mill's position was entanglement in his logic. I call it a consequence, and not the cause. We know that one of Mill's chief interests in logic as such was to discover if the method which had proved so successful in the natural sciences and their fields of investigation could be applied to the social studies in which the relations and the relata were much more variable and complex than in nature. It was more than a laudable motive; it was an imperative need in view of the fact that he was shedding his philosophy of natural law and coming towards a philosophy of history, even if that philosophy was that of institutional progress. Unfortunately, however, neither the motive nor the need was supported by the analysis. Mill was not clear about the meaning of the term 'method.' It is a model, a principle of causation or of successive movement, a rule and a contrivance as it suits him. This is the primary confusion. The secondary one goes deeper. I want to draw the attention of our historians to this point, because I

[5] *Autobiography*, p. 162.

feel that they are committing the same blunder in the assumption of their investigation as Mill did in his analysis. Now, in order that Mill's method can be true and adequate for the actual procedure of an empirical investigation, certain conditions, according to Miss Stebbing,[6] are to be fulfilled.

> These conditions are: (a) the total situation must be capable of being regarded as causally disconnected from another situation; (b) the cause-factors must be in one-one correspondence with the factors in the effect-complex; (c) one factor must be capable of being withdrawn (or added) without alteration of any factor; (d) there must be one, and only one, factor present in the one instance but absent from the other instance.

None of these conditions can be fulfilled in the course of a historical or social investigation. The investigator discovers, sooner or later, that it is a total situation, even if it were a record or an inscription, that confronts him; (in fact, a record or an inscription is only the congealed form or the dead end of a total situation), that a single cause-factor liberates or unleashes several cause-factors with which the one-one ratio cannot be struck; that no factor can be isolated, added, subtracted without altering the entire structure; (it is in this sense that the length of Cleopatra's nose is important in history); and that there will always be vestiges, hangovers, or causes going off half-cock, so to say, to be accounted for. So what will the investigator actually do? He deliberately reduces the organic nature of the social reality into a design answering the above conditions, in order to remain a scientist and make his study yield as much as it can. If he be honest he hopes that later on he would take up other factors one by one, constructing the summation in patience until it approximates to reality. But art is living and life is short. In the meantime, a convenience, or a contrivance rules and refuses to be dislodged. The result is that either the historian throws it violently and says that history cannot be reduced to a science, or he insinuates that history has no philosophy. But if one is genuinely interested in reality one will amend the method and come to a philosophy. Both these tasks were performed by other men. They used the dialectics and evolved a new philosophy of history.

6 *A Modern Introduction to Logic,* p. 336.

We have dwelt so long on John Stuart Mill because he is very typical, almost symbolic. His ideas marked the great divide of a great culture, just as his period did. The best Indian historians have not gone beyond Mill's methodology. We have seen how he fumbled between Bentham's radicalism and Coleridge's conservatism. Our historians do likewise with men who have influenced them most, mainly European scholars. But Mill failed to come over. This was due to his faulty logic and to his inability in evolving a philosophy of history. Progress was not enough; liberalism, radicalism, a sound heart and good brain—none was sufficient. He had boggled at the totality of reality and foundered in convenience. The contrivance had mastered him. Mill's is the tragedy of an honest man who wants to lift himself up by his shoes-laces to a position from which he can improve the world. Mill's age was congenial for a new philosophy of history, because the contradictions were very much there; but he failed to resolve them because he could not build up the requisite philosophy. The result was that an opportunity for England was lost. Personally, Mill remained the lost leader attacking himself inside the safe custody of academic interest. These are the lessons which our Indian historians must needs learn unless they choose to allow the history of India to be run by others less equipped with the sense of history.

The work of laying the foundations of a philosophy of history suitable to the world of hectic change initiated by the Industrial Revolution was left to others, the German romantics and the French thinkers. The former, for the historical necessity of forming a nation out of numerous, particularist states so long under the heel of Napoleon, threw up what may be called a philosophy of national history; and the latter, viz., the French thinkers, under the influence of the doctrines of the French Revolution, developed a devastating critique of capitalism but without any constructive philosophy beyond an amalgam of idealism, positivism and materialism. It was left to Hegel to supply the missing link to the French and English criticisms. From Hegel the modern philosophy of history begins in the west. The lectures which were presented in book-form by Prof. Gaus were from Hegel's lectures of 1830-31; but the first of these two were at the 1822-23 and 1823-24 sessions.

Before I close this section—'what is the expectation from

history which is not usually fulfilled and which philosophy can satisfy?'—I want to make only a few brief remarks in regard to Hegel's classics. In the first place, it should be placed in the context of the period and the needs of the country. A nation, and a strong nation, and a strong nation under the hegemony of Prussia, had to be positively and deliberately created by an effort of the national will. The national will had not yet been institutionalised; but Fichte and Herder were looking to its formation as an idea. On the other hand, it was a period when industrialisation had just started, but the country was still in the rural-handicraft stage and existed as an appendage to feudalism, lay and clerical. The German states had come under French domination, and it was on the whole a liberalising force. Almost simultaneously with Hegel's lecture, events were moving in France and elsewhere towards the crisis of 1832. In short, there was a discrepancy between the objective situation in Germany and the subjective fermentation of ideas. The idealism of German philosophers, the romanticism of German musicians, economists and historians of the period—all conspired to build what Marshall calls 'an empire in the air' as a sort of compensation for the failure or, if that be an inappropriate word, as the correlate of the desire, to build an empire on the earth. This discrepancy between the subjective and the objective situations explains much of what has happened in Germany. It has made the whole of German history shaky and unreal. How many times have the Germans sought but failed to unite! What terrible contradictions there are in German thought, its classicism and sentimentality, its noble abstractions and crude realism, its particularism and cultural expansion, its theological bearings and non-human practices? No wonder that German philosophies of history are a hotch-potch, a pauper's broth of incompatibles. No wonder also that Marx found Hegel as the founder of dialectics, but rejected the Hegelianism of the Hegelians. He was saved by the French and the British critical social philosophy and succeeded in building up a philosophy of history which avoided the idealism of Hegel and the mechanical materialism of French thinkers and of Feuerbach. This philosophy of history was dialectical materialism. Whatever may be the metaphysical loopholes in this, it had the virtue of being able to push people over the fence by making the sitting on it an uncomfortable position for the sitter; it had the merit of giving these people the will to act, thus abolishing the gap between theory and practice; and it had the privilege of enthusing people over things material and concrete instead of crying for the moon. All these advantages accrued from the fact that the Marxian philosophy of history was derived from historical needs of the day and was a pointer to the next historical step. This was a net gain for the society that was showing very wide gaps in its structure.

What I have said so far is only a sort of clearing the approach to the question. With the help of preceding historical examples one trail is discovered. It is a faint one, but we may follow it. Whenever the actual business of living in a changing society churns up live problems that are sought to be systematised into some form of philosophy, the solution of the problems is once more referred to history, i.e., historical living and acting. The process is essentially a dialectical one. All problems arise from living; at a certain stage, it appears that problems have an autonomy of their own and that they can be solved on the philosophic level; isolation is prolonged, history merges itself into philosophy; but life goes on demanding solution which, for the simple reason that the world of pure thought is an abstraction and this human world is an impure, active one, can never be adequate for the common purpose. Thus it is that a sort of back reference is made by philosophy to history. In short, the history of text-books throws no light upon the quetsions that vex the common man; nor does the philosophy of text-books, when he turns his mind away from what the Romans or the Chinese or the Indians did or the Russians are doing. The common man expects history to help him gain an insight into, a way of looking at, his own problems in order that he may solve them and live better; or what comes to the same thing, he wants a way of living, or a view of life. That means philosophy in the broadest sense of the term. Philosophy itself is thus a historical study. History is the beginning and the end of ways of living. Like the insignificant coral polyps the man in the street is busy building an island below the sea surface. History and philosophy both have ignored him, and he wants them to be guides for his living. Therefore, my charge against history, as it has been written so far, is that it has generally failed to tell you and me to make history. History which has no philosophy running through it cannot teach us how to do so, because philosophy regulates the conditions under which live issues are solved.

II

We now come to the second question which guards the approach to our fundamental problem. What are the main defects of Indian history so far written which can be removed by philosophy, either Indian or western? Obviously, I shall be treading on delicate ground. But if my object is to bring out the defects which are removable by philosophy, then my sins may be pardoned. By 'Indian history so far written' I mean the running accounts as well as the reconstruction of periods. I make no distinction between Indian and European scholars. Travellers' descriptions like those of Megasthenes, Huen Tsang, Al Bureni, Tavernier or Bernier, or the invaluable documents like the *Ain-i-Akbari* or *Sair-Mutakharin* of the Muslim period, or the diaries and despatches of the British, are excluded. They are valuable contributions no doubt, but my idea is to look at and swim in the whole and the full stream of Indian history, and not to get bogged up in the backwaters.

I find that the business of writing Indian history had had a history. It is alleged to have started with the impulse given by the Asiatic Societies of Bengal and Bombay. Illustrious English names are to be found among their founders. This has led to much sentimental talk about the impact of the west upon the east and vice versa. It is not my intention to take away anything from the praise which is due to the pioneers. As a sociologist, however, I find that whatever may have been the personal stimulus of scholars like Sir William Jones, the social drive behind the search for knowledge of oriental history and culture was the urgency felt by commercial interests suddenly called upon to combine trading with ruling to carry on both enterprises with the minimum disturbance to the onerous undertaking. People had to be governed well in order that commerce might flourish. Good government in those days of Bentham and Smith meant non-interference with the habits and customs of the people. So those habits and customs had to be studied. They could be studied in two ways: (a) by reading the texts, which meant translation by the pundits of the Fort, and also hunting them out; and (b) by observation. The first led to oriental scholarship and Indology, and the second to ethnology. It is very interesting to note how the early English settlers and officials took to ethnology, how the early proceedings of the Asiatic Societies are full of ethnological materials, how the older museums and the attached libraries seem to overemphasise them. In fact, Indology and ethnology stem off the same trunk, viz., the need to rule in such a way that commerce is not hindered and may flourish.

With Prinsep and Cunningham we can take the later names of Lyell and Crooke. If this almost simultaneous evolution of Indology and Indian ethnology were peculiar to India we could have traced it to an accident or the shock given by primitive and barbarous Indian customs to young British officials who had inherited the genius for locality in their small and intimate homeland. But one finds great interest for ancient history and local customs shown by Dutch and French colonial officers in the East Indies and French Indo-China. In British Africa the same thing is happening in the limited field of anthropology, but that is probably because Africa is reputed to have no history. Although it is unsafe to generalise, we may simply leave the matter by saying that the beginnings of modern Indian historiography were laid in the period of colonial commerce. Other factors must have contributed, but the main compulsion seems to have originated from the exigencies of the new economic situation that had brought about a few administrative and political responsibilities.

I wonder whether the implications of such beginnings have been fully realised. Interest in Hindu, Islamic and aboriginal laws and customs was no doubt aroused, but the long period effects were not always quite happy. Let us take Bengal. Pandits and ulemas were appointed by the Supreme Court to translate masterpieces of jurisprudence. They created a monster, Samskritised Bengali, which was completely removed from the language spoken and written by the people. Bengali prose used in the court became stylised with the double accretion of Samskrit and Persian terms, and with its prestige it soon became the model. It required more than a century for Bengali writers of genius to shake off the shackles and come closer to the language spoken. Even then the Bengali of Bengali literature is not always the language of the people. Those who know how the *pai hua* movement in China was the essence of the Chinese renaissance will appreciate this point. In the interpretation of the laws we can guess how the venerable pandits and maulavis blocked the path of progress in social reform by judicial means. Young British officials could not but trust the native advisers. I shall not refer to the many misrepresentations of customs and beliefs one notices in the early advent into ethnology. These are but a few results of the first attempts at Indology. But on one point later scholars have to yield before the founders. The founders knew the people more, and in so far as the process of ossification had not yet set in, the people were probably made of other stuff. With more knowledge, with fresher mind than what is to be found among recent officials, and with the enthusiasm caught from an unfolding period in their own civilization, and having fewer commitments to the preservation of law, order and balance and more to making them, these officials, including the military, pioneers realised that the history of India could not be separated from the habits and customs of Indians. Even when I do not claim on their behalf any deep understanding and clear formulation of the processes, I credit them with the realisation of a cardinal idea that Indian antiquity was a live thing, and not a mere search for pillars and inscriptions, monuments and old sites. Of course, as individuals, the pioneers would not be able to carry the credit, yet as a group of workers on the Indian field they deserve it. Probably, a better way of putting the same thing will be to refer to their work as a complex or a pattern in which history and ethnology, or anthropology, (the word sociology had not yet been coined although the caste-system aroused curiosity) were more or less organically related. This is an important point to remember.

Indian history, they realised, was not dead, but was continuous, not just a matter of records or of chronology, but was being lived by millions of people then and there and everywhere, not like a single shaft of culture but radiation and a spread. Indian history, they appreciated, was made living through its myths and legends, the exploits of its religious avatars and heroes, its folk-tales, all of which the people knew intimately, thanks to the epics and the festivals, the roving dramatic parties and singers. I strongly submit that if it could be properly developed, modern scientific historians and archaeologists would not have had to frantically search for continuity and the unity of Indian history, a search which when it fails is compensated by sentiments not always scientific. The fact of the matter is this: India has a history; this history is the history of Indian customs, beliefs, traditions as they are entertained by the people. It may include Asoka and Akbar, but they are decorations. The real base is the life of the people. Modern historians of India have missed the essence of India. It is one of the few countries whose history is continuous, because its people have been living history every moment of their life, a history that comprehends the future, a history that is related to the individual by strong bonds, viz., the ethical and religious injunctions in terms of actions and advice of avatars and heroes, in interpretations or *smriti*, a history that looks with indifference at this conqueror or that, that considers Delhi to be far away; in short, a history that is continuous, specific, solid and social. Indian history is Indian culture, that is to say, Indian history is shot through and through by philosophy which, as you know, is not mere metaphysics but *darshan*, a code of conduct pointing towards the Absolute or whatever it is. But turn over the pages of any good college text-book, and you will find that after the political description of a period, say the Gupta, the Turkish or the Mughal, only a few pages are insinuated, almost apologetically, in memory of the cultural activities such as the state of literature, architecture and systems of philosophy. I have not been able to trace any reference to rituals, customs, myths and legends there, not to speak of their changes if any. Mention of Nagarjun, Sankaracharya may be found, but of the practical philosophy, which is the most vital aspect of philosophy, none. This, to my mind, is a serious loss to Indian historiography. Our historians should never have been ashamed of their own people. One of them when faced with that charge replied that if they had not shown the political greatness of Ancient India, India's stock in the world would have gone down and we would have been dubbed as barbarians, primitives, unfit for self-government.

Well, this reply brings me to the second stage of Indian history itself, the first being what has been loosely described as the colonial-commercial. We are in the middle of the nineteenth century by now. The Indian press is born, and it has begun to ventilate administrative grievances and a few political demands. If you look into the old files of contemporary newspapers and journals, some of which reached a high standard of dignified expression, you will often come across hits at Christian missionaries for some derogatory remarks against Hinduism, and not unoften a protest or two against an official's feeling of superiority over the ruled. At the same time, you will also observe the notice of a dramatic performance, a meeting of pundits, a summary of the proceedings of a club composed of eminent Indians and Europeans devoted to the noble object of improving the material, moral, cultural or spiritual condition of India. By that time the after-effects of the 'Sepoy Revolt' were smudged out except in one important particular, which I shall mention soon. The country was clearly in for a period of consolidated British rule. A class of people had risen mostly from among the ranks of those who had derived or sought benefit from British connection, and that class dug their money in landownership and/or took to English education which was getting popular. Those among them who could write and speak English with ease and came from respectable families got jobs with the government. Some of them were very able men, but their prospects were not commensurate with their ability. Usually they were steeped in English culture, but they reacted against the full-blooded westernisation advocated by men of the thirties. It is difficult to demarcate the boundaries of personal disappointment and social conviction. But uncharitable remarks of foreigners often tilted the balance against the west.

About the seventies, both in Bombay and in Bengal, industrialisation had started, and from all reports it was growing fast. Bombay had 8 cotton factories; in '73-'74, in Bombay city alone the number went up to 28; elsewhere 8. Exported cotton goods jumped from £1,91,336 to £2,54,571 in a year. Heavy and cotton stuff stopped coming into India and Indian cotton products were being sold in China, Russia and America. In Bengal too 15 mills were working in the decade along the Hooghly. The import of machinery shot up from £ 3,00,000 in 1870 to £ 1.5 m. in 1875; and there was agitation in the English press, in Manchester and in the House of Commons, to abolish the very moderate duty of about 7.5 per cent *ad valorem* on British textiles which the Indian government had imposed in 1864. Not only that: British textile interests agitated for excise duty on Indian cotton goods and for factory legislation to protect the poor Indian women and children. Naturally, the textile and jute companies in India, British and Indian alike, did not like this. The following quotation may be of interest. 'Give Manchester what she wants or go....that is what Lord Salisbury (the Secretary of State of India) demanded of the Viceroy.'[7]

[7] Lord Northbrook is the Viceroy, and the reference is to the Tariff Act of 1875 passed at Simla by which 7.5 per cent *ad valorem*, on imports was reduced only to 5 per cent, which Lord Salisbury objected as insufficient for several reasons, one of which being

What can be more scandalous, to avail ourselves of Lord Salisbury's own words, than for an English minister deliberately to sell India to Manchester? Yet this is what the Secretary of State proposed to do.' The above passage is from the *Bombay Gazette*, (28 February 1876) of which the editor was one Mr. MacLean who was later on to transfer his affection to Manchester and be the spokesman of Manchester in the House of Commons.

I consider this to be an important quotation. It shows how in Bombay at least non-Indians, for their own reasons, helped the Indian case against the English government. But of superior significance is the pattern of the period, its date and make-up. The pattern is fixed by certain administrative factors which were supposed to negative the Queen's Proclamation, a definite feeling of resentment against unconsidered attacks on Hinduism, mainly by Christain missionaries, the rise of Hindu sects, and the phenomenal appearance of the factory-system and industrialisation in regions which had taken advantage of English education. Naturally, the English educated, be it said to their credit, secured by dint of their ability many things which were not within the avowed purpose of English thought and of European happenings. In Bengal particularly, it was fairly strong as is proved by the journalistic literature of the period. Probably the reasons of the emphasis on ideas in Bengal were the disintegration of the commercial class into permanent settlement zamindars and the unwillingness of these gentlemen to invest money in industrial undertakings. Bombay had no permanent settlement and capital was not so shy. Be that as it may, the acquisition of new thought, which was not in the bargain, did help the growth of nationalist ideas. The examples of Italy and Germany were not lost sight of. Mazzini and Garibaldi continued to remain almost Indian heroes quite late in the day. Such was the pattern, and the date was the eve of the formation of the Indian National Congress. The Indian atmosphere was charged with nationalism. It was not unconnected with Hindu resurgence and with industrialisation. Its psychological drive was self-respect. When people want to acquire self-respect they may adopt various means,

expressly political. Salisbury wrote, 'The entire removal of the duty should, however, not be adjourned for an indefinite period but the provision should be made for it within a fixed term of years.'

one of which is a trip to ancient times where food for self-respect is abundant. This happened in Germany where the Romantic Historical School of the same period furnished the background of German national unity in the tribal origins and in the German soul, in Frederick the Great and the uniqueness of Germany fighting single-handed against the Roman and Christian barbarians. I do not suggest that our patriots were students of German historians. What I mean to point out is the naturalness of the phenomenon.

So, nationalism is the context of Indian historiography of the second stage. Its imprint is all over the historical writing of the period. There also one finds all the strength and the weakness of our nationalism. References to Plassey drain, opposition to any British proposal for reduction by the Indian government of cotton import duty or for imposition of cotton excise, criticism of army expenditure, demand for simultaneous examination, researches into Hindu periods of Indian history, Rajput or Marhatta particularly, and interpretations of Hindu system of philosophy, band together and form an easily recognisable pattern. We may now proceed to evaluate it.

(a) The first trait one notices is a glorification of the past the treasures of which in monuments and other antiquities had been partly revealed. At this time more claims were made on behalf of Hindu philosophy than even the *rishis* dared. Everything Hindu was sacrosanct. Certain reformist sects had no doubt entered a few caveats, but either the number of their adherents were small, or their opposition was self-negated by their assertion that their reformism was a return to the purity of the *Vedas* and the *Upanishads*. We should not forget what happened to Keshab Chandra Sen's attempt at synthesis, the New Dispensation, which was understood by a number of otherwise sympathetic people as an unwarranted move away from Indian traditions. The Arya Samaj openly based its philosophy upon the Vedas. Contrariwise, Swami Vivekananda's severe indictment of Indian superstitions and prejudices was forgotten and his great speech at Chicago thrilled India. This mental climate persisted in the otherwise dispassionate historical writings of Ranade and Romesh Chander Dutt who share with Dadabhai Naoroji the distinction of being the progenitors of Indian nationalist economy. I wonder if it is well known outside Bengal that Romesh Chander was no mean historical novelist. His subjects were the rise and fall of the Mahratta power. Probably, Sir Ram Krishna Bhandarkar most successfully escaped the nationalist pressure. Even then his excellent researches must have titillated our pride. Obviously, the glorification of Ancient India fulfilled a psychological need, viz., the compensation for our sense of political and economic denial.

(b) The comparative neglect of the Muslim period was interesting. I do not suggest that the pro-Hindu policy of the government after the 'Sepoy Revolt' had anything to do with it. Nor can I prove definitely that it was a deliberate step taken by Indian historians. Yet, the journalistic sources of the period round about the eighties contain many uncharitable references to the Muslims which I do not want to repeat. Their substance is that India is the land of the Hindus only. I am afraid that this trait of nationalist opinion has not yet disappeared in spite of the best efforts of many eminent scholars who have drawn their inspiration from Sir Jadunath Sarkar. Authoritative textbooks written by European scholars repeat the same mistake, and are not above throwing a few *obiter dicta* which are at once seized upon by narrow minds. The old mischief has not yet been liquidated.

(c) The next weakness of the nationalist pattern is the preoccupation with political history (mixed with a dose of economic history of the British period) to the detriment of the social. Reference has already been made to the study of customs and beliefs made by scholars of the preceding age and to its supreme importance for Indian historiography. But, gradually, the ethnological interest recedes. It now becomes a hobby of certain officials with their leisure and intimacies of district work. Indian historians would not look at it. This neglect of social factors was not pardonable in view of the large number of mistakes in their accounts by foreigners and the patronising, and often the contemptuous, manner with which the Indian customs were treated. To my knowledge, only one book on that subject was written, viz., that by Akshay Kumar Datta in Bengali. Even today no reliable book is available on Hindu religious customs, beliefs, rituals, myths, legends, tables and tales. We depend mainly upon European authors. The same with Islamic customs. And yet, anybody with slightest acquaintance with Indian conditions past and present knows that the secret of the continuity of Indian history, of the mystery that the historical process has not stopped from functioning despite vicissitudes, of the fact that it has held together within the four corners so symbolically laid down by Asoka by his pillars, Sankaracharya by his *math* and Sher Shah and Akbar by their public works and monuments has not been lost. I say that the very active principle of our history up till late in the day has been the patient, stubborn, silent social process. We did not evolve any definite pattern of relations between the state and the people; nor had we any counterpart of the Church. The people were held together in the socius, and the socius utilised the myths and legends and mythologies as living history. I want to stress this point from a slightly different angle. The importance of the *Puranas* has been recognised by modern scholars for the purpose of ancient Indian history; some of them are *pucca* records dressed in the garb of mythology, others have been dismissed and caution has been urged against all. All this is good so far as it goes; but it does not go to the roots of the manner in which the people understand the past. My point is that the manner of understanding the past in the present is a part of history. Go to the villages and you will find that the past in the shape of ideal types of conduct represented by mythical and legendary heroes is being actually lived and practised from day-to-day. This no doubt is traditionalism, but is not a big portion of historical living just this? It is didactic history, and the true significance of philosophy understood in India is the capacity of traditions to mould individual and group-conduct. And then, all mythological and legendary heores whom the Indian people daily remember are like their compeers in other lands, essentially culture-heroes. Rama fights Ravana, the Pandavas fight the Kuruas, Indra fights Brittasur, Krishna fights Kansa, Jarasandha, Kala Yavana and Paundraka. Each such fight represents the conflict of culture-patterns and all that it means in the way of expansion, diffusion and consolidation of the higher type. Yes, almost in every case, it is the triumph of the higher type of ideology and social organisation, including probably the economic one also. By higher type I mean (i) a gradual synthesis of the different tribal rituals, traditions and beliefs, e.g., the Vedic and the non-Vedic or the Aryan and the non-or pre-Aryan, the monotheistic, the polytheistic and the devotional; (ii) a solution of fresh problems of status and functions created by the increasing groups of people in terms of a hierarchy which, be it noted, was based upon the twin principles of social assimilation and economic division of labour; and (iii) a fairly workable social mechanism to stabilise the new order. There is no doubt of the fact that the caste system was an improvement upon the older type of organisation by *bis* and *kula*. Its stability would prove it once for all. What is equally, if not more, important however is the strength and the resilience of the tapestry of Indian ideas. It would be no exaggeration to say that the tapestry woven by the culture-heroes of the past, instead of being torn by Indo-Greeks, Huns, Kushans, Turks and Mughals, went on acquiring beauty in variety and complexity, until the West came and introduced new threads. I am not praising the past for the sake of the past; what I mean is that our culture-heroes fixed our culture-pattern very efficiently, and as such, a sociological analysis of their achievement should form an essential element of the nationalist history of a country whose daily living still continued to be governed by ancient norms. I repeat Tagore's injunction that in so far as the materials of India's history are not the same as those of a modern political entity like England, France or the U.S.A., the approach and the method of Indian history will have to be different with regard to the refined apparatus of interpretation, criticism and construction. Our historians of the second stage were nationalists; but they did not fully realise the implications of their nationalism in the art of writing history.

I can hardly resist the temptation of pointing out two more important deficiencies of the nationalist history. One was the non-recognition of the fact by the historians in their assumptions, attitudes and achievement that this mosaic of Indian history consisted of autonomous segments. Indian history being co-terminous with Indian culture was multiformal—this conviction between form and content was not apparent to our historians. It could not be, because the compulsion behind the historiography was partly a protest against the claim that India had been driven into warring states in the pre-British days and partly that the British rule had introduced administrative and legal unity for the first time in Indian history. The protest took the shape of a counter-claim that India was one and had always been one. It was not given to the nationalist historians of those days to distinguish between processes towards unification and the fact of static unity, nor between the social agencies of fusion and the political factors of fission and disruption. And yet it should have been clear that the so-called downfall of the political empires right from the time of Asoka to that of Aurangzeb meant the assertion of the integrity of nationalities. I use the phrase 'so-called downfall' for certain sociological reasons. First, every formation of an empire government in India was in a sense an attempt at the establishment of a central government with the help of a courtly nobility made up of willing feudal chiefs combining military duties with administrative supervision. The rest of the feudal nobility owed nominal fief to the sovereign, but otherwise administered their areas as of old. In these areas the active allegiance was to the immediate superior. Naturally the bonds of the court at the big capital were weak and those of the local courts were strong. In these local areas, administrative and cultural homogeneity, decentralised village-community and a community of language and traditions, ruled. This community, in spite of outside influences to disrupt it, was an organic one. In short, the region remained a whole in every aspect of living. Thus it is that the downfall of empires was essentially an assertion of zonal cultures and organic regions and seldom interfered with the habits of living in the long run. The formation of kingdoms in the Mughal *subas* and the former opposition to their creation were both joint efforts of Muslims and Hindus. The way in which Pathan rulers in complete alliance with their Hindu chiefs opposed the Mughal invasions is as well known as the alliance between the Hindus and Muslims in the new kingdoms that arose after Aurangzeb. It happened in Bengal, Oudh, Gujarat, and the Nizamat of Hyder Ali, in every *suba* which was more organic than in the British provinces of today.

The second missing implication was the neglect of the genuine bonds of India—caste, family-life, the village community, and a particular type of religious dynamics. The first three were common to all who had made India their home, and they stressed the aspect of social and moral obligation in preference to any scheme of rights. One real base of Indian unity has been that of sense of obligation with its philosophical counterpart of Karmic pre-destination. Hindus, Muslims, Buddhists, Jains —all are bound by the same tie. And the religious dynamics which have kept Indian unity safe from degenerating into mechanical uniformity and civic death, came from the protestant mystics who streamed down the ages. Today we know how they kept open the door of a more or less stable, closed society with its fairly fixed patterns of material living by insisting upon the individual's direct contact with the godhead and the idea and practice of spontaneous love and devotion, by doing away with old rituals and Sanskrit mantras, in fact, by pushing aside priestcraft, caste prejudice, communal feeling and other forms of inequality including the sexual. Our nationalist historians in their obsession with politics ignored the social processes of Indian history and grossly neglected the magnificent contributions of the so-called 'depressed classes' and of the Muslims, the *sadhus* and *sants*, to the building up of Indian culture. We reap today the consequence of the political obsession and the blindness it conditioned.

Gradually, the second epoch matured until we come to this century. The aggressive attitude was modified by scholarship. Historians of our days of studentship had become scholars in the European sense of the term. They would refer to documents, inscriptions on plates and monuments, contemporary records and sift them with care. But all that technique was subservient to 'nationalism.' Think of the subjects: Indian shipping, local government, greater India, democratic rule, empires, and the whole of pre-Muslim India. The study of the Buddhist period became popular. On reading again some of the classsics of this period I find that our scholars seemed to have been suffering from what the abnormal psychologists call in their studies *dèjà vu*, the certain feeling of experiencing all that before and yet not being able to recall where and how it happened. The patient notices some similarity and is very certain that it actually happens. On analysis, it has been found that in such cases differences are suppressed; that the suppression in its turn creates the feeling of strangeness which again reacts in the way of loud assertion. A similar thing is to be noticed in the writings of our historians. We had democracy, we had empire, even imperialism; we had science, in fact, we could conclude with some assurance that we forestalled the West by a few centuries. As most of the historians are living I shall only limit myself to the statement that they were unconsciously suppressing a vital difference between the past and the present, viz., the passage of time and the process of becoming. In short, our historians erred not merely the use of social processes but also the notion of time, the notion of history as becoming. In other words, they had no philosophy.

Let me hasten to remove a misapprehension that may arise on a point of fact. About the period of intense nationalism, say between 1905 and 1920, a definite step was taken in Bengal to construct a philosophy of nationalism. The pages of the *Bande Mataram*, the *Karma Yogin*, the *Yugantar*, contained the first philosophical statement of the Indian nationalist position. Most of the articles came from the pen of Sri Aurobindo, and Bepin Chunder Pal would often develop his and similar ideas in speech and writing. Later on, the *Arya* continued to expand the original thesis. The remarkable articles that appeared then (in 1918) have since been printed as the *Renaissance in India*. Therefore it would not be quite correct to say that nationalism did not crystallize itself into some form of philosophy which the historians could exploit for their own benefit. In fact, I know definitely that at least three scholars of ancient India came into close touch with Sri Aurobindo. But, unfortunately, the direct influence of Sri Aurobindo on historiography is not traceable. The reason however is not far to seek. Sri Aurobindo's conception of patriotism was not metaphysical, but spiritual. He believed in the genius of a specific culture, and also that the genius of Indian culture being essentially spiritual its renaissance should be governed by the principle of spirituality. For him spirituality was no doubt integral, all-inclusive; it did not ignore the material, vital, or the mental life. At the same time, it was more than the mere sum total of life's expressions. It posited spirit as the first truth and connected it with life in the dialectic of ascent of life into divinity and the descent of divinity into life. Said he:

> Politics, society, economy, are in the first form of human life simply an arrangement by which men collectively can live, produce, satisfy their desires, enjoy, progress in bodily vital and mental efficiency; but the spiritual aim makes them much more than this, first, a framework of life within which man can seek for and grow into his real self and divinity and secondly, an increasing embodiment of the divine laws being in life, thirdly, a collective advance towards the light, power and peace, unity, harmony of the diviner nature of humanity which the race is trying to evolve. This and nothing more but nothing less, this, in all its potentialities, is what we mean by a spiritual culture and the application of spirituality to life.

Obviously, Sri Aurobindo's spirituality is poles apart from religion and metaphysics. After stating emphatically that spirituality takes all our aims and activities and endows them with a diviner, a more intimate sense, he proceeds:

> Philosophy is in the Western way of dealing with it a dispassionate enquiry by the light of the reason into the first truths of existence, which we shall get at either by observing the facts science places at our disposal or by a

careful dialectical scrutiny of the concepts of the reason or a mixture of the two methods. But from the spiritual viewpoint truth of existence is to be found by intuition and inner experience and not only by the reason and by scientific observation; the work of philosophy is to arrange the data given by the various means of knowledge, excluding none, and put them into their synthetic relation to the one Truth, the one supreme and universal reality.

You will probably wonder how such a spiritual interpretation of Indian culture could at all stimulate historical writing. Logically, however, it was possible. For example, it could, as it was doing in Europe at more or less the same time, create an intuitive approach to history. It could easily create a school on the lines of the modern Christian philosophies of history like Gilson on the Middle Ages, Berdayev on Russia and Sturzo on the church and the state. It could certainly give an integral vision of India. But nothing of their spiritual intutitive approach is to be found among Indian historians. (Elsewhere it made its appearance, as in Bepin Chunder Pal's *Soul of Bengal,* a book evidently written under the inspiration of Aurobindo's teachings.) This is strange if Indian culture is really as spiritual as all that. But there is no room for surprise in history. The compulsion of the age was patriotism on the material level; and if people were ready to make a religion of nationalism it was because of the fact that they found it a convenient substitute for the decay in their spirituality and in their understanding of the significance of Indian culture. This religious aspect of our nationalism, as filling the vacuum created by loss of spirituality, should not be neglected. If you want to hear the same remark in a different language, I shall say that our patriotism being essentially the creation of a specious class remained out of touch with the roots of Indian culture and searched for them everywhere except where they lay. Remember the pseudo-spiritualism and the scientific religiosity of the period. My submission is that Sri Aurobindo's ideas were not selected to survive by the material needs of the people; and yet the bourgeois historians, and others too, would not admit the importance of material needs as they felt on the basis of a lingering prejudice that materialism was India's taboo. But as Sri Aurobindo put it: 'There was never a national idea of poverty as some would have us believe, nor was bareness or squalor the essential setting of her spirituality.'

The above explanation is on the level of sociology. Difficulties in the processes of permeation of Sri Aurobindo's philosophy appeared also on the level of historiography. That philosophy possessed certain features which were foreign to the approach and the object of Indian nationalist historians. Sri Aurobindo's views are scattered in the pages of his *Renaissance, Psychology of Social Development, Evolution* and in three volumes of the *Life Divine.* In the latest *Sri Aurobindo Mandir Annual,*[8] there is a suggestive essay, 'The Integral Vision of History' by Sisir K. Mitra. These alone are the sources of what may be called Sri Aurobindo's philosophy of history. It is frankly idealistic, if one chooses to use the Western term. Essentially, it is an integral vision of the aeonic march of humanity towards divine life. History in that context cannot but be a world history; its march becomes equivalent to progress and its motive the establishment of a perfect community. Its reason is the plan divine. Obviously, such an integral vision was much beyond the scope, method and object of our scholars. They were interested in certain facts and aspects of the past of this country, and not interested with the evolution of ideas or of humanity. Most probably none of them believed in progress and perfection. For them it was a regression from some golden age, at least, as a sub-sumption. In a sense, this lack of faith in progress and perfection was the last pull of the religious attitude which, as you know, looks back, and therefore looks up to, some form of Ram Rajya. Conversely, it shows a weak grasp of the spirit of science which must needs have a forward gaze and believe in perfecting human nature and society. At least, that is what the thought of the French Revolution period tells us. Thus the whole context, the entire ambit of Sri Aurobindo's philosophy of history, was missed. But a few details were accepted. Sri Aurobindo had mentioned the specificity of certain culture, such as the Chinese, Indian, and the Western, each with a pattern and emphasis of its own, contributing its own share to the stream of life. He had also described the stages of historical development, the symbolic, the philosophical, the ethical, the conventional, then back again via individualism and science to the higher ones. As a result of this double approach, the typical and the historical, one thing emerged that could be seized more easily by our historians than the integral vision of human evolution. It was

[8] No. 4, 15 August 1945.

the specificity of Indian culture, the genius of the people. Our historians of the nationalist phase adopted this seminal idea as their first assumption. I use the word assumption advisedly. The pages of learned journals do not show it; nor do the more ambitious researches into any particular period for that matter. And yet these scrappy articles, periodwise probings and sectional visions, were held together by the faith in the uniqueness of Indian culture. Elsewhere, as in the history of Indian philosophy, the history of Indian art, the history of Sanskrit, Hindi, Urdu, Bengali, Gujarati literatures, that assumption of India's specificity, the genius of her people, was patent. Still more patent was it in the actual burgeoning, in the so-called Bengal school of painting, in the popularity of classical music, and finally, in the new orientation of Indian politics by Mahatma Gandhi. But here I must stop lest I wheedle you into believing that the specificity of Indian culture has been fully understood or worked out by our professional historians. 'Scientific method' with its mechanical causation, its evening out of all individualities for the sake of generalisation, and its great prestige, stood in the way. The method mastered the man; and the man rationalised his defeat by believing with Freeman that history is one, i.e., history of India is to be judged on the basis of the history of Great Britain, France, Germany, Italy, the USA, the latest being the USSR.

I do not propose to take up Tagore's view of history here lest you think that Tagore has become my King Charles' head. But a few broad hints may as well be given. He believed (i) that the materials of Indian history were different from those of West European history. Ours are myths, legends, folk-tales, epics and the various *shastras*. Therefore, the approach should be different. He did not use the word sociological, but that was what he meant. (ii) That education of India would remain incomplete unless such an authentic history of India was written. It would bring Indians closer to India by abolishing the barrier of false history written by foreign historians, and it would bridge the artificial gulfs between the pre-British and the British period. In short, he wanted the continuity of the trunk as well as the spread of the shade. When our historians failed to do either he attempted the task himself in his essay, '*Kalantar*,' which to my mind is a most penetrating analysis of India's historical fortunes. (iii) That India had a message which he, unfortunately for the superficial reader, called 'The Message of the Forest.' This message was essentially Upanishadic and spiritual. In terms of history, it meant that this land of ours had evolved a pattern of many threads, a unity in the midst of diversity, a system of culture that was coordinated with a hierarchy of values in which the material and the social were impregnated and informed by the spirit. The spirit in its turn was humanised by rituals, customs, mores and folkways. That was Tagore's view of Indian history. It was very similar to Sri Aurobindo's. And the reasons why Tagore's ideas were not heartily taken up were also not different. Add to these reasons the fact that both were outsiders, and the picture of our failure is complete. Tagore cried, 'We are waiting in the midst of this darkness to welcome the historian who will incarnate the whole of India before us.... O, Historian, show us the treasure-house of our capacities to offer to the world, open its gates.' This cry was lost in the wilderness. The gates still remain closed, and darkness enfolds us in its thick layers. Our history has not yet been written. A band of Indian historians has appeared; but their Indianness I question. Their nationalism is political; their scientific attitude is mechanistic; and their sense of history, not being grounded upon proper materials, is partial and non-directive. In short, they have no philosophy of history.

III

The latest phase, that which we are passing through, is that of 'scientific' history. At last, nationalism is officially abjured and Indian history is freed from sentiments, feelings, etc. It moves towards neutrality. We at last find that its scope has been extended to include periods other than the ancient Hindu and the Buddhist, such as the Kusan, the Gurjara Pratihar, the Chola and Chalukya, the Muslim and the beginning of the British period. Slowly but surely, the gaps are being filled by meticulous research; the pre-Aryans are coming to their own; and cautious effort is being made to have a picture of the interactions of cultures inside India and outside, China, Java, or what in a relapse into nationalism, is called Greater India. Probably, the greatest single contribution of the scientific phase is the light thrown on the Muslim period. But a more flattering compliment is the application of the principles of higher criticism to such cultural aspects as the Epics, particularly, the *Ma-*

habharata, the *Dharma Shastras*, to monuments and paintings. It is no exaggeration to say that the best work of our scientific historians compares favourably with the choicest examples of the work of European scholars on similar subjects.

At the same time, we must point out some glaring inadequacies in the achievements of our new historians, not in a carping spirit but in the larger interests of India and her historiography. We shall not dwell upon such lingering prejudices as those of a Kayastha historian *against* the Brahmin and *for* the Kshatriya contribution, or vice versa, or that of Muslim historians against Maratha rule, and vice versa again. That is unavoidable in so far as the historian remains a human being; despite his objectivity, his attitude itself forms a part of the historical process. More pertinent are the inadequacies which arise from what our historians believe science and scientific spirit to be. There was a time in Europe when science meant only the collection, observation and collation of data, their quantitative measurement, a working hypothesis and then its enlargement or rejection and a reaching out towards broader generalisations or statement of tendencies. And it did wonders. But just when this meaning of science was most popular and well established certain philosophers and historians protested against its all-embracing claims. They said that in view of the complexity of human behaviour involved in history, with the impossibility of setting all the relevant data and the absence of any opportunity for controlled experiment, and also in so far as a historical norm for the universe was an absurdity when distinct units were at different stages and levels of development, history could not be a science in the hitherto accepted sense. The result was interesting. Some historians began to call their operations artistic while others came closer to philosophy. Not that the vigour of scientific scrutiny was discarded, but that with the help of the scientific apparatus the unfolding of the deeper layers and the underlying configurations of a general culture-trait or a particular unit began to be considered the legitimate object of history. There were various schools among these new historians, but their common function, in my opinion, was the search for meaning. It would be the meaning or the expression of an epoch or of a country's whole structure, of a great man's activities, or the common people's actions and beliefs.

The history of art and ideas was a clear manifestation of this urge for meaning. Naturally, without shifting the base of the method, viz., scientific observation, etc., something like an intuitive approach towards the essence of the subject, its nature and structure, had to be adopted. In a sense, however, it promised a break with the methods of the natural sciences as understood. The point of departure was understanding. The word 'understanding' is a technical term. It is more than intellection. As Dilthey would have it: Everywhere we understand before we explain, and understand more than we explain. In this connection we can do nothing better than to draw our historian's attention to Prof. Hodge's excellent introduction to Dilthey's work. In the selected passages given at the end of the book,[9] there is the master's own account of 'understanding.' All that I can do here is to hint at it.

Dilthey distinguishes the natural sciences from humanistic studies in their method, attitude and tasks, primarily on the basis of understanding. Understanding, for Dilthey, is the apprehension of the meaning of a portion of history but in all the parts of that portion in relation to the vital movement of the whole as also the apprehension of the mental fact or process signified by it. Understanding can only be of the type or the individual, of something mental, never of the general law or anything merely physical, or sensual. The task is to discover a living unity in the given; and its process is the individual's projection into the past, the re-living and reproduction. I shall not raise the question whether such a view of the special features of historical understanding and expression could lead to anything more than a psychology of history. I shall content myself by saying that its corollary was a *weltanschauung*, a philosophical outlook comprising (a) beliefs and convictions about the nature of life and the world, (b) emotional habits, and tendencies based on these, and (c) a system of purposes, preferences and principles governing action and giving life its unity and meaning. The *weltanschauung* of a person or a type of society includes that person or that society's answer to the fundamental questions of destiny, which Dilthey calls the riddle of life. Dilthey, however, would not believe in a philosophy, (the singular is used as a raw material for being an abstraction). Says he: 'If we are to speak of a philosophy of history, it can only mean historical research with a philosophical aim and with philosophical aids.' Dilthey was thus driven by realisation of the scientific method in regard to history and humanities into

[9] Pp. 117-124.

the arms of some discipline which we call philosophy. (Our own scientific historians seldom cared to enquire into the methodology of science and hastily abrogated philosophy. The result is that Indians cannot *re-live* their history and thus fail to notice the living unity of the Indian type of culture.)

It was not merely the quest for unity in this mad world or the innate instinctive urge of man for the universal which prompted the European historian to question the methods he had followed in conjuring up the past. Philosophy had always been warning the scientific against mechanical causation. It had pointed out times without number that the scientist was by his very method isolating both his observation and the object of observation from the context of human experience. Philosophy never failed to expose the claim of scientists that they alone represented common-sense, and stood the democratic evidence of the man in the street as the arbiters of the truth or otherwise of an observation or a conclusion. In fact, we now find that it was science that was rearing up an abstraction and philosophy that was pleading for common-sense and experience. Not only that: philosophy was always burrowing at the foundations of scientific methodology by a searching analysis of its terms like facts, observation, causation, its whole logic of hypothesis and inference. In unmistakable terms philosophy told science not to transgress its limits. It reminded science that at every step of its hypothesis-making it was making a judgment, that even the rejection of hypothesis in the light of new facts was a clarification of values, and that this tendency was towards a monistic explanation of the universe.

Some European scholars understood the value of these warnings and changed their technique of historiography, Troeltsch and Toynbee, for example. At this stage, chronologically somewhat later, philosophy was reinforced in its great task by a later development of sociology, viz., the sociology of knowledge. In the hands of Scheler and Mannheim, to name two only, it has assumed considerable dignity. The main contention of these sociologists is that an idea, the ruling form of understanding, i.e., knowledge, is an integral part of living; and as living is the content of history, as history is not an account of experience that never was, but one of something which happens to go down the ages, knowledge has to be understood as a part of the social, i.e., historical experience. Now this view cuts across the scientific view of history by which an event or a fact is taken in vacuums. May I add that it also teaches humility to philosophy by keeping it in its place in history. Be that as it may, this sociology of knowledge has proved a great help to modern historial thought to restore the equilibrium which mechanistic science had upset.

A third help came from science itself. I refer to the growth of biology which strongly challenged the prestige of the chemico-physical sciences and indirectly the methods they had been grounded upon. Here I cannot resist the temptation of quoting from a fine book, Erich Kahler's *Man the Measure*. It is one of the best books on the history of ideas in the West. After tracing the evolutionary laws he writes:

> While natural laws then were becoming historical, history was becoming mechanised. Historiography felt rather ashamed of being valued as a second-rate discipline, a not quite serious, not quite scientific discipline, somehow related to romance and story-telling, since it was not easy to explain historical developments by mere mechanical causality. At any rate, historians also paid their tribute to mechanical causality by splitting the live stream of historical processes into innumerable petty causes and tracing every cause to another cause, into an infinite past, which meant the disintegration and explaining away of history. This brought about explanation by origins, and origins of origins, a method that is known as historicism. And everywhere in the humanities the search for a mechanical causality had the same levelling and disintegrating effect. It prevented a distinction between the essential and the non-essential, by rating all phenomena alike and distrusting and excluding any criterion but that of material evidence. Any judging of material was considered speculative, and what a scholar of the present generation has called 'the total suspicion of ideology' began to prevail, that is to say, every author and every scientific group was suspected of ideological prejudices. It began long before Marxism, and from the nineteenth century on, has dominated all learning and the intellectual outlook of all classes of population.

An interesting view is in their 'total suspicion of ideology.' 'Ideology' in this sense is nothing else than evaluation, which is the very soul of critical philosophy. Anyhow, the fact is that our best historians who have built up this scientific edifice of Indian history on Mill's principles of applicability of natural laws to the study of human affairs failed to realise that thanks to the growth of non-physical sciences in these years the natural laws were themselves being infected by historicity. This failure to utilise the historicity of natural laws has not helped in creating the sense of history which, I submit, is the legitimate object of the historian. The tragedy has a lining of irony. Our historians are all idealists, if you ask them privately; and yet if there is any crude materialism anywhere it is to be found in this naive assumption of a mechanical causation in the human process. Dilthey our historians have passed by.

Before I pass on to a discussion of the third fundamental question—viz., can there be any philosophy of history at all?—I shall mention two more criticisms of the methodology of our scientific historians. I have already mentioned how in the second phase, i.e., the nationalist one, historiography was being separated from the history, customs, life and habits of the people. The bourgeois tendency was strengthened by the abstraction implicit in the regnant scientific method. Nowhere do the people as such write their history. They just live it; i.e., they allow historical forces to pass through them, or as often happened in India, pass over them. At best, they create myths, legends and epics which, as I have said, are the vertical coordinate of people's history. If one looks deep into the question, however, one finds that the indifference of the people is really towards political history. But there is one exception. Sometimes the people revolt against tyranny and change the government. In India the records of popular resistance are few and far between. I do not think that a definite theory of popular resistance can be constructed out of Indian materials before, say, the 'Sepoy Revolt' or the *satyagraha* movement. The Sepoy Revolt so called was a popular movement, but I do not think that it had a theory. This absence may be explained in various ways: the smooth tenor of our socio-economic existence, the hedging in of kingship by customs, councils, and Brahminical injunctions and interpretations. The very spaciousness of India also had something to do with it. So, excluding the political sphere, the subjection of people to historical forces is a universal phenomenon. And yet people have changed. The noticeable changes have been effected in a comparatively stable and closed society like that of India, mostly through religion. Our religious movements have been social revolutions. But the abstract scientific method is seldom congenial to their study. Their tokens are non-material, impalpable values; their influence cannot be measured; and they are not quite tractable to the laws of reason, being by their nature irrational or supra-rational. Apart from the general unsuitability of the method to the material there was the sense of shame in an implied recognition of the charge that India had lost her independence through her preoccupation with affairs of the spirit. That shame need not have been there. In fact, the pride in our spirituality which characterised the nationalist phase should have overcome it. But it did not. The influence and the prestige of Western thought and politics generated this nucleus of guilt and fostered it in the name of science. The result was a complete neglect of the bonds of the people, *dharma*, religion. No history of the people, which in India is the same thing as the history of culture, could be written, because the only sign of revolt, resistance and life here against religions and rituals could thus be written. Let me repeat: Our numerous religious sects were so many rebellions. In Russia, the Slavophils and the Narodniks evolved an ideology of the people. He who divorced himself from the people disowned his god; he who denied his god dissociated himself from the people: such was the conviction of men who heralded the Russian revolution.

Here also it could be done on the authority of texts and practice. This *panthah*, way, is the social binder-religion—that which binds; and this *mahajana* is not great men but the people, according to the commentator Nilkantha. And in regard to practices, there was the whole field of Islam with its active principle of social democracy, and there was the magnificent contribution of the so-called depressed classes who kept the flag of people's freedom flying with their emphasis of individual salvation, the rejection of priestcraft, their doctrine of love, the blessings of their mystics and saints, their stand for women and vernacular. These practices were dismissed as esoteric. But that meant shyness, and nothing more. It was the clear duty of our scientific historians to coax them out of the secretiveness and the reticence of our esoteric sects. They had done a thing or two in that line. They would dig into the mound but not into the mind of the people. Their method stood in the way, the role of the depressed classes was thus not understood, the function of religion was thus neglected, and the continuity of Indian history was broken into bits, segmented into political history, and atomised into the biographies of great men—Asoka, Chandragupta, Harsha, Akbar and a few others. If we are politically suffering from the resentment of communities, the Achuts in particular, our Indian historians cannot be exonerated. It is their scientific method which made them fear the touch of the people, and that fear also haunts our political and economic attitude.

One of the main charges against this mechanistic methodology is that in the name of objectivity, disinterested pursuit of knowledge, neutrality before values, science was split up into two separate kingdoms of theory and practice. It was the old Christian duality, the kingdom in heaven and the kingdom of earth in a new guise. Theorists annexed the heaven and left the earth to technologists, foremen and *coolies*. If the theorists really knew the history of science they would have found that the beginning and the end of science were the needs and urges of human life and action. It was only at some stage in the middle that theory assumed an autonomy of its own. Assumed is the word, because it was not a genuine separation. One could find without difficulty a large-scale correspondence between the movement of theoretical science and the movement of society. Whenever theoretical science had taken a pronounced turn, one could notice a big change in the socio-economic structure. This is the finding of the sociology of knowledge and of economic history. Ultimately, however, theory comes home to roost in the human needs. Often it does not, but that is due to certain social factors which stand in the way, the historic rush of profit, for example. When it does, the ground ceases to be neutral. You know what an amount of irresponsibility this neutrality has created in the mind of scientists. They save their conscience by saying that the scientist, as an individual, must not intrude into his observation, experiment and conclusion. Well, it is easier said than done. The scientist does intrude. I quote again to satisfy your curiosity and fortify your confidence. Edgar Wind in his contribution to the volume presented to Ernest Cassirer writes:

> ... The investigator intrudes into the process that he is investigating. This is what the supreme rule of methodology demands. In order to study physics, one must be physically affected; pure mind does not study physics. A body is needed—however much the mind may 'interpret'—which transmits the signals that are to be interpreted. Otherwise, there would be no contact with the surrounding world that is to be investigated.

I had better continue this quotation, because Wind's concern is the same as mine, viz., the contact between natural science and history.

> Nor does pure mind study history. For that purpose one must be historically affected; caught by the mass of past experience that intrudes into the present in the shape of 'tradition': demanding, compelling, often only narrating, reporting; pointing to other past experience which has not as yet been unfolded... If the physicists were nothing but a physical apparatus, there would be no physics; nor would history exist, if the historian were merely an historical document. (The very formulation of these sentences contains a contradiction, for the words 'apparatus' and 'document' cannot be defined at all without relation to some one who uses them for some purpose).

Now I am not asking you to attend to the subject, the person called some one, the scientist, historian as the source of light, I would want you to concentrate on the word 'use.' The scientist and the historian both are averse from use and usefulness when they want to keep themselves shut inside the laboratory or the library. They remind one of the Roman patrician's epicurean desire to lunch on the edge of the Vesuvius. They are subsidiary to this science for the sake of science, a doctrine older than that of art for art's sake. The doctrine, to put it bluntly, was the reflection of a desire not to recognise class-conflict. This horror of usefulness beautifully liberated men in power from the responsibility of making changes in life and knowledge. Thus it is that mechanistic science actually prevented our Indian historians from contributing to the making of Indian history. And this is my most serious charge. Indian people have not known from those who could tell how to change over to the new phase of Indian history. I call it a betrayal. When I look at the results I cannot but grieve over it and appeal for an entirely different attitude towards history, an attitude which to be effective, must needs be unpregnated by philosophy. I do not ask you to adopt an attitude, as men adopt a pose. I ask for development out of a stern reality.

Behind this attitude lies the cardinal fact that history has a philosophy. History is human history, and man is interested in history because he is not a thing; in a sense, he has no nature; he has history, in fact, history is all that he has. What else does he possess but the past, the present and the future? As an individual being he is connected with the past by memory, with the present by intuition and with the future by expectation. But this flow of time has a unity transcending all breaks and throw-backs. It is crystallised, represented, condensed into the sense of the Now; its significance for the future is determined by re-collection; its recollection is coloured by the forward look. Individual mind is not a clean slate for automatic writing. It is the focusing point, the point of intersection, the start, the plank to dive into the stream of living. And in so far as the view of history is a part of history, history must have at least a philosophy of time.

That is not all, however. History must have some meaning. Surely history is something more than a subject in the school and college curriculum or for research thesis. It may or may not serve a divine purpose or a dictator's whim; but because man has nothing else but history he has a deep interest in history. And interest is the root of meaning. Man's interests give rise to beliefs, action, hopes, etc., to what is called *weltanschauung*, an outlook towards this riddle of life. The outlook itself is not sufficient; it requires amendment in the light of shifts in interests and values. The human being places a particular outlook in the entire context of his past experience, judges its adequacy for the present adjustment and tests it in the crucible of expectations. Therefore, it must needs be a critical outlook. And herein comes science. Real scientific spirit corrects the impressions of the past, scrutinises the present and indicates, but does nothing more than indicate, the tendencies which can be exploited for building or making the future. But here also comes philosophy, simultaneously, by its criticism of the methodology of historical understanding. I ask what else is philosophy but the knowledge of unity, its precise formulation for testing, the seeking of meaning, a *weltanschauung*, and a critique and revaluation? If your answer be in the affirmative then you will agree with me that history has a philosophy. The compulsion is central; it springs from the condition of man. If you have a well conceived standpoint of opinion you cannot escape it. The philosophy of history is implicit in our politics, economics, social life. Of course, the knowledge has to be assimilated to enter into our active will. That is why conscious assimilation is so necessary. As Prof. Woodburn has beautifully put it[10]:

[10] *Purpose of History*, p. 89.

History is, then, not only the conserving, the remembering, and the understanding of what has happened. And since in man history is consciously lived, the completing of what has happened is also the attempt to carry it to what he calls perfection. He looks at a wilderness, but even, as he looks, beholds a garden. For him, consequently, the purpose of history is not a secret he vainly tries to find, but a kind of life his reason enables him to live. As he lives it well, the fragments of existence are completed and illumined in the visions they 'reveal.'

Now I ask this straight question to our historians: Have you tried to convert this wilderness into a garden? Have you made us collect the fragments of Indian existence? Have you helped us to live rationally and live better? The answer is no and the reason is that you fight shy of philosophy. We must consciously have a philosophy of history.

The last part of this lecture is therefore concerned with the issue that I raised in framing the final question, viz., which philosophy? What I have stated so long is this: If the history of India has been for various reasons unsatisfactory then to remove the defects it will have to take recourse to philosophy. It may be argued that the remedy should be more science, and not philosophy. My answer to that is simple: So far as the gaps in our knowledge are concerned the principles of elementary science will be useful, although not in every case. Particularly, in certain stages, hypothesis-making on a low level of probability, or intuition, as it is vulgarly called, has achieved great results. But it must not be forgotten that even in the matter of texts and inscription, the elementary scientific principles are usually illumined by brilliant flashes of interpretation. Modern historiographs have patiently built up hermeneutics or the science of interpretation. I have no time to discuss this new development beyond pointing out that in the final stage of interpretation when the accordance is plausible enough to appear to be the truth and nothing but the truth there is still a chasm to be bridged, and it is bridged by the sense of relevance to the entire configuration. This arc of the gestalt is completed by the momentum of experience towards unity, which is the soul of philosophy. In any case, better science, by which I mean a method free from the limitation of mechanistic, unilinear causation, is of better service in the filling up of the gaps in India's historical materials.

One word about these gaps: they are mostly political. In other spheres, e.g., in social, religious, ideological and cultural spheres of life of the people, they do not exist. On the contrary, they are almost monotonous in their continuance. You cannot say that the hold of traditions over Indians is a stranglehold and at the same breath talk of lacunae in Indian history. So much about the need for elementary scientific principles.

What about philosophy? We know for certain that in the West there have been various systems of philosophy nursed by the dominant group interests. Idealism, for example, in one of its later phases, was positively used as a cloak for the status quo. Similarly materialism, if not as a well formulated system, is very often the way of life of the common people. Those who wanted change, but not a fundamental one, would waver between these two primary systems, often mixing the two and expecting a release of energy out of the incompatible mixture. Materialism, however, has served the people's cause from the point of view of the people. I am aware of many exceptions. But I am speaking of the main tendency. It has often surprised me why in spite of the paucity of the literature of Hindu materialism, quite a number of Sanskrit texts of Indian philosophy take so much pains to rebut Charvaka and the Lokayata. None had any metaphysics to work. The only reason to my mind seems to be that the sponsors and interpreters of other systems, I mean the idealists, were fighting against the way of life of the people. On putting these systems of philosophy against the social background of the age, (in India the economic background remained more or less constant) one feels like concluding that they primarily served certain social agencies and forces, and after having served them they did their best to remain in power. Continued power continuously corrupts. The carry-over period was full of refinement and still amazes us by their virtuosity. But its main achievement was the complete separation of philosophy from the needs of people, a separation that was never intended, because like science philosophy arose to fulfil the demands of the common man. The people themselves never cared for these subtleties which were imposed on them. They lived with their practical philosophy.

In India the persistence of spirituality or religion or theology as the major ingredient of philosophy helped rather than hindered the people in their way of living. At least they were spared the theological squabbles on such abstruse problems like the number of angels that could dance on a needlehead, and their political consequences thereof, to put it in another way. Indian philosophy on account of some pull from above or behind, the Absolute or the Earthy, remained highly activist, experimental, instrumentalist, almost empirical. William Archer was not very far from truth when he said that India did not have a full-fledged metaphysics. Yes, we were more interested in life than in knowledge, although the idealists did their best to deny living and its purpose. On these grounds the answer to the question which philosophy, philosophy for what and for whom, is clear. Philosophy must not be for the professor of philosophy or for the exploiters and the authorities in power to be used as a cloak for their sectional, anti-social and reactionary purposes. It must be for change, a fundamental overhauling of the life and habits of the people, in this case, the Indian people. It must be subordinated to human needs, and all types of needs, material and immaterial. It must serve man, man in India, because man, I repeat, has nothing but history, and the man in India has only a broken bit of history, the conserving and the remembering part of it. Hence the primary requisite of a philosophy for Indian history at this juncture is that it should be human and helpful towards completing the process of Indian history, in the first instance. The corollary is that it should break the partition between theory and practice. Obviously, such a philosophy must be a philosophy of change, our life's change, social change, economic change, political change, change of this material world. It will not be sufficient if it only effects a change in the life of one man. It must recondition all Indians. Now, I am not very sure if the well known systems of Indian philosophy can answer this collective need. I speak with caution. Our philosophical speculations are so fertile that it is not difficult to collect fragments from here and there and prove that ours is enough unto the day. But that will be eclecticism, and eclecticism is always of the surface.

Let me state my position in regard to the suitability of our philosophies for the making of Indian history. I can approach the subject in two ways: (i) as discussed by various *acharyas* and scholars and their sub-divisions. This has been done by Pandit Naran Chandra Bhattacharya in his *Kala Siddhanta Dharshini*, by Dr. Pandit Gopinath Kaviraj and other scholars, or (ii) as understood by the people in their beliefs and practices. I find from the little that I have read of the first is that the concept of time or *kala*, which is the marrow of the speculations, is either that of a 'blind and insentient power, much like the western conceptions of fate, necessity and destiny or as the supreme conscious power identical with the absolute reality or even as subordinate power immediately responsive to the supreme will.' In fact, there was no unanimity about the nature of *kala*, except on a point or two mentioned later on. In the 'Shantiparva' of the *Mahabharata* there are three uses of the word, one interpreted as *avyakta*, another as *jiva*, and a third as *maya shabala brahma*.

> The Nyayikas, Vaisesikas and Mimanisakas conceived it as a static principle, substantial, eternal and ubiquitous in character and held it responsible for our notions of priority and posteriority—temporal sequence or succession; whereas according to the exponents of the Agama it is the supreme dynamic principle lying at the root of the cosmic process, both of creation and destruction. To the *yogin* of the Patanjali school, however, it is only a mental construction based on a sense of succession and has no value in reality.

We need not go into other schools like the Jainas, the Shaiva, the Bhagabat and Shakta conceptions. Their multiplicity is bewildering, but there are a few common features. *Kala*'s function as the source of nature's dynamism is one, while the ascent of the soul through various stages to a stage when time is transcended (known as *kalatyag*) and becomes one with the absolute reality, is another. Apparently, such a transcendental view of *kala* is most useful for individual salvation, evolution and conversion; it has a philosophy of change, but the change is of the individual. Now if you think that Indian philosophy is very individualistic you are closing the discussion. As a student of Indian history I do not think it necessary. Speculative philosophy may steer clear of the collective need, but practical philosophy does not. People always want a philosophy of *kriya* to support the concept of *kala*. This, of course, our philosophies sought to do through their concept of *bisvakalyana*, the external manifestation of *kriya-shakti* keeping its own nature as *svatmabisyanta* (self-contained) by virtue of its capacity to represent the *svatantra-shakti* (supreme freedom) of the Absolute. Some philosophers built up time and space upon this *kriya-shakti* or *prana*. But it is one thing to speculate upon *kriya-shakti* and *prana* as time's purchase and another thing to quicken the life of the people with *kriya-shakti* and *prana*. The last duty remained unperformed because the social life had been so stabilised that it looked almost changeless. Almost, but not quite, because Indian society was like rivers of ice that appear to be steady and immobile on the surface but actually move surely and inevitably.

There were a number of crises in our history which they called *manvantar*. These had to be accounted for. Besides, after the crises the stream again looked placid. Great men had intervened, the *avatars* who appeared at every crisis, but on the whole there was a sort of social entrophy, a dispersion of energy, a loss in quality in time. Such a state of affairs could be met by the concepts of *kalpas* and *yugas*, *manvantars*, *avatars*, and the doctrine of *karma*, a doctrine, be it noted, is different from that of *kriya-shakti*. In short, the people's philosophy of time was a variation of the theme of predestination and recurrence. For the Indian people, the curve of history was cyclical. Sociologically speaking, it was unilinear and therefore quantitative. Its quality was related to the individual, but for the people it offered no quality other than patience, which is another name for taking it as a static, objective entity, i.e., time as it is. This will not do for the Indian of today. So the second requisite for the new philosophy will be such a concept of time that it will not be a euphemism for recurrence, not be along one direction, that it will not be cyclical; it will be neither the Greenwich time nor the twinkle of Brahma's eye, but that it will be open, responsive to deliberate changes of collective efforts and living, very human, dialectical, and materialist, in the first instance. Through this change from transcendental to human time philosophy will become one with history; or if that appears to be a bold statement, philosophy will be worthy of history in the making. And that is the least of what we want today from our historians.

The third and the fourth requisites for the proper philosophy I have mentioned before. It will examine the methodological foundations of historical knowledge in order to create historical understanding. And then it will have to be a critique of every aspect of people's life, how it is being trusted and how it can be bettered. This positive, creative and collective significance of the word 'critique' should not be unknown to students of Western and Indian philosophy. The nineteenth century philosophers of Europe used it in that sense; and so did our Nyayikas for whom *nyaya* was *anvikhiki vidya* (constructive approach to the Absolute) and *abhava* or negation was *satgunatmaka* (positive). Let us not be afraid of having a critique. I enter a strong plea for a critique of Indian history. The need is great. I wonder if our intellectuals have fully realised it. This India of ours has a history, a design, a pattern, a configuration of its own. Mighty forces are beating on it. If the core of the pattern is stubborn it will resist. But resistance is not enough. The question of questions is if it will be recreated through this joint adventure, which is our history and world history. In the process of re-creation many tumults will occur; but India need not be afraid. She has faced many a *manvantar* fairly and squarely. If an alien culture tries to sweep her, critical history will save her. Otherwise she will go ahead recreating herself and others. In short, our history has to be made in order that the future generation may behold a garden where there was a desert and a cactus land. It is in this crucible that the art of the science of Indian historiography will have to be tested.

PART THREE

SOCIOLOGY

6. *The New Humanism*

It would not be wrong to assert that certain symptoms of life's renewal are noticeable here and there in the midst of destruction and despair. The UNO may not be a success as yet, but that it has overcome so many near-crises is significant. In Europe, France and Yugoslavia have been reborn, Czechoslovakia will soon get going and Great Britain, despite Indian prophecies, is determined to reconstruct its social structure and thereby acquire a fresh lease of life. The USSR's influence is already acting as a leaven to a few moldy countries. The Middle East is now more than a strategic position, and the Near East is definitely aroused. Sooner or later, India and China will meet, and in that mighty upheaval extraordinary energies will be released.

No doubt, the counter-forces are there, imperialism is not yet dead nor is fascism. The development of American finance capital is a danger; and so is the back-kick of British, French and Dutch imperialism. And yet, the resurgence of the human spirit should be patent to all but those who have lost their sense of values in the immediacies of conflict or submerged it in their hatred of the West. The East is renascent, but the West is not deceased. The West may be exploitative, but the East today is not merely the exploited. Together they are opening a new chapter in the Book of Life. Human spirit has not finished itself in the orgies of violence and power-lust. It still has large tracts for creative endeavour.

The symptoms of renewal are unmistakable in the sphere of ideas. If we take Western Europe as our starting point for its prestige value, the 'twenties marked the nadir of spiritual depression. A miasma of frustration hung over young minds. The wasteland was spreading fast, and all the resistances of old were being eroded. In the creative arts, fantastic experiments were boosted as achievements; philosophy, being reduced either to logic or to psychology, lost its reason for existence; history shrank to the dimensions of nation-states; and economics became a plea for protection and bilateral agreements. The sciences too were diminished to national science and national service. Such was the general tendency which overrode the minor pressures of exceptional individuals. Even the best works of the 'thirties had no certain heart beating inside them.

Although faith was lost, the hankering after faith remained to torment the soul of the Western European in the 'thirties. The USSR was stabilised at last, and the progressive section of the European community found there a port in the storm. Communism felt that the kingdom of spirit was to be built by human beings on this earth and not by angels and saints in heaven. But when the enamelling of revolutionary ardour was knocked off by work and sacrifice, the same progressives concluded that communism was not for them, the civilised ones, but for barbarous Asiatic hordes who were used to dictatorship from times immemorial.

Before the 'forties began, intellectuals were shying at Stalinism. Hitler knew of it and sent Ribbentrop; *Mien Kampf* displaced *Das Kapital.* It was not a sudden transformation. Yeats had written, 'Things fall apart; the centre cannot hold'; and he prescribed the cult of the strong, silent man with eagle's mind. In France, the Action Francaise had prepared the ground. So blood and land, leader and one party, 'a good strong cause and blow are delight'—became the substitute for social equality in the matter of faith. If communism was too rational for anybody's taste, he could take to the doctrine of irrationalism served by Rosenberg.

Yet another sheet-anchor was found in the Papal Encyclicals. These sought to charge Christianity with modern relevance. A number of brilliant writers tried to connect the teachings of Jesus with up-to-date notions of social justice. The task was successful in showing up the limitations of a private morality into which Christianity had been reduced as also in exposing the propaganda that socialism was an atheistic and an irreligious doctrine. But failure marked all efforts to restore the original supra-national foundations of the Church and place it once more at the base of the European civilisation. The Catholic philosophers were unable to stem the fissiparous tendencies in thought that had been aggravated by nationalism.

So in place of the Church, the nation-state exacted all the

religious loyalties of peoples. The vision of a Gilson or a Maritain, the learning of a Dawson or Sturzo, or even the spirituality of a Péguy or a Bernanos could not make the slightest indentation upon the cult of statism. Other Christian thinkers shared the same fate. Karl Barth's influence was still a coterie; Niebuhr's name was known only to a few intellectuals; Schwietzer had left for Africa, a philosophic Rimbaud. Naturally, the religious attitude of a number of spiritual seekers degenerated into the mysticism of an utterly irrational type.

The above process, however, was not that of sublimation. Its atavism is clear from its affiliations to psycho-analysis and the study of the unconscious. Surrealism in art, nation-state in politics, race in anthropology, protectionism in economics, élan-vital in philosophy, mutation in biology, indeterminism in physics and mysticism in religion were blood brothers. They belonged to the breed of the unconscious. Those who were influenced by Jung's collective unconscious and archetypes found allies in Frazer's pupils. Together, they conspired to cross the breed of mechanistic psychology with a respectable strain, but the 'sport' became a throw-back. The entire work of man's national efforts was drowned in the deeps of the unconscious, and reason was degraded into the status of a disagreeable censor.

However noble might have been the motive of the psycho-analyst—and the search for integration was no mean impulse—the net result of his efforts was a loss of the dignity of man by a lowering of the status of his reasoning faculty. The Western Man felt it, but he could do nothing about it, totally beseiged as he was by all the irrational forces marching with the nation-state at their head. He succumbed, and the story of his surrender is the global war. But surrender is not suicide, let us make no mistake about that. The Western Man is carrying on guerilla warfare against the alien occupation. He is resisting with all the strength of his magnificent traditions, his Christianity, his scientific outlook and love of personal freedom as amended by social equality in the light of the Soviet civilisation and original Christian traditions.

On the other side of the Atlantic, the influence of unreason over ideas was probably less. Not that funny cults and crazy enthusiasms were in the doldrums—they flourished as well as ever—but certain tendencies kept American culture on an even keel. Of them, the older empirical habits of thought, the seed of which was planted by Pierce, should be given the palm. Those habits and attitudes were fixed by eminent philosophers, economists, sociologists and psychologists. If one name were to be taken, it would be that of Dewey. He ruled the period between the two wars. One notices his shade in all types of American thinking that relate means to ends. Names apart, the checking of theories by experiments and statistics saved American culture from the slough of despondency. The New Deal gave great assistance. President Roosevelt's four administrations prevented American thought from the sorry pass into which European thought found itself. By the conversion of the trough of economic depression into a field for economic experiments, like the T.V.A., the pace for rational enquiry was admirably set.

The Hollywood *ashram* of English intellectuals is outside the pale of American culture as it has been evolving these years. Whatever may be said about its other qualities, American culture has not abdicated reason, although it has imbibed a number of recent West European prejudices. One such may be mentioned because of its relevance to India.

Three American thinkers seem to hold some sway over their respective fields: Max Eastman, Edmund Wilson and James Burnham. (We cannot measure the depth of their influence in the States; we only summarise on the basis of their circulation in this country.) Each of the above three writers has told his readers that Stalin's USSR has gone behind the original impulse of Marx, Engels and Lenin.

The indirect conclusion is that the programme of world revolution of the First and the Third International must have been correct. In other words, the general impression left by modern representative American books is that Trotsky's idea of permanent revolution was any day better than socialism in one country in one step. It is not difficult for us to imagine what the reactions of American intellectuals would have been if Trotsky had triumphed over Stalin or Earl Browder was a greater figure than he is. They would then have quoted Stalin. Now, this is pure and simple prejudice begotten by an innate romantic ardour for change for its own sake. It is those who do not care for change that nurse such vague desires. Be that as it may, the romantic strand occasionally peeps out through even the seasoned American thought. Is it because of the fact that the American culture is only just adult? But even if it were so it would be, as it is, fresher than the blasé, stale European culture of the thirties. The best evidence is in American literature. There something is happening. If we leave the French resistance literature (Aragon, Malraux, Vercors, Kessel, for example) there is nothing in the world today which is comparable to the American literary creation in vigour and variety. Unfortunately, it was Hemingway who had represented the new American to Europe so long.

It is in this context of American creativeness on the one side and the European despondency on the other side of the Atlantic that the need, course and future of European thought has to be appreciated. Apparently, that thought has to be more than Euro-American thought pattern with an Atlantic civilisation for a social frame. Its texture cannot be the same as we perceive it in the works of Henry James, T. S. Eliot or Julian Green, for example, fine and finicky, atmospheric and impalpable, confusing truth with the punctilious observance of an esoteric ritual. Before the last war the Euro-American synthesis was a surrender to the older values. American culture went its way in reaction, and it has been a long way. Today American thought has nearly shed its nostalgia.

So when it will impinge upon the postwar European pattern of thought, it will do so as a vigorous and confident person impinges on a man past his prime, ripe with wisdom and charged with despondency. The American hold over Europe will probably aggravate the situation, but essentially the transaction will be one of interpenetration. Between a possible religious revival in Europe as a cure for frustration and the probable recrudescence of idealism in the States to cover the intoxication of success and power, a balance is likely to be struck. Its pivot will be Man. Euro-American culture-process will be humanistic in the idealistic fashion. In fact, from both the sides the pressure is moving towards it. Erich Kahler's *Man the Measure*, Lewis Mumford's *Condition of Man*, Beradyev's *Destiny of Man*, Malraux and Silone's latest works are handshakes across the waters.

Can we, however, call it genuinely spiritual, because no spirit but that of God exists or is relevant? In other words, if human history is taken as an interlude in the divine unfolding or an interpolated account of the fall of man and the working out of his sinfulness, then the revival is not spiritual at all. In our opinion revival it is in any case. First, because it is a move away from the mood of despondency and a triumph of some philosophy over 'the death instinct' that has seized the West European who had so long set the pace for life and thought and provided their models; and secondly, because it stabilises the American empiricism and gives the ballast of some philosophy. Blind faith in trial and error, experiment for the sake of experiment, search for its own sake, facts and figures on their own merit have received a shock; the flight into the upper stratosphere or the lower depths of the psyche is no longer easily condoned, even if it be for art and integrity.

We say 'some philosophy,' because humanism is more an attitude, a way of living than a metaphysic, because it is the attitude that governs metaphysic. But this Atlantic humanism must pass a stiff test at once. The supreme test of the unmistakable movement of humanism in the Atlantic world of ideas will be that world's attitude towards man in regions outside. Racial contempt and imperialist greed of the Western Man have dominated so long that they will demand herculean efforts on the part of the African and the Asiatic to dissolve them. Religious conversion of the Euro-American by his own efforts is a pious wish.

So a worldwide revolt is a very necessary aid in the transformation of the Atlantic pride into humanistic humility. That aid is being offered today. But the spirit in which it is being offered partakes of the nature in which this long drawn domination has worked. The mood is one of sulking discontent seeking the first outlet to hatred. For the first time, the Indian and the Indonesian, the African and the Chinese, the Burmese and the Siamese, have begun to hate. The ways and means to repress the popular movements have also for the first time been prompted by hatred. Once it was the anger of a stern father chiding the family and bringing it back to orderliness; now it is vindictiveness. Much of it is inevitable; but what is inevitable in the sphere of politics may be harmful for a moral and spiritual movement.

Our immediate concern is with Asia. We leave Japan, because we feel that Japan is far too committed to the Western techniques of resistance to be included in the Asiatic fold. China and India form a recognisable pattern. In China the resistance is still on a moral plane, despite these long years of suffering, feud and war. China's secret is the stronghold of social etiquette and Confucian morals. Some poison was sought to be injected into the anti-Japanese feeling, but it was a temporary measure. The anti-foreign propaganda was tried in China, and it led to a few riots. In the years to come, the need for reconstruction will stimulate Chinese humanism to do without it. The Atlantic world may depend upon China to resist its domination with the utmost dignity.

India's case is on par with China's. The problems are almost similar, and the solutions too. British rule is a special factor, no doubt, but the dynamics of change overweight it. Besides, India has had the benefit of Mahatma Gandhi's message for a quarter of a century by now. That message is non-violence, which, in ethical terms, means control of hatred in thought, word and deed and its final elimination. It is not difficult to notice the philosophic weakness of the message, nor does it require any special study of the *Gita* and the *Tantras* to discover that violence with a pure, selfless and disinterested heart has a definite place in Hindu and Islamic philosophy, codes and habits.

But a criticism of the message on the score of its inapplicability to the modern world is irrelevant. It misunderstands the nature of such a message; it insults human nature; and it ignores the march of the human spirit. That message is meant to make it impossible for any Indian to hate his oppressor, for any Congressman to hate a Muslim Leaguer, for the proletariat to hate the landlord or the capitalist. May be that it does not make it equally impossible for the capitalist to exploit the labourer, the landlord the *kisan*, or for the average Congressman to hate the Indian Communist. Still it has moralised the Indian struggle as nothing else has done. Gandhiji has been greatly helped by the spirit of the Indian social traditions which have tolerated social injustice but never permitted them to be solved on the animal plane of hatred. It is interesting to note how he talks of prayer and discipline when bitterness is being whipped up in the name of nationalism. Probably, Indian nationalism will pass him by, but it will be a betrayal of the genius of India, the potentiality of Asia and even the reborn humanism of the Atlantic civilisation. He is very necessary for Man.

One may at once retort that if Gandhiji fails Stalin will succeed; that if moralised politics are found wanting socialised politics will fulfil. It is a very pertinent answer. Socialism, not to use the word communism in the Indian context, is certainly an offshoot of humanism. It is equally democratic, and equally scientific. But the humanism of India and China differs from the socialist-humanism of the West in one important particular. The Asiatic type is theo-centric whereas the western is anthropo-centric. There are a number of western, mostly Catholic, thinkers who believe that an anthropo-centric humanism does not offer adequate stability.

But we are referring to the type as it has emerged in Western Europe out of the Renaissance. The Indian renaissances have never turned the mind and achievements of Man away from the Absolute, Personal or the Impersonal. It was only the last renaissance that wanted to push the Indian away from it. Even then it did not succeed. As against the political secularisation of the nineteenth century, India has had a number of religious revivals. Today, Gandhiji is once more trying to restore the lost equilibrium. Nevertheless, the man-centred humanism of socialism is a force to reckon with. It is going to be stronger in the days to come. Which type will win one cannot predict. All that one can say is that the success or failure of world civilisation will depend upon the manner of resolving the conflict between the two types. Probably the Asiatic type will have to wait till its newcomer shows tangible results more than what it has done so far. For modern man, it is not a matter of choosing one or rejecting the other. It is one of organic development in which decision is the simultaneous act of the person at different levels.

7. *Western Influence on Indian Culture*

August 1948, which celebrates the first anniversary of India's independence, is doubly significant for an analysis of the processes involved in the synthesis of Indian culture. First, the unassimilated portion of the Islamic pattern of values and living has led to Pakistan via the theory that Indian Muslims are a different cultural entity, a 'nation'; and secondly, political freedom now being stabilised, after a short period of strain, is likely to create special dispositions in the background of which India's attitude to the West and the West's attitude to India may be reorientated. None of these propositions indicates any finality in the process. Despite its religious basis Pakistan may eventually understand a now resentful India under the pressure of common social dynamics; and India is far too committed to Western values to change over to the so-called purely Indian ones at once. In the process of institutionalising political freedom, India has already registered a running transaction with the West in various ways, of which the adoption of the British, or Anglo-American constitutional model and British, or Anglo-American ideas of law and justice are the most important. Economically, the ties of both India and Pakistan to the West are very much closer. What might have been construed as Gandhiji's abjuration of the West in the interest of India's soul has been pushed behind the attempts at reviving and strengthening India's body on Western lines. Gone for ever is the indigenous impulse of the Gandhian constructive programme before the Western faith in state action. Yet new angles will surely be taken by a sovereign India towards Islamic and Western cultures. Here our concern is with the second aspect of this two-fold problem, as the importance of the first recedes in the background. Today the de-Indianisation of Islam and the de-Islamisation of India have conspired to halt, if not undo, the process of synthesis. Both India and Pakistan are afraid of acculturation. It is needless to say that conversion and re-conversion are examples of absorption rather than of assimilation.

All are agreed that India entered into a new lease of life in the nineteenth century. The spurt of vitality came from the West through various channels like commerce and trade, increased facilities for communication, western learning, administrative unity, etc. For the first time, historians assert, an alien civilisation impinged upon every detail of Indian life, changed its pattern and created new values. Thus India's wealth ceased to become treasure; money became capital, goods became commodities, land became a source of monopoly-rent, and the self-sufficiency of rural economy was transformed into the inter-dependence of urban and world economy. Similarly, the vision of the average Indian, so long closed like that of the frog in the well, was enlarged. Horizons extended beyond the nucleated village and the walled town to the sprawling city, and from the Indian city to the spires of Oxford and the willows on the Cam, the quads of the Inns, the banks of the Avon and the Thames, up there to the lakes in the north. Education no longer centred in rhetoric, and now included European history, politics and metaphysics. The broad march of the English constitution, the glory of the French Revolution, the finality of the American War of Independence, the romance of the Italian, and the cold, ruthless realism of the German unity brought enlightenment into the dark nooks of the Indian mind thus far denied of any sense of history and politics. At the same time, western philosophy and science introduced reason into daily habits and made Indians realise the meaninglessness of many ancient customs and prejudices. Western vitality and empiricism gave lessons on the virtue of activity. Above all, India became one, from Kashmir to Cape Comorin, and developed nationalism. Culturally, there was an all-round progress. Vernacular literatures, painting and music blossomed in all splendour; scientific research, Indology, journalism, university life, clubs and associations, female emancipation, social reforms, even new religions, flourished in the abundance of youthfulness; and the thus educated Indian became a lover of freedom and a humanist.[1] In short, so the historians assert and many others will still have it, India was renascent. A study of the quality of this renais-

[1] A further list is in O'Malley's *Modern India and the West.*

sance will reveal the degree of India's assimilation of the western influence.

For a proper appraisal of this estimate, however, we should remember that the nineteenth century renaissance is only one, and the last one, of a series of renaissances that India has enjoyed in the long course of her history. We know of at least five previous major periods of momentous changes bearing all the signs of new life: the Vedic-Aryan, the Buddhist, the Gupta, the Harsha and Vikramaditya, and the Muslim, which included the glorious one of medieval saints and prophets of Bhakti cult. Subsidiary movements are greater in number. Each such period brought about an expansion of the human spirit and intelligence, produced critical scholarship and creative work in arts and crafts, collected disparate sects and schools of thought into working syntheses, begot a new type of man, encyclopaedic in range and synoptic in vision, curious to know and able to feel the whole gamut of experience, having a conception of the non-material tinged by the colours of the earth and an ambition for the earth uplifted by hopes of realising the ultra-mundane, here and now. Each such epoch proclaimed the adequacy of Man, his competence, his resourcefulness and sufficiency in all spheres, including the religious. Every time Man acquired youthful confidence in his own powers. He felt that he could master the elements, create gods and works of art in their image, dissent from traditions, frame new codes, discover self and soul, ride the course of events, plunge into action, fight, preach, trade and traffic, and yet keep the poise that was the token of his god-linked aristocracy. He would carry every mental endeavour to its extremity and still possess the desire and energy to come back to the centre or the point of intersection between time and eternity, and gain fresh accession of strength for reaching new levels of equilibrium. In all these symptoms the pre-British Indian renaissances were similar to themselves and also to the pre-industrial renaissances of the West. Humanism and enlightenment as such are well known social phenomena in the history of India.

And yet a difference is noticeable. The last Indian renaissance, as a movement, was more secular than religious. True that a number of saints were born in the last century and that a sort of religious revival took place; still the religious life of India was not the same even as it was in the fifteenth and sixteenth centuries when Islam struck full blast upon a defensive

Hinduism which a retreating Buddhism had done its best to weaken. Now it acquired features of its own. Thus, for example, the new sects, e.g., the Brahmo Samaj, the Arya Samaj, the Prarthana Samaj, the Theosophists, the Rama-krishna Society, to name a few only, had not that mass appeal which Kabir-Panth, Bengal Vaishnavism, or Sikhism commanded. Even the simulated interest in Bhakti was confined to the 'middle-classes' or *bhadraloks*. A part of it was traceable to a general sense of political frustration, as would be evident from the large number of *bhaktas* among Indian politicians. Certain sects had premises too intellectual for the average Hindu idol-worshipper, while others dressed up the old metaphysics and theology in a garb whose newness wore out soon for the common Indian. The result was that practically all the new religious movements were absorbed by the old society, which but for a few in the upper strata, did not materially change in the process. Mysticism, which had been a genuine revolutionary agency in a closed society, was now reduced to the status of other carriers of tradition, other agencies for change by permeation from the top, such as education and the like. Chaitanya, Kabir, Dadu, Nanak, Chisti, and others had a definite conception of the people and their spiritual needs. They were not interested in poverty or illiteracy, nor in 'progress' and 'reform.' People for them meant sons and daughters of God, children of eternity, a colony of souls hungry for light and peace, and for whom God was equally hungry. At the same time, for the earlier mystics, 'people' connoted concrete living entities performing collective functions according to status, i.e., *swadharma*, and personal ones in the light of *swabhava*. Be it noted that although the emphasis varied as between *swadharma* and *swabhava*, no Indian mystic-revolutionary ever preached against the collective, 'popular' reality of the person, or against his occupation. Some had gone against caste, no doubt, but none against 'community' or its material bases. The nineteenth century sects were, of course, not poor in their missionary zeal; in fact, they had better means of propaganda; they also wanted to reach out to the people; only, for them, the people were there to be reformed out of their superstitious ways in the interest of progress and humanity. Shatov, the peasant in the *Possessed*, shouts, 'And he who has no people has no God. You may be sure that all who cease to understand their own people and lose their connection with them at once lose to the same extent the faith of their fathers and become atheistic or indifferent. I am speaking the truth! This is a fact which will be realised.' It is difficult to share Shatov's certainty of faith today, but a sociological study of our last renaissance reveals that the original quality of spirituality, which the founders of sects and systems possessed in abundant measure, soon exhausted itself in social reform and ideas of human progress by inadequate, though sympathetic, radiation through the new elite. The detumescence of spirituality into social zeal is peculiar to the Indian renaissance of the last and the present century. In earlier days, the primal impulse had clogged itself in rituals only: now it was exhaustion, or attenuation. To put the difference sharply: while the irony of the last renaissance lay in the idea of social good without a conception of the people, which produced a tension leading to a cleft culture and split personality, the tragedy of the older ones was in the acceptance of society without an idea of the good, which produced a vacuum between the urges of the spirit and the needs of common living, between the material content of spirituality and the forms of religions prescribed for the commoner. But in no earlier instance did Indian renaissance reveal the conflict between the good and the evil, the sacred and the profane, the kingdom in heaven and the kingdom in earth, Caesar and what is not Caesar's, sin and redemption—a conflict which was at the heart of the renaissance and humanism in Christian Europe. These concepts were alien to the Vedic and the early Puranic Hinduism, and also to early Buddhism. Some sociologists would call them Semitic traits and thus attach them to Islam. In the Islamic culture of Indian peoples, however, they were not very marked up till the other day. They are recent accretions to Indian culture; note the Brahmo concept of *apapa biddham,* Gandhiji's explanation of the Bihar earthquake as the wages of sin, the common notion of the division of India as immoral, and the split psyche of any westernised Indian of the liberal professions. Still Indian culture abides, witness the behaviour of a large number of Indian capitalists who sin without conceiving, particularly when they are not educated in the western fashion.

II

A very striking feature of the nineteenth century renaissance in India was the note of nationalism. It pervaded every sphere of activity, including the religious. Indians felt that their genius had been insulted. Some stupid remarks had no doubt been made by some missionaries and administrators. But when we remember that many of the Indian protagonists of ancient values were either government servants, or otherwise not averse from a foreign government's patronage and any European approval of their efforts, the springs of their new culture can be partly traced to wounded national pride. But probably a better explanation lies in the fear of alien values threatening the traditional ones, and in the consequent unconscious realisation of the necessity for a fundamental framework of values to resist, at least to bear, the pressure of a mechanised unification by a foreign civilisation operating through a soulless administration. The cultural framework to act as the counterpart of administrative unification was there: ramshackle might be, but ready for repair and still believed to be possessing the structural strength to support the novel ways of living which western civilisation had introduced via the British rule. Naturally, the nineteenth century renaissance conveyed the spirit of protest and a loudness of tone, both carry-overs of a reaction. Informed by the lessons of European history and British political philosophy (it is not strange that German or French political thought had comparatively less influence on the Indian intellectual), the new cultural renaissance soon developed political interests. As days passed, Indian culture became less concerned with such affairs of the spirit as the person's soul and its discovery, and made instead a religion of politics, which culminated in transforming India into a mother-goddess, saints into political leaders and leaders into saints and heroes. Patriotism became the 'religion' of renascent India. It flowered from the need of restoring a cultural alter-ego to the awakened political ego. But, probably, the Buddha, Kabir, Chaitanya, Nanak could not have recognised it as a cognate experiment. At best, they would have called it a 'moral' upheaval. Morality for India, however, is only one constituent of religion, in fact, a weakening of its spiritual marrow. Sri Aurobindo tried to spiritualise nationalism, but social forces worked against his attempts and supported those that have since made of Indian nationalism a potpourri of religion, ethics and power politics with profit making as the meat. Wisely did Sri Aurobindo herald the coming age as the Gandhian era. But Gandhiji also was soon to state that while for him non-violence was *dharma*, for his followers it was expediency. In the history of Muslim nationalism in India, known as politics for Pakistan, there has been no spirituality and plenty of religion mixed with power. It would be, however, wrong to say that the Muslim League introduced religion into politics. The course of Indian nationalism itself had facilitated that introduction. The British policy towards the communities was greatly responsible for this peculiar religiosity of Indian politics.

Yet a third feature of the last renaissance. In a sense individualism is a late arrival in India. The Indian intellectual now loves to think of himself as an individual, in the British way. We would, however, do well to remember that the British way had matured under the sunshine of capitalism in its heyday, although the vintage belonged to the age of Adam Smith, Edmund Burke, Jeremy Bentham and his school of philosophical radicals and the early utilitarians. The strength of the doctrine of individual freedom came from the assertion of a particular type of freedom that took its cue from the laissez faire demands and practices of the rising bourgeoisie. It was freedom *against* encroachment by a government to which the old suspicion *against* the King's party still clung: it was freedom *against* the social curiosity of a class and its tendency to trespass: it was the freedom of an atomised unit, a romantic wife *against* her husband's conventional family, a citizen *against* the policeman, an adventurous son *against* his cautious father, a playwright *against* the censor, any producer and any seller *against* any producer and any seller. So the main positive significance of freedom was submerged in the *against* relation of the individual. In another language, the freedom of British individualism was freedom *from* an external authority, but not *to* an inner one. With the British such a relation did not lead to any serious conflict, and for two simple reasons, viz., (a) that the external authority was the making of the individuals themselves, or their elected representatives, and (b) that the individuals were prosperous enough to stop worrying about the positive inner content of freedom. The positive inner content, however, if the individuals remembered their Christianity, was spiritual; but they did not; hence political freedom and economic laissez faire were taken to be identical with individual freedom. Thus it was that although British individualism had no apparent ground for external conflict, it had a centre of weakness. To cover it, either a return to Christianity was wanted—

it was the way of Cardinal Newman, Keble and Pusey, or an Empire had to be built by the Gordons and the Cecil Rhodes, (or defended by the Lionel Curtises and Lord Halifaxes), all holy men, all Christians devout. Catholicism and/or imperialism could be the only escape from the heart of conflict.[2] Similarly in India: aggressive, orthodox Hinduism and/or political terrorism became the only alternative conclusions of India's adaptation to British individualism. If aggressiveness were more aggressive here than in Great Britain, it was due as much to the political subjection of the country and the frustration that it bred among the people as to the peculiar social composition of the class that gave expression to it. The Indian 'middle class,' being a new creation or an uprooted class, were not the bourgeoisie of Manchester and Birmingham who had their roots in history.[3] The Indian educated had no such limitations. But, and here is the point, only he who stands on the soil can be alone and an individual; he who hangs like Trishanku in the air should either look up or below for his surety. If personalism be the name of the former's social philosophy, individualism would be that of the latter. Indian culture knows of personality. The roots of Indian personality spring from above like those of the Indian tree of life: its branches spread over all life's doings, in the realms of art and science, in family life and in the larger spheres of society and in all traffics of the spirit. Individuality seeking for its roots down below would shoot through the soil and spread itself over the same area of living space as personality does; but it stands against another such individuality in isolation unless all individualities are placed in a ring, as of the state, machine, class, vested interests, etc., to lend verisimilitude to unity. The Christian renaissance in Europe had also started with personality, but it ended in individuality, as von Martin has shown in the *Sociology of the Renaissance*, by the inner conflicts of its society. Here too the same thing happened, but under the pressure of derived

[2] Now that the days of the old type of imperialism are over, the urgencies of Catholicism are dominant, *vide* Christopher Dawson in England, Eliot and Arnold Toynbee, and Gilson, Maritain and Sturzo in the Continent.

[3] Toynbee's remark, viz., '....it is clear that what is a crisis for the key minority (Western middle class) is inevitably also a crisis for the rest of the world,' (*Civilization on Trial*, p. 21), does not hold good of India, whatever may be its validity in its own immediate field of observation.

ideas. Original thinkers like Tagore and Iqbal, saints and sages like Vivekananda and Aurobindo, noticed the differences, but the grafting had already set with the result that today many Indian intellectuals believe that democracy should mean individualism. Individualism, however, is the milkman's version of the milk of personality.

It was, of course, natural that many special features of the last Indian renaissance should flow from the fact that the West came to India through England. The good and the bad alike were derived from the England of that period of first contact. It was a glorious age for England indeed. England had solved the problem of the Church and the State. She was expanding: she had achieved constitutional stability and the rule of law. She had capitalised agriculture and was breaking the restrictions of the mercantilist epoch to usher in the industrial revolution. She had been firmly established as the first national state and was the hub of world's credit and commerce and going to be the workshop of the world. She was turning to free trade. For the first time, she was casting a steady gaze across Europe to Asia and Africa. A corollary to this was the expansion of England's spirit. It too was to become a steady expansion; because at home liberties were secure, the backbone of the society, viz., the middle class, was formed, and the disposition of political forces in Europe was balanced in favour of England by virtue of Europe's dependence on English coal and iron, investment and technical skill. A measure of this growing steadiness can be gauged from the manner in which England had stood the onslaught of ideas of the French Revolution and its other consequences. Tom Paine, Godwin, Shelley and Fox were freaks, while the conservative Irish Burke was English. Edmund Burke still rules a semi-socialist England through his creative precedentism. But there was adventure in this steadiness. In the realm of knowledge and intellectual discipline, England stood for scientific attitude based on a daring honesty of mind and a faith in the universality of causality. Bacon had laid the foundation; Newton had built on it; and a host of first-rate scientists and philosophers extended the bounds of induction's territory. True that the region of extra-sensory perception, deduction and absolute values shrank, but the emphasis on sensory proofs and inductive analysis was a token of a valuable type of intellectual integrity and courage. Such was the cautious-audacious intellectual climate of the country that brought the West to India. In fact, England and the West became co-terminous even for Europe and America.[4] England became the 'ideal type' of the western civilization. Voltaire had accepted it as such, and many more from Emerson to Henry James were to do it later. The makers of the Indian renaissance were similarly affected. They laughed and coughed, thought and dreamt, dressed and dined in the English style. They behaved like strangers in India. But they affected India, even though by permeation from the top. No wonder that on the credit side of the western influence in India Tagore mentioned three major items, viz., (a) enlargement of India's vision beyond India's frontiers: it had been limited by the caste system in the preceding ages; (b) faith in the dignity of man as such: the dignity had been circumscribed before by function; and (c) trust in the ability of human intellect to solve human problems: previously, it was an outside agency; at least, it was not the mind of man that could do it. Tagore found these the main springs of modern India's renaissance. His objection was that in the name of law and order these springs had been allowed to dry up. The British rule of India, in his view, was a moral betrayal of western culture. An examination of these items would further bring out the quality of the last renaissance and the degree of India's assimilation of western culture.

III

India's vision has certainly been enlarged by the West. The Aryans, the Sakas and Hunas, the Tartars and the Arabs were an incoming force: they all came and stayed; the western peoples, chiefly the British, have come and gone: they are an outgoing, horizon-seeking force. Admitted, but with two small provisos: (a) Indian Buddhist monks and Indian merchants had always gone out of India and spread Indian influence; and (b) in the Muslim period, when Indian society had closed itself in self-defence fairly completely, some contact was still being maintained with the world, e.g., with Persia, Central Asia,

[4] M. K. Gandhi went to England to study law and 'see England, the land of philosophers and poets, the very centre of civilization.' Today, therefore, we should not criticise young men if either the USSR or the USA excites them in a similar fashion. Glamour comes easy to youth. Does wisdom of the free come always to the old? It did in Gandhiji's case early. But what about others?

Africa, and spasmodically with Europe. But the real quality of the extended vision of Indian mind is not so much spatial as cultural. We may now examine the quality of this cultural vision. All visions do not posit sight. If insight is also a form of sight, India's gain has been an insight into her past. European scholars assert that India had never possessed any sense of history, not even 'history.' The Indian conception of history, however, was not linear, positivistic and progressive. It was not to be 'recorded,' but to be stamped on the heart of the people so that their daily conduct bore the mark of ideals as represented by the heroes and heroines of legends and epics. It was in a sense vertical. Its defect lay in the inability of the people to change the course of events. But to what extent has India profited by the western horizontal view of history as a spring of certain events in time? The western gift of insight into the past did not so far enable the Indian people to make history except using the knowledge of her past culture as a source of self-respect and in the matter of quotations, imitations and holding British statesmen to their sentiments and pledges. On the contrary, many of those who have made India's history have had little or no western 'sense of history' at all. (Gandhiji had none. His conception was essentially Indian, i.e., qualitative, vertical, 'heroic,' and moral.) Besides, Indian history written by Indian scholars on the western model is either a clever exercise in nationalist obscurantism, or a fresher's attempt to apply scientific method to facts, facts and nothing but facts, excluding urges, motives, laws and values. Is not Gradgrind's 'insight' as superficial as the romantic's? If India has made history, it is through the Indian technique of satyagraha, a means always practised by Indians but never mentioned in any book on Indian history. This remark should not be misconstrued. Although India's freedom may have been secured by the Indian technique the maintenance of that freedom may demand the use of the non-Indian concept of history as making and changing. An independent India will find the western view of world history extremely useful.

Still, insight has had a different significance in India. Either it is valuable, or it has no value. Most Indians feel that it is valuable; in which case, they may, and do argue that western civilization has not enhanced it. Others who think that it is valueless still feel that insight into the laws of history, for them an adequate substitude for spiritual insight, has been blurred, if not blinded, by the behaviour of the West, i.e., England, towards India. Educated Indians once did not equate western imperialist exploitation with western civilization, thanks to their rational liberalism. But today, such is the effect of their long inurement to imperialist domination, the exploitative West is for most Indians a decaying West, a West doomed to extinction. Recent events in Malaya, Indonesia, Indo-China and in the Middle East, the new concerted drive of the West in Africa, the racial arrogance in South Africa in particular, have their lessons which are seldom missed by an educated Indian, for the matter of that, any informed Asiatic. But this understanding is purely on the political and economic level. Therefore it is hard to conclude that an enlarged vision has been permitted to be followed by a deepening of spiritual insight. What, however, must needs be said on behalf of such an enlarged vision is that it has stimulated an insight into the temporal historical processes of change in consequence of which there has been a general desire to speed them up lest independence breed complacence. With a number of young people, however, the processes of change in the recent life of the West are held to be universally true and, therefore, applicable in toto to Indian living.[5] Such a version too obviously ignores the existence of Indian culture itself, and thus also underestimates its pull against doctrinaire change and all attempts at history 'making' according to a universal, absolutist paradigm dictated by the 'natural laws of history.'

Scientific approach is the next major item on the credit side. Science, as experimental truth in regard to those aspects of matter which lend themselves to quantitative measurements, is the great gift of the West and has passed to us through England. Naturally, physics and chemistry grew fairly fast in

[5] The references are to the socialist and the communist youth in particular. Socialists admit the continuity of historical processes, but they would shorten their duration or otherwise deal with them in the light of the variety, data and tempo of social and constitutional evolution. Indian Communists who would jump over them with the help of their reading of historical changes are proceeding *per saltum*. That Russia is their spiritual homeland or model is not a philosophical charge. England had been the spiritual homeland and model of our patriotic forbears only a few years ago. The real questions are: (i) if biological mutations have their counterpart in human history, and (ii) whether history is one, has its universal, natural laws; or it is a generalisation of specific histories, each with its pattern of place, folk, work and tradition.

India. Other sciences like physiology and biology, however, did not. Applied sciences like medicine and engineering, would not also easily strike root. In short, sciences having direct connection with human beings and life did not keep pace with the advance in those having no immediate contact with daily existence. If economics, politics, jurisprudence, and sociology be given the name of science, then India's contribution to the thoughts of these social sciences has been next to nothing. Looking closely, we discover three cardinal reasons for the unequal speed in the growth of various branches of scientific knowledge: (a) the resistance that came from the system of Indian social institutions; (b) the attitudes which the new machinery of education induced against the desirable spread of scientific attitude among even the English educated; and (c) the colonial economy of the country. It is a historical fact that the old policy of social reform at government initiative was given the go-by after the 1857 mutiny, and neutrality in such matters became the watch-word with the result that the teeth of institutional opposition were not broken. Wicked men have attributed deep political motives to this policy of so-called non-interference. Be that as it may, the persistence of prejudices that blocked the progress of scientific attitude was as much due to the government's neutrality as it was to the western scholars' pandering to all the conservative forces in the name of appreciation of Indian culture. These scholars and lovers of India's past claimed more than even the *rishis* dared. Their panegyrics became the stock-in-trade of all the nationalist obscurantists in search of self-respect. Others of the West, not so scholarly, who thought that they knew India in virtue of their stay and 'experience' either as missionaries, officials or tourists, played a different tune about India's past, present and future. Their comments, however, created the same effect as those of admirers. India began to look back, a posture not quite favourable to the acquisition of scientific attitude. Positively, the culpability of the foreign administrative machinery for education in starving scientific research and technical education was as great as its bias towards literary education. So long as the policy was to create clerks, scientific education was not necessary. As long as it was desirable to keep India as a store-house of raw materials and a market for Manchester, technical education was undesirable. Besides, had not a general interest in science been a prelude to the revolution in France only the other day? So let scientific attitude be confirmed to faddists in the laboratory where, of course, by a little manipulation they could be kept in their places under their white superiors. The fact of the matter was this: although brilliant individual scientists[6] worked against odds and made their genius felt, the seizure of the whole people by the scientific spirit, if not the whole people, at least, of the English educated community, remains a different story, independent of the number of Nobel laureates and Fellows of the Royal Society. And it was this story that was not permitted to unfold itself by the executive of interests completely uninterested in the spread of scientific attitude among the people, nay, antagonistic to it. That such hostility was not uncommon in Europe is an irrelevant consideration. There, the needs of industrial progress partly countered the hostility. Here, scientific attitude would sharpen the critical attitude towards the ruling powers—literary education had been bad enough;[7] it would mean industrialisation—not a safe state of affairs; it would mean social revolution —where then would the devout common man, the loyal Rajahs, Knights, Rai Bahadurs and Khan Bahadurs, go? So, naturally, the immediate effect of the incidence of the West upon India as colonial economy was against scientific attitude and its permeation. The side effect was the wonderful spectacle of science graduates being the repositories of all the worst prejudices that priestcraft had ever concocted. It is extraordinary how they discovered the latest discoveries in the ancient texts, how they defended the indefensible social customs in the name of western science, how they Indianised science. Luckily, that attitude has changed. The latest phase seems to be a naive faith in the mechanistic approach and a type of scientific snobbishness, an attitude that the West has wisely discarded.[8] The

[6] The biographies of Sir P. C. Ray and Sir J. C. Bose may be read in this connection.

[7] Here a few words on the so-called literary education may not be out of place. That it was meant primarily to produce loyal citizens who could imitate the English and be clerks to carry on the drudgery of their administration is historically true. But literary education really meant a taste for the humanities, which was not in the bargain. That India has derived great benefit from this so-called literary, but essentially humanistic bias cannot be disputed.

[8] No action, however, is without reaction. Some Indians have utilised the idealistic reaction against science for their own purposes. The principle of indetermination, as interpreted by Eddington and Jeans, is grist to their mill.

situation is no doubt improving. But, assuredly, it is not due to the West of India's intimacy. It is improving in spite of it, thanks to the growing needs of Indian industrialism and the national desire to improve the standard of living of the people.[9]

IV

Space forbids any discussion of intellectual daring. It is an unvarnished truth that many Indian philosophers had pushed their intellect to the farthest land, removing all cobwebs including the gods and the *Vedas* in the process. They believed in logic, and often dismissed the absolute, God, mind, matter, substance, as they chose. Most of them came back to the ineffable, and were dumb. When they reasoned, they remained rational; when they stepped out, they declared the area as out of bounds for intellect. Spiritual affairs were matters of direct experience, and there they not only dared but did. All that can be said is that Indian thinkers had not taken the trouble of boldly and rigorously applying their reason to the affairs of the world as the only, and the final, entity. Contact with the West should have been fully working that way, but the effect of western practice in regard to India had so long run in the opposite direction. In practical affairs, the western attitude, up till 1948, was that Indians being a highly metaphysical and spiritual people should not be bothered with the conduct of such material things as were involved in mere existence, for which a western government was better fitted and ever willing. And the tragedy was that we almost accepted the West's valuation of ourselves and its own institutions. But false values do not stick in times of transubstantiation. Scientific attitude, intellectual courage, faith in causality—they are one and the same—is a habit of mind that can come only at times of crisis in the ways of living. Such a crisis is social, all-comprehensive. It is not intellectual in the usual sense of the term. The French dared in 1789, the English in 1688, the Germans in 1848, and the Russians in 1917. That was daring. For the first time in several centuries India has a chance to dare.

[9] Here too the emerging situation has a few unpleasant possibilities, the not remote one arising out of scientific endowments by big firms for research and fellowships. It seems that in the hectic search for funds our scientists gloss over the 'conditions' of big American trusts as also the story of patents. State 'interference' in scientific pursuits in today's India is less menacing than state-sponsored institutes of the social sciences.

Lastly, the dignity of man has been described to be the gift of the West. In the context of some of the worst features of the caste system, the gift is great. But doubts begin at once. Did the West demolish the caste system? Did it succeed in its attempts? Were the British sincere and deliberate? We have already referred to the policy of administrative neutrality in social matters. We know that whenever an Indian sought to introduce any bill for social reform the Indian government shelved it to a committee, circulated it for eliciting public opinion, nay actively opposed it in the name of being too advanced or too limited or too large in scope, badly framed and what not. On the other hand, there are many instances of lower castes adopting the superstitions and ancient habits of the upper castes as also the 'miscellaneous' items of higher standards of living of the westernised lower middle class in cities. Still, western influence has corroded the status basis of the caste system; only, in that process it has isolated the person to gravitate towards government offices, mercantile firms, and mills in cities where it has been easier for him to imbibe new ideas and to lose dignity incidentally. No positive social, civic function has emerged to act as a substitute for the old, unless tending to files and machines be called one. One is not sure if the destruction of old values without their substitution by a system of comparatively stable ones should be cited as an instance of assimilation or a gift. At best, it is an impact without the necessary satisfying response. Naturally, no question of dignity apart from the dignity of protest could arise. But the right to protest is indicative of a versus-relation of rights, and not of the 'of-through-and out' relation of obligations, which is the meaning of India's social texture.

Be it remembered in this connection that India has had no counterpart of the Roman concept of 'natural right' before Tilak coined that ringing phrase. After the Surat Congress of 1907, 'birthright,' an allotropy of 'natural right,' came to stay in India's political vocabulary. This may be illustrative of India's assimilation of western influence, because that concept has often been the slogan of the dispossessed in the West. Yet, Indian thought has always preferred the 'cosmic cyclic law' to 'natural law,' and within that spacious ambit it has considered the pursuit of duties flowing from functions fixed at birth as the best active policy. This has also been the sociological basis of the Indian judicial pattern. One type of jurisprudence was the 'multilateral character of jural regulation constituting its imperative-attributive structure:' and 'only by a collective recognition of social facts which realise values, is it possible to establish a close interconnection between claims and duties. Only if the rules of law are not entirely autonomous is it possible to have a guarantee that this interconnection will be effective.' If this Petrazizky's test of jural regulation be true of India, then the introduction of the Austinian jurisprudence by England may be held to be responsible for separating responsibilities from claims, and for disrupting the collective, multilateral character of jural experience—the real significance of Hindu customary law—through the emphasis on unilateral, imperative structure of positive, state-law. It is small consolation to be reminded of the fact that civilization passes from status to contract when we know that such development has injured the social reality of jural experience and separated law from morality. Through perfectly legal contracts the war-profiteers killed nearly a million and half of men (unofficially three millions) in Bengal alone. Through perfectly legal means, i.e., under one section of the Act alone, more than a lakh of acres were seized from the tenants by the landlords in the U.P. within three years of the war. Of course, contract confers dignity upon the contractors, but we are speaking of the dignity of man. The author did not see much dignity in those hungry eyes; nor could he spy it in the behaviour of an Indo-European club-member. The dignity of a protesting modern wife or an up-to-date daughter-in-law is not worth the price of cosmetics used to keep it up. Dignity is not common to the average westernised Indian. His national dignity, his professional dignity, his Hindu dignity is loud, like the cry of empty canister. And the reason has been mentioned. he is cut off from traditions; he is a liberal, and therefore, partly a romantic and partly a schizophrenic; he suffers from inferiority-complex; he is rational at the top and hankers after solid values of integration in the bottom of his heart; he is not a whole; he is full of tensions; he cannot resolve. Such a state is not conducive to the natural dignity of self, and so it is hostile to the dignity of concrete human beings. When it is not openly so, it covers its hollowness inside the capital letters of MAN. True Indian humanism may be similar to Christian humanism divested of its Christian specialities, but the Indian humanism of the last renaissance is tainted by individualism, which, as we have suggested before, is more of a policy than a principle. If dignity has been attained at all, it has been as a result of a protest against British rule and western influence, the very sharpness of which may be said to have converted its negative character into something ethical and psychological at best. Gandhiji's role has been tremendous in this connection. By the Indian technique of satyagraha,[10] he sought to confer moral dignity. Yet complete dignity has still to be won. We have yet to add intellectual dignity to the ethical one, and also to fill out the vacuum created by the removal of fear of the British or of the West. Until then, we are adolescents in dignity. Probably, the un-westernised, common Indian still retains his dignity and still respects manhood. At least, that is the author's experience.

There is one big item, however, on the credit side of the western influence on India which must be mentioned again. The West came close to India driven by the urge of British commercial and industrial capitalism using the Indian administration as its agency. It released certain forces and killed others. Among the released forces are some which now act against the agency and the original drives. They centre in the pattern of attitudes known as anti-imperialism. Others are positive, the most important of them being the growing conviction that the future of man belongs to the weak, the oppressed, and the dis-

[10] *Satyagraha* should not be confused with either non-resistance or passive resistance. For Gandhiji himself *satyagraha* was a whole philosophy of life with *satya* (truth) = God as its theology and *agraha* (insistence, holding on to, hankering, earnest search, heightened interest all combined) as the human, experiential, hence experimental and empirical psychologic content. A discussion of Gandhiji's originality in regard to civil resistance or civil disobedience, which is included in *satyagraha* as a collective technique of operation against injustice, is interesting but academic. Its negative aspect, the one that made up his political following, was probably more western of the dissenting, non-conformist Protestant Christian type than Indian. But its positive aspect, which is dear now to none but a devoted handful, is more Indian than otherwise. Probably, his ethics too were not quite in the Indian tradition of *riti, niti*. His conception of morality was certainly not *achar-siddhata*, i.e., merit by correct performance of rituals, though he greatly believed in discipline. In any case, *dharna* is an ancient, popular protest of the weak, and every home-made Indian wife practises it even now with almost ritualistic fervour and some artistry. Gandhiji was very feminine indeed in this sense. The maleness of his political following indicates a strengthening of ardour (*agraha*), though there seems to have been a weakening in the holding on to his object of that ardour, viz., *satya*, possibly as a result of its gradual substitution by ideals more germane to the western spirit, e.g., parliamentarianism.

possessed, as Tagore has said in one of his noble poems. These forces are neither western nor Indian; but they have begun to operate in India, because India has so long been the only remaining first class colony and is vitally interested in their operation. Once these forces start, the West and India will not be opposed to each other. Then, and then only, will the scientific spirit, the daring intellect, the faith in causality, the dignity of man, his enlarged vision and deepened insight cease to become a luxury of the few and be transmuted into a common treasure. Cultural exchange will then be barter, and not a matter of accounting or balance of payments between two parties who have got tired of competition and come to a 'business-understanding.' It is not a matter of gift, influence, and all the various aspects of a static relation. It is another type of relation starting from the very base of living and reaching out further than it ever did. Materialism, in the sense of *anna* as *Brahma*, not *Brahma* as *anna*, of man with unlimited potentialities, not as God's potential, of men reaching out to men, but not through intermediaries, of men making their own destiny through the manipulation of forces of social change, but not through any gift of the West, may be a partial view, but it has been very necessary as a corrective to the unbalanced development of Indian culture. India is learning through her contact with the West the emphasis it has given to certain vital traits of common life she had so long neglected. What India makes of that emphasis, how she integrates it with the values she has cherished and refined will be the supreme test of evolving Indian culture in its next phase. Let us not minimise the danger of this emphasis. The oppressed often carry memories of past denials and deprivations; a socialist upheaval may as well spring from envy and frustration. But then the way out is easier and clearer than what has been permitted so far by the limitations of Indian culture.

* * *

Has any unfairness been done to the West in this all-too-short account? When the House of Commons reeks with complacence at the passage of the Independence Act, when a new chapter is being declared to have been opened in the history of Britain's relation with India, when the British themselves are describing this Act as the greatest act in history, when the virtues of the Commonwealth are being sung indelicately, when

India has been divided and Balkanised, even when the doyen of western powers continues to malign India and interfere with her affairs (*vide* Hyderabad issue) in different forms, when there looms the danger of India's being involved, again against her best will, in a conflict which the West has done nothing to resolve, more critical remarks could have been pardoned. But the author's object and spirit are otherwise. Here are two mighty forces reorientating their relations, and we on our side should know where we stand. The British political rule has been the shortest one on India's record, but is that going to be true of western culture and its influence? Much evidence of the West's decline has been advanced. It has fallen in line with our wishes. But is it reliable? Some time of trouble has come there; Great Britain is on the defensive; France is almost down; Germany is *hors d'combat;* and Italy too is out of the picture. But Great Britain has tremendous moral reserves; France still retains its clarity and logic; Germany will be helped to recoup; Italy may have another renaissance; Atlantic civilization is in the offing under the lead of the United States; and Eastern Europe is resurgent under the impulse of a typical western order. We can, therefore, rightly say that the western civilization has retired to rally. On the other side, in the East, political democracy, capitalism, socialism, the products of machine-civilization, have come to stay. Western civilization will continue to affect the life of peoples here, as it will rejuvenate itself in its own territory. Whether the assimilation will be a synthesis or not will depend upon the capacity of India and the East to discover themselves before they are dragged into another internecine conflict as a result of which there will be no West, no western return and rally, and so no western influence worth mentioning. The time has come for a conscious planning of development and assimilation on both sides to reach synthesis. Up till now it has been left to the blind forces of profit-seeking. Will the UNO help? Can it, when its chief members are sabotaging it with obscene cunning? This author suggests a deep-layer prospecting of the sources of India's strength simultaneously with the pegging of its relationships far and wide.

8. *Notes on Indian Culture*

Something of unusual importance has happened to our country. It has acquired a large measure of self-government over nearly all the major sectors of life and at a time when opinion has accepted the virtues of nation-states. A long chain of reactions has been unleashed thereby. While some of them have immediately exploded, others have been delayed, making us nervous of their time of discharge and possible consequences. Probably, such a situation is nothing peculiar to India. It is attendant upon every significant change in any country: which by itself should teach us humility and give us the opportunity of profiting by the experience of all countries in similar situations. Yet, now that that situation is facing us, we should address ourselves to the task of harnessing the energies released. History tells us however that self-government is a challenge before which many peoples have succumbed, either because the strength of their response was inadequate or their wealth was insufficient. The latter possibility may be excluded. Our material resources are enormous. The problem is also not of human material. We have an initial advantage in numbers, probably a little more than is easily manageable. And one is not sure if we have really lost our talents by disuse: at the worst, they have rusted. There is a wealth of intelligence in the country. What is more, there is a reserve fund of disinterested, contemplative attitude which, however close it may be to fatalistic escapism, is, under proper training, likely to help us through the period of preparation. For the present, I discount the factor of will even against the advice of our leaders. That faculty is a by-product of the occasion, and not its solution; that philosophy is dangerous inasmuch as it is auxiliary to the cult of power. What is therefore primarily needed for a collective, vigilant response to the challenge of self-government is consciousness. And consciousness, in the psychological sense, is born of predicament and nursed by crisis. Obviously, many people cannot be aware of crisis; even the intensities of awareness vary. But when a great political event overtakes us, or when a major economic upset occurs, the awareness is generalised. Many emotions cluster round it. They may sharpen or distort it, or even sap its strength. I submit that it is the primary function of a party, an elite-group, or the intelligentsia, or a convention like this, to see that the general awareness is not dissipated in any manner, and positively, that it spreads and enhances its quality, in intensity, form and content. In short, awareness is to be transformed into a sense of urgency with a little more direction, a little more of subject-matter, and with much more of organic proportion than what prompted its being. There is nothing wrong in 'criticism' except in the wrong selection of the crisis to bend our awareness to.

Frustration has seized us all, barring our leaders who are admirably maintaining their courage against odds. The youth, and I am expected to know more of them, have not yet been pessimistic, although they feel that their services are not being fully utilised. How much of this residual optimism is due to the expanded prospects of employment and how much to their physiology, I cannot measure. But they are being very critical of our national policies. Recently, in a university debate on the draft constitution it was difficult to find a young man to defend it. A sharper, and a more negative criticism comes from the sympathisers of the Hindu Mahasabha and the R.S.S. who make up their intellectual vagueness by emotional clarity. The 'leftist' youth are in a quandary. They dislike the present policies but do not know which others they would like, with the result that they have become dislikers in general, not a state of affairs congenial to the specific feeling of urgency. It is difficult to discover today considerable number of intelligent young men who by conviction are either Congressmen or honest supporters of government policies. Yet there must have been many a few years ago, at least, when they were asked to avoid slave-factories like poison. But that indecision may largely be a consequence of the general ignorance of data to support an alternative policy, because today, as they were on the day before yesterday, all data are in government files.

The general picture includes senior men, lawyers and government servants, doctors, engineers and the like. In a recent visit to Allahabad, I had a chance of meeting a cross-section of professional classes. Their bitterness of feeling was amazing. That it enveloped the reputed intellectual capital of this province and the home town of Pandit Nehru was the irony of it. No argument in defence of the foreign policy, no enumeration of the difficulties, no list of achievements of the central or the provincial government weighed against it. Probably, the little men, the worker and the peasant are in no better mood. For them the high cost of living is a bigger obstacle to appreciation than ignorant prejudice. I do not propose to further darken this gloom. My concern is with the implications of such defeatism for culture and with the clarification of issues in order that your convention may deliberate on measures for countering such defeatism in the morning of self-government. I consider this darkening of spirit to be unworthy of human beings, not to speak of Indians in the year 1949. It wounds human dignity.

Some analysis is necessary at this stage. One explanation of our mental shape is fatigue after fight, aggravated by the abnormal conditions of the war. I find it difficult to accept this. For one, your efforts were neither total nor long-drawn. We should not delude ourselves into believing that our self-imposed sacrifices and sufferings for freedom were unequalled in history, or that they engaged all sections of the people equally, fully and completely. China alone could give a lie to that fond belief. And then, one is not quite sure if it was all our doing. The days of imperialism were nearing their end. One empire, the British, realised it. The tempo of our efforts coincided with the speed of that realisation. For another, even if, as has been said by T. S. Eliot in his 'Notes Towards the Definition of Culture,' 'The danger of freedom is deliquescence; the danger of strict order is petrifaction,' we have no excuse for not consciously perpetuating and enlarging the opportunities and conditions for the process of crystallisation just begun. At present, there is certainly a solid nucleus of high constructive endeavour and informed sagacity in the statesmanship of our leaders. But the real danger is that of its being lost in the surrounding liquifaction. Therefore, an explanation in terms of fatigue is no explanation at all. It is merely a statement of fact, which unfortunately seems also to absolve us of any responsibility. I do not propose to refer to the very common analysis of our defeatism in terms of the moral failure of our leaders. I have no data to support the wild charges of corruption and moral lapses against them. You may have them, although I have my doubts if you have sifted the evidence from hearsay. Besides, I suspect if at any given stage of our struggle Indians as a whole were more moral than what they are today. It is vanity to conclude that we the common men have remained moral while those in charge of government have suddenly become immoral through the exercise of power. I also question the assumption that any political fight has ever been waged on the moral level. It is very true that Gandhiji was a moral genius and pitched his immediate followers on to a high key. But if one accepts all the implications of this combined statement, then a lowering of pitch so soon after his death, in fact a few months before it, is a criticism of his approach and leadership. Your criticism will mean that he was unrealistic, that the potter did not recognise the common clay.

What in reality happens in every case, and has actually happened in ours, is that a new motive, a new attitude has been imposed upon our traditions. It makes them appear to be a fresh disposition of forces guiding our action. In the political fights of colonial countries the new motive takes the shape of patriotism, national interest, anti-imperialism, and the like. But patriotism, insofar as it has never been a tradition with us, cannot be virtue or morality in the sense of *rita,* which is the Indian sense. Thus it is that the so-called corruption by power is only an instance of the very natural dropping out of the novel motive or attitude from the new artificial pattern after its purpose has been served. Such a dropping of the pilot motive after the crossing of shoals is natural and expected. We need not therefore make much of the sudden loss of moral fervour if we only remember that the idea of nationalism was a new emotion not quite in consonance with our mores and folkways. Nationalism has never been a habit of Indian glands nor a vital section of Indian habits. It has never been our stereotype. In our hearts we do not like it; we resent it. Hence we have carried over the fear of a foreign concept to the fear of freedom, a freedom which has been brought about by nationalism.

Once this analysis appears sensible, you will not wonder why our national movement has not stimulated our culture to any considerable extent. Indian culture had thus far been another name for Indian *riti,* a derivative of *rita;* it was wound up with *dharma* and *achar.* Now, when patriotism became new *dharma,* it had to develop its own *achar,* which for various reasons it could not. Gandhiji stuck to *riti,* and sought to unfold a *niti* not very different from the old. But the political and social undercurrents proved too strong for the general acceptance of Gandhiji's *riti* and *niti*. Thus it is that our patriotism, in a special sense, became a symptom of the decay of our religious feelings and hence, of our earlier cultural values. This latter decay showed itself in another manner. Both the corpus and the quality of literature, music, painting, sculpture, in fact all that is commonly known as culture, are poor both absolutely and in comparison with what little was achieved before 1920 in the different regions of India, Bengal, Maharashtra, Andhra and Gujarat. It almost seems that the extension of the national consciousness in area and quantity has been at the expense of the quality of culture. The extension has been a big thing, but it has been mainly in the political aspect of our life, which, as I have said, had never exhausted, or even vitally touched the fullness of our being. Increase in the quantity of the movement certainly involved a penetration into the lower, hitherto unaffected, stratum of the middle class, but it did not break the barrier that separated the entire body of the middle class from the mass.

This situation has to be fully seized to appreciate the nature of our present malaise. Putting it sharply, its constituent elements are the following: (a) Nationalism being a substitute-religion has tended to produce an ersatz-culture, that is, a culture without a strong framework of *achar* capable of doing duty for the old. This fact, more than any other, accounts for the reported loss of moral tone among Congressmen, a loss which is really a degeneration of style. (b) The regional feeling, which is usually intense and exciting, because it is more integrated with the ways of living—which is the true meaning of culture—has had to yield place to a somewhat vague all-India feeling the national movement demanded. The result has been a weakening of regional cultures without a corresponding increase in the strength of Indian culture. (c) The culture of middle classes, being a spurious product, has not been transmitted beyond the limit of the middle class. Attempts have been made to do so both by agitation and education. They had not fully succeeded, because the institution in charge of the national movement itself has been similarly limited. If liberal education had wanted to improve the cultural equipments of the people from the top, the Congress movement wanted to carry the masses with the help of patriotic ardour. The Congress movement treated the mass as an addendum and succeeded in converting it into a crowd. And through the crowd it wanted to reach out to the people. This approach was inevitable, but it has left its legacy in certain cultural distempers. Thus it is that the patriotic literature of this period is loud with the rhetoric of hustings. It is not firmly grounded upon the interests of the people which alone can give content and stability to the national movement. The result is that our 'populism' in literature and music is thin and sentimental, that our folk-songs of the period are vapid. Into this gap between the regional and the all-India culture, between the culture of the people and of the middle class, the national movement has fallen with a thump. If a happy balance could have been struck between the needs of regional culture and those of Indian culture, if the masses could be approached on the basis of their own, material and economic interests, then probably the present sense of frustration could have been avoided and our cultural output worth mentioning before the bar of the world. I say this because a plausible view of moral degeneration is the absence of an adequate framework. If culture is the way of life and morality is essentially traditional, then the relation between cultural decay and moral slackness of the day will be evident.

I have used the word consciousness before and leaned upon it a great deal. I have suggested that it is born out of crisis and it grows as the sense of crisis is intensified. But crisis as such does not guarantee the quality of consciousness. Often has a crisis pulled down the quality and staggered the focus of consciousness. To correct this possibility analysis based upon a knowledge of the main trends of societal evolution is essential. This is the intellectual aspect of consciousness. Having been fortunate enough to know some of our leaders I cannot, for the life of me, minimise their intellectual acumen and abilities. Yet it is a fact that in their effort to create and spread political consciousness, the case of historical reasoning has gone by default. A proper historical analysis would have revealed the various class-urges of our national awakening, its regional basis, its dissociation from traditional values, and thus exposed a few and encouraged others. Pandit Jawaharlal Nehru probably understood it better than others; but he was handicapped in the application of his historical sense to the moulding of events, first by his spatial, geographical, panoramic, and slightly Churchillian view of history as drama, and secondly, by his loyalty to the immediate issue of making the Congress strong through unity. Marxist leaders, if I am not mistaken, have had little say in the matter of policy-formation of the Congress. I am taking names as a concession to the public notion that our leaders alone have made our history, that is, to the exclusion of social forces. May be that our social forces were not helpful either. But a naive faith in the maturity of objective conditions is also deterministic, if not fatalistic. In any case, some analysis by the Congress of the social stress and strain was called for and it was not done well enough to have informed the consciousness of the rank and file of the organisation, and through them, the people who were only too willing to follow. With such analysis every crisis would have enriched the general consciousness. There are instances when whatever analysis was there was not allowed to touch the masses, or when they were not helped in understanding it. At least, that is my impression. Incidentally, the masses never find it difficult to understand social or historical analysis; it is only we who do. Thus it is that the Indian revolution, like many others before it but unlike a few by its side, has been an anti-intellectual movement and left us ill-equipped to take advantage of the logic and the tempo of events.

The foreign government mistrusted intellect for various reasons: it was dangerous for order; it was foreign to the empirical genius and the instinctive ground of the Anglo-Saxon character. But Indian culture had never fought shy of intellect, not even its absurdities and non-worldly abstrations. It seems that along with parliamentarianism and priggishness we have retained the Anglo-Saxon mental suspicion of intellect. This legacy may be good for political or economic deals, but it may be mischievous for culture. I do not want to put on record the evidence of insulting mistrust of intellect or analysis. I do not make a grievance of such insults. After all, there must be some people to be insulted even by a national government. I only state that our national movement skimmed away a part of our consciousness, the political one, and left the rest high and dry, unsupported by any new scaffolding of behaviours and *achars*, with the result that our reasoning is working unrelated to the context, in a sort of vacuum. My assumption must have been obvious to you by now. Culture is an affair of total consciousness; it engages consciousness in its entirety; or it is lost in the sands of sentimentality. Have you not noticed how our film-songs, our short stories, our novels reek with emotions? Cheap sentiments are those that arise from splintered, divided, lonely consciousness. Even our socialistic literature is very romantic. I do not minimise the social importance of romanticism. But a bit of analysis could give it the body it lacks, even if it could not thereby give it the finished form.

In another language, this means that our politics has ruined our culture. Let me not be misunderstood. In a colonial country like ours, politics had a place more important than what it occupies elsewhere. But in our preoccupation with political action we lost a few things, including the need of a political theory. We plunged into action in the abandon of sacrifice, even of despair, and often without the necessary intellectual equipment. Those who had it in an ample measure could not preserve the necessary detachment. The biographies of the intellectual section of our leaders are littered with examples of compromises in the name of loyalty, and what is equally sad, of reality. Once upon a time social stability was so assured that men of knowledge could direct policies without being involved in them. We are now in for a prolonged period of insecurity and brisker circulation in inter-group behaviour. We cannot therefore have a class of Mandarins or Brahmins. Nor do I think that such a class can be created by a fiat of the government overnight. Even if it can be done, the principle of birth, which is very much with us in the shape of nepotism, will convert a brains-trust of planners into a caste. Yet the necessity for such a group will always be there. Provided that proper precautionary measures against the possible degeneration of such an elite group, either by the contamination of the caste system or by the tendency towards unrelated, unreal sectional and bureaucratic specialisation and similar other evils, can be assured, a body of men devoted to the enrichment of popular consciousness through the prestige of their own disinterested, detached, scientific analysis would be very useful in saving our culture from the degrading pull of partisanship. Here again I must make one point clear. The taking of sides on an issue is not by its nature unscientific. The so-called scientific attitude of neutrality is not borne out by the conduct of the scientist with reference to his experiment. He is fully committed to the law of causality even when he is compelled to seek the assistance of other laws to explain an aberrant behaviour. He does it with the help of statistical mechanics. What passes as scientific neutrality is really legal advocacy of the status quo in a subtle manner. It is perfectly possible to have a detached view of things when you are otherwise attached to a view of how things are likely to shape. Thus it is possible for a realist in literature by practice to appreciate the agony of romantic poetry, for a socialist to understand and benefit from the complex mechanism of capitalist production, for a modern painter to enjoy and profit from an early Christian painting. It is a difficult job indeed, but one has to be on razor's edge at critical times. Therefore, along with the historical sense I plead for a scientific attitude to rescue culture from the clutches of political partisanship.

Will such a body of men plan culture? In my view, culture as such cannot be fully planned. If culture comprehends the whole of life, then surely would a large segment of living formed by the unconscious have to be recognised, respected and allowed freedom. This is true of individuals, more true of groups, and still more so of those strata of people whose living is one long pervasive obedience to traditions. Take a craftsman first: he is bound to his materials, pigment and canvas, words and stones. In overcoming their brute resistance, he follows certain rules which have been handed down to him by his forefathers or by his teachers. After a certain stage, he masters these rules by implicit obedience to the texture of materials and technical rules. Then something happens to him: he wants to convey an idea or a design which he calls his own. Then his technical mastery becomes an instrument. In the process of communication an additional factor intervenes. Call it motive, or genius, sense of form, anything you like, but it is there. It is a new factor. It may be the net result of his experience, which in its turn may be personal, familiar or collective. This is where the group, the class, the tribe, race, and sometimes the nation to which he belongs, comes in to frame his general attitude and give a direction to it. The influence of each is a compound mixture of conscious training and unconscious inheritance. Too much consciousness makes the composite product artificial. This is the defect of much of modern art where a consciously formulated purpose or design or theory is imposed upon the act of creation and does not fit in with, or runs contrary to, the deeper patterns in the unconscious. The centre of gravity of formulated ideas does not, in many modern examples, fall in line with the meta-centre of the upward surge of the unconscious. The result is instability, just as in dynamics. This is the real functional defect of propagandist art. There is no other valid criticism of propagandist art. The *Upanishads*, the *Ramayana*, the *Mahabharata*, each propagandises its cult, but in each the conscious part is integrated with the unconscious. A study of their symbols should clearly prove it. So if socialist literature proclaiming the victory of the proletariat is dubbed propagandist it is mainly because of the lack of integration between these two parts of culture, a lack which is conspicuous in the absence of symbols therein. Yet, the conscious and the unconscious are not two distinct entities inimical to each other. The one can be driven into the other, or brought out of it. It demands patience on both sides. But, and here is a point I make: a critical situation, if it can generate a sense of crisis, may extend and enrich the feeling of urgency by historical analysis and scientific habits of thought, may shorten this period of maladjustment and make of it a period of fruitful exchange. The area and sharpness of conflict may also be lessened and transformed for creative purposes. So long as a revolutionary situation is dependent on spontaneity, it is the unconscious that scores over the conscious. But it need not be so. If it is a counterrevolution, the same thing happens. Hence the need for a forward-looking vision for the historical sense, which is the dynamics of progressive literature. The only sensible attitude therefore, is to scientifically plan and advance into that submerged region with the utmost caution. In other words, though that part of culture which belongs to the unconscious cannot be planned every effort should be made to infiltrate there and bring it out of its lair. It is just here that T. S. Eliot goes wrong. Planning of culture means creating the conditions of culture. It is hardly necessary for me to point out that the unconscious to which I am referring is nothing mystical or mysterious. Being the precipitate of history, it is not outside history.

The conditions of culture signify freedom, because, as Malinowski has said in his final and maturest book,—*Freedom and Civilization*—freedom is the gift of culture. Freedom involves choice, which relates to purpose-formation, instrumentalities, which relate to the means for achieving the purpose, and full enjoyment of the ends achieved and controlled. The first demands freedom of discussion and opinion, the second freedom of association and action, and the third freedom for securing distributive justice by removing fear of want and obstacles to the enjoyment of prosperity. These sectors of freedom are the very conditions of a culture-system. To quote Malinowski:

> A culture functions . . . by means of a system of related institutions. The values of a culture are embodied in its ideals, mythologies, political constitution and economic ideology; its instrumentalities function through the balanced coordination and working of institutions. The standard of existence and quality of living depend on the scope, range, distribution and enjoyment of wealth, rights, power, art, science and religion. Each member of an institution enjoys his own differential freedom in the measure to which he has a part in the planning, a full access to the means of execution, and a share in the rewards. Even in its smallest and most insignificant manifestations, freedom gives any and every member of a society the sense of achievement, and through this the sense of personal value. In a free culture people can form their purpose, undertake activities and enterprises, and enjoy the gains from work thus undertaken.

You will at once see that the approach here is essentially pragmatic. I have quoted from an eminent sociologist to avoid any other suspect theoretical basis. I can safely recommend this view to you to enable you to understand the relation between freedom and culture and to apply its tests to the facts of freedom gained and of culture inherited. Implict in this view are some stresses and strains of culture meaning freedom and certain aspects of freedom. I shall frame a few questions to apprise you of certain menacing possibilities. Let us take the institutions first, the family, caste, village-communities, city-life, universities, etc. Once upon a time, the first three were related. Are they so today? Can we say now that they are working in balanced coordination? Are these institutions and instrumentalities framed for the functioning of culture? The religious-proprietary basis of joint-family, the birth-test of caste, the self-sufficiency of village life, are all being shaken by new forces for the absorption or mobilisation of which the traditional culture-system is not equipped. We knew that a large number of our cities have failed to develop a character, those which do only retain their old flavour, like Lucknow or Banaras, others like Kanpur, just cannot achieve cultural integration. Slums, high rates of mortality, municipal intrigues in modern Indian cities, are only indices of the ruling disequilibrium between the old and the newly born institutions. Have we reached a new equilibrium level? Are our cultural values embodied in our political constitution and economic ideology? You will remember in this connection the sharp retort of our law minister to the claims of the village panchayat to be incorporated in the constitution. That condemnation contained a half-truth. India still possesses a frame-work of rural culture: even our modern values are tied up with the rural ones. The truth of that remark lay in the fact that the rural frame-work was likely to be a brake upon that evolving pattern of values which the constitution was meant to provide. Yet the concession to the claim is realistic. Nobody knows how long our countryside will retain its character. It will have to fight for its existence in days to come and be transformed in that process. Till then that section of the constitution will remain. I for one cannot swear to the eternal verities of rural values as they are today. Our culture is being daily urbanised; and the sooner we plan out the maladjustments the better will be the transition to a new phase of culture.

And then this matter of economic ideology. If you mean by ideology a vague desire, then India's economic ideology is certainly socialistic. If, on the contrary, it be a force compelling certain action and prohibiting others, then at best, it is one of private, free enterprise minus the attendant evils. The directive economic and social principles of the constitution are pious wishes. When they will succeed in establishing a norm of economic behaviour then will their ideology be culturally compulsive. Till then, a more positive help from the state as the only going, major comprehensive institution of its kind would have been welcome. I fail to see how the present state of wealth and its distribution and enjoyment can assure to each individual of an institution 'the enjoyment of his own differential freedom in the measure to which he has a part in planning, a full access to the means of execution, and a share in the awards,' i.e., the preliminary conditions of culture. How can an individual in the present set-up acquire the 'sense of achievement, and through this the sense of personal value'? The freedom of private enterprise is not a condition of culture; it is the privacy that kills the freedom. Nor is the freedom to vote, which with its mechanical conformity to other people's wishes is all that adult franchise may confer upon an individual. This is the umbilical cord that binds culture with democracy and socialism. At present, culture is a class-luxury.

I am sorry to have taxed your patience. In any case, I had

warned you against my unpracticality and inconclusiveness, I had wanted to analyse a few ideas: you will develop them. I would thus request you here and now to examine the national movement that has given us a chance to administer ourselves without being equally successful in changing our ways of living, i.e., our culture, which had been left to the tender mercies of spontaneous forces and minor voluntary agencies. Then your duty becomes the rectification of errors and the support of its abiding elements. In this self-examination, criticism of leaders has no place. It should be an objective, historical analysis. The next urgent matter is an enquiry into the methods now being discussed or adopted to give us the adequate cultural framework for our freedom. That enquiry has to be rigorously scientific. On one point I would like you to concentrate. Strident calls for unity are to be heard from all sides. Politicians, language enthusiasts and employers, all want unity, the first as loyal adherents to every important decision of a new born state (or is it an old party?) in difficulty, the second in the name of a need for cultural homogeneity, and the third for uniform conditions of production. I want you to consider carefully if this type of uniformity is sanctioned by Indian history, even though it be a grave need of the hour. That is to say, you should examine the well-advertised thesis that India rose when there was a central, administrative unity as under the Hindu, Buddhist, Muslim emperors, and declined and fell when that unity was broken up into separate entities. This theory of decline and fall is questionable. You are also to enquire into the corollary of the above, viz., the ecology and value of regional cultures, if they have or have not actually contributed to or can still influence the mosaic of culture, or if their descent into the level of sub-cultures will or will not lower the quality of Indian culture itself. You may also have to relate Indian culture to the world context. On the nature of your findings will depend your attitude to a few burning topics of the day. Thirdly, I would request you to think about the extent to which culture can be planned. Will you leave that large, powerful segment of the unconscious alone, or make such a habit of your conscious thought that it becomes in course of time a part of the unconscious? Remember that the unconscious can behave as if it had its own ways of selection and survival; and such ways are usually more powerful and subtle than those of reason or intellection. The recrudescence of the R.S.S. and the Mahasabha only illustrates the cunningness of the unconscious. Beware of loose talk about it. Culture is always artificial and human. It must pay for the penalty of its existence in its eternal tension with the denizens of the deep. All that we can do is to mitigate the psychoses. How we are going to do it is the final question. That way of living which is called capitalistic culture increases the number and the intensities of psychosis through unequal opportunities, wage-slavery and loss of dignity. It does not provide opportunities to personality to develop. The freedom it refers to is not the freedom of choice. It does not confer the right to work and enjoy the fruits of that work. It does not help the common man to build up institutions and use them as instrumentalities for good and better ways of living. So you will have to decide how far you, as artists and craftsmen, and as citizens, are going to be socialists by conviction. The question of propaganda is a minor issue. Propaganda is only a proof of partial conviction. He who is convinced is not loud but quiet, and in quietness lies the quality of art and thought.

Need I point out to you again that the remedy for frustration I have suggested is essentially anticipatory, forward-looking and end-seeking? The type of historical analysis I have in view is not digging into the past, however valuable that may be. While it is essential for us to fill up the gaps of our knowledge by means of what is usually known as research but which is essentially an archaeological exercise, the sole purpose of historical analysis is to know the fundamental nature of historical processes. That nature is change, the change that is involved in invasion of the past into the living, throbbing and contemporary present. This too is not enough, because history is not exhausted in our activities. It moves on into the future, sometimes with a rush and often in halting steps. Numerous instances of petrified existence of entire communities can be quoted. They have been permitted to remain by sheer inertia. Surely it is not desirable that Indian culture should remain where it was. Much less desirable will it be if it wants to go back like a detained child to its mother's womb into the dark recesses of nescient safety and fantasy. In short, no manner of revivalism is a cure for frustration. It is an offence against the laws of change. The withdrawal into inner resources, which Toynbee recommends for the crisis in culture today, is permissible only when it is a preparation for a rally for the step ahead. This path, however, is not a straight one, nor are the travellers always moving ahead. The general direction must always be forward. Our heritage, if one understands it properly, does not allow us to bury the talents but to invest them in risks and uncertainties. As the *Upanishad* says, '*Charaibeti.*'

9. *Asian Nationalism —A Cultural Interpretation*

AT GREAT MOMENTS OF SOCIAL CRISIS HUMAN FEELINGS RANGE between the anguish of the Apocalypse or the millenial hopes of the kingdom to come, to the cynicism of the procurator of Judea who did not remember Jesus but recalled Magdalene, in Anatole France's great satire, or to the indifference of the sightseer suffering from toothache at the Crucifixation, in Strindberg's bitter tale. In between comes the daily grouse of self-complacency of millions of common men and women to diffuse or absorb the shocks of the crisis. When shocks are too violent and unbearable, common men and women want a saviour. If their traditional outlook is religious, the saviour will be an *avatar;* if religious traditions have been sufficiently loosened by secular forces, the saviour will be a dictator. In earlier days, the two types would blend in Caesar Augustus; today, they are apart. Such has been the gamut of human feelings at the great turn of events.

What is the place of thinking in such predicaments? Modern researches do not clearly establish either that in every case revolutionary, thought preceded revolutionary action or that revolutionary practices immediately generated revolutionary thought. It is well known how great ideas remained mere premonitions till later generations discovered their continuity. Instances of upheavals without churning up any significant new ideas are also not rare. Probably, revolutionary ideas conspire with general discontent to generate a system of ideas, which ultimately becomes thought. That thought in its turn sometimes becomes an excuse or a defence of further action. This process of interdependence and mutual conditioning is much about all that can be said with a fair degree of certainty in such matters on a general level.

One specific feature has been observed: the decay of the old elite representing the ruling stratum and the uprise of a new elite representing the one that heaves up from below the surface. This relates to the agency of further action rather than to that of further thought, because it is not unoften that the originators and carriers of new ideas belong to the older ruling stratum. Such men de-class themselves by imagination or historical knowledge. So it will not be accurate to say that the case for ideas, if not that for thought, goes by default at junctures of history. Obviously, emotions storm the ideas and drive them pell mell at such times. Very rarely do ideas by themselves take control of emotions to convert cynicism, indifference, grouse and complacency into positive fervour. But when they do—and they usually do so when (*a*) they are personified and/ or (*b*) they represent and focus the interests of the new class—revolutions succeed. Crisis is usually either an old maid or a barren woman till the bridegroom cometh.

There are, however, some special features of the crisis that faces Asia's mankind today. It is continuous. It began with an eastern power's resounding victory over a mighty western power. Japan proved that Asia need not remain backward. Her success was assured because she had adopted all the techniques of the west. Along with the awakening of the spirit of Asia had to be measured technology in terms of material prosperity. It would, however, be unhistorical to conclude that the victory of Japan did anything more than shake up Asia from its dogmatic slumber and indirectly help the release of a secular trend in Asia's spheres of thought. No Asian who lived consciously in the first decade of this century would fail to remember the thrill of that event and minimise its significance. At the same time, the Asian trend towards secularity was not the same thing as formed the background of the earlier Renaissance and Reformation or the subsequent capitalism in Europe.

For one, in Asia, the element of rationality in secularism could not wean itself away from the earlier high intellectual traditions, although the rationalistic ethics of Confucianism made it easier for China to fight the Indian, particularly, the Buddhist mystical and metaphysical strands in Chinese thought. For another, the necessary concomitant of rationalism, namely, individualism, received more resistance from collectivist ideas and habits of community life, still strong in most parts of Asia, than it did in western Europe, where the remnants of community life had by then almost disappeared and large-scale industrialisation had atomised society into individuals and converted them into mass. Finally, rationalism had to meet a new enemy in Asia in the irrationalism of nationalism, which stimulated the romantic conception of history, race and 'the genius of the people'. On this point, the development of ideas in the east in the present century has been similar to that in the west in the last, with this difference that whereas in the west nationalism with all its intellectual irrationalities could be said to follow as a reaction to the rationality of the Enlightenment and the message of the French revolution, in the east it has not been the result of a reaction to any marked intellectual movement. There were no Encyclopædists worth speaking of in Asia. Asian nationalism as a protest against imperialism had little to do with Japan's victory. It came only after the First World War. So far as this writer knows, there was no real understanding of the nature of imperialism, either of Japan or of the west, in any Asian country before 1917.

This irrationality continued throughout. Meanwhile wars, both in the west and the east, became recurrent. A basic socio-economic transformation was taking place. But it was interpreted as the political transformation of colonies in terms of nationalism. There was a coating of racial feeling over it, which only heightened the irrationalities. These two combined to bring about a cultural interpretation. The east was convinced that it was culturally ancient and superior to the west. And the west often flattered the eastern vanity in its own interests. But the cultural interpretation divided the community into two camps of ideas, one openly hostile to the western influences, and the other, absorbent of western science, rationalism, individualism (and parliamentary democracy). But they were one in one vital matter, viz., lack of historical understanding. Historical scholarship was no doubt undergoing a change. It was no more a plea for past national greatness. Modern methods of research were adopted; many gaps in knowledge were filled by archæology, numismatics and textual criticism. Yet the study of historical process remained incomplete in the absence of a genuine appreciation of history as a social process, as distinct from history as a panorama of interesting political events. History of the lives of the peoples was not taken as the basic factor; they were the great givers of history; no change was noticed in their activities and attitudes. As such, change could only come from outside agencies. One speaks of a wide field like this with infinite caution.

Yet it would not be very wrong to say that the factors held responsible for historical change by Asian historians were foreign influence or invasion, dynastic change, or the Grace Abounding of great men and *avatars*. All these factors, be it noted, were exogenous. Even national saints and *avatars* were not given their social context. The Buddha, the Prophet, the Vaishnava saints, Nanak, Chaitanya, and other 'heroes' in Asian history, seemed to come in these scholarly pages from outside worldly life to initiate worldly change. None appeared to have emerged from social necessity. In other words, endogenous forces were not considered. Cosmic forces were treated by Sri Aurobindo in India; but then his concept of national history was only a part, though an integral part, of the cosmic cycle and the cosmic scheme. His was spiritual understanding rather than historical understanding. In the Middle East, where Islam was being re-valued in practice, historical understanding should have been easier because of the great Arab and Islamic traditions of historical scholarship. Yet nothing significant was achieved in the appreciation of historical and social forces. There was a feeling of change in the air: but that the roots of change lay inside the womb of society was only dimly sensed. Naturally, rationality did not have full chance for development. Such equipment was hardly adequate for meeting the recurrence and the continuity of crisis in a continent which had to meet the west on its own grounds.

The result was that for Asia crisis became comprehensive, all-pervasive and deep. Without being a Jeremiah one can still compare the almost total disintegration of values of this century to that at the turn of the Christian era in the west, when Græco-Roman culture collapsed and, what Toynbee calls the internal and external proletariat, pressed on the existing order. There was one redeeming feature then, Platonic thought, which entered into Christianity and gave it intellectual substance. Even if the close of the Middle Ages is cited as a parallel, the revival of Græco-Roman culture and the marvellous intellectual structure of scholastic thought would distinguish it from the present crisis. In addition, the great system of mathematics and philosophy built in the century of geniuses that followed, saved

Europe from the effects of disintegration. The next century built up science and spread scientific attitude.

Today, none of these conditions exists in Asia. So far as India is concerned, we are still waiting for the day when old Indian thought will be reorientated to suit modern times, as Aristotelianism was reorientated in western Europe in the Middle Ages. Is Confucianism being re-conditioned on a large-scale to suit Chinese conditions? We hear that it is being done. But how many thinkers are 're-constructing' Islam? Barring Iqbal, no Muslim in this sub-continent is known to have thought it out. Hindu revivalism is well-known; but which system of Hindu thought can be related to modern Indian conditions is not known to many Indians. The result is frightful. There is no branch of India's intellectual activity in which ideas are not derivative or imported, which does not inevitably succumb to a foreign dogma, or which draws its sap from the soil. Being modern only means being fashionable.

Ideas really do not have the frame work of a homogeneous temporal series; they function in sociological time in which there are lags, suspensions and spurts according to the nature of social development. If this determining factor is neglected, easy communicability remains the only attribute of modernity. It then means craze for the latest. By then, understanding has been reduced to the search for sensations. And this is exactly what has happened in every field where historical and social understanding has not come to the rescue of man. The vulgarity of Indian films is only the visually logical extension of the utter inability of the modern Indian to face this crisis. If progressive Indian poetry, painting, political thinking, is nothing more than strings of cliches, the absence of historical and social understanding is the cause. Similarly with revivalism: its history is atavism, and its sociality is compensatory nostalgia for an imaginary past.

Yet it need not have been so. The Russian revolution had a consistent body of thought behind it, viz., Marxism. Leninism offered a historical analysis of imperialism. But it was misunderstood by most of the Asians who were radicals. Instead of studying the course of the Russian revolution, how the internationalism of Marxism was conditioned by Russian history and Russian society, that is, by Russia's needs and developments, most Asian radicals regarded it in terms of Comintern, as an international dogma true of all countries and at all times. The faith behind their dogma was in the oneness of the historical process. Thereby the Asian radicals ran counter to those specificities of their histories which could transmute their dogma into living faith.

The Indian revolution had no such consistent system to impel it. Yet Gandhiji was rooted in the soil of society; and Jawaharlal had some notion of historicity. Unfortunately, sociality and historicity did not coalesce here, as they did in China. The result is that despite social vision the crisis is deeper here than in China where the element of historical understanding is stronger. Chinese revolution has not only an intellectual base in rationalism; its rationalism is not only embodied in ethics but, at the same time, it is trying through collective action to adapt historical understanding to its traditional rational ethics. Indian revolution has not had that advantage. On the other hand, it has other advantages, e.g., a new technique which has proved successful in India and is full of promise in South Africa from which it sprang. Though it is too early to pronounce judgment on its universal efficacy, its applicability under certain conditions seems to have been justified. The two basic assumptions of the application of the new technique of satyagraha are (*a*) the unchangeability of human nature, and (*b*) its basic urge for moral perfection, irrespective of contexts and contingencies. So the only concession to change in this technique is that which is implicit in the course of moral perfection and in the experiments pertaining thereto.

Obviously, the philosophy involved here is that of moral and psychological change independent of the material conditions that make for such change. This philosophy works on the notion that time is a homogeneous, irreversible series tapering to and merging in eternity without being affected by happenings in social time. In so far as it is not firmly grounded on the material conditions which modify morality in social time, it cannot perceive that means are ends and ends are means. Not to understand the dialectical relation between this pair is clear evidence of the essentially absolutist assumptions of the technique. On the concrete level, the evidence is more dramatic. It should be no exaggeration to say that after the achievement of its immediate objective, wrongly called end, namely, political freedom, the *agraha* for *satya* has not spread to the extent that was necessary for moral upheaval and psychological transformation, which was the declared end.

If today any symptom of mass enthusiasm for constructive endeavour is noticeable, it cannot be traced to the new technique. The large number of schemes of national construction, like the dams and the community projects, in particular, are not traceable to the technique that achieved the objective and owe greatly to another philosophy of life, call it welfare, planning or planned social development if you like. They establish the proposition that satyagraha has had no philosophy of history, that while it was efficacious for a certain limited purpose, however urgent and noble it might have been, yet it carries no guarantee of a philosophy of life suitable for the next historical stage, or for the matter of that, for the next higher level of the same stage. So, if this technique does not develop a suitable philosophy of history, India's crisis may last longer and leave Indians to the mercy of dictators. The Middle East is a warning to all Indians.

In short, the crisis of the modern age is the crisis in historical knowledge. Discursive, practical, speculative reasoning, as also social sympathy and vision, will have to be transformed into historical-cum-social understanding if we Indians are to come out of the deepening crisis to save certain values and create new ones. This writer believes, perhaps fondly, that universities have a part to play in this transformation. Values are too valuable to be trusted entirely to politicians banking on the old technique.

10. *Mahatma Gandhi's Views on Machines and Technology*

THIS PAPER COMES OUT OF THE CONVICTION THAT A STUDY OF THE social changes of technology should be based primarily on an understanding of the conditions of the society which brings about the contact and also of the society on which the impact takes place. If these conditions are crystallised in two systems of values, one which has accepted, and the other which has not accepted 'technical progress' as desirable or technological advance as 'a self-evident good'[1], and further, if the strains of technological advance, which any scheme of technological assistance brings in its wake, must needs be reduced or eliminated for the assistance to be genuinely effective, then one of the chief concerns of the sociologist as well as of the technical administrator is the discovery of the terms of the normative system of the country that assists or radiates technological values and the country that is assisted or influenced thereby. This does not preclude the various types of specific researches on the social effects of technological change; on the contrary, the normative study may be fortified by their scientific conclusions. What is stressed here is the methodological issue, viz., that in a matter like the impact of machines or technology, which is associated with western Europe, on Asian countries, which are believed to belong to a pre-technical stage, the underlying axiological assumption that technological advance is a 'self-evident good' should be brought to the surface. Once that is done the way is clear for the comparative normative approach. It is heartening to know that eminent western sociologists[2] have recognised the importance of this approach from the end of industrial societies.

[1] R. K. Merton, *Socialist Theory and Social Structure*, p. 317.

[2] Talcott Parsons in his *Essays in Sociological Theory;* Prof. W. E. Moore in his paper 'Social Consequences of Technical Change from the Socioligical Standpoint', published in the *International Social Science Bulletin,* Summer, 1952, Vol. IV, No. 2.; and the

Equally disheartening is the absence of any formulation of the eastern value-system by an eastern sociologist, who one would suppose to have been more interested in the matter. One reason for this deficiency may be the psychological fact that Eastern people are yet too deeply involved in their system and therefore, the technological impact on their basic values is yet superficial. Another reason may as well be that those among them who could formulate and compare the value-systems are the very people who believe in technical advance as a 'self-evident good' and therefore, do not worry about the problem at all beyond the stage of annoyance with temporary maladjustments which, in their view, a Welfare State, or a similar agency or agencies, would benevolently remove sooner or later. Certain economic interests in India, in particular, also seem to be far too committed to technological advance to be anxious to study the conflict of value-systems involved in the resultant strain. Though one hears about cottage industries and their place in Indian life and notices earnest administrative encouragements, the importance attached to them seems to be mainly on the score of their being able to provide 'some' employment to those who are being thrown out of 'employment' by technological advance.

Gandhiji, however, was deeply and primarily concerned with the value-systems. There were others too, but they are less known. Gandhiji put his views very sharply indeed. One may not like the manner of his posing the problem, one may consider it as partial, one may dismiss it, if one chooses, as many 'educated' men and industrialists of India have chosen. But his statements remain a challenge to the entire problem of technological change and schemes of technical assistance. They should be taken seriously, because many new disturbing features of Indian life cannot be explained, or removed otherwise. From them one might also infer that the term 'underdeveloped economy,' which is the excuse of technical assistance, was inappropriate insofar as it confused the coexistence of two different value-systems by placing them on the assembly-line of historical development in which economic growth being the supreme value

excellent manual prepared by the World Federation of Mental Health (edited by Margaret Mead), *Cultural Patterns and Technical Change*—all have laid great emphasis on the pattern of beliefs and attitudes, or traditional values, of the people who are exposed to such change.

was subservient to and dependent only upon technological advance. Perhaps, Gandhiji was unfair to the European civilization; it may also be that he did not subscribe to the unilinear concept of history. But it is certain that he had other values, and his understanding of India at least, was unerring. We Indians love to think that Gandhiji's views correctly represent the unformulated values of the vast majority of the Indian population towards social changes. They, as he would say, would welcome change on their own human terms.

Let us know exactly what he said in regard to machines and when. (He never used the word 'technology,' but it is clear that he meant it.) Much misunderstanding of his position prevails everywhere. But he did not want to be misunderstood; in fact, the very clarity of his style leaves no room for misunderstanding. The first unequivocal statement of his position occurs in *Hind Swaraj* or 'Indian Home Rule,' written originally in Gujarati, in the return voyage from London to South Africa in 1908 'in answer to the Indian school of violence and its prototype in South Africa.' It was first published in the columns of the *Indian Opinion* of South Africa in the form of the editor's answers to the reader's queries. In this period, Gandhiji was finding himself through many a personal and a few social experiments. Violence had become the desperate creed of Indian nationalists. He was analysing this creed all the time, digging its base, so to say, and reaching towards an alternative moral creed. *Hind Swaraj* was the first formulation and bears all the marks of religious conversion. The subsequent history of the book is interesting, but not quite relevant here. But it is on record that in January 1921 (*Young India*) Gandhiji would 'withdraw nothing except one word of it, and that in deference to a lady friend.' As Mahadev Desai wrote in his preface to the 1938 edition, 'Even in 1938 he would alter nothing in the book, except perhaps the language in some parts.' We will see, however, that certain alterations were made, but they were more in the nature of elaboration in terms of reality, e.g., the relative unpreparedness of Indian people for the practice of 'a higher simplicity and renunciation,' which he knew to be India's values, than as deviations from a fundamental position. As Babu Rajendra Prasad said in his presidential address to the Sevagram Conference[3] in March 1948:

[3] *The Harijan*, 4 April 1948.

> Naturally, his whole life was a series of experiments and he rightly named his autobiography as *Experiments with Truth*. As is to be expected in these circumstances, his mind was not static but was growing with experience in life.... This is not what is ordinarily called inconsistency, but the characteristic of one who has fixed principles by which he judged the problems as they arose and was not afraid to take different views at different times, so long as the fundamental principle is not in any way violated.

This admirably sums up not only the man Gandhiji but the position of Gandhiji vis-a-vis the machine-civilization of the West. His writings show[4] that his opposition to England or to the western or even the European civilization, was not merely on the limited ground of political and economic subjection but on the much wider issue of the conflict of civilizational values. Here is a fairly long extract from *Hind Swaraj* (Ch. XIII):

> *Reader*: You have denounced railways, lawyers and doctors. I can see that you will discard all machinery. What, then, is civilization?
>
> *Editor*: The answer to that question is not difficult. I believe that the civilization India has evolved is not to be beaten in the world.... It is a charge against India that her people are so uncivilized, ignorant and stolid, that it is not possible to induce them to adopt any changes. It is a charge really against our merit. What we have tested and found true on the anvil of experience, we dare not change. Many thrust their advice upon India, and she remains steady. This is her beauty: it is the sheet-anchor of our hope.
>
> Civilization is that mode of conduct which points out to man the path of duty. Performance of duty and observance of morality are convertible terms. To observe morality is to attain mastery over our mind and our passions. So doing, we know ourselves. The Gujarati equivalent for civilization means 'good conduct.'
>
> If this definition be correct, then India, as so many writers have shown, has nothing to learn from anybody else, and this is as it should be. We notice that the mind is a restless bird; the more it gets the more it wants, and still more unbridled they become. Our ancestors, therefore, set a limit to our indulgences. They saw that happiness was largely a neutral condition.... We have had no system of

[4] Letter to a friend, quoted in *Mahatma*, Vol. I, pp. 129-30.

life-corroding competition. Each followed his own occupation or trade and charged a regulation wage. It was not that we did not know how to invent machinery, but our forefathers knew that, if we set our hearts after such things, we would become slaves and lose our moral fibre. They, therefore, after due deliberation decided that we should only do what we could with our hands and feet. They further reasoned that large cities were a snare and a useless encumbrance. They were, therefore, satisfied with small villages. They saw that kings and their swords were inferior to the sword of ethics, and they, therefore, held the sovereign of the earth to be inferior to the *rishis* and the *fakirs*....

And where this cursed modern civilization has not reached, India remains as it was before. The inhabitants of that part of India will properly laugh at your new fangled notions. The English do not rule over them, nor will you ever rule over them. Those in whose name we speak we do not know, nor do they know us.... Now you see what I consider to be real civilization.... The tendency of the Indian civilization is to elevate the moral being, that of the Western civilization is to propagate immorality. The latter is Godless, the former is based on a belief in God. So understanding and so believing, it behoves every lover of India to cling to the old Indian civilization even as a child clings to the mother's breast.

The views expressed here would appear to be extravagant. In fact, G. K. Gokhale, whom Gandhiji called his master, thought so when he read the book in English translation. Many historians and sociologists would not accept these statements. They would be cautious about India's ancestry, about her deliberate wisdom in rejecting machinery, city life and the evils thereof. They would question the latent virtuous assumptions about India's past and her society. They would attribute them mostly to lack of opportunities and the incurable human habit of making a virtue of necessity. They would also not fail to detect a high order of spiritual values in the western, European, or modern civilization and a low order of social values prevailing in the East, in India old and new. But here at last was the Indian positing of a felt contrast in the fierce clarity of exaggeration. The exaggeration was similar to that of a rebel slave who would assert with vehemence his own human dignity and clothe it in historical terms. At the same time, it was not a metaphysical rebellion, so typical of India and the East. It was not a protest against the universal condition of man whose life is interrupted by disease, old age, or death, as was that of Buddha. It was essentially a moral rebellion, couched in the social terms of civilization, which Gandhiji defined as good conduct with the entire weight on performance of duty and observance of morality. And the supreme duty was to attain the mastery over mind and passions in the performance of which we know ourselves, that is, knowledge accrues. The performance implied proper use of hands and feet and the process led to the limitation of indulgences, reduction of wants and simplification of life. All these ideas formed a whole pattern of thought, beliefs, attitude and action which placed Indian civilization in sharp opposition to what he sometimes called the western, at other times, the European, but what was really the modern civilization clustered round material values.

Let us follow the development of Gandhiji's ideas. In October 1924, soon after he had broken one of his famous fasts, he gave an interview[5] to a student from Santiniketan, Sri Ramchandran, who questioned him on his views on the place of art in national regeneration and on machinery. Ramchandran asked:

> *R*: Are you against all machinery?
>
> *G*: How can I be when I know that even this body is a delicate piece of machinery? The spinning wheel itself is a machine; a little tooth-pick is a machine. What I object to is the craze for machinery, not machinery as such. The craze is for what they call labour-saving machinery. Men go on 'saving labour' till thousands are without work and thrown on the streets to die of starvation. I want to save time and labour, not for a fraction of mankind, but for all. I want the concentration of wealth, not in the hands of a few, but in the hands of all. Today machinery helps a few to ride on the backs of millions. The impetus behind it is not the philanthropy to save labour, but greed. It is against this constitution of things that I am fighting with all my might.
>
> *R*: Then you are fighting not against machinery as such, but against its abuses, which are so much in evidence today?
>
> *G*: I would unhesitatingly say yes; but I would add that scientific truths and discoveries should first cease to be mere instruments of greed. Then labourers will not be

[5] *Mahatma*, Vol. II, p. 212.

overworked and machinery instead of becoming a hindrance will be a help. I am aiming not at eradication of all machinery, but limitation.

R: When logically argued out, that would imply that all complicated power-driven machinery should go.

G: It might have to go, but I must make one thing clear. The supreme consideration is man. The machine should not tend to keep atrophied the limbs of man. For instance, I would make intelligent exceptions. Take the case of the Singer Sewing Machine. It is one of the few useful things ever invented, and there is a romance about the device itself. Singer saw his wife labouring over the tedious process of sewing and seaming with her own hands, and simply out of his love for her, he devised the sewing machine in order to save her from unnecessary labour. He, however, saved not only her labour, but also the labour of everyone who could purchase a sewing machine.

R: But, in that case, there would have to be a factory for making these Singer Sewing Machines, and it would have to contain power-driven machinery of ordinary type.

G: Yes, surely. But I am socialist enough to say that such factories should be nationalized or state-controlled. They ought only to be working under the most attractive and ideal conditions, not for profit, but for the benefit of humanity, love taking on the place of greed as the motive. It is an alteration in the conditions of labour that I want. This mad rush for wealth must cease and the labourer must be assured not only of a living wage but a daily task that is not a mere drudgery. The machine will, under these conditions, be as much a help to the man working it as to the state, or the man who owns it. The present mad rush will cease and the labourer will work, as I have said, under attractive and ideal conditions. This is but one of the exceptions I have in mind. The sewing machine had love at its back. The individual is the one supreme consideration. The saving of labour of the individual should be the object and honest humanitarian considerations, and not greed the motive.... Therefore, replace greed by love and everything will come right.

Next morning the interview was continued. Ramchandran persisted:

R: If you make an exception of the Singer Sewing Machine and your spindle, where would these exceptions end?

G: Just where they cease to help the individual and encroach upon his individuality. The machine should not be allowed to cripple the limbs of man.

R: But I was not thinking just now of the practical side. Ideally would you not rule out all machinery? When you except the sewing machine, you will have to make exceptions of the bicycle, the motor-car, etc.

G: No, I don't because they do not satisfy any of the primary wants of man;.... Ideally, however, I would rule out all machinery, even as I would reject this very body, which is not helpful to salvation and seek the absolute liberation of the soul. From that point of view, I would reject all machinery, but machines will remain because like the body, they are inevitable. The body itself, as I told you, is the purest piece of mechanism; but if it is a hindrance to the highest flights of the soul, it has to be rejected.

The long quotation is important from many points of view. The views expressed in 1924 seem to mark a departure from those of 1908. Gandhiji was a realist in the best sense of the term. The seeds that had been laid in the *Hind Swaraj* grew into a plant in the upturned soil of India. Gandhiji had started the non-cooperation movement and the Khilafat movement, but he realized that the people of India were not yet ripe for the supreme renunciation his values demanded. Non-violence and truth could not be the bread of the masses. That was the bitter lesson of Chauri Chaura (1922). The masses wanted bread, and for them 'God was bread and bread was God.' A terrible famine raged in Orissa, and it haunted his dreams. In various cities of India strikes occurred; and their lesson was not lost on him. His sense of limits, a gift which every moral genius must possess, came into play. And in that process he realized a few basic truths. It was clear to him that the impetus behind the large-scale use of machinery was profit or 'greed'—which was 'in the constitution of things' as they were, and not philanthropy or love; 'today machinery helps a few to ride on the backs of millions; the labourer must get a living wage and a secure daily task and his labour should not be drudgery; and above all, man, that is, the labourer, was the supreme consideration. These were his postulates. In Gandhiji's view, man was the producer, the bread-worker by hand, an idea which he had imbibed early in his career in South Africa from Ruskin's *Unto This Last,* which he had translated as *Sarvodaya.* Gandhiji, be it underlined, would have nationalised or state-controlled factories of power-driven machinery to control the profit and 'produce for the benefit of humanity,' love taking the place of greed as the motive. At this point, Gandhiji presumably believed that the state was, and would be, an agency for transforming greed into a love for humanity, though elsewhere he was less hopeful. All this appears to be a move away from the uncompromising position taken up in the *Hind Swaraj*.[6] Be that as it may, it was not a sacrifice of his basic, or he called it, the 'ideal' position. 'Ideally, however, I would rule out all machinery, even as I would reject this very body, (the purest piece of machinery) which is not helpful to salvation and seek the absolute liberation of the soul.' This idea of salvation and absolute liberation from the body is, in my view, the key-note of Gandhian values, or Indian values, as Gandhiji and many others would interpret them. In short, Gandhiji would have welcomed the 'natural destruction' of machinery and mills, together with law courts, railways and hospitals, but not a violent destruction. By 'natural' he appeared to have meant the potential nature of the scholastics—the nature that sprang from love, purity, simplicity, and flowered in fulfilment and renunciation. His exceptions arose from the 'actual' nature of man in India, his unpreparedness.[7] Truly could Gandhiji say, 'Ripeness is all.'

These values, it is obvious, centred in renunciation and non-possession. The Hindu idea of renunciation is not *vairagya*, which is probably a Buddhist concept incorporated into Hinduism to make it suitable for its eminently practical *varnasram* and *purusharatha*. Renunciation in the Hindu sense is *aparigraha* (non-possession) of the *Geeta*, as Acharya Vinoba Bhave has pointed out more than once in the pages of the *Harijan*. The concept of love, or altruism, the good of all, as opposed to the hedonistic calculus of the greatest good of the greatest number,[8] was probably a mixture of Vaishnava, Christian and later Buddhist ideas. Whatever its origins, it worked very well indeed, particularly as a means of propaganda of Gandhiji's ideas among

[6] For western readers the change is like that from Tolstoy to William Morris. One would not like to recall here Ruskin's glorification of war in his address to the Royal Military Academy, Woolwhich, 1865, since published in *The Crown of Wild Olive*.

[7] 'A Word of Explanation', *Young India*, January, 1921.

[8] Cf. *Autobiography*, Pt. iv, Ch. viii, and *Young India*, 12 September, 1926.

the masses. In other words, the 'ideal' pattern of Hindu values was never forsaken by Gandhiji. It was woven round 'wantlessness.' How could technology and machines, geared to the production of goods for the satisfaction of wants, which created more wants, joint wants, derived wants, the infinite hyperbola of wants, be consonant with the pattern of Indian norms? How could such norms square, for that matter, with economics, grounded as it was on wants and their satisfaction? If absolute liberation of the soul from the body be the utter sum of existence, then Gandhiji, and with him, every Hindu who was aware of his ancestry, would raise the eternal query: Why this craze for machinery? Why machine-civilization at all? Other problems such as machines helping a few to ride on the back of millions, the concentration of power and wealth, of justice for the labourer as man, securing attractive conditions of life for him and of giving him security of employment, etc., would be subsidiary. These latter, in Gandhiji's opinion, ultimately hinged upon non-possession, *aparigraha,* wantlessness, subordination of body and bodily wants to the need of the soul's liberation from its physical encasement, which was the *end.*

II

These subsidiary problems, however, were far from socially insignificant. In the Gandhian view of life, they were related to the means. To many 'educated' Indians they were the ends, or the primary values. Gandhiji had many opportunities of discussing them with those who were more sensitive to the needs and ideas of the day. Rabindranath Tagore's objection was of a different type, but it was met by the logic of means. The poet had written in 1925 against the *charkha* (the spinning wheel), because he felt that it would bring about a death-like sameness in the nation. Gandhiji met this argument on the highest level. Taking his cue from the Hindu philosophical conception of oneness, identity, or sameness, which Sankara had carried to its logical extreme, Gandhiji held that 'behind a variety of occupations there is an indispensable sameness also of occupation.' After inveighing for a while against exploitation, both by European and Indian manufacturers, Gandhiji conceded:[9]

[9] *Mahatma,* Vol. II, p. 283.

> Machinery has its place; it has come to stay. But it must not be allowed to displace the necessary human labour. An important plough is a good thing. But if by some chance one man could plough up by some mechanical invention the whole of the land of India and control all the agricultural produce and if the millions had no other occupation, they would starve, and being idle, they would become dunces, as many have already become. There is hourly danger of many more being reduced to that unenviable state. I would welcome every improvement in the cottage machine but I know that it is criminal to displace the hand labour by the introduction of power-driven spindles unless one is at the same time ready to give millions of farmers some other occupation in their homes.

Here was argument on the purely economic level of means, that is, of employment and unemployment. To a modern western economist it may appear to be old-fashioned. He thinks that he has devised excellent measures against various types of unemployment, cyclical, structural, frictional, seasonal, and all that, and he is not worried if even under full employment two to five per cent are unemployed. But Gandhiji was not to be deluded by such theories and measures emerging out of the practices of countries that had been wedded to industrial and technical civilization, that had colonies to exploit and accepted competitive values in production, trade and commerce. The essence of Gandhiji's concession in this open letter to Tagore is, however, historical. That is to say, so long as 'some other occupation in their homes' was not available—and it was not likely to be available in that historical context, or in the near future, because imperialist exploitation would not allow India to create alternative occupations—Gandhiji would stick to the spinning wheel and be against the displacement of labour by machinery. In other words, India in her present context should have labour-intensive economy for the sake of full employment.

Gandhiji was very respectful towards Tagore, and as we have seen, met the poet's cultural charge with economic arguments. But he was not so soft towards the Indian Communist M.P., Mr. Saklatwala. He duly published his appeal in the *Young India*. The differences with Tagore were not vital, but with Mr. Saklatwala they were. Gandhiji wrote in *Young India* under the caption 'No and Yes':

> His facts are fiction and his deductions based upon fic-

> tion are necessarily baseless. And where these are true, my whole energy is concentrated upon nullifying their, to me, poisonous results. I am sorry, but we do stand at opposite poles. There is, however, one great thing common between us. Both claim to have the good of the country and humanity as our only goal. Though we may for the moment seem to be going in opposite directions, I expect we shall meet some day. I promise to make amends when I discover my error. Meanwhile, my error, since I do not recognize it as such, must be my child and my solace.

Having said this in true humility—and there is not the slightest reason to doubt it—Gandhiji reveals himself in the full panoply of his original, uncompromising, absolute, non-historical faith. He wrote:

> For unlike Saklatwala, I do not believe that multiplication of wants and machinery contrived to supply them is taking the world a single step nearer its goal. Comrade Saklatwala swears by the modern rush. I whole-heartedly detest this mad desire to destroy distance and time, to increase animal appetites and go to the ends of the earth in search of their satisfaction. If modern civilization stands for all this, and I have understood it to do so, I call it satanic and with it the present system of government, its best exponent.

Then follow some sentences which would remind one of the wrath of prophets, but with a difference:

> I would destroy that system today, if I had the power. I would use the most deadly weapons, if I believed that they would destroy it. I refrain only because the use of such weapons could only perpetuate the system though it may destroy its present administration. Those, who seek to destroy men rather than their manners, adopt the latter and become worse than those whom they destroy under the mistaken belief that the manners will die with the men. They do not know the root of the evil.

The last paragraph seems to retain its pertinence today in spheres wider than the Indian. The points to be noticed in Gandhiji's reply to Saklatwala's appeal are Gandhiji's firm faith in wantlessness as a cardinal human virtue, and his objection only to the 'modern rush,' by which he included both the western and the Indian values of the day. We may further note his association of modernism with the British government in India.

Strictly from the point of view of the propagation of an answering faith, this mixture of basic values with nationalism was excellent. A sociologist would not cavil at it. Technological values are usually associated with the nationalist values, particularly in the eastern countries in the period of their anti-imperialist struggle. It centres in their opposition to the obstacles that imperialism places in their economic growth, and also in the period of economic advance which is held to be possible only with the help of technology. But it is equally understandable that nationalist, anti-subjectionist motives and attitudes should be integrated with the basic values which are, or are interpreted to be, specific to the culture of the nation. While it is true that in this extract no reference is made to the Indian-ness of the objection to the modern rush and the argument appears to rest on the personal level, it is apparent, as it certainly was to the Indian of 1925, that it was a typically Indian argument securely grounded on the Indian philosophy of life, *aparigraha,* non-possession, enjoyment through giving away, *tyaktena bhunjitha.*

We must repeat that Gandhiji collected other arguments round this basic, axiological objection to machines. They were mainly what we would call sociological arguments, on the score of excessive population on land, of idle labour, of bad distribution of wealth, benefit to the nation, that is to say, the welfare of the people. He referred to unemployment again and again, to bad health, unwholesome food, and to the decay of art. He categorically stated that labour had a unique place in swaraj, or independence, and formed its content. Each argument depended on another and the whole formed a pattern of positive values. In 1935, on April 23, he said after opening the first All-India Village Industries Exhibition at Indore:

> The reason why our average life-rate is deplorably low, the reason why we are getting more and more impoverished is that we have neglected our 100,000 villages. We have indeed thought of them, but only to the extent of exploiting them. We read thrilling accounts of the 'glory that was Ind,' of the land that was flowing with milk and honey; but today it is a land of starving millions. We are sitting in this fine pandal under a blaze of electric lights, but we do not know that we are burning these lights at the expense of the poor. We have no right to use the lights if we forget that we owe these to them.

Gandhiji would seldom forget to remind his audience of their responsibility towards the people. The word 'owe these to them' is an English rendering of the Hindu concept of *rina* or debts, contracted by every individual at his birth to his ancestors, his gods, sages, and to nature, the universe or society, debts which must be duly discharged in the course of existence. Hindu social organisation is built on the principle of obligations which Gandhiji insisted on resuscitating in all social and economic spheres of activity, *vide* his concept of rich men holding their riches on trusteeship for the poor. Only in the sphere of political struggle against foreign rule would he allow the exercise of the western sense of rights, and these too hedged in by the sense of social obligations, which was one vital significance of non-violence. Gandhiji continued: 'There is a difference between the civilization of the East—the civilization of India—and that of the West.' We may once again remind ourselves that formerly he had contrasted only the modern civilization with the earlier, pre-technical one, and minimised, if not ignored this distinction between the East and the West. However, this again is not quite a shift in position; in fact, he was also speaking to the West. And he was only referring to the defects of the tendencies of the western civilization, and not to its inherent nature, as Mahadev Desai pointed out in his preface to the 1938 edition of *Hind Swaraj*:

> It is not generally realised wherein the difference lies. Our geography is different, our history is different, our ways of life are different. Our continent, though vast is a speck on the globe, but it is the most thickly populated, barring China. Well, the economics and the civilization of a country where the pressure of population on land is greatest, are and must be different from those of a country where the pressure is the least. Sparsely populated America may have need of the machinery. India may not need it at all. When there are millions upon millions of units of idle labour, it is no use thinking of labour-saving devices.... The reason of our poverty is the extinction of (cottage) industries, and our consequent unemployment.

There follow certain figures about the increasing dependence on land as a result of the destruction of cottage industries and the loss of health through the elimination of vitamins in grain after being ground in machines. Gandhiji's context was the first exhibition of village industries which he was building up as the base of his constructive programme. He was an anti-machinist with a purpose, and the language of his argument was suitable to the masses hearing him.

Gandhiji seemed to have been perpetually alive to this problem of unemployment. On 22 October 1937, he inaugurated the Educational Conference at Wardha and developed his ideas of education through handicrafts. It was a new setting for his constructive programme—an integration of living in love, with efficiency and independence, without exploitation, conflict and poverty, and with education of the body and mind. In expounding his thesis, he said:[10]

> Then, take the question of machinery. I wish that machinery is not necessary for us at all. We should use khadi (home-spun cloth); and, therefore, we do not require mills. We should try to produce all the necessary cloth in villages, and we need not be the slaves of machines.... I am afraid, by working with machines we have become machines ourselves, having lost all sense of art and handwork. If you still think that we cannot do without machines, the scheme (of new education) I have placed before you will be futile. You wish to keep our village alive by means of machines and think of imparting education to the village children through them. Machines will only help in making all the thirty-five crores of people unemployed. If you think that machines are really indispensable, you must reject the scheme and suggest a new one.

In 1946 India was passing through a severe food crisis. Gandhiji offered advice to those who sought it. There were suggestions and counter-suggestions. Even in those dire days he would not move from his fundamental ground. In one of his replies he said:[11]

> I regard the existence of power wheels for the grinding of corn in thousands of villages as the limit of our helplessness. I suppose India does not produce all the engines and grinding machines.... The planting of such machinery and engines on a large scale in villages (a suggestion made by a correspondent for resolving the food crisis) is also a sign of greed. Is it proper to fill one's pockets in this manner at the expense of the poor? Every such machinery puts thousands of hand *chakkis* (grindstones for corn) out of work,

[10] *Mahatma*, Vol. IV, pp. 238-39.
[11] *Ibid.*, Vol. VII, pp. 71-72.

and takes away employment from thousands of house-wives and artisans who make these *chakkis*. Moreover, the process is infective and spreads to every village industry. The decay of the latter spells too the decay of art. If it meant the replacement of the old crafts by the new ones, one might not have much to say against it. But this is not what is happening. In the thousands of villages, where power-machinery exists, one misses the sweet music in the early morning of the grinders at work. But to come to the main point. Whilst I hold that these power engines are at present being put to wrong use, it would be some compensation if these engines, in addition to their present use, were also used to pump water out of the rivers, tanks and wells for irrigation.

Probably, a very reasonable account of the place of machinery in the context of independence was written by Gandhiji in the *Harijan* of 15 July 1946. It was a clarification of his concept of independence for the benefit of Congressmen. He painted a glorious picture of self-sufficient villages, giving free and voluntary play to mutual forces, highly cultured in the sense that there every man and woman knows what he or she wants and, what is more, knows that no one should want anything that the others cannot have with equal labour, a society based on the living force of truth and non-violence, a society not like a pyramid but like 'an oceanic circle.'[12]

> I may be taunted with the retort that this is all utopian and, therefore, not worth a single thought. If Euclid's point, though incapable of being drawn by any human agency, has an imperishable value, my picture has its own for mankind to live. Let India live for this true picture, though never realisable in its completeness.... In it, there is no room for machines that would displace human labour and that would concentrate power in a few hands. Labour has its unique place in a cultured human family. Every machine that helps every individual has a place. But I must confess that I have never sat down to think out what that machine can be. I have thought of Singer's Sewing Machine. But even that is perfunctory. I do not need it to fill in my picture.

On 31 July 1946, Gandhiji addressed a conference of ministers of industries of different states in Poona. There he clarified

[12] *Ibid.*, pp. 201-02.

his conception of village industries and referred to the imbalance between town and village economies and the need for establishing justice in their relation. In that connection, he came to a fairly elaborate explanation of what he meant by machines. Sri D. G. Tendulkar, the author of *Mahatma,* gives the following summary:[18]

> 'Ours has been described as the machine age,' remarked Gandhi, 'because the machine dominates our economy. What is a machine? One may ask. In a sense, man is the worst wonderful machine in creation. It can neither be duplicated nor copied.' He had, however, used the word not in its wider sense, but in the sense of an appliance that tended to displace the human or animal labour instead of supplementing it, or merely increasing its efficiency. That was the first differential characteristic of the machine. The second characteristic was that there was no limit to its growth or evolution. That could not be said of the human labour. There was a limit beyond which its capacity or mechanical efficiency could not go. Out of this circumstance arose the third characteristic of the machine. It seemed to be possessed of a will or genius of its own. Machine was antagonistic to man's labour. Thus, it tended more to displace man, one machine doing the work of hundred, if not a thousand, who went to swell the army of unemployed and underemployed, not because it was desirable, but because that was its law. In America it had perhaps reached the extreme limit. He had been opposed to it not from today, but even before 1909, when he was in South Africa surrounded by machines. Their onward march had not only not impressed him, but had repelled him.
>
> 'It then dawned upon me that to suppress and exploit the millions, the machine was the device par excellence; it had no place in man's economy, if, as social units, all men were to be equal. It is my belief that machine has not added to man's stature and it will not serve the world, but disrupt it, unless it is put in its proper place. Then I read Ruskin's *Unto This Last*. . . . I saw clearly that if mankind was to progress and to realize the idea of equality and brotherhood, it must act on the principle of *Unto This Last.*'
>
> In the machine age, this principle had no place. Under it the fittest alone survived, to the exclusion and at the cost of the weak. 'But that is not my picture of independence,

[18] *Ibid.,* pp. 210–15.

in which there is room even for the weakest,' observed Gandhi. 'That requires that we must realise all available human labour, before we entertain the idea of employing mechanical power.'

III

We have traced the development of Gandhiji's ideas on machines and on machine-civilization and found that despite many concessions to the 'proper' use of machines his values were definitely opposed to those which make for technological civilization and are made by it. By 'proper' he meant, positively, that which was prompted by love and good for humanity, and negatively, what did not lead to concentration of wealth in a few hands and inequality, to centralisation of power, to urbanisation, to unemployment, to political, economic and social exploitation. These evils, which in his view, were the characteristics of the modern society, with its American apogee, were the consequences of the large-scale use of machines, and they had to be fought with vigour. To that extent he was placing Indian (eastern) against western (Euro-American, modern) values. It was certainly not a case of revivalism, but a clear statement of a principle of social organisation which was different from the one that had succeeded in imposing itself on the strength of political suzerainty. His minimal idea was to establish coexistence of different social systems on the basis of equality, though the prophetic strain that came to him in the course of his experiments with truth led him to think that the values he propagated would also be good for the western world. We will leave it to the western sociologist to ponder over this issue. An Indian sociologist can only mention that Gandhiji's protagonism of Indian values was not an exercise or the romantic agony of nationalist historians, nor was it a reactionary, obscurantist throw-back. It is submitted here that he was a revolutionary and what a revolutionary in India should be, viz., an Indian revolutionary, that is, one who would first be steeped in Indian norms and realities and then evaluate the nature of changes in social realities in order to create fresh norms. Gandhiji did not go to the past: in fact, he was not an Indologist; he only went to the roots and the sources. And 'the deeper you go to the root the more radical you become.'

At this stage, it will be relevant to note the revolutionary elements in his views. Their importance arises from the problem before us—viz. that we here must consider the conditions under which technological change can take place without causing the various tensions and frustrations which bring about aggression, violence and war, and which lead to mental unhealth. In other words, we must ask ourselves whether technology should always depend upon wants and their increase and bring about a state of culture in which material wants are the king. The inner significance of Gandhiji's concessions to the use of machines, that is to say, the logical meaning of the term 'proper' use, is that they do not, and need not, go together. It is perfectly possible, in Gandhiji's opinion; and it is also logical to assume, under stated conditions, that technology can be introduced into India without upsetting the Indian pattern of values. These conditions are non-possession, *aparigraha,* the 'oceanic' constitution of Indian independence in terms of self-sufficient villages with their group-existence fulfilled through the panchayats, bread-labour, *sharir-srama,* with its concomitant of the dignity of labour symbolized in khadi, *sarvodaya,* that is, total awakening or uplift, and of course, non-violence and truth, that is *satyagraha.* Of these, *aparigraha,* non-possession, or wantlessness and *srama* or labour, alone are selected for discussion. (Gandhiji would have emphasised truth). Now, non-possession in the context of human history has been an individual value, and at best, an 'ideal' value for the elite-group, known as the Brahmin caste, to be perpetually practised by it. Others practised it, but the Brahmin was the specialist. Gandhiji would institutionalise it in the State that would own, and not possess it for greed or profit. To this extent he was a socialist,—or even a Communist as he called himself before Mr. Louis Fischer[14]—but with this difference that his socialism did not grow out of industrial civilization, technological values, class-conflict, or according to the operations of the laws of dialectics. (That it could only be social expression of truth; non-violence and faith in God, is important, but not relevant to our selected purpose). It was to grow out of agriculture, cottage industries, and 'oceanic' rural organisation, into a non-possessive state which would be wedded to public good and be a guarantee of non-exploitation by large machinery in the hands of the rich. Meanwhile, Gandhiji would

[14] *Ibid.*, p. 190.

ask the rich and the fortunate few to hold their fortunes in trusteeship, practising *aparigraha* themselves. Trusteeship, however, for Gandhiji, was an interim measure sanctioned by Indian traditions. A second revolutionary element in Gandhiji's prescription is the concept of *srama* or manual work. So far as this writer knows, *srama* or the value of the dignity of labour, was not quite an Indian value. In a hierarchical society, types of work are defined and relegated to different strata on the two assumptions: (1) that spiritual 'work,' that is, pure contemplation, is the highest type; and (2) that each stratum, or caste, which is fixed by birth, has its own '*swadharma*' ('bond,' 'religion'), the practice of which means fulfilment of personality, and the departure of which means 'destruction' of self. But Gandhiji had a different conception of labour. He writes:[15]

> The law, that to live man must work, first came home to me upon reading Tolstoy's writing on bread-labour. But even before that I had begun to pay homage to it after reading Ruskin's *Unto This Last. The Divine Law*, that man must earn his bread by labouring with his own hands, was first stressed by a Russian writer named T. M. Boudaref. Tolstoy advertised it and gave it wider publicity. In my view, the same principle has been set forth in the third chapter of the *Gita*, where we are told, that he who eats without offering sacrifice eats stolen food. Sacrifice here can only mean bread-labour. (A sociologist may not agree. Gandhiji was at best Indianising a foreign conception). Reason too leads us to an identical conclusion. How can a man, who does not do body-labour, have the right to eat? 'In the sweat of the brow shalt thou eat thy bread,' says the Bible.... And invidious distinctions of rank would be abolished, when every one without exception acknowledged the obligation of bread-labour. There is a world-wide conflict between capital and labour, and the poor envy the rich. If all worked for their bread, distinctions of rank would be obliterated; the rich would still be there, but they would deem themselves only trustees of their property, and would use it mainly in the public interest. The ideal body-labour is agriculture, but the next best would be spinning, weaving, carpentry and smithery; and the logical, common body-labour is scavenging.... Scavenging, thus intelligently taken up, will help one to a true appreciation of the equality of man.

[15] *Yervada Mandir*, Ch. IX.

Surely, this is not the Indian value. The dissociation of body-labour from mental and spiritual labour has had a long history, which Gandhiji did not take into account. His attitude towards what is known as the caste-system cannot be discussed here. But on this matter of bread-labour bringing about economic equality, he was anti-caste and, therefore, a revolutionary, almost a socialist. In other words, if the socialist gave up the usual western assumption, viz., no high technology, no socialism, and remained content with the use of certain special types of machinery, which would not displace labour, or exploit human beings for greed, or concentrate power, etc., then Gandhiji would bless him. If further, the socialist accepted this idea of bread-labour and would build on the revolutionary content of this view, viz., the ending of the separation of physical labour, now the only duty of a whole class of people who form the majority, from mental labour, now the monopoly of the few, then the difference between him and Gandhiji would not exist except in the matter of wantlessness. One could argue here that there was a danger in this concept of bread-labour, viz., the possibility of lowering the impulse and the level of intellectual work by making the intellectual workers work physically for bread without raising the intellectual level and stimulating the impulse of physical workers. But Gandhiji would reply that it could be averted.

Thus the Gandhian conclusion in regard to machines and technology is logical if one accepts the postulates that (a) India has a separate norm of values with the hidden assumption that values determine conduct, that (b) she has a separate principle of social organisation which would be disturbed, and even destroyed, by large-scale use of machinery for greed and profit, that (c) a proper use would presuppose certain requisite attitudes, some traditional and others not, but all working in alliance, and also that (d) a type of state would own and control large machineries, if they were indispensable for defined purposes. Otherwise, the machineries to be used would be of a special type suitable for removing the drudgery of handicraft and improving its quality. They would operate in the general context of decentralised economy, in close alliance with agriculture. Gandhiji would thus remove the stings of capitalism and socialism alike.

In this author's opinion, Gandhiji's views have to be carefully studied before any scheme of technical assistance and large-scale technological development is initiated. While it is very true that among certain strata and sections of the Indian people these views appear strange, even though lip service and homage is paid to them, and that such sections and strata would want and initiate rapid technological change in the name of economic advance, evolution and progress, of historical forces of the modern age, it is also clear that an unintelligent injection of technology would so disturb the existing social pattern of human relations that work would cease to be associated with joy and workmanship, that skill would be replaced by efficiency, that 'the public identity of the job' would be lost, that scientific management and discipline would squeeze the labourer of all humaneness, and that a new instrument of social power would 'teach docility' or 'break the intransigence of workers,' all the time keeping greed, profit and more profit in the background, beyond the sight of those who are to be immediately benefited by higher wages, better conditions of living, welfare measures and the like.[16] In other words, the sociologist would do well to study the sociology of the demand for, and may one add, the sociology of the *supply* of technology to India. Fortunately, the Indian masses are not yet fully taken in by the technological values. They are being acted upon by technology, and they are showing healthy, normal reactions to the injection by absenteeism, inattentiveness, a sort of lackadaisical attitude towards work in the factories, unpunctuality, the so-called absence of pride in work and workmanship, but unfortunately, quite often in accidents and ill-health. Even strikes, which are bemoaned as symptoms of industrial conflict, can be traced to the search of the soil-bound peasantry of India for mental and social peace in holiday, away from the scene of work, the din of factories and technology, to the villages where the pattern which they know and instinctively feel to be right, rules even today. An Indian sociologist cannot thus help questioning the manner and the possible hidden motivations of a technological advance of those who want it and those who supply it. He can at least categorically state, with Gandhiji, that if change is inevitable, let it come in the shape of certain types of machines, at the proper time, in the proper context; and that if large-scale use of machinery is unavoidable, let it be owned and managed by the state, a new form of state. Judging from experience, he

[16] Cf. R. K. Merton, *Social Theory and Social Structure*, pp. 319-22.

cannot share Gandhiji's hope of an interim trusteeship by the fortunate few. In short, the whole problem of technological advance in India, which, let it be repeated, is undeveloped only in the purely technological sense, and, therefore, in the sense of being more socially integrated and less fragmentised, has to be studied from the points of view of both the types of machinery to be introduced and of the types of people who would accept them, with due regard to the motivations of introduction. In India, human beings are not yet atomistically individuated so that no functional specification in the most common productive processes is possible. Nor has it occurred in many industries. In India, no productive section of society is 'universalistic'; that is, only very few 'criteria possibly present in any segment of the population without regard to previous social relationships or membership in irrelevant groups' are available. In India, human relations are affective rather than rational and impersonal.[17] The normative system suitable for the industrial mode of production through large-scale use of machines is thus not the normative system of India. A matter of additional importance is the fact that this normative system has combined with nationalism, anti-imperialism, and Gandhiji's interpretation of independence, to convince some people that it is still valuable. So change must take account of these facts in order not to produce the same evil to which the west has been an heir.

[17] See Moore in *International Social Science Bulletin,* Vol. IV, No. 2 (1952).

11. *Indian Tradition and Social Change*

THERE ARE OTHERS WHO ARE BETTER, AND BETTER KNOWN, sociologists and more devoted to their field of study than I am. Sociology was not my first love, nor have I been its constant lover. I had come to it because, being interested in developing my personality through knowledge, I realised that none of the social or the natural sciences I had to study in my earlier days, could give me, at one and the same time, the synoptic view, the large vision and the understanding of the milieu of knowledge which were necessary for the fulfilment of my being. It has all been a personal affair, not a matter of sociology for the sake of sociology.

Not only that: soon after I began to think for myself it was also borne in upon me that I was an Indian, that I could not but be an Indian, that I could develop my personality only by understanding Indian culture. And Indian culture I found to be essentially social. I also felt that the Indian history I knew was merely political history, that the Indian economics and politics I studied were detached from the context of Indian institutions, and further, that the western metaphysics in which I became interested in the process of my social studies, did not suit my modes of thinking, feeling and being. My mind worked in this way: India might or might not have had history in the western sense of the term; of politics, again in that sense, India had had little experience—she was becoming political only recently; her economics had been 'unproductive' and subsistential; and her metaphysics, again in the western sense, was poor. Positively, my conviction grew that India had had society, and very little else. In fact, she had too much of it. Her history, her economics and even her philosophy, I realised, had always centred in social groups, and at best, in socialised persons. Yet, this elementary fact was missing from the books I read. The scholars were competent in their own fields, but because of the indifference to that solar fact of Indian culture, viz., its rootedness in the social realities which made up India's social system of action, their work appeared to be narrow, circumscribed, fragmented and partial in outlook and treatment. I could not appreciate this type of closed scholarship, its unrealism and its complacency. At the same time, their profession was mine, and with my limited talents, I could not do anything about it.

Sociology showed me the way out. This does not mean that for me sociology is the final science. Perhaps, some day I shall realise that sociology too is not enough for me, unless it is differently orientated. Please pardon me for this personal note. My main purpose is to tell you frankly that I am not a sociologist as sociologists would like me to be. So I guess that deep below my acceptability to the conveners of the conference flows the common feeling that knowing is more important than knowledge, that living comprehends knowing, that for an Indian, this business of living, despite India's increasing involvement in the world, is primarily Indian living which, in its turn, is essentially social living, that is, living in groups through stages of growth, until one is to be so socialised that freedom will have become co-terminous with existence and institutions turned into agencies of growth.

This autobiographical beginning lays down certain basic postulates of sociology as I have been growing to understand it, and naturally, as I would like to see it develop in India. Sociology has a floor and a ceiling, like any other science; but its speciality consists in its floor being the ground-floor of all types of social disciplines, and in its ceiling remaining open to the sky. Neglect of the social base often leads to arid abstractions, as in recent economics. On the other hand, much of empirical research in anthropology and in psychology has been rendered futile because its fields have so far been kept covered. Yet within this mansion of sociology the different social disciplines live. In so far as they live on the same floor they are bound to come into conflict with each other in the name of autonomy. To pursue the analogy, they seek to divide the house and close the door against each other. But a stage comes when exclusiveness ceases to pay. Such a stage seems to have been reached by nearly all the social sciences.

So the restless spirits among the social scientists are trying to discover interrelations, and the bolder ones among them are building up systems. Much heart-searching is going on among them today to attain to some form of unity in diversity. I do not mean that the barriers have been demolished, or that the unity has been established. But the dissatisfaction is divine. This development in the social sciences is illustrated by the search for (a) some basic, neutral and lowest common multiple concepts, e.g., human group, status, mobility, solidarity or cohesion, sympathy, conflict, cooperation, community, etc., in sociology; propensity, welfare, preference, indifference in economics; power and again welfare, in politics; (b) some common methodological principles derived from modern refinements of logic: (c) reorientations and ways of interrelations, or cross-breedings; and (d) a philosophical approach. Each type of search has its own merits and demerits, and it is the duty of a trained mind to avoid the pitfalls associated with the method adopted. The popularity of a method is often dependent on academic fashion.

The philosophical approach is at present out of court. The large sale of Toynbee's works is indicative of religious frustration rather than of a mounting philosophical temper. In certain American universities, and also under the auspices of the UNESCO, a genuine effort is being made towards discovering the interrelations of the social sciences. Even there, the logical approach as such is not much cultivated, because it is generally considered to be futile. It seems that the debate between the logic of the natural and the logic of the social sciences continues without coming to any conclusion which could be useful either for research or for policy. The effort is thus mainly directed towards bringing the experiences and techniques of different social disciplines to bear upon relatively small, concrete, specific problems. Recently, the Indian government, through its education ministry, has drawn our attention to this aspect of the matter.

There are numerous difficulties in the way of making the effort a success at once. All social disciplines are not of the same level; experts are not always used to team-work; and each discipline is apt to build vested interests round a department inside a faculty. Requisite personnel who can rise above specialist interests are also rare. But, in my opinion, the real difficulty comes from the growing indifference to theory. When I say theory I do not mean 'an isolated proposition, summarising observed uniformities of relationships between two or more variables,' however useful and precise the establishment of such a proposition may be; I mean by theory another type of generalisation which logically hangs together, from which 'statements of invariance' can be derived, and into which the type of isolated propositions mentioned above can be logically fitted. Most modern sociologists are averse to such theory and are content with isolated propositions between two or more variables. In this they find the statistical apparatus very handy. The exceptions, like Max Weber, von Wiese, Karl Mannheim, Becker, T. Parsons, and Merton, are not content with isolated propositions. One could, of course, dismiss them as Teutonic.

But I must confess that an Indian sociologist finds 'theory' congenial to his temperament and traditions. I also suspect that in the course of its 'flight from philosophy', which is almost always used pejoratively in these days, scientific social research has been hopelessly dispersed. As an Indian, I find it impossible to discover any life-meaning in the jungle of the so-called empirical social research monographs. While statistics seek to give some sort of precision in trends, precision becomes non-significant in the absence of any theory and direction. In India, the danger arising out of the aversion from 'philosophy' is much less than in Europe or the USA, though I am not sure how long it will remain so under the high-powered pressure of modern academic fashion. Therefore, I would like to think that if Indian sociologists really tried, they could materially contribute to this vexed question of interrelationships of the social sciences.

Indian sociologists would not be true to their temperament in feeling apologetic for their pre-disposition to theory, or, philosophy, as it is loosely called. If they are sure of their ground, which is offered by social traditions in the main, and if they still retain the traditional gift of logic and theory, they may soon be doing things to which the restless and the bold spirits among the western sociologists are aspiring today. In the social disciplines at least, the knowledge of traditions shows the way to break them with the least social cost, if that is necessary or inevitable. We Indians have the advantage of being pre-scientific in our thought, just as we have that of backwardness in our economy. We need not traverse the whole path of western evolution, step by step, of knowledge and economy. It is uneconomical to reject theory in the name of science and then come back to it when science has failed to produce a synoptic view and generate understanding.

The first task for us, therefore, is to study the social traditions to which we have been born and in which we have had our being. This task includes the study of the changes in traditions by internal and external pressures. The latter are mostly economic, and we know what they are. But the way in which the economic pressures work is not that of a mechanical force moving dead matter. Traditions have great powers of resistance and absorption. Unless the economic force is extraordinarily strong—and it is that strong only when the modes of production are altered, traditions survive by adjustments. The capacity for adjustment is the measure of the vitality of traditions. One can have a full measure of this vitality only by immediate experience. Thus it is that I give top priority to the understanding (in Dilthey's sense) of traditions even for the study of their changes. In other words, the study of Indian traditions, which, in my view, is the first and immediate duty of the Indian sociologist, should precede the socialist interpretations of changes in the Indian traditions in terms of economic forces.

It has been held that participation, not to speak of lifelong participation, is the enemy of 'scientific detachment.' I know how our scholars are taken in by that mysterious phrase. *Nishkam* will not do for them, oh no! But weighing the two in the balance, viz., the advantage of insight that comes from participation and that of being in the swing and being internationally recognised as scholars in accordance with a supposedly common standard of 'scientific' technique, I find it tilting on behalf of insight. In any case, participation by long conditioning, which is the first requisite of understanding, should make it less possible to pass on the most jejune and vapid generalisations about Indian problems with which we are being familiarised today in the name of scientific research. I do not in the least suggest that foreign scholars should be barred out of Indian problems, but I am only referring to the greater ease of insight and understanding that can be secured by the sociologist when he is saturated in his own traditions. His capacity to judge is a matter of acquired discipline, but in the matter of understanding, empathy precedes sympathy.

Thus it is that it is not enough for the Indian sociologist to be a sociologist. He must be an Indian first, that is, he is to share in the folk-ways, mores, customs and traditions for the purpose of understanding his social system and what lies beneath it and beyond it. He should be steeped in the Indian lore, both high and low. For the high ones Sanskrit is essential, and for the low ones the local dialects. Anthropologists and ethnologists try to pick up the latter, and sometimes succeed in doing so. Yet the spirit is often missing and the letters alone abide. I do not think that many social scientists operating on Indian problems today know Sanskrit; and none care for Persian or Arabic. This state of affairs is deplorable. Unless sociological training in India is grounded on Sanskrit, or any such language in which the traditions have been embodied as symbols, social research in India will be a pale imitation of what others are doing. It pains me to observe how our Indian scholars succumb to the lure of modern 'scientific' techniques imported from outside as a part of technical aid and 'know-how,' without resistance and dignity. In the intellectual transactions which are taking place, it seems that we have no terms to offer, no ground to stand upon.

You will pardon me if I unfold my mind a little more on this vital matter. I am not equating sociology with the cultural anthropology of the modern man. So long as the generalised relationship between culture and social structure is not more clearly understood, that equation does not hold. With Parsons I maintain that 'a "system of culture" is a different order of abstraction from a "social system" though it is to a large degree abstraction from the same concrete phenomena.' My interest is merely to bring to the urgent notice of fellow sociologists only two major points: (a) the common concrete phenomena of which both the social system and the culture are 'abstractions' are the subject matter of sociology; and (b) in so far as the Indian society is concerned, those common concrete phenomena had best be studied through group-action and group-traditions.

This is not the occasion for an elaborate thesis. I can only offer a few hints of the way my mind has been moving towards that conclusion. I have a feeling that the frame of reference, which is the first requisite of a theory, is not the 'actor-situation,' as Parsons would have it, for the simple reason that the unit of the Indian social system is *not* 'the individual as actor, as an entity which has the basic characteristics of striving toward the attainment of "goals," of "reacting" emotionally or affectively toward objects and events and of to a greater or less degree, cognitively knowing or understanding his situation, his goals and himself.'

Action for the Indian is not individualistic in that sense; it is 'inherently structured on a normative, teleological,' but *not* on a 'voluntaristic system of coordinates or axes,' with the result that the failure to attain it does not lead to 'frustration.' The Indian has no such fear of loneliness. We too have our axes in *purushartha*, but the operational system seldom permits any 'voluntarism' on the ground of individual desires. The individual, if such a term is permissible in the Indian context, no doubt, desires to protest against the system of action traditionally prescribed for the attainment of his desires. But the common Indian 'individual's' pattern of desires is more or less rigidly fixed by his socio-cultural group-pattern, and he hardly deviates from it except under severe economic duress.

Protestants there have been many in our history, but very, very few of them have abjured the wider group-traditions. Every saint has sought to prove that he is in the line of great masters —*purvasuri, acharya.* This accounts for the curious fact that each one of the thousand and one sects has dissented only to come back to the fold within about three generations contributing its own special technique of normative, teleological, goal-seeking patterns of behaviour to the broad, general stream of the Indian design. In this sense, India's religion is the traditional way of living; so is her culture. Hence her social system is basically a normative orientation of group, sect, or caste-action, but not of 'voluntaristic' individual action. So there is no escape from traditions if you are an Indian, and additionally, an Indian sociologist. I make little difference between the Hindu and the Muslim, the Christian and the Buddhist in this matter.

Of course, 'voluntarism' is coming up, particularly among the middle classes in the cities, towns and their fringes. But they form an interesting special study for the Indian sociologist. They are vocally important, but if you watch their behaviour closely, you will find that their anti-traditional individualism is also developing a tradition of its own, a tradition of revolt which tends to become a little boring. In my view, the real reason why we have not done more than what we have done through planning—and we have done none too badly—is the yet unresolved conflict between the traditions which are the principle of *dhriti*, that is, *dharma*, that which holds, maintains and continues, and the new traditions which the urban middle class have been trying to build up in the last hundred years or so. Bureaucracy is not the villain of the piece.

The sociologist would look at it from the point of view of the growth of traditions through conflict. Be that as it may, the absence of voluntaristic action has done Indian society one good at least. Excluding the middle classes, if you will, the absence of frustration that leads to all manner of psychoses is a remarkable phenomenon of Indian life. The poise of the Indian peasant and the head of the family is there for all to see. Perhaps it is on the low 'level of aspirations,' as the psychologist would call it, but the point is that the level is still being governed by traditions which set the level of culture and values for most Indians. This should not be missed in our urge for uplifting the level of wants.

One point I want to make here in passing. It will be said that if the group is still the unit of action, aspiration and orientation, normative, affective and cognitive alike, then the Indian social life is the life of bees and beavers, regimented, totalitarian, in fact, almost communistic. I almost accept that argument. We are a very regimented people, but the beauty of it is that barring a stratum of people who repeat 'individual values,' 'freedom,' 'cultural freedom,' like parrots, or who have become morbid by their very un-Indianness, the majority of us do *not* feel regimented. In fact, quite a number of honest and true men have felt free, and they are not fellow-travellers either. They are men like Sri Aurobindo, Ramana Maharashi, Ramakrishna, Dayanand, not to go further back. And not all Indian women either; it is they who count most do not always feel, as an eminent politician put it, 'oppressed, suppressed, repressed and depressed.'

Our conception of freedom is different, because our conception of man is *purusha* and *not* the individual, or *vyakti*. I wonder how many times the word *vyakti* occurs in our religious texts or in the sayings of the saints. This, however, would be a small point if the whole paraphernalia of modern communications were not trained on us to make us belong to a 'free' society of individuals each exercising his right of choice despite advertisements, press-chains, chain stores, and empty purse too, which, you must admit, does not leave much scope for 'consumer's sovereignty.'

The Indian sociologist thus, I am afraid, will have to accept the group as his unit and reject the individual. He should, however, launch on his career with open eyes. If science deals with facts and with nothing else, then he cannot be a 'scientist'; if, similarly, history is the study of facts and hardly anything else, then he cannot be a historian of social change either. In other words, he will have to brave the brave new scientific world and be unpopular. Tradition, which will be his central theme, is not a fact; it is a forgotten fact. As it has been aptly said, 'In fact it is generally when the tradition is no longer a description of an actual fact and when it has become somewhat evanescent as a rule of conduct that it most clearly justifies its name and performs its real functions.' Strictly speaking, the study of traditions need not be unscientific, at least, in the modern sense of science which has trade and traffic with quite a number of 'somewhat evanescent' things. In the mid-passage of this century, it is a little out of date to dismiss that rather vague world of fact and values, norms and symbols, as outside the pale of closely logical scrutiny, which, after all, is all that matters.

About the study of traditions being non-historical, it should be enough to remember that tradition comes from the root 'tradere,' which means to transmit. The Sanskrit equivalent of tradition is either *parampara*, that is, succession, or *aitihya*, which has the same root as *itihas*, or history. Traditions are supposed to have emanated from a source, which may be scriptures, sages (*apta vakya*), mythical heroes with or without names. Whatever may be the source, the 'historicity' of traditions is recognised by most people. They are quoted, recalled, esteemed; in fact, their age-long succession becomes an assurance of value which has already accrued in the process of its instrumental functioning as a constituent of social cohesion or social solidarity.

In Roman law, 'traders' also signifies safe keeping and deposit of something precious; and so it involves confidence-worthy persons whose normal and legal duty is to preserve the precious thing intact. The Sanskrit equivalents of each term used above will at once occur to us all. The persons are either the Brahmins, or the *sampradaya*, which is the corporate custodian; the succession is by birth, or initiation; the preciousness is of the order of sacredness; and the methods of keeping the traditions intact are correct speech, or pronunciation of sacred texts, psychological fixations to maintain the social structure and vice versa, mainly by the caste-system with the custodians on top.

In short, the chain of traditions, *sampradaya parampara*, has been the true historicity of the Indian social system so far. Through the normative system thus evolved has the continuity of the Indian social system been maintained so long. As I have no time to go further into this question, I can only mention that both sound and sight have been harnessed for this work of tradition-conservation. The role of sound is best manifest in *Om,* and *nama japa,* while that of sight is in the images, or *deva-rupa.* The two are combined in the idea that the sage is the seer of *mantram,* which is to be repeated for one's own hearing and imparted only to the initiate. In India, the highest value has been given to rectitude, which is correct pronunciation, correct technique, correct initiation, correct conduct and correct meditation. The overtone of the word *rt* is rectitude. No wonder that the style of writing and the style of behaviour are both called *riti.*

One easy conclusion from the above is likely to be the idea that tradition is nothing but the act of conserving, hence conservative. But that conclusion will be wrong, as I have hinted before. Traditions do change. I am excluding the external factors of change in this address. Among the endogenous ones also, I am not taking into account the class-relations, and for two reasons; (a) in our society class conflict has so long been smoothed and covered by caste-traditions and the new class-relations have not yet sharply emerged; and (b) we are more or less ignorant of the socio-economic history of India. (Here lies a fertile field of study in the interrelations of social sciences.)

In India, a full account of the subtle methods of the internal, non-economic changes would thus be the immediate occupation of dynamic sociology. I guess that it would probably be an object-lesson to those who are legitimately proud of having produced revolutions by consent and without much blood-shed, by the democratic procedure of parliamentary government. So far as I have been able to find out, three principles of change are recognised in our traditions, *sruti, smriti* and *anubhava.* It is *anubhava* or personal experience, which is the revolutionary principle. Certain *Upanishads* are almost entirely based on it. But the matter did not end there.

Personal experience was no doubt the root, but it soon flowered into collective experience. The entire history of collective dissent throughout the Middle Ages down to modern times, proclaims the supremacy of generalised *anubhava* as the principle of change. If we care to know the origins of the numerous sects, *panths,* we find that their saint-founders started with their own experience, had little or no account with rituals, temples and priests, spoke in dialects, and *not* in Sanskrit, to the lower classes and castes, gave an equal status to the women and preached the doctrine of love, *prem* and *sahaj,* spontaneity, which came like a tidal wave flooding the soil and leaving a rich deposit on the banks of time and tradition. The high traditions were predominantly intellectual and centred in *smriti* and *sruti* where the principle of change was supplied by dialectical exegesis. We find more or less the same process among the Indian Muslims. The *sufis* among them have always laid great stress on love and experience. I think, reason, in the western sense, has not been the highest category with us. *Nyaya,* or dialectical skill, was no doubt exercised with extraordinary subtlety, but it will be improper to say that discursive reason, *buddhi-vichar,* has been historically superior to *anubhava,* experience, or love, *prem,* as an agency of change of traditions.

Rationality has not had much chance in our social system except through philosophical speculation and the rules of exegesis. Interpretations have sometimes sabotaged traditions, but in almost every case, the interpreters seem to have fought shy of the implications of their deeds. Even Sankara, whose philosophy dismisses life and the social system once and for all, puts it within the ambit of Vedic traditions. So when the high and the low intellectual traditions, to use Turner's phrase, had a chance of coming into conflict, they were comprehended and brought together within some abstract modes of thought and feeling. Here the well-established elite-group reasserted its power and all the revolutionary experimental urges were sucked into its orbit of influence. Tradition was victorious once again.

Indian social action has so far proceeded in that fashion. It has given latitude to rebel within the limits of the constitution. An excellent example of squaring tradition with experimental ardour indeed! The result has been a caste-society, a society that has prevented the formation of classes and burked all forms of class-consciousness *without* the religion of 'free enterprise.' You may like it or dislike it, but there it is. My information is that in most Indian elections class-consciousness is often sumberged by caste-feeling.

I have so far followed Turner's simple classification of traditions into high and low. But one could, on the basis of the argument carried thus far, come close to what Gurvitch has called the 'depth analysis' of social reality. This analysis starts from the surface, goes down the various levels of traditions and traditional lore to the deepest level of spritual values and their collective, immediate and integral experience, involving spritual and sense data alike. Even on the surface of human geography and demographic pattern, traditions have a role to play in the transfiguration of physical adjustments and biological urges. In India, for example, things like city-planning and family-planning are so bound up with traditions that the architect and the social reformer can ignore them only at the peril of their pet schemes. Lower down are the organised and the unorganised superstructures operating through rituals, *achar*, *kria*, which consolidate collective behaviour and give it style.

Here, usually, the dynamic element of traditions stops for most Indians. But if the social symbols, which are really and truly 'presences,' hiding and seeking, revealing by concealing and concealing by revealing both the spiritual and the social reality, render these rituals active—and in my experience they do it for many Indians—then the dynamics may proceed. Now begins the creative aspect of symbols. Symbols are neither signs, nor expressions, nor appearances of certain things. They are the things themselves. Symbols have no syntax; they have no subject, object, predicate, and no preposition. Of course, there are symbols and symbols, some of them social and others not so social:

> Social symbols are inadequate expressions of the spiritual realm adapted to concrete social situations, to typical social structures, and to definite collective mentalities, in which different aspects of the spirit realize themselves and by which it is grasped. Social symbols are thus simultaneously conditioned by social reality and the spirit which realises itself therein: they vary in function to this spirit. That is why symbols are at one and the same time products and producers of social reality and why they are the principal object of the sociology of the human spirit.

Most of you, like me, will react sharply against this kind of mystical jargon and say that sociology came out of this mumbo-jumbo long ago. And you will be right. But we will be very wrong if we miss the meaning of it in our dislike of the terms. That meaning is simple: the study of sociology is principally the study of traditions; the study of traditions, in the ultimate analysis, involves that of symbols which, under certain conditions and on particular levels, are explosively creative and dynamic; and, therefore, the values and norms retain and enrich their noetic connection with specific social structures and concrete historical situations. All this is very relevant to Indian conditions.

In my view, the genuine relation of the social sciences to each other is ultimately established through the understanding of the different levels and layers of the way the person works in, through, and out of society. Gurvitch, as you know, calls it depth-sociology on the lines of depth-psychology. An Indian who thinks of *patal* down below would like to give it another name. Whatever that name is, the descent to the deeps and the ascent to the heights are relative activities. The point is this: sociology should *ultimately* show the way out of the social system by analysing the processes of transformation. And, I think, the Indian society and the Indian sociology—all our *shastras* are sociological—both do it excellently, but in the limited sphere of non-economic endogenous group-action.

As a corollary, I may state that as different philosophical systems of India mark the different stages of the spiritual growth of people and men, so the different social disciplines appear to the Indian person as rings of the tree of life, which for him, has its roots up above, with no Ygdrasil to burrow from below. Sciences have begun to disagree since the western society began to disintegrate. The Indian society too is changing, but without much disintegration. This is an advantage for the Indian sociologist. So, naturally, Indian sociology, for yet some more time to come, cannot but be interpretative with greater dependence upon the method of insight that comes from active participation in the Indian system of social action than was permitted by nineteenth century science. Investigation will always be there, but it will have to be investigation into the spirit of things observed, that is to say, symbols. Other investigations are necessary, but subsidiary.

If this address were to be delivered a few years ago my emphasis on the need of the study of traditions would have been much less sharp. Meanwhile, I have seen how our progressive groups have failed in the field of intellect, and hence also in economic and political action, chiefly on account of their ignorance of and unrootedness in India's social reality.

Besides, the study of traditions by dependent people could degenerate into an argument for traditionalism via the need for self-respect and national vanity. For a free young people who are apt to get groggy with the fumes of progress, however, the study of their own traditions may be a guarantee of steady and balanced growth. Revolution is often a leap, but after every leap one must stand steady and sane. And there is plenty of room for sanity in this mad world.

Even if one chooses to take sanity on the stride, is it not true that the deeper down you go to the roots the more radical you become? That saying of Marx is good enough for me in this context. And if Marx is considered backdatish along with Marxism, I shall go further back in history to be up-to-date, to Cato, whose approval was for all lost causes. But is the cause of spirit, which functions in the context of traditions, really a lost cause? Is the method of insight an altogether decadent, futile method? Is interpretation useless in modern human knowledge? I do not quite know. If it is not, then Indian sociologists should take courage in both hands and openly say that the study of the Indian social system, in so far as it has been functioning till now, requires a different approach to sociology because of its special traditions, its special symbols and its special patterns of culture and social actions. The impact of economic and technological changes on Indian traditions, culture and symbol, follows thereafter. In my view, the thing changing is more real and objective than change per se.

12. *The Intellectuals in India*

So far as is known to this author no systematic treatise or research monograph exists on the evolution, status and functions of the intellectual elite groups of India on the basis of which any scientific generalisation for the purpose of comparative study could be made without damage to academic conscience. While it is true that the rights and duties of an ideal type of the Brahmins (and also in part of the Kshatriyas, who together formed the elite group of early India) have been written down for the benefit of the rest, one has to depend upon the logic of attenuated inference to have a view of the manner in which that extraordinary intellectual group continued to function throughout the ages down to the period when India really began to feel the impact of the West. All that one might say is that the realities did not always conform to the ideal type of the Brahmin busy in the performance of graded duties keeping identity with the Brahman as the goal. At the same time, the persistence of the type acted as a genuine social force against the social disintegration that comes from the destruction of elite. Generally speaking, the two processes of withdrawal and rally in the face of strong and receding pressures are noticeable. The secret of the perpetual hold of the 'ideal type' from the point of view of sociology lay in the gift of compromise and the powers of assimilation which the upholders of tradition possessed in ample measure. Through interpretations of texts, even of completely heterodox ideologies, the obduracy of social realities was respected keeping the status of the interpreters intact. A wider flexibility operated in the matter of adjustments to local customs than in the field of ideas. Here too the Brahmin elite maintained its prestige, but through a shift in its functions to priestly activities. The story of the Brahmins keeping themselves distinct from the affairs of the state and of the world is not true. Yet there was no complete involvement for them. Opinions may differ about the degrees of attachment, but the persistent idea that the ideal virtues consist in detachment helped in the persistence of the qualities associated with an elite, viz., the social and psychological distance, the uniqueness of recognised functions and the prestige in the due discharge thereof. This state of affairs was the rule the other day. Under the impact of Islam and Islamic rule the status and the functions of the Brahmins did not materially change anywhere except in the courtly centres. There too the Brahmin was respected for his trade and traffic with the powers beyond the earth, the omens and the stars. The history of India in the Muslim period is replete with instances of the Brahmin hegemony in certain spheres. In the villages, it was as complete as ever, if not more so because of the fact that Hindu way of life had to be defended against the corrosive influences of the courts and cities. Serious challenges to the Brahminical elite came from the saints and founders of unorthodox sects. But their subsequent history shows how the position and prestige of the Brahmins survived. The Brahmins led the counter-revolution against revolutionary doctrines of *Bhakti* and *Prem* (devotion and love). If anything, the well-known rigidity of Hindu social system was the result of this counter-reformation, one of the incidental results of which was the strengthening of the position of the Brahmin in the social hierarchy.

One of the curiosities of history is the fact that while the shock of such strong ideological pressures as Buddhism and Islam was absorbed with no basic changes in the status, structure and functioning of the intellectual elite in particular and the Indian society in general, the influence of the West, which percolated into India through channels other than the ideological, shook the Indian elite to its very foundations. If *post facto* explanations are permissible, the only plausible reason was the gradual decay in the vitality of the Hindu society, on the one hand, and the totally different type of culture it had to face by the end of the eighteenth century, on the other. So when Raja Rammohun Roy accepted English education, it was in a sense a confession of the defeat of the old elite. There was no doubt a reaction to it; even a series of sincere attempts at synthesis were made. Yet the various revivalist movements of the nineteenth century did not possess the ardour and the appeal of the earlier ones; nor did the syntheses have the integrity of their medieval counterparts. They, however, performed the necessary task of keeping Indian culture from slipping out of the rails—a danger which Japan, for example, was facing at that time—although they could not change the direction which had been set by the West. Since then there has been no turning back for the elite.

The West has changed the axis of Indian culture as it had moved so far. This has been done, among other ways, by the creation of a new 'class,' the 'middle class,' who differ from the industrial bourgeoisie by being 'non-productive', and from the earlier Indian bourgeoisie, by being 'non-commercial.' They belong to the limited number of liberal professions thrown open to the English educated Indians by the British government. The complaint of these gentlemen against the British rule was chiefly centred in the limited opportunities for higher government services and in trade and commerce. Industry was at the periphery. As days passed, the nature of the foreign rule was divulged and its economic implications were slowly realised. But there was hardly a leader of note then who abjured the West in blind reaction. In fact, the new middle class, which was essentially the creation of political and administrative exigencies, accepted the Western values as symptoms of progress. These values were rationality with its corollary of science, democracy of the parliamentary type, and a special type of liberal individualism which the British had thrown up in their own country. It must be said to the credit of the new middle class that these values were sedulously learned. The learning of this new elite displayed in their writings and speeches was of a high standard. It was not in the bargain, but excellent use was made of the knowledge of English, which was the first test of the new Anglo-Indian culture. Through English flowed the stream of British thought, its history, politics and its philosophy. Science came rather late. The mixture of idealism and empiricism which characterised British thought of the nineteenth century led to the spirit of reformism. Most of the new elite were social and political reformers. Like the British, they believed in the slow processes of evolution and permeation. In scholarship, they adopted the British model with this difference that while the British pattern subtly advertised the merits and the glories of British achievement, Indian scholarship, in history, for example, and it was one of the first branches of knowledge to be taken up by Indian scholars, was openly patriotic, as it were to make amends for the loss of respect involved in political subjection. But the real achievement was in literature. Throughout the period creative literary activity was brisk. All the modern Indian languages earned new leases of life from their contact with English literature. Both form and content came from the West. This author can speak with a certain amount of confidence with one Indian language, which is his mother tongue, viz., Bengali. Bengali literature as it is known today is shot through with Western ideas and values. Creative literature, however, was not the only literary activity. Journalism was an important literary vocation. The elite were all writers for the press. This extraordinary urge of self expression has been described as a renaissance. The point to be noted here is that as the expression, when it was not in English, was through a language which had been processed in English, the self remained divided. There was no severance, nor was there a complete integration except with some rare individuals. Nehru writes only in English, and he has said that he belongs to two worlds. In this matter of divided loyalty to values and temperament, he is only a typically Indian intellectual. That explains a good deal of his appeal to the Indian middle class. Does it seem that divided personality can be a good working hypothesis for creative work? At any rate, it gives time to think, feel and act.

The present day Indian owes a deep debt to this new elite. As there is a chance of counting the beginning date of modern India from the advent of Gandhiji in the Indian field, it is good to remember the linkages. At the same time, the deficiencies of the new elite should not be ignored, if not for anything else, at least for the fact that they still cling to most Indian intellectuals, vide their opposition to Hindi as a medium of instruction on the ostensible ground of its inadequacies for international contact but essentially on account of their own total conditioning through the English language. The chief deficiency was their social and psychological distance from the people, that is to say, from those who did not know English. And as these formed more than ninety per cent of the people, the elite looked like strangers to the country. The reaction, fortunately enough, was not contempt—the feudal towards the *canaille*—but an attitude of benevolent reform which, later on, was to develop into a sort of romantic identification not dissimilar to that of the *narodniki* with the Russian *moujik*, including the necessary dose of terrorism. In fact, romanticism was built into the very mental structure of the new elite. While a part of it had been done by the

English romantic poets, another part was endogenous to the very situation of social disassociation, which is one of the breeding grounds of romanticism. The best instance of the process of further degeneration is the cloying sentimentality of much of modern Indian literature, painting and music, and most, if not all, Indian films. Sentimentality is sentiment clothed in an ill-conceived idea, the idea of reaching out to the reality that has been missed.

The second major flaw was, in a sense, a corollary of the first. As a consequence of the social and psychological distance implicit in the knowledge of English, the sap of the original culture could not ascend. This had not happened in the Muslim period. For one, Arabic/Persian and Sanskrit were more or less on par in regard to utility or dis-utility. They were both useless in all matters but a few, affairs of the state for Persian and affairs of the soul for Arabic and Sanskrit. The world of utility belonged to the derivative local languages. Both Sanskrit and Arabic/Persian had highly developed patterns of symbols and myths; and though the two did not coalesce, they had easy coexistence (The Hindi-Urdu controversy is a phenomenon under the British rule). But the relation between English, on the one hand, and Sanskrit or Arabic/Persian on the other, was one of the two levels of existence, two modes of thought, two directions altogether. So when the new elite made its choice, it meant the exclusion of Sanskrit (and later on, of Persian), and hence the prospective loss of contact with life-maintaining symbols. It took some time for Sanskrit to fade out, but the significant fact is that it did. Hardly one per cent of the best products of the university today, be they lawyers, doctors, scholars, engineers, or government servants, has had the elementary training in Sanskrit. The case of the Indian Muslim was so far slightly better. Among the legislators hardly a dozen can quote from the texts in defence of legislative changes in Hindu marriage. Of course, there are pockets of Sanskrit and Persian/Arabic learning in out of the way places. But judging from the status of *Pandits* and *Maulavis* in schools and colleges, one would say that Sanskrit and Arabic/Persian are in disorderly retreat. The costs of this state of affairs have been more or less intangible, but in the field of culture the intangible are not the insignificant. The precision of English prose could not be learnt in the way that English was taught; and in the process of learning English the rigorous precision of Sanskrit was not learnt. Much of the woolliness of modern Indian thinking and writing can be traced to the replacement of Sanskrit by English. Things might have been worse if the intellectual traditions had not, as they fortunately had, passed into the currency of popular knowledge. Even the popular beliefs, the myths, legends and folklore have stood in the way of further mischief. The contribution of the conservative and non-English knowing and often illiterate woman in putting a brake upon the rushing consequences of the displacement of the language has been really great.

There is another matter which calls for some notice in this context. The elite who owed so much to the English language and thought shared the limitations of British culture. Compared to the immediate Indian past, the horizon of that culture was broad. But compared to that of the contemporary West, it was insular and limited. There were very few Indians who were directly familiar with the main currents of contemporary European thought except those that flowed through English translations. The culture-lag between Europe and England even when England was limited but great, as she was in the nineteenth century, was a fact; that between India and England was equally so, only more patent; and hence that between India and the Continent was gaping. It was only after 1910 or thereabout that the gaps began to close. But India lost valuable time in coming to know the West. Even now, when the latest Continental books are in every drawing-room of the elite, one cannot be sure if the almost instantaneous familiarity with the latest of the West (including America) is based on any understanding of the Western values. This author has a feeling that without some saturation in Christian dogma, thought and values, particularly the Catholic ones, the total spirit of the Western civilization cannot be fully seized. One can extend this generalisation to include the Greek Orthodox Church traditions to enable one to understand the inner significance of the happenings in the area which is now put beyond the pale of Western civilization. In this sense, the English language and literature which the Indian elite learnt, the Anglo-Saxon ideas which it imbibed and the mores which it imitated through it, acted as a sort of iron curtain against the infiltrations of Continental ideas, both religious and secular. It was an item on the debit side of the British rule; culturally, it was a flaw in the act of assimilation of the elite. The Indian intellectuals were not westernized; they were only Anglicized.

Such then was the general picture of the Indian elite during the British regime. Whatever the quality of intellect of the English educated middle class as a whole, it succeeded in throwing up some very remarkable men. But strictly speaking, it was not an intellectual class, as the Brahmins or the mandarins or the clergy were. Beyond the common preoccupation with the English values there was no other cultural bond. Even the more advanced among the political section of the modern elite could hardly go beyond the British parliament and the British trade union movement, the British type of nationalisation and welfare. In the shape of middle class jobs, and to some extent occupations, it was a loosely knit interest group. Political consciousness, that is, nationalism, was a bond, but then nationalism itself was never quite an Indian value. The difference between the new elite and the remnants of the old never disappeared. They sometimes looked similar. Thus, for example, the new intermediary class of landlords or the zamindars, who mostly belonged to the upper castes, took to English education. In those regions where permanent settlement had been introduced, the process of identification was precipitated. It was very late in the day that some landlords began to invest money in business or industrial enterprises. The net result was that the ideality of the type of elite we are discussing was set by the successful government servant, lawyer, doctor, etc., that is to say, the top men of the liberal professions. The intellectuals, such as writers and professors, belonged to this group. Teachers and professors as such never formed a sociologically identifiable sub-group. Their status was the same as a whole, though the teachers, writers and speakers of English had always a superior position. The middle class had a social ranking of its own. The lower middle classes were to remain distinct until the two wars abolished the distinction by sheer economic pressure.

The first world war and the following years witnessed structural and functional changes of the elite. High prices hit the professional group badly. War demands stimulated Indian investment in new enterprises. A new industrial bourgeoisie appeared on the scene. They had been there in Bombay, in the textile industry, particularly, but they expanded their activities after the war. When after the war the spirit of nationalism was stimulated, the bourgeoisie became the national bourgeoisie. It was also the period when the labour movement came in full tide. In the meantime, Gandhiji had come to India and was feeling his way towards giving a new orientation. It is impossible to do justice to his leadership in a short space; but a few notable points relevant to our issue can be briefly mentioned. He broke the back of the preceding elite in the following manner. His ideology was entirely different from, and totally opposed to, the current one. He condemned Western civilization in toto and asked every Indian to reject it. Along with it, he abjured both terrorism and the habit of political mendicancy. And he wanted self-help and identification with the masses. He cursed college education with bell, book and candle, and called the universities slave-factories. His symbol was the spinning wheel, his myth was simplicity of living and high morality, and his folklore was *Ramrajya,* the rule of justice amidst plenty. What made matters worse for the elite was that Gandhiji practised what he preached, a sequence which was unfamiliar to the older leaders whose verbalised intellection left room for a certain amount of inconsistency. His programme was less integrated than consistent. There was an inexorable logic in his action which consolidated his expression, gave it clarity, and simplified his instructions. Naturally, the then ruling elite failed to discover any system in his thought. Of course, he was no thinker. He was at first sought to be dismissed as an idealist, almost a crank, because his reality was not the reality of the elite. His means were different, his ends were different, and his emphasis on the purity of means was a strange gesture. The fact of opposition to Gandhiji when he initiated the movement is not now generally discussed, but it was very much there. Only without a grounding in the Indian realities the opposition had no depth. It only stood out and served the nation by waiting. The orthodox never accepted Gandhiji, though Gandhiji was probably more Indian than they. We all know the story of his supreme sacrifice. In short, even the insecure ground on which the elite took its stand was knocked off by Gandhiji's movement. Since then, the political elite has been the ruling one in conjunction with, or vis-a-vis, the bourgeoisie. (The beginning of a subtle change in the conjunction is a later, and a very recent development). From now on the elite need not consist of the members of the liberal professions. Those who could sacrifice their middle class comforts and sever their intellectual affiliations, alone would be at the heart of the group. The college and university intellectuals found Gandhism too serious, too puritanic, too business-like, too arduous, and too idealistic, yet, without 'ideas,' and many of them found it difficult to absorb it. A number of the intelligentsia found Marxism more satisfying. Events in Russia had popularised Marxism. It was neither Moscow gold nor sheer perversity that made the Indian Marxists critical of Gandhism; and much less was it the paucity of patriotic feeling. The Indian Marxist intellectuals thought that Gandhism had no 'philosophy,' by which they meant dialectical materialism; and the Gandhian movement left it mostly to Gandhiji to formulate a philosophy which he did in his own way. An attempt was made by M. N. Roy to interpret Marxism in the light of India's status as an evolving colony, but no Indian Marxist offered an Indian version of Marxism that could be a substitute for Gandhism. So the triumph of Gandhism was more or less complete.

It was not fully complete. The outright condemnation of the *Hind Swaraj* against the western civilization did not catch. Today it may be said that the original anti-westernism of Gandhiji has failed. Instead, it is Tagore's attitude that seems to have come to stay. His attitude was absorption through positions of strength; and by strength he meant more or less the same things as Gandhiji meant, but saturation in the highest Indian cultural traditions was added to them. It is not suggested that the Indian intellectuals, barring a few in Bengal, were influenced by Tagore's views. Strangely enough, he was known to most educated Indians chiefly as an anti-imperialist who was also a poet and got the Nobel prize. It is also not meant that the Indian intellectuals of today are steeped in the *Upanishads*, as Tagore was. Only Dr. Radhakrishnan and a few others are. What is implied is that most Indian intellectuals have come to believe that the West is very much with us, that it need not be condemned, that it should be assimilated, and that it can be assimilated only if one's cultural roots are strong; and that is what Tagore and before him, Raja Rammohun Roy and many others of the pre-Gandhian era, had preached and practised. Nehru's voyage of discovery of India is very typical of this attitude. Being an attitude, the strands of its beliefs are not so strong as to become convictions that translate themselves into spontaneous action. And being an attitude of such a class, it would spell eclecticism for the majority of the elite. And so it does. To have the best of both worlds is often indicative of a pre-adult state of mind. The adult stand on their own world to negotiate with the other. Judging from conduct apart from verbalisation, the Indian intellectual does not yet seem to be fully awakened to his own heritage. He still has to find his moorings.

Events immediately after independence were not directly helpful to the intellectual class as such. They were immediately suspected of desertion, if not betrayal, during the struggle for independence. When they were trying to survive it, the abolition of landlordism came to reduce the income and lower the prestige of lawyers who had so long been the vanguard of the national movement. The teachers were particularly badly hit by the rocketing prices. Their salaries had always been low, and the dearness allowances, when they were given, did not add up to the cost of subsistence plus standard. The doctors did not suffer much. But the engineers and technicians who had been thrown out of employment after the cessation of the war still remained unemployed. The partition of India wrought a revolutionary change in the attitude of the middle classes. They became anti-Muslim, and forgot and forgave the British misdeeds even when they included the creation of conditions for an inevitable partition. Anti-Muslim attitude was a denial of the composite nature of Indian culture, the intertwining of its Hindu and Muslim strands; and its simultaneity meant the shedding of the sense of shame and guilt which was associated with appreciation of the British in any form. For a year or so, the gratitude toward them led to an exaggerated form of pro-British feeling which the British did their best to foster. One of the methods was, and still is, the cult of British statesmanship in 'granting' independence to India, whereas in reality, they just could not maintain India by force many days after the war. Be that as it may, the English educated middle classes could, if they would, laugh in their sleeves. The contact between them and the British has become closer both in business and culture since then. As the contact is no more between the rulers and the ruled, it may be more dignified than before. One cannot but admire the processes by which the anti-British feeling of the middle class was transformed, or canalized, into anti-Muslim feeling after the partition. That feeling, thanks to the genuine statesmanship of Nehru, has, however, subsided. It is all a-piece with Nehru's foreign policy of the quest for peace to which the overwhelming majority of the Indian intellectuals subscribe. Nehru is an important cultural fact and force.

Closely following the integration of the feudal and decrepit Indian states and the fixing of the administrative machinery which had been badly shaken by the British withdrawal and the partition, came the Five Year Plan. This is not the place for a discussion with the middle class elite groups. Government servants of the higher cadre had been recruited by open competition and an efficient bureaucracy had been evolved. Some of its members were men of high intellectual calibre and had wide intellectual interests. Their quality had no doubt deteriorated in the period when all their energies were engaged in maintaining law and order, that is, holding the balance between the Hindu and the Muslim which the imperialist policy was designed to upset. Thus shrinkage in cultural interests has continued due to no fault of the officers. They are still openly recruited and form the cream of youth. The nature of their work has, however, changed in quantity and quality. The district officers and those near the seats of the State governments are the most harried creatures to be found anywhere. Between pleasing the bosses and the public they have no time to work and think. And when the policy is not certain or changes quickly, a thin pall of futility hangs over their activities. At the same time, the change-over from being the servants of a government that is keen to serve the people marks a new orientation of the middle class mentality. Intellectually, it involves an empirical approach which is not always congenial to thinking in terms of ideas. But the gain in the feeling for Indian realities acquired in the process of village level activities is a solid one. All indications point to the possibility that when the Second Five Year Plan is in full operation, this new feeling will be the driving force for new thinking. Two of these may be mentioned. Indian economists spent years to learn their Keynes. Faced with the issues connected with the implementation of the Five Year Plan, they spent another few years in unlearning their Keynes. Recently, they seem to have been stirred to think on their own. The frame of the draft of the next plan, called physical planning, shows a degree of realism that was absent. The second indication is the Indian engineers' ability to adjust their knowledge to local situations. Unless the goal of 'a socialistic pattern of society' is lost in domestic and international party politics or in the tanglewood of unemployment where fascism grows, the situation bears the promise of offering the realistic base of India's intellectual adventure. Slowly but surely, other sections of the intelligentsia are being drawn into the ever expanding orbit of the Plan. The realism is likely to be further strengthened by the pronounced slant towards technical and scientific knowledge in recent years. Engineers, technicians, scientists, statisticians, and economists have acquired confidence from the atmosphere of planning.

Yet the importance of certain forces operating against the promising reorientation of intellectual values is not to be minimised. With the abolition of the zamindari, the intermediary character of the middle classes has no doubt gone, but the possibility of a wide rural middle class has emerged. So long as the landless agricultural proletariat are not rehabilitated, the social influence of this rural class may not always act as the background of an intellectual uprising. The presumption of this proposition is that the future shape of Indian culture will have to be less urban and more rural, and that to make the rural bias effective the impulse must needs come from the entire rural population. The second danger comes from urban unemployment. The very large number of unemployed graduates and trained personnel in certain fields is a drag when it is not positively mischievous. If we add the young urban refugees to that number the danger becomes a menace. A certain dose of frustration may be good for a particular type of literary and political activity, but the type of frustration one notices among the educated unemployed and the refugees does not meet the demands of the situation. The third danger arises from the loss of contact with modern knowledge involved in the hasty introduction of Hindi in higher instruction and the consequent loss of attention to English which is now the most important international medium of higher knowledge. There is a lot of confusion on this issue. Hindi and other Indian languages cannot certainly compete with English. At the same time, if it is true that the mother tongue is the best channel of release of one's thoughts, and further, if it is true that one's own thoughts are the best materials of intellectual endeavour, then it is difficult to see how creative intellectual work will suffer in the long run by the displacement of English in education. The danger is in the short run. But then it becomes a challenge to creativity, and not a damper. In the long run, the individuals are dead, but not the nation. Probably, the shift of interest towards the mother tongue means a shift from information and derivative knowledge, so long cultivated through English, to creative work and genuine thinking. One wonders if information and scholarship should be enough for India. Even creative work in science is not a different story.

Sufficient indications have been given about the nature of the problems facing the groups that owe account to intellectual values. One thing must have been clear, viz., the mobility and the re-formation of the middle classes. This fact alone would have been sufficient to explain the breaches in the exclusiveness of any one group, particularly the intelligentsia. Insecurity and unemployment add poignancy to that fact. It is apparent in the spread of the trade-union spirit among the white-collared gentry. But the mobility has a limited range. The middle classes have spilled over to the lower middle strata without crossing them. Questions of social prestige are still important.

If anything, the state is increasingly working through the middle classes and enhancing their prestige. It no doubt aims at a classless society. But that is a long way to go. Such aims take time to be realised. Meanwhile, certain important forms of state activities may work in a different way. Welfare and planning activities extend the range of the middle classes, create a new, and a more popular type of government officers, particularly on the village-level; and they fix the bureaucrat-manager as the ideal type to which youthful ambitions are hitched. (The change from the selfless, fearless type of nationalist worker is important). This is more or less inevitable. So long as planning comes mainly from the top, as it has come till today, the movement towards the socialistic pattern of society, which is the objective of the Indian state, will be still a middle class affair. With the extension of the range of bureaucratic activities the horizon of interests of the enlarged middle class will certainly be broadened. But it may at the same time create a state of affairs in which playing for safety is more paying for the bureaucracy than dangerous thought and perilous initiative. The same danger lurks outside the sphere of direct action through government servants. While it is true that governments are recruiting Indian experts or frequently consulting them, this type of advisory and non-effective functioning, howsoever useful to the experts or useless to the governments, is not always conducive to the spirit of creative thought in clusters which, if one has not misread history, has been the impulse behind the formation of an intellectual class. It is not so much a matter of free enterprise or planned order, democracy or authoritarianism, as of the social, as distinct from the economic, recognition of the role of invention in a Welfare State. Experts alone cannot do the trick. Like the bureaucrats, theirs too are often derivative minds. Here, according to this writer, is the first problem of those who are given to ideas, viz., the search and the working for conditions in which creative work is possible. It appears that some eccentricities will have to be cultivated, some non-expertise non-uniformities fostered, some dangerous thoughts to be taught, a few reckless adventures undertaken and some syntheses of knowledge attempted. The universities should be the arena of a few of these forays into the unknown. At present, unfortunately, they are not. There is much too much of dull uniformity and too little of adventure in our groves. Even the best of youth are apt to play for safety and slither into lethargy after a period of romantic frustration. The incentives are not always there; and what is worse, the wrong incentives are much to the fore. If it is possible to enter and rise in the scale by pleasing the powers that be than by producing a paper, a thesis, or a book by sheer hard labour and a little discipline, and further, if the powers that be owe more account to the cult of power and its practice than to academic values, then instead of pushing back the frontiers of knowledge in gay insouciance, the university intellectuals, like ordinary mortals, would do their best to close them. Add to it the factor and influence of inside and outside bureaucracy, the vested interests of the so-called specialisations entrenched in every department, and the general isolation—one would like to call it alienation—from all currents of life but the political, and you get a realistic picture of the level of achievement of university intellectuals in India today. It is not that there is a paucity of intelligence or good intentions; it is the gravitational pull of normalcy that prevents a leap into the dark. But all this is a sociological, almost an environmentalist, explanation. The endogenous cause seems to lie in the fact that the intellectuals do not as yet seem to have any problems to tackle, except on the purely physical or the merely academic plane of writing theses for the doctorate. Most of these latter are jejune, vapid and vague. As yet—and here is a ray of hope. Problems, which are real problems, come from shocks which a changing reality alone can give. And we have been shocked into freedom and rocked into the current. India is on the march, and the general dynamic situation may be trusted to create that measure of instability and un-balance which is one of the premises of the creative spirit. Of course, moving points of equilibrium are not the essence of dynamics, nor is dynamics a magic word. In a sense, faith in the dynamic situation might mean an alibi for intellect and the intellectuals. It might involve surrender to the rationalist fallacy of whatever is, is right. But our situation is not so dynamic as all that. It is moving; it is probably progressive without being revolutionary. So it appears that the Indian intellectuals may have quite a few unorthodox functions to perform to rectify the irony of the situation, viz., the more successful and the more extensive in its operations the government is, the more the conditions of uniformity it tends to generate. On the other hand, the Indian intellectuals cannot step out of a planned movement towards the socialistic pattern of society. So here is the basic tension. And an 'underdeveloped' country thrown into the vortex of world events after a long course of arrested growth and hibernation is an interesting field of intellectual adventure.

Another aspect of the same problem is that of squaring the principles of change by which India has lived and moved so far with those by which India is going to keep step with the world. At long last, new windows of a closed, musty room seem to have been thrown open to all the winds of heaven. No more does the atmosphere generate claustrophobia. At the same time, it appears that the airing is going to blow away the furniture. Proportionate attention is not being paid to those of India's traditions that have saved India and enabled her to survive the stormy political vicissitudes and the stealthy corrosions of her history. Every culture has its own principles and mechanisms of effecting change in its traditions. These principles and mechanisms appear to be going by default, and those that are adopted are supposed to belong to history without specificity. And this despite the belief that no assimilation of modern culture to enrich Indian culture is possible without being rooted. The author used to think that only the Communists among the Indian intellectuals were not Indians in this sense. He now suspects that the anti-Communist and the neutralist intellectuals may be equally neglectful of the secrets of India's survival and India's adaptability. Indian intellectuals have not yet clearly thought out any philosophy of history. And mere world-view can hardly be enough. It is either very vague and sentimental, or too simple and mechanical, or just eclectic.

Recently, there has been a reaction to the mechanical simplification of vulgar Marxist thought. When that reaction has not leaned back too sharply to the equally mechanical simplification of anti-communism or to moral rearmament, it has made for eclecticism. It is arguable that it has some relation to the current economic ideology of mixed economy and the political one of neutrality. The rationalisation of non-involvement may take the form of the scientific vantage-point of detachment from which the merits of both sides can be observed and cultivated and the demerits noted and abjured. The line between static and dynamic neutrality is chiefly a matter of action and goal; but for the intellectuals it is a matter of high discrimination and clarification of the goal, and ultimately, of choice. From what one can see, these duties have not yet been self-imposed. Probably, it is too early to expect the Indian intellectuals to be so highly conscious of their functions. The present analysis can only indicate the situation and hint at the possibilities. If the problem of unemployment can be intelligently tackled and the liberal fervour of the government continues for a decade more, and if, of course mankind survives, then the Indian intellectuals have a fair chance of coming to their own even against other heavy odds. And as regards choice, Indian history, particularly of the recent years, has made it a little easy. The acts which are the means of choosing hinge on non-violence. Only let not the cost of non-violence, like those of civil suits, be as unbearable as those of violence and criminal cases.

13. *Anthropology and Cultural Reconstruction*

THE SUBJECT OF MY PAPER IS SO COMPREHENSIVE THAT ONLY A large committee of experts could do justice to it. Even if we keep anthropology and culture within bounds, the territory enclosed still remains a continent. Says Malinowski:

> Culture consists of the body of commodities and instruments as well as of customs and bodily or mental habits which work directly or indirectly for the satisfaction of human needs. All the elements of culture... must be at work, functioning, active, efficient. The essentially dynamic character of cultural elements and of their relations suggests that it is in the study of cultural function that the most important task of anthropology consists. The primary concern of functional anthropology is with the function of institutions, customs, implements and ideas. It holds that the cultural process is subject to laws and that the laws are to be formed in the function of the real elements of culture.

Obviously, this functional approach apart from its merits and demerits, is a delimitation of anthropology as a study of origins with its hitherto accepted affiliations to archæology and history including the evolution of moral ideas and artifacts, language and arts. But in spite of such a circumscription of the scope, the chances to stray remain numerous. Culture continues to embrace 'all the manifestations of social habits of a community' plus 'the reactions of the individual as affected by the habits of the group in which he lives, and the products of human activities as determined by these habits.' So if I feel nervous before the subject you will pardon me and put it to a sort of agoraphobia—the horror of space.

My difficulty is enhanced by the pronounced attitudes of a number of revered anthropologists. They have told us that 'the anthropologist is a man of science, and is therefore not called upon to play the philosopher and interpret history from the standpoint of the ideal.' In fact, most of the academic anthropologists are singularly value-free. So, unless I choose to abjure my profession I should not discuss the question of 'reconstruction' at all. The task of 'reconstruction' must no doubt be preceded by analysis, but it is generally allotted to administrators, social reformers and similar active beings. Besides, reconstruction posits values and ideals, things which are considered not germane to 'scientific method,' if not hostile to it. In any case, he who would reconstruct culture must have faith in social progress. But an anthropologist who is a Simon-pure scientist cannot afford to fritter his energies in such emotional beliefs.

On the other hand, however, I am supported by the respectable opinion of Prof. Franz Boas. He is firmly of the opinion that 'a knowledge of anthropology may guide us in many of our policies,' although he takes care to point out that knowledge does not help in predicting the ultimate results of human action. His argument is simple. For him culture is not a

> mystic entity that exists outside the society of its individual carriers, and that moves by its own force. The life of a society is carried on by individuals who act singly or jointly under the stress of the tradition in which they have grown up and surrounded by the products of their own activities and those of their forbears.... The forces that bring about the changes are active in the individuals composing the social group, not in the abstract culture.

It is a very reasonable position. It avoids the concept of 'group-mind,' and yet does not consider that the individual is the seat of all trends and forces. Which probably explains why Prof. Boas brings to bear his training and knowledge in anthropology upon such vexing problems of modern civilization as nationalism and crime, education and eugenic selection, the interrelation of races, marriage and leadership. I shall not refer to the uses of anthropology for purposes of administration to support my feeble attempt at connecting anthropology with cultural reconstruction. These uses have not yet shed their political designs. It is not easy to forget that the policy of indirect rule in colonial Africa was the impulse behind the so-called scientific anthropology.

But opinions may now be left aside and a positive stand may be taken on other grounds. The study of anthropology, be it of the evolutionary or the functional school, equips the student with certain definite principles of knowledge, and therefore, of action and reconstruction.

The very first impression which anthropology creates is the bewildering variety of customs, beliefs and codes of conduct. There are very few culture-traits to which an exception can be detected. Sexual customs range from 'near licence' *via* group marriage to almost puritanic chastity after marriage. Even the the instincts are not safe. If mating is controlled by hunger in one tribe, hunger is modified by customary respect in another. The status of the woman may be high or low; jealousy may be present or absent; incest is generally tabooed, but something very similar may be found at odd places. Common participation and private property, acute sense of ownership and reckless generosity, ranking and equality, fear and courage, faith and doubt, coexist. It is a welter that almost refuses to be orderly. But along with that impression of bewilderment which descriptive anthropology makes on a young mind, rises another, viz., that of toleration. Gradually the idea dawns that variety, being a fact of human life, has to be accepted. On the islands of New Britain, human flesh is openly sold, man-hunt and cannibalism flourish in the Congo region, the Lhopa of Upper Bhutan kill the mother of the bride at the wedding if a wild man is not caught. Homosexuality is a regular ritual among the Kadiak off the Behring sea. It is widely prevalent with the Chukchi of Central Asia, the Bataks of Sumatra, the Marshall Islanders, the Tartars and the Karatchai of Caucasus. Pederasty is common with the women of certain tribes of Iceland, Zanzibar and Bali. When one knows such things one can appreciate why the Miranha chief told a missionary:

> You whites will not eat crocodiles and apes, although they taste well. If you did not have so many pigs and crabs you would eat crocodiles and apes, for hunger hurts. It is all a matter of habit. When I have killed an enemy it is better to eat him than to let him go to waste. Big game is rare because it does not lay eggs like turtles. The bad thing is not being eaten, but death; if I am slain, it matters not whether our tribal enemy eats me or not. I know of no game which tastes better than men. You whites are really too dainty.

Here, a student of anthropology has every right to question, 'Are they?' And as regards homosexuality, he will certainly refuse to be shocked by M. Charlus' conduct in Marcel Proust's novels or to agree with the censor in banning the *Wells of Loneliness*. Anthropology is a great shock-absorber.

The next step to which anthropology leads is the conviction that we are not as civilised as we look or think ourselves to be. It is a revolutionary step indeed. Are we civilised? asks every student with Prof. Lowie. There is hardly a single custom which is not a palimpsest. Below the magnificent Vedic *mantrams* uttered by the Hindu couple at the time of marriage lie the rites, known as *'stri-achar'*, which are certainly pre-Vedic, if not primitive. The taboos on the menstruating Hindu girl of today have their parallel in those of primitive tribes. Children suffering from infantile paralysis, women from hysteria, and retired high officials seeking to place their sons or those active ones whose promotion has been stopped, are exorcised of their ghosts, spirits, influence of stars, and what not. A glance at the newspapers will convince. Talisman-making is a lucrative profession. In this war, the stock in 'astrology' went up, and a number of reputable newspapers in Great Britain ran a regular weekly prediction column. Going deeper than mere examples, there are unmistakable evidences of what has been called primitive mentality in the functioning of a modern man's mind. It is not necessary to fully accept M. Levy-Bruhl's explanations and laws of the primitive mind's thinking, but he who has observed the behaviour of crowds in political meetings would be prone to revise his objections to the mystical character of collective representations in the primitives' perceptions. Levy-Bruhl's ideas about the nature of 'participation' or his views on name as a part doing the duty of the whole may be amended, but the manner in which we actually react to certain personalities, ideas and names, shows that there is an unmistakable strand of the pre-logical, if not of the a-logical, in most of us despite the high degree of sophistication.

At this point, however, a possible source of misunderstanding may be removed. The words 'level' and 'palimpsest' have been used, but they should not convey the idea of one layer laid upon another. Unfortunately, the study of primitive mentality is still carried on in the old fashion of static psychology. Even the equation of the modern man's unconscious with its archetypes to the primitive man's mental workings suffers from the defect of mechanistic, if not a deterministic, approach. We have no reason to believe, however, that the primitives' perceptions function on one plane and in one groove at a time. The perceptions are not inelastic. So, in terms of dynamic psychology, the layers may be described as fluid. They tend to harden in isolation, no doubt, but within their sphere they intermingle 'to create field.' In fact, there is no more of fusion in their perceptions than in ours with the result that their sense of the wholeness of patterns is more acute than ours. To put it differently, the primitive reactions to a given situation are more 'integral' insofar as they engage a more total personality than ours. But when some of the modern diverse forces are kept back, coordinated or sharply focused by high tension emotions, then the layers disappear. If that be so, then one may conclude that mass violence, which appears to be the strongest emotion today, is not a throw-back, or atavism as it is called, but an expression of the 'man of peace', who is also the man of violence. This lesson of anthropology should act as a corrective to the cruder theories of pacifism. Far be it for me to insult the primitive man by describing his life as nasty, brutish and short. All that is insinuated is that the course of culture is not monolinear in that man has passed or is likely to pass from violence to non-violence along a single track. A further conclusion may be drawn, viz., that the Western Man is not vitally different from, and therefore, neither inferior nor superior to, the Eastern Man. Anthropology teaches us to abolish the old world distinctions between us and them! Anthropology is a grand school for humility. The capacity for 'recognising' variety and absorbing unfamiliar shocks leads to the proper attitude towards broadening the base of culture. That attitude is now called scientific, but 'toleration' equally serves the purpose of reconstruction.

The third contribution of anthropology is the conception of 'pattern', for which credit is mainly due to the American anthropologists, particularly to Dr. Ruth Benedict. In a way, it is a crossing of the concept of the *gestalt* in modern psychology with that of function in modern anthropology. The pattern of culture is not a circle with a clear outline; it is a mobile arc that is constantly tending towards the shape of a circle yet seldom reaching it once and for all. In this *disposition to a design,* the singular traits, the specific tendencies, the instincts and behaviours are coordinated. What a fruitful idea it can be for purposes of writing history! None but a historian with a sound training in anthropology can write about this marvellous pattern of Indian culture, the interweaving of its numerous strands, with a hard, stubborn core, and the viscous pattern and the fluid fringes. Within that ambit the history of Bengal has a specificity of its own marked by its rice-culture and its shifting river-beds, and above all, its frontier-culture in which the weak hold of Aryan traditions is compensated by a multiplicity of traditions, pre-Aryan, post-Aryan, Buddhist and Jain remnants, the Islamic, the Arakanese, the Dutch, the Portuguese and the English continuities. No environmentalism can explain this pattern of Bengali culture. Georgraphy can fix it, but it can hardly account for its mobility, or for that peculiar quality named emotionalism which historians have attributed to Chaitanya and his school of Vaishnavism. If today Bengali literature is more full of experiments than most other provincial literatures, the determining conditions of that trait should be traced to the greater complexity and the consequent fluidity of the pattern of a frontier culture. It has not always been to the good of Bengal, but some merit it has conferred on that outlying province. Compared to an average Bengali's reactions to new forms of poetry or to new calls of politics, those of the Madhyadesa appear to be almost conservative. But the converse proposition is also true, viz., that the greater the uniformity of culture, the stabler the general state of mind and its attitudes.

A corollary to the above is the general persistence of cultural traditions in and through political or economic experiments. The so-called political backwardness, i.e., the uneducability of certain peoples in democratic habits, which has been advanced as an argument for doses and degrees of self-government, is essentially a misreading of the strength of the culture-pattern. The misreading occurs in two ways. If the resistance of the pattern is strong, the community is declared unworthy, or it is kept in a sort of quarantine in the name of 'preservation' against the deleterious effects of contacts with alien and higher cultures. The resistance of a pattern is there for all to see. The recent controversy between the Western type of democracy and the Soviet type of democracy, when the latter is not dismissed as just totalitarianism, is a case in point. Resistance takes various shapes. Before this, War Communism was declared by no less a person than Mr. Winston Churchill as a noxious weed, a pestilential epidemic. He is repeating it even today in another manner. In India, communism was interpreted as promiscuous intercourse, an invasion upon the sacredness of religion, and of course, upon property. And we were all duly afraid, and we still are. Fear, however, is not the only expression of resistance. Hatred of the foreigner is another. In Bombay and Calcutta, the foreigner's lot was not happy during the riots. Occasionally, new resistance is offered through new myths and symbols. *Jai Hind* has practically substituted *Bande Mataram;* the I.N.A. hero the average Congress worker; and the legend of Subash Babu quite a number of familiar ones. This means that resistance has been shifted or raised to another level. Resistance, however, continues. The cry of Asia for the Asians has been taken up by millions of people who have been disabused of other aspects of the Japanese propaganda. The positive side of resistance is of course the persistence of the pattern, which is a very precious quality indeed. It serves as a norm, an instrument of adaptation and social selection and a store of values, a criterion of judgment of experiments.

We must not forget that social change takes place in spite of the unyielding core of the pattern. Within that large but loose circumference, acculturation goes on between the so-called primitives and the civilised. The process of acculturation in different parts of India has been very competently described by Dr. D. N. Mazumdar in the North and Dr. Ghurye in the South. The Gonds in the Bastar State in the C.P. have been acquiring new traits from their more sophisticated neighbours. The Bhumij of Bihar is already a caste well within the Hindu fold. The Rajbanshis of Bengal, the Tharus, the Cheros of the U.P. show distinct signs of acculturation. On the other hand, a retroactive process of acculturation is also noticeable among the Hos and the Mundas of Chota Nagpur. There are numerous cases to testify to the process of acculturation, slow or fast, positive or negative. Prof. Hersokovits has analysed the functions of acculturation and classified its results into acceptance, adaptation and reaction. Dr. Majumdar has accepted that classification and given various examples for each stage of the process from his first-hand knowledge of tribes in the U.P., C.P., Bengal and Chota Nagpur. I have very little to add to these facts. Only on one point I should like to lay some emphasis. The proneness to acculturation is conditioned by such factors as the utilitarian value of the innovations, the comparative levels and types of the interacting units, and the previous history of their relations, e.g., sympathy, antipathy, prestige or hostility. These modify the attitude towards innovations as also the *rate* of their acceptance. In fact, it is the *rate of change* which is mostly signified in Herskovit's terminology; otherwise the old word 'accommodation' used by Prof. S. Park and Burgess and endorsed by Dr. Hiller, would have sufficed. The reason for my emphasis on the fact of *proneness,* i.e., the rate of change and its conditioning factors, is not far to seek. In my humble opinion, one particular attitude towards the problem of primitive tribes in India suffers from an unfortunate deficiency in the analysis of the actual process of acculturation which anthropology reveals. The fact of the matter is the *tempo* of accommodation depending, among other factors, upon the *degree* of similitudes between the contacting parties. Probably, the same analysis may account for the increasing bitterness between the two major communities of India. The rate of change effected in the behaviour-patterns of converts to Islam is so fast as to appear as an overnight rupture with the very folkways and mores of the person. And yet, cultural diffusion between the Hindus and the Muslims has gone on for centuries, and it is impossible to isolate the Muslim element from the so-called Muslim dress, the Hindu element from say *darbari kanada* or *mian ki todi,* or from the food habits of a Kayastha or a Kashmiri pandit in the U.P., or even from the worship of Satya Narayan by an orthodox, upper-caste Hindu widow of an eastern Indian. In short, acculturation, as the anthropologist knows it, may take place on various levels, but at different rates for each. It may be that on one level the rate of accommodation is fast while on another reaction rules. In such cases, it is best to take as the unit of observation the whole pattern of interchange between the parties concerned.

I can hardly resist the temptation of pointing out in this connection that despite the recent increasing bitterness between the Hindus and the Muslims, quite independently of the two-nations theory, the acculturation-process is going as merrily as ever. The technique of electioneering, the popularity of socialistic ideas with the rank and file, the political programmes, the realisation of the need for drastic economic and social changes, and above all, a gradual understanding of the actual functioning of the institution of imperialism—all these and many more agencies are working against those that make for enhancing the social distance between the Hindus and the Muslims. Anthropology always stresses the continuous process of acculturation at some level or the other.

I have so far discussed the lessons one can draw from the study of anthropology inasmuch as it unfolds the variety and the complexity of the processes of cultural changes. But overriding them all is the cardinal theme of anthropology, viz., that culture is man-made. In other words, anthropology is the Science of Man. All behaviours intersect in the social human being, and the social human being is the only creature that can step beyond the given social pattern, and yet survive. Naturally, such a subject deserves a whole science to itself. But unfortunately, what V. F. Calverton has called the 'cultural compulsives,' that is to say, the vested interests that determine the culture complex, or what Prof. Mannheim describes as 'ideologies,' have been working so insidiously that a very valuable corrective of the scientific method itself has been missed by even the most honest among the anthropologists. The history of social sciences is littered with examples of the working of such compulsions as account for the prestige of Westermarck's views on marriage and incest with the middle class and academic circles, or Morgan's notions about the origins of family, marriage and property in the U.S.S.R., and their primary non-acceptance elsewhere. It is not my intention to suggest that these vested interests and class-mores alone determine the method of approach or the validity of conclusions. The culture-lag between the natural sciences and the humanistic studies also plays an important part. I have noticed with regret the neglect of 'modern' scientific methodology among our historians, economists and anthropologists. More often than not their 'scientific method' belongs to the nineteenth century when a high premium was put upon induction and the laws of syllogisms, and the entire 'philosophical attitude' was abjured. Many a student of the social sciences is only too proud to proclaim that he is not a philosopher. Well, philosophy too has been changing materially in the hands of the psychologists and particularly, the logical positivists. Still the need for a philosophical approach abides. In fact, it should be resuscitated. As N. Berdyaev puts it in the *Destiny of Man*: 'Philosophy may get rid of psychologism, for aught one knows, but it cannot get rid of man. Philosophy must be consciously and not instinctively anthropological.'

The time has come to impregnate all social sciences, anthropology and history in particular, with philosophy. How it can be done cannot be discussed within the compass of a paper. But one short statement may be ventured to indicate the direction of my desire. M. Scheler refers to four main types of anthropological theory: the Jewish-Christian, the Hellenic, the scientific, i.e., the evolutionary, and the modern theory of decadence. But if Indian culture has a pattern of its own, which I believe it has, then the Indian conception of the role and destiny of man, i.e. to say, the philosophy of Indian history, should help in the formulation of the appropriate approach of Indian anthropologists. This view does not abrogate science; it only rectifies its defects, fills it out where it sags, modifies its claims and informs it with an outlook the absence of which has reduced anthropology to the mere study of primitives and the presence of which is the first condition of the cultural reconstruction of India. In fact, I respectfully submit that Indian culture can be re-made with the help of a proper anthropological approach to Indian history.

If this be granted, then the actual work of cultural reconstruction falls into its place. The word 'reconstruction' is unfortunate. It suggests a machine, which life is not. But probably, the meaning is clear. The reference is to the life-pattern itself, the preservation and enrichment of its values, and the elimination of its dis-utilities and obstructive survivals by the application of the principles of anthropology. The principles are that culture is varied, that it is man-made, that it is a running business, that it is not one man's job, that it is neither a single trait nor a bundle of traits but a whole pattern with a hard core but a soft fringe, and that culture is for man through whom every thread of the pattern passes. The corollary-principles are that though there are types and stages in the evolution of culture, it is not permissible to hold that one is superior to the other; that though the political or the economic aspect may assume dominance, its provenance is in the culture-pattern and the promise is in its growth and development. Obviously, these principles of anthropology, at least so far as I have understood them, can be very well utilised in every sphere of Indian life today, in the matter of the Hindu-Muslim relation, the Indo-British connection, the problems of the 'depressed' classes and the primitive tribes.

In conclusion, I assert my faith in the very basic assumptions of the subject, 'Anthropology and Cultural Reconstruction.' As I take it, the premise is that knowledge must need be related to living. If knowledge be its own reward, then anthropology had better be left to some teacher leading an apologetic existence in some musty museum. There is no such thing as anthropology for the sake of anthropology. Its only function is to make and remake culture. Man is a culture-making animal. As Dr. Ruth Benedict so beautifully put it:

> We do not stand to lose by this tolerant and objective view of man's institutions and morals and ways of thought .... We know all culture changes. It is one of its claims upon our interest. We hope, a little, that whereas change has hitherto been blind, at the mercy of unconscious patternings, it will be possible gradually, insofar as we become genuinely culture-conscious, that it shall be guided by intelligence. For what is the meaning of life except that by the discipline of thought and emotion, by living life to its fullest, we shall make of it always a more flexible instrument, accepting new relativities, divesting ourselves of traditional absolutes? To this end we need for our scientific equipment something of the anthropologist's way of looking at human behaviour, something of respect for the epic of our own culture, something of fine tolerance for the values that have been elaborated in other cultures than our own. •

The only comment I want to make on these words is that for the Indian anthropologist, a deliberate and planned application of anthropological knowledge to the remaking of Indian culture is immediately necessary in addition to the fine tolerance for the relativity of cultures. We must not forget that the Sanskrit equivalent of culture is *sanskriti,* which means reorientation, or recreation. Other Sanskrit equivalents of culture have been used, like *baidagdhya, parishilan,* but these terms came into currency at a time when the individual had become sophisticated enough to be aware of the social distance between himself and the rest of the people.

No better support for the Indian anthropologist in this onerous task of cultural reconstruction can be received than what is furnished by the broad march of the Indian social process. For reasons that need not be gone into, acculturation in this country has proceeded more on the lines of acceptance, adaptation, accommodation and assimilation than on those of conflict, which, as is well known, is also a form of social relation. That large historical tendency has been built up by a number of patterns, sometimes regional and at other times popular. Occupations or economic functions have often cut across them, but generally speaking, they have worked within the region through guilds and castes. In fact, the process may be described as symbiotic of nature and the development of society. It is not suggested that stresses and the strains have been absent. In fact, they are implicit in such cases as the *mela-bandhan* of Debibar, the earlier reformation of Raghunandan, and the rigid restrictions against pollution in its various forms. And yet cultural symbiosis is the outstanding feature of India's cultural reconstruction. It is to be clearly noticed in the specific culture-patterns of the *arya-bhumi* and the *anarya-pradesha,* of Bengal, Gujarat, Maharashtra and Tamil Nad. We submit that these regional symbiotic patterns are the true significance of the term 'nationalities' in India. Our nationalism, in its political sense, may be a gift of industrial capitalism and all that it means in the way of extending the rights of the individual person to those of a state, but the student of Indian history with the proper approach will find the meaning of nationalism in every case of the formation of culture-patterns. Viewed in this light, anthropology may also help in the day-to-day task of political reconstruction. How exactly the work will be done belongs to the science and art of administration. But our leaders should know that anthropology has ceased to be merely a study of primitive tribes. It must now be recognised as at least one of the sciences of human relations.

14. *Standards in Education*

If there is one opinion about higher education in recent years more dearly held than another, it is the decline of its standards. All sections hold it, the teachers propagate it, and the government circles are nervous about it. A young M.A., who has passed out in May meets his professor in July and speaks about the deterioration since his days. Much of it is the *Satya Yuga* mentality in reverse, or just a sudden realisation that the *Kali Yuga* has come. But mental tricks apart, the seriousness of the matter is unquestionable. Ultimately, it means the social function of knowledge. The immediate significance is the role of the state in the maintenance of general standards within which academic standards can be maintained and raised, or from the opposite angle, the maintenance and raising of academic standards by schools, colleges and universities with the help of which the general standard of intellectual achievement and efficiency of the nation and the state can be kept up and uplifted. Today the two propositions should not differ materially, because past political sacrifice is fast ceasing to become the passport to office and the available so-called best products of the universities are being absorbed in state services.

On a deeper level, the two aspects are really one. It all depends on the nature of the state. If it be class state then the academic standards will be the reflection of the social standards of the class, with emphasis on leisure, classical and liberal education open to the privileged few; if it be democratic, socialist state, then the academic standards will depend upon the speed with which the socialist society absorbs scientific and technical knowledge for the improvement of its standards of living through new modes of production liberating human beings from bondage to leisure for creative, liberal pursuits. The nature of the Indian state, however, is not yet fully developed.

All that can be said about it is that it certainly is not a socialist state and that the dominant pressure on it is towards the direction of a class-state, despite the directives of the Constitution and the subjective good intentions of the ruling party. Thus it is that the purpose of the article is limited.

One preliminary remark may be permitted at this stage. The crystallising agency for the conclusions in this article is eight weeks' careful reading of about six hundred answer books of postgraduate students of half-a-dozen universities, in addition to *viva voce* examinations and the scrutiny of quite a few doctoral dissertations on various aspects of social sciences. As most of the results are already out, what follows need not be misconstrued as betrayal of confidence. No examiner's reports are being written here. In any case, the issue is of such vital importance to the nation that it should be openly discussed. Nothing less than the life of the nation is at stake. And time is of the essence of the contract between India and her fate. India, of course, means the rising generation who alone can rectify the mistakes of the government, if any, by their knowledge and enthusiasm, and whose frustration is an evil of the first magnitude. And India's fate is a matter of social architecture in which the structure of stone and steel must need subserve the rules of design and the beauty of form. We need not define either the form or the design, because we know them both, even if vaguely.

The point is the rules of the technique. Education is just that and nothing more. So if it is said that academic standards, which were never too high in the last hundred years, is falling fast, all that is intended to convey is the idea that either the old rules are not being imparted to the young, or that we teachers have not been able to formulate new rules for the novel needs of an independent country in a strange set-up. In other words, it is unfair to blame the youth. They have lost touch with the old rules and standards, which we cannot maintain and they do not know, because they have not been told by us what the new standards should be. The young are hovering between two worlds, one dead, and to change the phrase, the other whose birth the elders do not know or are afraid to recognise yet.

Let the decks be cleared. This fall in standards, which is to be regretfully admitted, is not due to the adoption of Hindi.

For one, only a few universities are giving instructions in Hindi in the under-graduate classes, and the answer books are of post-graduate students who have been instructed in English. For another, it is a sociological fact that expression is a general quality and communication is only a specific skill. And expression sets the standard, and not communication. Those who write well in English can, and often do, write well in their vernacular. This has been established by many experts in their reports, including Sri Paranjpaye's report of the Bombay university. The fall is also not due to any sudden lowering of inherent ability, because none knows what it was, none can dogmatise about heredity, and none can jump to the conclusion that ability had dried up from the day that the British left and Pandit Nehru formed the government—and that was hardly three years ago. The last argument means (1) that the conditions of subjection were propitious for high intellectual standards, which really takes away a lot for the grounds of independence; and (2) that colleges and universities should revert to their function of producing such students as would be intelligent clerks and officers and forget all that they learnt in the course of noting and drafting and sitting over files, for that was the implication and outcome of high standards. The fall, therefore, has nothing to do with independence, not even with the reported general lowering of competence in governmental affairs, because the universities and colleges at least, enjoy autonomy in the determination of academic standards, even if the schools do not. There too it cannot be proved that the State governments desire the fall directly.

Indirectly, however, the state may be held responsible. Poor wages to teachers, permission to take in more than the optimal number of students in the class, the lack of room, materials of study and experiments, the small number of teachers and lecturers in proportion to that of students, each is conditioned by government grants. If the government again is poor in funds or confuses short period balancing of budget with the equation of administrative revenue with social expenditure, then the indirect responsibility becomes almost direct. So far as the schools are the feeding ground, the fall in standards at the university stage can be traced to the niggardliness of the state. But constituent colleges are another story. Barring a few, they are run more or less on competitive business lines. Once business principles come in standards go out. Such has been the experience of many inspectors of colleges and examiners.

The atmosphere of intrigue is merely applied economics. In a department of a university the standard is set usually by the head and the professor in charge. He has always been well paid. A thousand rupees a month is the average salary of a professor. There is besides no rule or ordinance to this writer's knowledge which compels the head to take in more students than his staff can manage. Pressure is sometimes exerted over him to admit the unworthy. But it is not irresistible, at least in the senior classes. If he yields, which he does too readily mostly for vanity or to score over a sister department, then neither the argument on the score of money nor on that of smallness of staff, etc., holds true. If, in addition, he worships quantity in production and calls it research, or pushes his ill thought out ideas down the gullets of young graduates who are only too willing to oblige him because he is the examiner in half, and sometimes, more than half the number of papers, then the government can hardly be blamed for this sorry state of affairs. Therefore, the sphere of indirect responsibility of the state is only limited to the schools.

Another plausible way in which the state has been implicated for the decline of standards has been offered. It has not yet been clearly formulated, but its vagueness should not be counted against it. Two forms are noticeable: (a) India government has considerably slowed down the tempo of movement which brought it into power; as such, the youth are frustrated. The fall in academic standards is a consequence of such frustration. Obversely, if the tempo had been kept up, the standard would have gone high on the strength of revolutionary enthusiasm. (b) Which is a Marxist variation of the same, there has been no unity of thought and action in our culture with the result that it has been completely alienated from our life. Of late, the alienation of the youth from the nation's work has increased because of the alienation of the Indian state from the realities of living and the historical situation; (which, in the opinion of many Marxist intellectuals, means Anglo-American imperialism on the one hand and class-conflict at home on the other). As these two theses have not been officially promulgated the writer hopes to be excused for his defective formulation.

The large element of truth contained therein should be obvious to any thinking person. That frustration is due to the slowing of the tempo of the movement, that the youth are frustrated today, that without enthusiasm for the new state nothing can be achieved, and that with its help creative activity spurts on to further endeavours, all these are so generally true that they are almost platitudes. Similarly, it should be equally admitted by any serious student of the history of ideas that crises occur at a time when needs, practice and action cannot be contained within old ideas. It is indisputable that our intellectuals are divorced from all types of realities except the reality of professional existence, and that the knowledge they purvey is miles apart from what the Indians need really and truly. In the teaching of social sciences, of which this writer has had experience, the dichotomy is nearly complete.

No academic theories of consumption, production, distribution, or exchange holds wholly true here, and no economist is intimately concerned with the extent of the exceptions to, or departures and aberrations from, the academic normals and models. That imperfect competition of the crudest type obtains in every type of market within this country, that marginal productivity theory, the concept of full employment, savings-investment equation do not fit in with our facts, are tardily admitted, but no attempt has yet been made to build up ideas that are rooted in Indian realities. Young men are simply bewildered by modern economic analysis. This does not mean that economic analysis should be discarded; on the contrary, it should be studied with greater earnestness. The subtleties of modern economic thought are an excellent training ground for Indian intellect. Only these subtleties are not being used as an apparatus of realistic thinking. If they are applied, their limitations are sure to be exposed. That too will not be enough, because 'application' is an exercise of static thinking whereas what is needed is dynamic, that is, historical and comparative thinking.

History of physics, chemistry, biology, and other natural sciences is just not taught, and history of politics, economics, and literature has been reduced to a catalogue of names. Is it not strange for a new country that neither historiography nor philosophy of history forms a part of the history curriculum of any of its universities? Is it not tragic that only a dwindling number of post-graduate students have had any trade or traffic with Sanskrit or modern world history? Every student thinks of history as the decline and fall of empires and is blissfully ignorant of the course of social forces. And who is to blame him? That way history is not taught. Neither is sociology, nor politics, nor jurisprudence, nor economics. The young man, if anything, is dynamic. He has little immediate interest in static analysis. In any case, static analysis is an acquired trait or taste.

Yet doubts arise about this dynamic explanation. What is the tempo the Indian national movement is supposed to have possessed and the national government is alleged to have halted? Three impulses worked for it; Indian capitalism on the rise, British imperialism on the fall, and Gandhi's leadership. The first two contradicted each other and the contradictions manifested themselves in the political movement. They are embodied in the present state policy. Like the child of a maladjusted couple, they are a product, and not a resolution. Progressive thinking, however, must go beyond this stage. Another level of contradiction existed, between Indian and western values, the moral leadership of Gandhiji and the a-moral, historical domination of capitalism, British imperialism on the retreat and American domination in gallop. The first is apparent in Hindi-English controversy, the second in charges of corruption and fall from Gandhian ideal, and the third, which is most hidden, is to be suspected in the attitudes towards the Indian policy of neutrality. These occupy the foreground of our attention and cover the background in which historical reality seems to have taken shelter. What is important to note here is that three initial impulses behind the tempo have been showing more points of agreement than disagreement. They were really bound by unbreakable ties, hence the Commonwealth link, hence the concept of trusteeship, and hence the boring moral exhortations which go by the name of momentous political statements.

The rise of Gandhian ethics was intimately connected with the transition from commercial capitalism to industrial capitalism. India's commerce capital was an ally of British capital in distributive trade; and a long apprenticeship was necessary to develop the real conflict with British industrial capital with its highly developed finance and services during which colonial capital had to remain a subordinate partner to metropolitan imperialism. Under these conditions our national movement had to work. It worked well, but on the basis of secondary sources of conflict, sources which by their nature were temporary and derivative. Now that these sources have finished their course, it is unfair to blame the present government for halting the tempo. That tempo was never really fast; its speed was mainly emotional and did not carry the nation to the next genuinely historical phase. Our independence is at best a halting place, a wayside station, and not the next junction. After all, every movement gets the state it deserves. It is a travesty of history to say that a revolution swallows its leaders as a tiger eats up the cubs. Our leaders were never revolutionary, because they were the products of, or at best manipulated the secondary conflicts. If this be more than a doubtful assertion, then the cause of frustration among the youth has little to do with such political factors, as the slowing down of the tempo, etc.

The youth were only emotionally enthusiastic. Their noble sacrifices had no intellectual content; neither had their leaders. They were asked to quit the colleges, and they readily quitted. They quitted books, ideas and thinking. Those splendid young men and women who plunged into action in 1942 or on earlier occasions did not particularly subscribe to very high standards. Man per man, the ICS recruits in the critical periods of the national movement, or the Communist youths during the first three or four years of the war, were academically superior to the present generation of the same. It thus seems that the relation between our national movement and academic standards was always a bit tenuous. The incessant calls to students for strike by our political leaders led to some worsening of discipline, but that was certainly not an irretrievable disaster.

In China and Russia, where there have also been revolutions, such calls were less frequent. If their academic standards have not fallen, and many neutral observers say that they are well maintained, it is neither because of the practice of self denial by their leaders nor because of the less number of young victims to revolution but because there were real revolutions. When this writer comes across examples of Chinese scholarship in agricultural economics or rural sociology carried on right in the midst of Japanese occupation, famine and pestilence, he feels bewildered. A few books on history and archæology written by Russian scholars in the very period when Hitler was pounding at Moscow, Leningrad and Stalingrad, have come to this author. Their standards are very high indeed. Surely, there must be something else than the reaction, 'collaboration,' 'counter-revolution,' to account for the present frustration and the consequential indifference of the Indian youth to quality.

Another doubt is on the score of frustration. Most people feel and many psychologists think that frustration arises out of broken pledges and suppressed potentialities. They are right so far as the origins of frustration and the conclusions thereof in neuroses are concerned. In other words, such beliefs relate to the proposition that frustration is a denial of the fulfilment of an original impulse. A number of questions arise here. Is there an original impulse or drive that is balked? No impulse, drive or wish seems to be original. If it is not, if it be impure or a mixture, then more than one course of its possibility is likely. Which course is blocked? Besides, has one impulse, if any, but a single track of its own? That too is not borne out by the experience of human behaviour, child behaviour in particular. Analysis of the conclusion of frustration, viz., neurotic condition, also does not reveal a single origin with mono-linear development. Behind the popular beliefs is also the presumption that the nature of frustration is the same as the nature of the impulse frustrated.

It may as well be that some frustration takes a new start and runs its independent course, like Lucifer ploughing his own way down the walks. Evil seems to follow its own laws. This may appear to be Manichean, but the career of hardened criminals, drug addicts, and those women whose life is one long unbroken exercise in self-pity, is a lesson. This writer has patiently observed the most vociferous critics of the government and come to feel that they thoroughly enjoy their condemnation. Such luxury can only be an evidence of the autonomy of the course of frustration. Probably, the only truth about frustration is that it is useful for correcting our idea of the nature of expectation and impulses that have gone awry. A difficult task, undoubtedly, because who loves to think critically on one's past deeds, who dares to question Gandhian leadership and ridicule Ramarajya, who cares to find out how much of our national movement was governed by thought and how much by emotions? In fact, not many really creative impulses have been represented so far. Some fond wishes and dreams have been, which is not a bad thing by itself. The authentic ones were seldom there; only words were. Thus it is that in this writer's opinion our present frustration has little to do with any impulse other than what it has released by itself. Our frustration is false, pseudo, at best, one of para-wishes. Its supreme foible is its touching preoccupation with its own self, very similar to a school vice.

The Marxist position, as usual, is stronger than that of

the politically radical psychologist. The elements of its strength have been indicated. There has been, and still there is, no unity of thought and action in our country. Perhaps the dissociation is greater today than before, perhaps not. Our education is very unreal, not merely by virtue of its non-vocational, over-literary, non-manipulative and urban character, but primarily because of its divorce from the conditions of living. None can guess our crude modes of production or its hide-bound relations from any page of the academic syllabus. But how far can unity of thought and action retrieve the situation? This question also raises a number of issues. The hard core of the position appears to be pragmatic. Thought originates in action; its validity is tested by action; it is organised by action from the point of view of outcome; it must needs end in some action, which is result. The corollary is that there can be no thought divorced from action.

Philosophers have pointed out the defects of this position. Pragmatism is a sub-species of idealism and full of fallacies. Instrumentalism stems out of it and refines its crudities. Concepts, at least, are instruments of action. Marxist position is similar to instrumentalism in many ways, but the difference is noteworthy. So far as this writer understands it, instead of priority of action over thought, the Marxist counts on their dialectical interplay. For him, the world is an objective reality independent of thought and ideas. He further grounds both thought and action on human behaviour, which by its nature is historical, and therefore relative in every way but in the spiralled search of the absolute. Within such historical relativity the status and function of knowledge is conditioned by class disposition because of the social division of labour. In the individual act of knowing, the Marxist is not immediately interested. But the status and function of knowledge really signify the climate of knowing. It is here that the Marxist explanation is pertinent and sound, because the climate of knowing sets the standard through criticism of the existing social order which supports an adequate corpus of knowledge. No criticism of agronomical theory can be so effective as that of farming practices, no general theory of employment or business cycles as the figures of the unemployed. If a dock labourer or an Indian agricultural labourer could speak frankly with leaders of economic thought, the latter's thinking could have come closer to reality.

The Marxist position is also true in another way. If we exclude among others the subtleties introduced by the process of individual knowing, we are led to conclude that there is a fair degree of correspondence between the progress or regress of theories and the march of material, living conditions. In broad sweeps and secular tendencies Marxist sociology of knowledge is largely true. One may even venture to say that barring those few cases of accidental inventions, nearly all the important ones which are the result of hard thinking have been occasioned by social crises. The relation between technical inventions and changes in modes of production is closer. Even intuitive flashes have their lowering clouds.

Admitting all that, the mentioning of unity of thought and action is still not clear. Thinking as distinct from thought and thought as distinct from theory increase the distance between thought and action. Thinking no doubt is mental action. In so far as it is dependent on (a) knowledge of the contradictions of the past or passing system of thought, and (b) language, that is concepts and symbols, it is a form of social action. But either is past social action although thinking is being done at present. From this angle all thinking is historical. But the historicity of the Marxist is another type. It is forward gazing; its action is essentially futurist.

Futurist action involves the transformation of present contributions into past one, and also the construction in accordance with some vision of the next step reached by understanding. So there must always be a lag between social action in terms of language and knowledge of past contradictions, and social action in terms of the potentialities of that historical knowledge which is charter of freedom from necessity; otherwise one will have to posit some sort of 'eternal content' running throughout all the motive forces of change and/or all the social orders hitherto existent. Such tie-ups with eternity the Marxist resists. His sociology is that of liberation, a sort of social *moksha*; hence its trace of millenialism. This is also one of its capacities to enthuse. As such, the levels of social action and thought are as different as those of *prabrtti* and *mukti*. The case of Janak is an ideal compromise, and not of genuine unity of thought and action. He had a family.

Unity therefore, can only mean a constant endeavour for the progress of thought to come closer to the march of action. Needless to say that vital thought and vital action are meant. We need not re-define vitality; the Marxist explanation is sufficient unto the day. But the closeness must be measured. So far as is known, no serious theoretical discussion of such approximation as would bring about change is forthcoming in Marxist literature. What is found is a post hoc explanation. The function of leadership is brought in for rescue, but in the ultimate analysis that peculiar matchmaking between knowledge of the historical process and the willed action remains the artist's secret.

Even Engels had to introduce the unknown in the famous passage: 'Every ideology, once it has arisen, develops in connection with the given concept-material, and develops this material further, otherwise it would cease to be an ideology, that is occupation with thoughts as with independent entities, developing independently, and subject only to its own laws. That the material life conditions of the persons inside whose heads this thought goes on, in the last resort determines the course of this process, remains of necessity unknown to these persons, for otherwise there would be an end to all ideology.' Apart from the unknown, the 'last resort' seems to dismiss the intermediate stages, e.g., the logic of thinking, which unless one accepts Durkheim, has acquired, since Aristotle and the dialecticism of less remote days, an objective validity with laws of its own. The intermediate stages are as important as the last resort, because Engels is concerned with 'thought process' and his strength lies in the analysis of the function of knowledge, function being both individual and social.

One would thus prefer to lay stress on the first paragraph in which 'the given concept material' and the development of this material are declared to be necessary for the development of ideology. 'The given concept material' betrays a belief in the possibility of a thought-system becoming detached, aye, independent of social reality and remaining useful, at least, in the interest of critiques and desirable changes. Ultimately, therefore, social usefulness is one and only one of the tests for objective truth. That being so, thought and action unite infrequently. They seem to have their own mating seasons, but they are unrecorded in calendars.

The relevance of these views to the matter of the fall in academic standards, and therefore, to that of raising them, is great. They have fallen very low, because there has been a counter-revolution instead. Therefore, and this is important, a revolution is necessary to raise them. Such a revolution would build up its adequate theories, which, in their turn, would create the necessary outlook and enthusiasm among the students. They would thus think and act and raise the standards by their own efforts. But, as this author holds, though our revolution went off half-cock, though our national movement had no understanding of the context to be changed or a general view of the social order to be brought about, yet intellectual life and intellection have normally an order and standard of their own. Therefore all that can be suggested for the improvement of academic standards now is to bring our academic theories closer to our realities, criticise their general hidden assumptions, which are the framework of the status quo, and above all, inject them, so to say, with the objective validity of the historical process of knowledge, social order and their interrelations. Beyond this begin the faults in the Marxian sociology of the unity of knowledge and action.

To conclude: direct administrative responsibility is mainly limited to the schools. In so far as they are the base of academic foundation, the state is duty bound to provide conditions for better teaching. Private colleges, which are at present run on competitive lines, have to be controlled, if not nationalised. In the universities, the optimal number of staff and students has to be adhered to. These, however, do not go deep into the nature of the problem. The curriculum has to be drastically changed. Its nucleus should be the history of ideas of every subject, including that of their method. That also should not be enough. History of ideas has to be shown, as far as is permissible, in relation to the history of social development. Both must needs be grounded in the objective validity of the historical process. Thereby the intellectual basis of the tempo and of the alienation from action will be secured. Teachers can only supply the rules of the game, and probably, a little infection. The role of the teachers is not as great as it is alleged. They are not *gurus*; they can at best be historically conscious. The responsibility of the state thus appears to be greater on the whole than any other units in the complex of education in the matter of creating the socially necessary conditions for preventing the rot and uplifting the standards in knowledge.

PART FOUR

SOCIAL PROBLEMS OF LITERATURE

15. Social Problems in Fiction*

Tagore has limited the scope of problems in fiction as a work of art in a number of letters and articles. The most important of them appeared in the *Parichaya* some time ago under the caption, '*Sahityer Matra*.' The substance of Tagore's argument is that no expression of opinions on problems should break up the composition of story. While admitting that human nature changes, that its interests are shifting towards a discussion of intellectual problems, and that such changes in interests should come out in a novel, which must needs depict life, Tagore insists that the primary interests of human beings are comparatively stable, that the basic rules of literary composition are more or less immutable, and that the enjoyment of literature is based on these permanent principles. Tagore continues that no opinions can be substituted for the creation of character, which is the chief concern of the novelist. The logical consistency of opinions on problems and an ethical conformity to external codes are equally irrelevant to the plot. The relevancy consists in balance and completeness of the whole. Such is the essence of life, original and fruitional; therefore, this is the essence of art as well. Problems are materials, and materials are not to be confused with the finished product. Tagore adds that significant form of the whole is the gift of creative imagination, and not of logic and ratiocination.

* A very interesting problem has been raised by Sri Dilip Kumar Roy in the appendix to his new novel, *Ranger Paras*. It is about the role of problems in modern fiction. I hasten to admit that I am not in a position to say how far the question arises from or is answered in the novel itself. My primary concern is with the appendix as such. The present essay is not to be taken as a review of *Ranger Paras*.

The above remarks are charged with the experience of ages. They set the norm for all arts, not to speak of fiction as a work of art. But in them there is a reproval of all violent departures and a toleration of minor changes. They are not aimed against the spirit of evolution: only they do not suffer mutation. It is particularly necessary to remember the qualifications in Tagore's essay—they are in the nature of minor adaptations. The three important ones are that (1) changing interests in our life should be and would be reflected in fiction; (2) our life carries a lot of cargo which is not essential for our spirit but essential for steady sailing; and (3) problems which are vital to the character, as in *Gora,* have a place in the pages of a novel.

Let me state the opposite point of view. The modern novel is co-extensive with modern modes of living. The appeal of *Gora* and *Ghare-Bayere* (Home and Outside) is considerably enhanced by the author's wonderful art of polemics. Certain characters, particularly those belonging to our class, best exhibit their inwardness through opinions on problems. Speech-making is nothing criminal; it is vital to the people of the age which has passed from reflexive action to reflective expression and discussion. Opinions and their statement mark a step in the gradual substitution of force by persuasion, which is the main contribution of civilization. We cannot go back to the age of the gods and the heroes—they were an unthinking lot! We cannot be satisfied with mere action, hence with mere plot. The plea of plot for plot's sake is on par with that of art for art's sake. There is no ground for admitting the identity of plot with art. In fact, this identity is extremely tenuous. Then again, problems are never purely emotional. Pure emotions have never been known to exist. The essence of problems is always intellectual. Emotions collect round a predicament, but the way out is never by emotion. Problems would never come in a novel unless the emotions of the characters have failed, as they must always fail, to find a way out. As characters are human beings, they cannot stew in the emotional juice for ever. Therefore, opinions on problems are absolutely vital to the characters. If there is no finality in the judgment, it is no fault of the writer. Judgment has a core of experience, but it can never be described. It is the reporting of the judgment that the writer is concerned with when he is writing. As has been well said by a suggestive essayist—'not experience itself but the author's judgment of his experience is the essential material of fiction; not what he observes but his intentions and speculations concerning it.' 'He is a poor master whose work surpasses his judgment; he alone is advancing towards the perfection of art whose judgment surpasses his work.' So wrote Leonardo da Vinci. The word 'judgment' in these two quotations cannot mean complete silence on crucial issues with which mere experiencing is satisfied. Experiences and events, in other words, situations, which portray character, may be as banally descriptive as statements of opinions. Of course, opinions would have to be interestingly put. But it is the quality of reporting the judgment that is important. A string of interesting statements would never mark a style. Judgment, as such, relates experiences better than emotions, which, by their nature, tend to make us all one and reduce our very individuality, the source of perennial social interests, to a statistical sample. Emotions are great levellers of character; they destroy the relations which are the subject-matter of the artistic process. The artist who is preoccupied with one type of character is not rich in his artistry; the rich one must have a variety of characters of minor and major shades, whom he would relate by his judgment. The most important relation is that of conflict, and the business of relating must take this fact into account. The conflict is always a problem as it always presupposes a value on one side, and on the other a fact or a situation. Hence a judgment or a problem is always problematic; can never satisfy all parties. A problem that is settled for a reader has ceased to disturb; a problem with which he is satisfied is a fact. So it is hardly fair to the novelist who posits a conflict and seeks to solve it according to his own light, intellect and judgment, and then reports it by bringing it into the universe of public course, to say about him that he is merely 'concerned with 'intellectual opinions' and preoccupied with the nonessential or the irrelevant. His interests are deeper than parading his modernity; his interests are no less than the solution of conflicts. If he does not resolve his maladjustments, he is not left in peace. The whole of the artistic process is to secure adequate adjustment between the artist's body and mind, between them, on the one hand, and situations which he has chosen or allowed to develop, on the other. I am told that the writing of a poem releases bodily tension, which is a physiological conflict, i.e., one on the vital plane, (as Dilip Kumar would probably like to call it). The reading of a poem performs a similar service to the reader, if we are to trust the authority of a pure and 'elegant' poet like Housman. No wonder, for the poet as an artist establishes connexions between interests hitherto suspected to be diverse. This is the essence of his craftsmanship as a maker of images. And the better the craftsmanship the more serious the nature of the conflict that it has attempted to solve. The so-called 'pure' poet selects images which do not contradict but fit in with each other, and thus emancipated from the vulgar touch of quotidian life causes no disturbance, no discomfort in the mind of the reader. The cloying sweetness thus produced is not poetry but its delusion. The bad 'pure' artists who avoided problems may have a certain degree of virtuosity, but it is not craftsmanship. The test of craftsmanship is the mastery of a difficulty, and not its avoidance. The suggestion to avoid virtuosity or pedantry may equally be offered to those who would not touch problems with a barge-pole, those who write amiable essays, sweet poems and harmonious fiction. They have energies left to be pedantic, not those who grapple with conflicts of life and seek to extend the old technique. The above remarks do not refer to tragic art alone. Yet, as tragic art is still considered to be great art, it may easily set the norm for all types, if any eternal principle of art were possible to discover at all.

The underlying assumptions of this discussion are more interesting than its form of articulation. The word 'story' is used by Tagore in the sense of a plan or plot, and the word 'problem' in the sense of content. I accept the words in his sense. The scope of the word 'art' should also be clear. When 'art' is mentioned in criticism we should be definite as to whether we are using the word from the point of view of the artist or of the reader (or spectator, or listener). In other words, we should make up our minds as to whether we are more interested in the process of creation or in the fact of achievement. I am convinced that a lot of confusion prevails on account of shifts in the meaning of words. In this discussion, so long as we refer to creative imagination consistently, we should concentrate on the process and not on the product. The consistency lies in the fact that the pages of a book have to be written one after another and turned over to come to the end-product, at which point only we are entitled to judge the whole. Retrospection is never before the last page is reached. The assumption is that we, as readers, do not jump from the beginning to the conclusion and skip over dull pages. Words are the materials which determine the technique of writing, and they do not overlap but run serially to make the sentence, the paragraph, the chapter, and the completed book. This temporal succession is the basis of literary technique. Therefore, in literature, the sense of the whole is postponed later than in painting or in sculpture or even in architecture, where, owing to the peculiar constitution of the eye, the form can be guessed at once, i.e., even when details are being studied. Thus deprived of the pleasure of dispersion and of the simultaneously immediate feeling for a structural unity, the process of the literary artist becomes more slow and processional. It is almost like a slow-motion picture of life. The process of assimilating the content naturally becomes the immediate preoccupation of the writer.

Now, it seems that there are at least two ways of writing, i.e., expressing the process of assimilation. One way is by planning ahead. Another way is by letting the subject or the content behave as it likes. Automatic writing, as in psychic experiments, is seldom literary. So far as planned writing is concerned, the following remarks may be offered:

> (1) So far as is known, there is hardly a single instance of the original plan remaining unchanged and ejected by exigencies of new ideas or new situations, which crop up inconveniently.
>
> (2) Even originally, there are plans more than one in number and the artist, for a good deal of time, remains hesitant. The plan itself is an exercise in the conditional mood.
>
> (3) The exigencies demand a good deal of attention, and it may well be that they earn a form at the cost of the main story. The artist may grow to love it so that it is handled in a much more careful manner than the main plot.
>
> (4) The characters and situations, the moment they are well-drawn, may assume independence and refuse to be drilled or regimented to the service of the main plot.

As has been indicated above, the plan or plot is the same thing as the form, and the plan is the only thing that the artist can from the beginning impose on the content, which is the artistic process of managing the materials, viz., problems and words; the rest grows and is checked along with the process of creation. Besides, there is some sense in the phrase—it is the height of art to hide itself. A plan must prepare for its own demise. That novel is really ill-written which shows the blue-print on every page. That 'elegant' lady is ill-dressed who shows her whale-bones.

So far as 'unplanned' writing is concerned, it should never be allowed to mean that there is not even a vague conception of a character or an apprehension of the story's doom or denouement. The legitimate meaning of the unplanned type of fiction is to be understood in terms of the writer's wishes. In this case, the general wish is to (1) keep the play of the mind more in the background; (2) allow the characters and incidents to speak for themselves; (3) accumulate details, each of which has a natural right to exist as a fact does in actual life, only indirectly related to another through living, but apparently isolated and dissociated; and, lastly, (4) give pleasure by surprise when the whole edifice emerges suddenly like a ship out of a yard.

Some of the best examples of the latter type of writing are the best fiction of modern times. The cumulative effect of the whole of a book like James Joyce's *Ulysses* is assuredly one within the range of aesthetic pleasures. The quantity of detail is no disparagement, for in accordance with the laws of process, quantity may twist into quality. Therefore, the seeming absence of an original plan, after a careful analysis, may reveal one of a type different from that of a 'constructed' novel. Here the critic comes in and performs a legitimate function in showing up the deceptive chaos, incidentally pointing out to the unwary that their absence of habitual response to a plan is not necessarily the absence of a plan. The plan of 'unplanned' novel is an emergent quality which cannot be posited at the start.

The two styles of writing have been separated at the instance of the opinions of novelists themselves. We have seen that the antithesis is hidden beneath almost similar practices. The greatest common measure is the pressure of the subject of characters and of situations. The more vital the subject, the more alive the character, the more complicated the situation, the greater is the degree of apostasy from the original motive and the orthodox execution. In other words, the very end of the artistic process, viz., the perfecting of materials, defeats itself at the very moment of perfection. The living content is always intransigent and intractable, I mean, the content that has received life from the artist. This particular tragic situation every artist has to meet at some stage or the other or his activity. The conclusion is that the plan, as the scientist may be conceded to possess it when he is working at the laboratory under controlled conditions, or the form, as the engineer draws it in a blueprint, is not essential to fiction as such. It has been present in most good novels. In others, the details have blurred it where it existed. In many cases, it is an invention, and not a discovery of the critic to satisfy those who seek to compensate their own irrationality by constantly looking for rationality in the mental processes of authors, the silent accused. So far from the point of view of the process of writing fiction.

The point of view of the critic is somewhat different at a later stage. At the beginning it is the same as when the critic is closely following the artist's unfolding. Then the critic's work is passively repetitive. But the critic soon becomes active and registers a different point of view. To measure this difference we must know that critics are of different types; at least, the same critic shifts his grounds constantly. There is the phase (or type) of technical scholarship when the critic looks to the facts and the events and at their relations, i.e., when he is a technician and exercises his sense of fact. Here slovenliness and inaccuracy in workmanship is the chief enemy. There is the phase of evaluation when the critic is a judge of values. Here the slips in psychology and sociology are to be pointed out. Then there is the aesthetic stage when the critic discovers canons of art. Here he is a metaphysician and talks in abstract language. An ideal critic would have a beautiful proportion of the necessary doses of the sense of fact, the sense of values and the sense of the abstract. The critic who possesses the first in a high degree would not usually care very much for planning, as he is more interested in details. The critic whose sense of values is strong is more likely to be pleased by a fiction constructed on a model. The philosopher of aesthetics would behave likewise, as the form is usually held to be more abstract than contents. Whether the form will bear the weight of philosophy or not is another matter. Usually, the philosopher is too high for poor particulars.

The difference between the points of view of the critic is smudged by the central feature of literary technique. It has been noticed before that words are the materials which determine the technique of writing, and they do not overlap but run serially. In other words, the writer writes serially and has to follow a temporal succession. Now, the critic, whichever type he may belong to, whichever stage he is in, is supposed to have read the book from the first page to the last. He records his impressions of the book, finds fault with it and appraises it after reading the whole book. The impression need not always be *of* the whole, but *after* reading the whole. Therefore, at the moment of writing he may be said to have made an escape from seriality. But it is a temporary escape, for he returns to his kill or his love. Even the aesthetic philosopher who loves to talk abstractly on the whole, or the form, cannot but relate his generalisations to the details and to the artistic process of relating those details, if he is to be taken seriously at all. The critic must always have a sense of fact, before he can have a sense of values, or a sense of the abstract. He can have it in an undeveloped form. Thus it is that the process of writing is important from either point of view. Therefore, the problem of form or content, in the light of the technical process of writing, is, really and truly, one of technique, i.e., one of handling the materials. The content is primary, in the sense that nothing more fixed and concrete is behind it.

A corollary to the above remarks: Significance is suitability to the purpose, particularly to the immediate purpose of creating, expressing, or 'operating,' as the Schoolmen said. Operating or making, which is the sphere of art, is to be distinguished from demonstrating, which is the work of the Man of Learning. If the chief reference of art is to the operating on materials, the meaning of the term 'significant' will be with reference to the operated materials themselves. Meaning of words does not exist before words are written or spoken. What comes out later should not be treated as cause. There is a temporality in this causal relation as well.

The above remarks are based on the assumption that the artist has a mind which operates on the materials, for otherwise artistic process is a misnomer and art is equated to being. In truth, it belongs to the sphere of becoming; or as the scholastics put it, *recta ratio factibilium*—'the undeviating determination of work to be done.' 'The process of artistic creation is an affair of the most severely practical intellect.' The word 'practical' is to be understood in the sense that all the faculties are to be used for a specific purpose, however vaguely conceived, by the artist who must have some intellect. The act of using our faculties is an expression of the dynamics of human appetite. Thus it is that artistic process and craftsmanship belong to the same genre. Another conclusion is that 'intellectual' problem is a tautology and that it has no existence apart from any other problem.

Nobody can predicate which type of fiction will yield a greater amount of pleasure, the planned or the unplanned one. But this has to be admitted that the emphasis on content is sanctioned by the modern temper. In this age reason is unpopular. The very hubbub about planning in a world of competition confirms my view. Living is found to bé discontinuous and no consolation in religion is being found. Scientific method does not assure continuity and the majority cannot make religion out of poetry. If we have any faith at all, it is in a chance collocation and fortuitous concourse. That is no faith, but its apology. Modern fiction cannot but reflect this attitude. The result is an emphasis on details and a corresponding staccato and syncopated development in fiction. The formlessness of life thus conceived has its parallel in a disbelief of artistic form. Probably, it is not pure anarchy. There is the promise of creation in the womb of this chaos. When the social content is such, at least one meaning of significance in the phrase 'significant form' is a corresponding formlessness. Is the universe so complete, formed and concluded that the novelist should come to a completion and give a form to this welter? Where is the stability of the content? The tempo is so fast nowadays that a year now is equivalent to a past decade.

Probably, it is 'creative imagination' that is expected to stabilise and reduce this welter to a shape. But much of this imagination which artists are supposed to possess as a special faculty is memory and a forward-looking tendency combined—'memory fringed with anticipation.' As to creation, more often than not it is the permutation and combination of old forms. What remains of creation is a reflection of new content for which the mirror of the mind is to be placed at a new angle. The newness consists in a preliminary unfamiliarity of the content to the public. The angle is the individual's, but only in the first instance. Of course, the clearer the face of the mirror, the better the reflection. The clearing process is not automatic. It is done by logic, by technique, by judgment. The logic is formal and dynamic. The formal logic usually proceeds by correspondence between propositions—which makes for lucidity of expression and ease of communication, in other words, which helps in the process of making the unfamiliar familiar; the dynamic logic proceeds by knowing the causes of changes in the social content, in other words, by understanding the nature of problems and conflicts.

It is then that the 'creative' artist goes on to solve them in a new synthesis. Creative imagination, even if it exists, is not opposed to logic, either formal or dynamic. When it is opposed, it can never offer a form to anything. There is a noble sentence in Shelley's 'Defence of Poetry'.... 'Sounds as well as thoughts have relation both between each other and towards that which they represent, and a perception of the order of the relations of thought.' When the order of the relations of thought is recognised in what is usually taken to be the sphere of the non-logical, viz., the poetic, it does not behove the pedestrian artist to rise superior to all considerations of logic. Creative imagination is not above logic. I wonder whether it is a special faculty at all. At best, it is a novel nomenclature for a very old thing, a high degree of technical efficiency which lends spontaneity and a glow to the finish. Its mysterious nature is probably due to the poverty of our technique for psychological analysis.

There is one other assumption of the discussion about which I want to make my position clear. It is that the artist obeys his own laws, and as such, is above all other social considerations. I now find that unless the position of the artist in the process of social change is properly understood, profitable discussion becomes impossible. Hence a few words are necessary.

It may be argued from what has been said in a previous paragraph about the artistic process that it is not different from social conduct inasmuch as both are practical, both demand intellectual efforts and both involve an 'undeviating determination of work to be done.' This equation is legitimate within certain limits. The artist is a social being, his logic of creation (whichever it might be, emotional or intellectual) is social, and his materials are social. The logical process of an individual is determined to a great extent by his social status and training. On the other hand, social conduct may be raised to an art, as it was in China. Yet there is a distinction. The scholastics gave the name of prudence to the principle of social conduct. Prudence and making (art), both have first to judge and then to command. The chief function of prudence is to command, which is the virtue of the aristocrat of the head of the Chinese family, nay, that of any family which has any high tone of social conduct; that of making is to judge, which is the virtue of the artist. Judgment is an intellectual exercise, even 'the suspension of judgment' is so. Prudence is an exercise of willing. Intellect belongs to the individual; the society *qua* society has no intellect. Besides, the very technique of writing in seclusion (even reading) makes for a certain exclusiveness for the writer (and the reader). He seems to think that he is exercising his own judgment and behaving in accordance with his own laws. An actor does not get this chance, nor does the Hindustani musician whose music is accompanied by the tom-tom. Much less so the head or any member of the family. But looking deeply into the artist's method, we find that certain habits, customs, mores are working through him. The words are not his creation, the syntax is not his, the meaning must be communicated. No individualist, no believer in personality can get round this objection that language, the very material and the medium of his art, is a social product. A poet may attribute a private meaning to his words, coin a phrase or an idiom, invert the order of sentences, may disobey syntactical rules, but there is a limit to his playing the truant. He must make himself understood by his own set at least. A fiction-writer has to address a larger public in any case. And though he, like Joyce, might seemingly go on uttering words and phrases as they come, he cannot cut off his moorings entirely. Words have roots; some roots go deep; others sprawl on the surface. In the case of Joyce they go as far down as Iceland. Similarly with syntax, which is determined by social experience, or, in term of the new psychology, the collective unconscious. The entire process of intellection is a generalisation from collective wisdom, if not the wisdom of society, at least that of a particular dominant section of it. Thus it is that the artist is a social being, and because he gives a twist to the words, adds to their meaning, arranges them in his way, he is still himself. The artistic process is conditioned by the social process, yet separated from it. The artist's forte is judgment, and not prudence. Naturally, he is not of the same category as a statesman or a political leader.

So far as 'the laws of being' are concerned, I doubt if there has ever been an artist who was born with a knowledge of them. If it were so, volumes would not have been written on the evolution of their 'mind and art.' Even Keats, who was a born poet if there is any such creature in English literature, took time to discover them. Tagore discovered them early enough, yet some time did elapse. And has he finished unfolding them or creating them? Most certainly not. Otherwise what is the secret of his perpetual youth, his ever-greenness, his adventurous journeys into the recesses of his deep self? If 'laws of being' could have been so easily formulated or unearthed, artists would have been plentiful like blackberries. That they are not only proves my thesis that the discovery or the framing of the laws of being is a rigorous discipline which lasts throughout the lifetime of all serious artists. I leave the question of success open, for I have not made up my mind as to whether there are any eternal laws, whether they can be discovered or set, and, if at all, whether they are by art or spiritual exercise. In other words, I am not sure whether art can be a substitute for spiritual discipline. With my present knowledge and experience I consider Richards' suggestion that poetry or art can act as a substitute for religion rather tenuous. Therefore, all that the artist can ever hope to do is to frame certain generalisations about his comparatively stable moods. There is no certainty about this stability nor is the stability desirable, for the artist who is always dictated by one law of his being bores in no time. And then the generalization need not be honest at all. Every generalization is an intellectual process; it is beset by all the dangerous trickeries of intellect for economising energy. The artist must note on the impermanent and the relatively stable. He builds on sands which are shifting slowly. Even Himalayan truths have floating bottoms.

The upshot is that no fiction writer, even as an artist, can avoid the social process. A mere writer accepts it on trust, a fashionable writer exercises prudence in using it for his popularity, and the supreme artist has a personal mode of expression besides. The social content is dynamic, therefore it is full of conflict. Conflict is the 'necessity' of the social order, and necessity can never avoid conflict as his subject-matter. His relationship with this conflict requires judgment in the selection of his attitude towards it. The solution of the conflict, no less than the release of his tension, is an intellectual exercise of the highest order. All problems are intellectual in that sense. It is by judgment on this that a fiction writer as an artist becomes the leader of society. He can never be a leader of society that is full of prejudices. He can only be a mouthpiece of that society. His potentiality corresponds to that of the society, for he is primarily a man of intellect and judgment, and not a man of will-power, command and prudence.

My conclusions can be reduced to the following categorical statements:

> That form is seldom imposed by the artist upon the content.
>
> That content is always social.
>
> That both content and form reflect the social process, and not society.
>
> That the social process is dialectic, creating problems at every step by opposition.
>
> That problems are the whole matter and their solution the whole manner of the art of fiction.
>
> That the solution is by knowledge or understanding as it is now called and not by a special faculty called creative imagination. Downey writes that 'valid imaginative reconstruction must develop from scientific insight.'
>
> That there is little distinction between art and craftsmanship; they have the same core, the problem of solving technical difficulties and conquering the opposition of matter. In art, the matter that opposes is the old form of art fixed and sanctified by old forms of society.

As such novels worthy of serious attention are *problematic*.

The need of solving the problems is the same for all; the artist's personality is in his personal solution. If the personal solution is accepted by the readers, present or future, he is allowed to continue as an artist or accepted as such. The point to be noted here is whether it is his personality or mere individuality. More important than these propositions is the fact that problems are the very texture of some fine modern novels, their very bone of bones, their flesh, their very own.

16. *Sociology of Indian Literature*

I

THE BASIC ASSUMPTIONS OF THE ARTICLE* ARE FEW AND SIMPLE. Literary traditions and experiments, which form the subject matter of both literary history and literature, are an expression and a very effective means of communication of cultural traditions and experiments, which in their turn, affect and are affected by the social process. Their relations are mutual transactions; but for the sake of convenience they may be understood either from the point of view of singular structure or total development. In so far as the need of an all-India approach and its correct analysis is urgent today, the discovery of the total form of Indian literary development subscribing to the general form of India's cultural change and subserving in the long run the overall social process is more purposive than any sectional partial view of a specific Indian literature, or a critical review of the achievement of literary artists therein. A general survey of Indian literature also posits a belief in the existence of its general form. Such a belief is warranted by philological and historical facts. Thus it is that the treatment here is dynamic, cultural and social, that is sociological.

The source of order in the diverse literary forms was Sanskrit literature, which was the creation of an élite group, while

* This essay was prepared about two years ago, primarily at the insistance of the representative of an American Foundation. As the scheme did not materialise, the essay in its revised form was taken over by the American University and the Fisk University of the USA. Even then I have not been able to locate it.

The study of social processes involved in literary ideas, literary techniques and literary situation is an unexplored tract in India. Articles published so far suffer from the following defects: (a) Unfamiliarity with the principles and methods of sociology, (b) The over-simplification of Marxist interpretation, and (c) Indifference the diversities arose out of the folk tales, rhymes and songs, which came from the people. The former often absorbed the latter and produced a composite literary order that lasted through centuries. The livingness of common social traditions, which the élite group had with their prestige established outside literature, was largely responsible for the continuity of literary forms in the midst of literary changes. These changes, it must be noted, were not large in number or momentous in quality. The relative permanence of social traditions was due to the following factors which the élite group intelligently utilised.

Various tribes and peoples lived together for ages in the context of political decentralisation which gave them freedom to exist as they willed, and thus removed one major impetus to

to what is happening to literatures other than that in the writer's mothertongue. The first two defects can be removed by a wider spread of sociology, but the removal of the last one, which is really a deficiency, depends partly on the literatures, and partly on the success of a research project under which representatives of different Indian literatures can be brought together to produce a joint-work of social and literary import. Sociology does not yet enjoy the prestige it deserves, though it is on the way to do so, thanks mainly to the presence in India of American experts in social sciences, who, however, are more of anthropologists than sociologists; nor is there any Indian institution which can undertake the scheme. Yet the time is propitious.

India, which has always been one, is more consciously one today than ever. The same social processes are working in almost every part of India, and more or less the same literary techniques are being adopted in every Indian literature. Literary magazines worth the name carry translations of literary work in other Indian languages. In short, Indian literatures are tending to become Indian literature. Sanskritic forms, the wide base of social solidarity, and a certain conformity to norms of behaviour and attitude once accounted for India's literary similarities. Now it is the impact of the world forces which the west has brought to India in the shape of new ideas and new modes of living. Old mores, folkways, customs and institutions are dissolving in every part of India, and the fact is apparent to all who read in their mothertongue. Perhaps it is more so in one area or better reflected in one literature than in another. Yet every Indain is an heir to change. This essay is built on that fact and is charged with the destiny it indicates. If it succeeds in its purpose, it should enjoy the additional advantage of focussing the attention of writers in the state language of India on the importance of regional languages and of heightening their consciousness of being Indian writers.

A few points in connection with the research on the sociology of an emergent Indian literature may be noted. After all, the essay is only an outline. It needs to be filled up by *particular* references. The author has actively participated in the formative processes of the Bengali literature alone; he has had indirect contact with Hindi, which he reads, and Urdu literature, which he does not read but which he has enjoyed through the medium of friends in the long revolutionary change. Their economic self-sufficiency in the context of rural needs, the undeveloped means of communication, and a comparatively less pronounced impact of urban life, which elsewhere made the villages yield their surplus to the cities in a stream and proved an incentive to changes in modes of production, bred an attitude of social acceptance. The institution of caste and family and guild apprenticeship in particular hardened the social crust. Intellectual traditions of Karma and a loose form of toleration, which in the absence of the Church permitted coexistence of sects, creeds and religions so long as they did not upset the social hierarchy, made for a certain degree of uniformity that burked the desire for material change.

At the same time, it would be unhistorical to ignore the exchange of forms and contents between the Sanskrit and

course of his stay at Lucknow, the famous seat of Urdu. Other literatures he knows still less. His contact with them has been established through correspondence and personal talks with writers and critics, and the histories or appraisals when they are written in English. So research should start by checking up the generalizations ventured here. If in that process they are discarded, the author will only be too pleased. Occasion will then arise to rewrite this essay. Meanwhile, it is no more than a working hypothesis, for which it is necessary that it should be more interesting than true.

The checking may proceed on the following lines:

Selection of any social attitude. It has to be traced in pre-British writings, which are usually poetic. Its first change during the initial impact with western ideas has then to be followed. Subsequent reactions are usually dichotomised into acceptance and rejection. These are depicted in *personal literary* situations, particularly in novels, stories and dramas. They have then to be connected with speeches and writings of social reformers and orthodox protagonists. (Public apathy or indifference is, however, important.) Then the features of the next phase of acceptance, i.e., the changes in the ideas brought about by relevant social forces and also the compromises, are to be obtained.

The spread of the ideas is to be then noticed and measured by (a) recurrence of the theme, and (b) the corresponding reading habit, if possible. Let us take the position of the girl-wife in the husband's family as an example. The conflict, when it arises, is usually threefold: (a) inter-familial, that is between the folkways of the girl's and husband's families; (b) intra-familial, that is commonly between the wife and the mother-in-law, or the elderly resident women relations of the husband; (c) intra-age, which revolves round the question of both physical and intellectual maturity. The conflict may be contrasted with the harmonious relations between the wife and her mates, young sisters of the husband or brother-in-law, their jokes and badinage. Rituals and the early familial training in role-taking are important agencies of harmony.

In natural families other conflicts arise, e.g., the eternal triangle, political ideas and the individualistic notions moving round the natural right of woman as such to freedom. The older methods

Prakrit literatures. The forms and contents were absorbed in classical Sanskrit literature. Indian aestheticians of poetry recognised regional styles or *riti*. 'Debased' language in the lips of common folk and women in particular, is common in classical Sanskrit dramas. On the other hand, Prakrit forms tended to approximate to the classic Sanskrit norms. These adjustments, however, did not disturb the placidity of the flow. In the process of slow accommodation, the Sanskritic tradition was almost always the dominant partner. Its dominance was established in ample measure in philosophical and musical literature as well. Indianization with the help of a Brahminical-Sanskrit culture led to the emergence of a recognisable totality. Even so late as the sixteenth century one Bengali author translated his work into Sanskrit to make it understood by Indian devotees.

The impact of Islam on Indian culture was marked. No sphere of cultural life remained untouched. Under the Muslim rule, which was much longer than the British rule, a cultural

of conflict-resolution are to be set against the new, e.g., escape into religion, escape into jobs, into party, singly or jointly. The part played by children in the resolution is important. References to divorce, companionate marriage, companionship or comradeship are to be arranged and the various attitudes scrutinised in the light of the literary situations as they develop and end. Intrusion of the author's views needs to be separated from the natural development of the story and characters. A very useful beginning has been made by Prof. G. S. Ghurye in his article on social change in Maharashtra in the *Sociological Bulletin* (Vol. 1. No. 1)

Once the outline is indicated, the next step should be the adoption of one or more suitable techniques for the measurement of attitudes. It is obvious that such techniques and questions should be amended in the light of local conditions. Probably, that too will not be enough. Two more corrections will be needed. The findings of literary attitudes have to be checked up by the survey of social attitudes conducted separately, though simultaneously. A comparison of these two sets of findings will lead to some reliable, that is, scientific generalizations in the sociology of Indian literature. The stress on scientific sociology can, however, be overdone; it can be rectified by history and by the biographical details of authors and readers. So far as readers are concerned, their reading habits require intensive study. A beginning may be made with school and college libraries and records of publishing houses when they are available, which usually they are not. One can, however, start with Lester Asheim's report on the conference on reading development published on behalf of the American Book Publishers Council. Failing that, the historical-critical method followed by Kellet on literary taste and George Orwell's essays on boys' literature in England or the historico-sociological method in Hauser's *Social History of Art* may be tried. The latter is apt to become impressionistic, but so long as no research-project is forthcoming, it is better than doing nothing.

synthesis was attained. For our purpose, the birth of Urdu and the resurgence of Bhakti and mystic cults are significant. Urdu is definitely an Indian language. Starting from camps and towns, it spread over a large part of northern India and certain regions in the south. Probably under court patronage and with the penetration of Muslim rule in the hinterland through the new revenue system and the judiciary, this new language came closer to the people in course of time. It almost acquired a new base by annexing certain forms of Hindi. Till the other day, Hindustani was almost indistinguishable from Urdu. Gradually, politics intervened; Hindus and Muslims were sought to be kept apart; and Urdu became more Persianised and Hindi more Sanskritised. Urdu imported signs and symbols from distant lands, and Hindi from distant times. The result is well known: Hindi, 'modernised' after independence, is not understood by the people of India; nor, one is sure, is 'modernised' Urdu by the average Pakistani. Six Bengali Pakistanis were shot during the Urdu-Bengali agitation. Thus one important means of communication between two religious communities—a means that was enriched both by Muslims and Hindus—has been severed. Be that as it may, Urdu was in a fair way of becoming an inter-regional language, at least so far as courtly behaviour was concerned.

The literary significance of Bhakti, however, consisted in the renaissance of regional languages with all that it meant in the way of cultural peculiarities of the different nationalities. Rama and Sita of the original Sanskrit *Ramayana* of Valmiki are not quite the same as the Rama and Sita of Tulsidas and Krittibas of the Muslim period. Other devotional poems and songs of the period belong to a genre different from that of the Vedic verses. In short, regional and folk elements at last got a chance. Mystic cults and literatures were more sharply dissident. Their emphasis on the individual was as much a protest against priestly rule as their doctrine of love was against the law of karma, the way of knowledge (*gnan-marga*) and rituals of the Brahmins. The very fact that mysticism, including Sufism, was the utmost limit of protest is an evidence of the closed nature of the society. In an open society other manifestations of protest and desired change are possible, but in a closed society mysticism appears to be the only way out of the shell. Thus it is that the balance of unity with diversity in literary forms was maintained over a large period of the Muslim rule with the help of mystic and Bhakti literatures catering for the peoples in the regions, Sanskrit litrature for the dwindling old élite group, and Urdu suited to the needs of those who lived near and in the courts. But it must be said that the final tilt of the balance was towards order and continuity.

Like mystic cults falling in line with the orthodox theology, the new forms of literature began to conform to the older ones. The social agency for the purpose was the flexibility of the caste system into which the new sects were slowly incorporated. (But the caste system drew its line on Muslims. The sects assimilated were Hindu-Muslim sects and were recruited from lower castes and classes.) Its literary counterpart was the Sanskritization of forms. In certain regions, a few literary forms emerged out of the impact of Islam while others were borrowed from its indigenous elements. The distinction coincided with the differences in the courtly and popular taste.

Basic material reasons of such comparative stability and continuity in the literary modes of communication are not far to seek. Historical research does not divulge any vital change in this period either in the productive or the social relations. No serious technological innovation is reported to have taken place. Feudal relations were only broadened and deepened; modes of production continued with minor changes at the fringe of agriculture; trade was facilitated and hampered alternately; currency muddles and unfair taxes often conspired; royal exactions were often heavy and uncertain. But, by and large, conditions of living were easy; trades moved to and fro, if not always safely; *hundies,* cheques of indigenous banks, enjoyed currency; wealth did not flow out of the land; and public works often came to the rescue of the people.

The real harm was the restriction of the horizon. Gone were the days of cultural expansion, and in came many movements of counter-reformation centering in the Smritis. Learned commentaries on academic points were written in elaborate forms, and they did duty for creative work. Indian society had turned inward, and the creativity of the people appeared to be on the downgrade. Only the defence-mechanism of Hindu institutions kept Indian cultural traditions going. Indian society, Indian culture, Indian literatures still comprehensive and rich, were too stable, too static, too formal at the time when the west probed into this land. The area of communication was shrinking and its lines were atrophied. The influence of the west on Indian society has been greater in scope and intensity than that of Islam. Muslim rule had not deeply affected Indian trade and commerce except on certain rare occasions when taxes were imposed on Hindus—and most traders were Hindu—or currencies were tampered with. It had never touched the village-community.

The East India Companies immediately harmed indigenous trade and commerce capital, and once the English company established itself it took no time to destroy the panchayat. Feudal relations were preserved in their pristine purity in the 'native' states despite, probably to consolidate, political annexation. In the important wealth-producing eastern regions, a new feudal class was imposed, but the imposition did not lead to any agricultural improvement or to a basic change in the feudal relations. If anything, the sector of production was limited. The zamindar lived on surplus revenue and drifted to the city. Along with the establishment of ownership, which was divorced from productivity and responsibility towards agricultural improvement, came the introduction of English literary education to create a class that would support a government equally divorced from society. These two classes, the landlord and the literati, formed the middle class, who were not the bourgeoisie of the west nor the Sethis of earlier India, neither quite the manorial lords of medieval Europe combining military and administrative duties with the exaction of feudal dues nor even the geographical middle of two sharp opposites. They were an uprooted class who were kept hanging in mid air. But the English educated middle class acted as a medium, a sort of transmission belt of western culture. Be it ever remembered with gratitude that the early Indian pioneers of western culture made the best of their social situation. Men like Raja Ram Mohan Roy were steeped in both types of culture and deliberately accepted the challenge of the west. And the west too had not yet declined. Western Europe was yet developing; capitalism was then a progressive force; science was on the march; and democracy, nationalism, humanism still had content and glamour.

It is interesting to note the depth of the western influence over the mind and behaviour of the first batch of Indian intellectuals. It reminds one of the Soviet fascination of the Indian youth; it was probably stronger. Even the opposition to that influence on the ground of materialism and of its being foreign, is strikingly similar to the present charge against Communism. Probably, the commonness is in the unreality and in the attempt of one stratum to transform it into reality. In any case, the social unreality of the first stage in the history of Indo-European contact was to haunt the Indo-British (or Anglo-Indian) culture for days to come. Perhaps the finest example of that attempt was the new literatures. Indian literatures after the British period developed along comparatively new lines. The hold of Sanskritic forms, though firm in the beginning, ultimately became weak because these forms would not recognise or could not even face the new social content. The time was ripe for laying a new cable. So long as it connected one segment of the Indian people with the west, it did not immediately matter if it did not connect with the rest.

II

The various new Indian literatures developed the following general features in course of time.

(1) *Enlargement of scope.* It was partly due to printing facilities, partly to expanding literary education, in which English literary political and philosophical traditions dominated, and partly to a type of compensation in terms of 'life-space', that is, for political subjection and economic helplessness. The literary forms now adopted were the novel, drama, travel-sketches, essays and diaries, story, sonnet, and epic. Barring the drama and the epic, they were new. Mythological dramas were often written and staged to express political feeling in 'non-actionable' forms. Novels were mainly about historical personages and events, and for the same reason. At least in Bengal, epics were written in blank verse and on European models. Even the heroes were reversed in the *Meghnad-badh Kavya,* an epical freak written by Michael Madhusudan Dutt whose model was Virgil, Milton and Tasso.

(2) *Gradual acquisition of new values.* There are cases of overnight adoption of western values as in the Bengali epic mentioned above, but the process was generally one of infiltration and weakening of resistance. The values related to ideas of liberty, equality and fraternity, nationalism science, and rationalism, in particular. Most of them were directed towards the problem of political subjection and civil liberties, but reformist religious movements facilitated their intrusion into social

affairs. The growth of rationalism was hampered by the neglect of scientific and technical education. So rationalism allied itself with the older traditions of humanism, which however, was religious rather than positivist or scientific in character. On the other hand, resistance was apparent. A reaction against the so-called gifts of the west, like Christianity, material prosperity, rationalism etc., set in. But adjustment went apace. Hindu customs, beliefs, mores and folkways were described and analysed as 'scientific; Hinduism, with the help of theosophy, was 'proved' to be socially and spiritually wiser than Christianity; its philosophy was of course more subtle and satisfying! The unperceived effect of the adjustment was that the Hindu religion which was an ensemble of rituals and customs began to be taken by the English educated as Hindu culture, a way of life, sanctioned by both human and divine reason. All the cultural processes of imitation, resistance, accommodation, radiation, adjustment and assimilation now became evident in the Indian literatures.

None of these axiological processes, however, could come to fruition without the corrosion of the Indian social base. That was done mostly by economic forces which had seeped into the foundation. Village communities with their economic self-sufficiency and minor democratic forms had wilted under the pressure of the new system of land tenure and decayed with the destruction of cottage-industries and the attenuation of rural finance. They receded further before the new 'local self-government.' Joint family life was directly attacked by notions of individualistic family life and indirectly by legal decisions and enactments. Official transfers of middle class officers and mobility of labour stressed the inability of heads of large joint families, or their only earning members to support the increasing number of hangers-on known to *Mitakshara* as co-partners. The caste-system was undergoing a double change; on the one hand, it was yielding its rigours; on the other hand, lower castes wanted to rise in the scale by adopting the rituals and customs of the upper castes, some of which were against mobility and positively illiberal. Railways and urbanisation helped the first change score over the second. All this made for re-valuation of notions of marriage, family and caste.

The net literary result was growth of romanticism including its love, passion and agony, side by side with a certain type of rationality and the spirit of adventure. Rituals, marriage and its attendant customs like child-betrothals, young widowhood, dowries and third party negotiations, as well as the priestly class who flourish on them, came in for a lot of criticism. Social relations revolving round individualistic, passionate, romantic love were encouraged. The eternal triangle became a popular theme. Woman's status was thus ideologically raised. She was no longer the chattel or the drudge; even the orthodox called her the eternal mother, wife or companion. But the new literature loved to look at her as the lover minus the body. None realised that this view was another form of the woman as passion's property, and that it was all a make-believe, because that property had been denuded of its physical content by puritanical fervour.

(3) The chief originator and carrier of the new values was the *new class of gentry, mostly belonging to liberal professions, including landownership*. They were educated in English, but thanks to the reaction and to subsequent revivalism, they were not fully involved in, or wholly committed to, western ideologies. What had once been the pure prestige of western values now became an opportunist technique of adjustment to the British rule. These English educated gentlemen, when they did not flock to liberal profession, were mostly absentee landlords, urban and urbanised, nationalist or nationalistic, non-capitalistic, and yet bourgeois in spirit and outlook. They formed the liaison officers of two cultures and they were hated and favoured by both. They adopted western standards of literary appreciation and modes of literary creation. Their great writers were called the Indian counterparts of Scott, Shelly and Byron. They played a progressive role in literature despite the derivativeness, verbosity, substitute-emotions and pseudo-enthusiasms of their creations. The genius of a few outshone the imitative adaptations of the rest. It was rarely, however, that the light they shed made the darkness below visible. The general uprootedness and parasitical nature of the imitators was as much a case of historical denial of 'manifest destiny' as one of struggling to escape the limits of fate. If their failure sprang from their cheap idealistic, rather non-materialistic, approach, their success was due to the vague, generalised recognition of the fact that India could not stay where he was and the western influence was an impulse for change. This dialectic of the socio-cultural situation was fully reflected in the polarisation of attitudes and beliefs in literature, hence too in its forms. Such

literature was essentially a class literature, and it flourished in its ignorance and neglect of the people's 'vulgar' literature, which in its turn withdrew further into its shell.

(4) *The effects of industrialism and technology* were not immediately apparent. It was only after the First World War that Indian literature recognised industrialism, and after the second, it sensed technology. But in the earlier period these two agencies of social change made for some economic literature in English, mostly dealing with the British drain of Indian wealth. Two of the famous Indian economists of that age wrote history or historical novels. Otherwise, such essays dealt with material progress and success in life and breathed rationality. The connection of rising capitalism with Calvinistic attitude and of succeeding capitalism with rationality cannot be definitely established in the history of modern Indian culture, but it can be sensed as a vague integument of ideas. After the First World War, however, the incidence of capitalism on Indian society was duly registered in Indian literature. The register ranged from rural romanticism to Marxist classicism. Go back to the villages, the mystique of the people, philosophical anarchism with its cult of individual freedom, decentralisation and federalism, economic interpretation, exploitation, increasing misery of the poor, dictatorship of the proletariat, and party discipline, these were the slogans. The vision of social justice in Marxist ideology began to appear in the tone and content of literature.

III

But we are anticipating. The beginnings of this century saw a deepening of the above social processes and a tendency of the consequential cultural and literary changes to develop 'form,' which was at once a store and a measure of literary values. The processes were further facilitated by Asia's awakening, notably expressed in the Japanese victory over a western power, Russia, and inaudibly murmured in the revolution of China and the Middle East. There was great sympathy with the Boers against England, Turkey against Italy, and for Moroccan resistance against the French. But that sympathy had little to do with any understanding of the nature of imperialism, though revolt against colonial political status was freely expressed. It thus collaborated with the upsurge of nationalism. If 'uncivilised' Japan of the other day could beat the west in its own game, what could not 'civilised' and multitudinous India do! The Japanese method was not properly studied, but it was generally held to mean science and technology. Another method was terrorism. Russian 'nihilist' stories were very popular in this period. One can easily detect Narodnik and Hameltic symptoms in the then patriotic literature of India. The national movement as such was based on the romantic conception of the nation having a moral mystique of its own that demanded personal human sacrifice. Mazzini's influence was unmistakable in the great political utterances of the day. Often was the nation identified with the Divine Mother who in certain parts of India is the pivot of power-cult. A highly spiritual philosophy of Indian nationalism was offered by Sri Aurobindo, but it made no headway against the middle class attitude towards the motherland, excepting probably in Bengal.

Be it noted, however, that while the literature of the Swadeshi movement was also volitional and activist, the romantic pressure was more evident. Even the philosophy of Will, or the doctrine of Shakti, could be very romantic. In literature, heroes of action were too ready to swoon into their ladies' arms at the critical moment, or retire into forests to establish *ashrams* after defeat and disappointment. Consequently, romantic individualism may be said to have been the ruling note. Indian literary content swung between collective mystique and personal action and settled at the specious point of individualism which the British ideology had introduced as an idea into this supremely totalitarian society. That point could not, however, be fixed before the middle class wanted to make up for their pointlessness, their uprootedness. The will, however, languished in the absence of adequate institutions for its growth. This phenomenon of pseudo-individualism spread out from Bengal, the rendezvous of middle class destiny, to other parts of India where the 'middle class' took time to grow. It also largely explains the influence of Bengali literature over other Indian literatures. But romantic individualism was a releasing social force. It certainly led to the consciousness of the fact of exploitation of woman by man, peasantry by the zamindar, lower middle class by the upper middle, and also labourers by the employers. These releases were manifested in literature in unequal degrees.

With every increase of self-importance of the middle class —which did not always cover their central lack of self-confidence —the new values became harder and more uniform throughout India. Naturally, the new literary forms became pronounced and similar. Simultaneously, there was a further recession of *prakrit* folk and sect literatures followed by a nostalgic search for them. One motive of the search was of course revivalist nationalism, but subtler factors came from the romantic concept of the people and the perception of the hollowness of Anglo-Indian culture. Yet the two literatures remained on two levels though some men of genius delved into the lower; they were parallel to the basic class divisions which the caste hierarchy was no longer competent to muffle.

Within the middle class, divisions tended to be smudged; and in certain parts of India, the upper sectors were pulled down without the abolition of their middle character, that is, without throwing them into the rank of the proletariat. The middle class attitude towards culture, though flexible within limits, still remained incrusted with prejudice. Its language was not understood by the people, nor was its literature. Strictly speaking, no new communication was established with the people and the old communication was snapped. At the same time, it will have to be remembered that social changes were extending throughout India, and the foundations of a modern Indian culture were being laid. It is true that regional literatures still differed from each other; and the reasons, apart from environmental factors, were the following:

(a) Historical influence of early European, commercial, hence, political settlements, including education through English.

(b) Dominance of commercial centres and ports for export of raw-materials from the hinterland.

(c) Growth of industrial areas and cities. These two formed the urban-rural transmission line of culture.

(d) Greater or less hold of Sanskritic, or Persian traditions in the already existing literatures. This is clear in the case of Hindi literature of India's heartland and Urdu literature in courtly pockets like Delhi, Lucknow and Hyderabad.

(e) Lastly, the tempo in the spread of communications and the press in particular. Despite these differences arising from the tempo and the spread of British rule, an outline of a new all-India literature can be recognised and the contents thereof safely indicated. In fine, while modern Indian culture became extensive, it was not intensive enough to penetrate beyond the values of the middle classes.

IV

The common social and cultural processes reviewed above were registered in the following general social faiths which motivated the literary beliefs and attitudes in their turn.

(1) *Faith in progress* was almost universal. Almost, because one of the orthodox counter theories was the cyclical concept of *yugantar*. The west was held to be the harbinger of *kali yuga*. Otherwise, faith in progress seldom wavered. It was to be brought about by science mainly. Yet mechanistic materialism was never adopted. The Indian attitude did not also square the old idealism. The attempts to do so were half-hearted. Probably, faith in collective human effort, which was another means of achieving progress, was equally strong or equally weak. In the agitational form of politics it was evident. In the economic sphere it was least manifest, except in the demand for restoration of village-communities and cottage-industries. Certain voluntary social reformist agencies had no doubt been functioning, but only in the general context of *laissez faire*. The government drew upon itself the entire demand of doing everything for the people.*

* In view of the common misunderstanding about the autocratic nature of Indian monarchy in the remote and the paternal benevolence of the British rule in the recent past, as also in view of the present malady of Indians to look up to the state for every good to be done or blame it for every bad that has been done, it is necessary to point out that Indian history always kept the state apart from society and that the Indian state, if ever there was a state in the Austinian sense, allowed the society to live in its own way. The scope of the so-called 'voluntary agencies' in India was eliminated, and they were established through institutions with the backing of a non-oecumenical religion. It was only when the East India Company's administration became the government and the government assumed the functions of a colonial state, that is, only when *laissez faire* for exploitation was accompanied by religious and social neutrality, that the Indian people replaced blind faith in a transcendental force by the all-powerful and all-good state. What were words and panegyrics to kings in the olden days became a settled habit of mind of the people. This habit persists today. It accounts for a good deal of frustration and defeatism, that is, for the loss of confidence in collective human effort.

In this vacuum it was the voluntary organisations that suffered. It is quite likely that the uncritical and unrealistic abandonment to socialist theory by a highly educated and intelligent group of young writers, known as progressives since the thirties, has its origins in the vacuum mentioned above. The truth of the matter is that the social forces making for change and progress were seldom analysed in India by Indians. If they were less religious they could have a religion of progress or of collective humanity. So their descendants wanted to build up a religion of history, which stands or falls by the faith in progress to be achieved by a certain type of collectivity and a certain type of conscious effort.

(2) *Faith in the individual.* Reference has already been made to the peculiar character of new Indian individualism, viz., that it did not have the social backing which the industrialised countries of the West had. Distinction has also to be made between this type of individualism and the personalism of earlier Hindu literature. Such personalism was developed through well-defined stages of social discipline and worked out into a final identification with the Absolute or a personal God, as in Viashnava *padavalis* and *sant* songs. The new individualism on the other hand, worked negatively against caste, family and political authority, and positively only for the rights of the 'individual.' In such a climate anarchist philosophy grew naturally. It will not be untrue to say that the literature produced in the Gandhian era of national movement could not come out from the anarchist ideological envelope and that even the literature produced under the influence of socialist thought has found in it a sort of Appleton layer.

(3) *Faith in reason.* Here again reason was not of one type. There were rationalists no doubt, but they confined their activities mostly to pamphleteering. The best use of reasoning was made in the critical interpretation of old documents, inscriptions and records. Fine pieces of historical scholarship appeared. Yet it was not quite 'historical reasoning.' Either it was 'scientific' in the usual sense, or it was 'nationalistic' defence or glorification of India's past and India's culture under the cover of scientific research. Above all, it was sectional and discontinuous, that is, dynastic, political and non-sociological. Rational thinking was also behind philosophical literature, but here too nationalist

defence of Hindu philosophy and its historical account formed the rule.

On the whole, rational approach operated against many religious superstitions and social beliefs without replacing them by any positive alternative. In reaction, intuitionalism appeared on the double support of traditional Indian psychology and the idealistic opposition to science recently led by western philosophers. Bergson, Eddington and Jeans put the young Indian rationalism into cold storage. Gandhiji's 'inner light' and charisma hastened the process. While it is true that pure reason can hardly be the sole impulse behind literary creation, rational approach can suffuse it, as it suffused classical French literature. Modern Indian literature was non-classical in the absence of formal unity and order no less than in its adjuration of traditional controls, or even self-control. Decay of social control facilitated the riot of sentiments.

V

We may now come to the corresponding literary beliefs. These are to be construed from creative practices and critical standards, but chiefly from the latter. Indian literary criticism in the early period of British contact was essentially didactic. The stress was mostly on moral values. It was double morality, however. While non-morality in western literature was pardonable, it was inexcusable in the Indian. The erotic and highly sensual elements in Sanskrit or Vaishnava literature were conveniently forgotten or explained away in terms of religious symbolism. Very little of formal criticism was indulged in. Yet a few critics held a high position by virtue of their learning and dignity. Later on, even these critical standards went overboard and new literary beliefs were formulated. The central one was art for art's sake. That popular dogma of the 'naughty nineties' appeared in India after the usual time-lag. Art was considered distinct from craftsmanship. It was unrelated to living, society and morality; hence it was the fruit of leisure and 'culture.'

Along with it grew the cult of the artificial and the fantastic, as also that of the ideal physical type of the artist, with flowing hair and dreamy eyes, a little looseness in morals and much slovenliness in habit, intellectually undisciplined, and otherwise a derelict. Creative impulse was therefore 'spontaneous.' Competent technique, it was held, could not be a substitute for the vigour of the native and noble impulse of genius which everybody was presumed to possess. It was no longer necessary to know the rules of the game to be its master. Experience was nothing more than impression. And once you have the artist's eye you need not care about the design. This literary belief spread over all the fine arts and was responsible for the dominance of literary values over painting and music. Romantic agony became the only test of sincerity.

Yet it meant an extraordinary release for literature, and also for fine arts. While it meant that religious faith was no longer a social bond and that old moral values were moribund, it also signified that the old aesthetic tradition could no longer contain the new poetic content. The release from literary bonds was effective to the extent that the new literary beliefs harnessed the new social attiudes which were those of non-acceptance and protest. Wives against husbands and mother-in-laws, sons against fathers, the young against the old, and the oppressed against the oppressors—that was the attitude which began with social sympathy and reformism and later on turned to a vague longing for revolutionary change. A fresh gust came from the west after World War I was over. Continental literature was in every young man's hands. Those who had never heard of *Kalidas* or *Bhavabhuti,* whose knowledge of the *Ramayana* and the *Mahabharata* was less than meagre, who considered Fielding and Dickens to be old fashioned, were familiar with the works of Ibsen and Hamsun, Tolstoy, Turgeniev, Dostoievsky, Chekov and Gorki, Bernard Shaw and H. G. Wells, Flaubert, Maupassant and Maeterlinck, D'Annunzio and Pirandello, Whitman, Sinclair Lewis, and Drieser. Not that there was any critical understanding of these authors; in fact, their context was often missed; but young Indian literateurs copied their form or formlessness and smuggled their content. The net result was a gain in humanism. True that it was still romantic, unreal and often exotic, yet the consequential humanist trend was unmistakable. By the thirties this trend acquired a direction and content.

Direction came from the study of Marxism which was initiated by the Russian revolution and helped by its chain reactions throughout the colonial world where anti-imperialism took the form of socialistic nationalism. The content was partly indigenous. By that time Indian capitalism had risen and the proletariat could be spotted. The trade-union movement was also growing. Young writers recognised these social forces and their conflict. Others separated themselves to live in what was called the ivory tower. This time the 'progressives went to the masses, the exploited class of the peasants, workers and petty bourgeoisie, with better historical understanding. But their form, being derivative, was loose and did not always fit the content. In this search the significance of folk-literature was discovered. More or less similar things happened in Europe. So the Indian literary movement of this period can also be described as a part of the wider movement. The world was convulsed and the convulsion was transmitted to India; and India was not wholly unready. Unconscious and conscious transmission of culture was at last possible, because now there were a few common grounds of social acceptance.

The corresponding literary attitudes have since then been clearer. Few now question the thesis that the function of literature is social, though critics have not yet analysed how the social processes enter into literary creation and what they do there or is done to them. There is also a general agreement that it must voice the aspirations of the downtrodden, like women, children and the scheduled castes, the poor peasantry, the industrial labourer and the white-collared clerks. Propaganda is often defended as more purposive and creative in the long run than disinterested pursuit of art for art's sake. An yet sharper articulation is found in the belief that literature must bring about social change instead of registering it as the naturalists of the twenties held, by understanding, focussing attention on, and thus exposing, the social contradictions in the system.

Some exaggeration has occurred here, but it is equally true that no philosophy of the historical social process has been forthcoming to excite creative endeavour as an alternative to Marxism. Hence the standards of appreciation and criticism, which always wait on creation, are in a general way Marxist, but seldom technically conscious. The usual lag between the social process and the cultural process, the inevitable amendment of the latter by literary artists, and also the persistence of traditional aesthetic values acting as cores of resistance and centres of rivalism, account for the present uncertain position of literary criticism. In any case, the social function and influence of literature are recognised to be wider and deeper today than ever before. The connection of modern Indian literature with the deeper significance of humanism on the plane of living is the secret which young Indian literatteurs are grouping to secure and are not likely to miss or sell once they know and understand India.

It must be admitted, however, that the methods of recognition and the agencies of influence are not yet working smoothly. India, in a sense, had no 'reading public.' Her method of transmission was verbal, that is, both oral and musical. Indian philosophy was orally taught; Indian epics were sung; and there were the ballads and devotional songs. Manucripts, no doubt, became plenty, and they travelled far and quick through wandering scholars. That tradition became very weak in course of time. On the other hand, India has not yet developed a publishing industry. Authorship is certainly more paying than before, but because it must need cater to a semi-literate public it can seldom afford to break new ground. Very few significant authors can thus maintain themselves by their writing. State publishing has not yet been undertaken; it has its dangers. The central government cannot do it; probably, it should not do it. Once these States are more culturally and linguistically organised, the way may be open for an intelligent approach to the question. Meanwhile, the sociology of Indian literatures indicates the need of building up relevant institutions round the literary beliefs and attitudes, the cultural and social process described before. If the great problem of the relation between state and society had been solved, such institutions could have been sponsored by the state and welcomed by writers. At present, therefore, only voluntary associations of authors and a vigilant attitude towards help from the state are indicated. State patronage of culture can hardly go beyond patronage so long as the state, society, and their relationships are what they are.

REFERENCES

Select General References (In English)

The Cultural Heritage of India, Vols. 1. 2. 3. (Ramakrishna Centenary Volumes. The new edition will contain ten volumes).

Majumdar, Raychaudhury and Dutta, *An Advanced History of India*

L. S. S. O'Malley, *Modern India and the West*

P. Griffiths, *The British Impact on India*
A. Yusuf Ali, *A Cultural History of India during British Period*
Jawaharlal Nehru, *Autobiography, Discovery of India*
Nirad Chaudhuri, *The Autobiography of an Unknown Indian*
D. P. Mukherji, *Modern Indian Culture*
I. N. Madan, *Modern Hindi Literature*
R. B. Saxena, *History of Urdu Literature*
D. C. Sen, *History of Bengali Language and Literature*
E. Thompson, *Rabindra Nath Tagore, Poet and Dramatist*
Iqbal Singh, *The Ardent Pilgrim*
K. M. Munshi, *Gujarata and Its Literature*
P. R. Sen, *Western Inflence on Bengali Literature*
G. S. Ghurye, 'Social Change in Maharashtra' (*Sociological Bulletin*)
S. A. Latif, *The Influence of English Literature on Urdu Literature*
S. A. Suharwardy, *Urdu Novel*
W. C. Smith, *Modern Islam in India*
P. T. Reji, *History of Telugu Literature*

Special References*

(a) *Bengali Literature*

The tradition of social novels, dramas, stories and essays is at least as old as the impact of the British rule in India. In the period before Tagore strode the scene for fifty years and more, the dramas of Michael Madhusudan Datta, Dinabandhu Mitra and Kaliprasanna Sinha, the essays of Raja Ram Mohan Roy, Vidyasagar, Bhudeb Mukherji, Bankim Chatterji, Shibnath Shastri, and the poems of Michael Madhusudan Datta, Hem Chandra, Rangalal breathed political and social reformist fervour. Political essays are numerous. One may, however, begin with Tagore who is the great divide in Indian literature.

(1) Tagore: His social novels, stories, some poems and essays are indispensable. His dramas often deal with social problems, but their symbolic garb may not unfold their social content to the unweary reader. Among his novels the following are to be read. (Titles are in Bengali). *Chokher Bali, Nauka Dubi, Gora, Ghare-Baire, Char-Adhyaya, Chaturanga.* English translations are available. The English titles may be obtained from the Viswabharati Bookshop, 6|3, Dwarkanath Tagore Lane, Calcutta. To this author's knowledge no English collection of Tagore's stories has appeared; nor that of his social essays. Besides Thompson's *Rabindra Nath Tagore, Poet and Dramatist, Tagore—a Study* by D. P. Mukherji (which is a short running account of the man's total achievement) may be glanced at.

---

* These references are not at all exhaustive. If any prominent name has been dropped, it is entirely due to the author's lapse of memory. Friends who have helped me in these references are not to blame. It has not been possible to collect materials and references for Maharashtra, Tamil, Telugu, Gujarati, Kanarese, Assamese, Oriya, Malayalee, Punjabi and other important languages, from Lucknow. The work is not one man's job. A full research project is necessary.

(2) Sarat Chandra Chatterji: All his novels and stories are of sociological interest. His sympathies were for the downtrodden and the vagabond. His acute sense of justice embraced all forms of life. S. Sengupta's *Sarat Chandra, Man and Artist* should be consulted.

(3) Pramatha Chaudhury: His stories and essays, written under the pen-name 'Birbal,' expose social and intellectual hypocrisies by the light of reason and wit. Only his *Char Yeari Katha* has been translated into English and published by the Viswabharati. It gives a brilliant sketch of the fantasies, follies and foibles of England-returned men of the upper class. His essays, which are gems of their kind, still await translation.

(4) Among modern living Bengali novelists and short story writers the following are relevant to the purpose: Naresh Sengupta, Premen Mitra, Buddhadeb Bose, Achintya Kumar Sengupta, Manik Bandopadhyaya, Bibhuti Bandopadhyaya, Dilip Kumar Ray, Banaful, Annanda Shankar Roy, Subodh Ghosh, Naren Mitra, and this author.

(5) There is lot of poetry in Bengal. Tagore was a great releasing force both for 'literary' poetry and for poetry of live issues. Leaving his contemporaries aside, and men like Satyen Dutta and Jatin Bagchi were no mean poets, one may begin with the study of Kazi Nazrul Islam, Mohit Lal Mazumdar, Sudhindra Datta, Premen Mitra, Buddhadeb Bose, Achintya Kumar Sengupta, Jibanand Das, Bishnu De, Amiya Chakravarty, and Subhash Mukherji. There are many others whose works may be taken up later.

(6) The dramatists contemporary with Tagore are Girish Chandra Ghose, Kshirod Vidyabinode, Dwijendra Lal Roy and Amrit Lal Bose. Their mythological and historical dramas are often the cover of modern political and social issues. As mentioned before, the real social dramatist was the late Dinabandhu Mitra. Sachin Sengupta's full-length dramas and Manmatha Ray's one-act plays are carrying on the tradition. Drama, thanks to the films, is in the doldrums in Bengali literature. Only Bengal and Maharashtra have had public stages.

(7) Amrit Lal Bose was a satirist in drama. Two great but gentle satirists need mentioning, the late Sukumar Roy, who wrote nonsense verses, and Raj Sekhar Bose (Parasuram), who has adopted the story-form. Unless one has mastered the Bengali language it is difficult to appreciate these two authors. Their exposure of social evils is very kind.

(8) Literary essayists and critics are too numerous to mention. The best of them were Tagore, Suresh Samajpati and Pramatha Chaudhury. Among living essayists the following have definitely adopted the sociological angle: Gopal Haldar, Niren Chaudhury, Amit Sen, and this author. The best literary essayists like Atul Chandra Gupta, Sudhindra N. Datta, Buddhadeb Bose, Annanda Shankar Ray, Mohit Lal Mazumdar, Bishnu De, Sajani Kanta Das, Hiran K. Sanyal, and Bimala Prasad Mukhopadhyaya, have not been able to ignore the significance of the social context. Social

changes haunt them all. Some have faced them while others seem to have been apalled by them.

(b) *Hindi*

The following authors are significant. Barring a few of Prem Chand's stories, no major Hindi work seems to have been translated into English.

(1) P. N. Srivastava, the author of *Vida,* in which the conflict of a newly married couple is delineated with sympathy.

(2) Ugra, the author of *Delhi Ka Dalal,* a novel of immoral traffic of women; and *Badhua Ki Beti,* a novel of untouchability.

(3) Nirala, (the famous poet) the author of *Apsara,* a story of woman who is naturally free; *Billeswar Ki Bakhariya* (the Goat-herd) is a social satire.

(4) Prem Chand: All his novels and stories, particularly the *Seva-Sadan,* the story of a forsaken girl; *Ranga-Bhumi,* which deals with three groups, the peasantry as represented by Sur Das, the blind beggar, Sophia, the Indian Christian girl, and the Hindu family of Vinay; *Premasrama,* where the conflict of the landlord and the tenants is the motif; *Karma Bhumi* is a socio-political novel with a bias for non-violence. *Gabana* is a departure inasmuch as it seeks to expose middle class respectability through Ramakant who belongs to the lower middle class and wants to climb through fantasy. *Godan* was his most mature novel. Here he is conscious of class-conflict. Prem Chand's stories are gems, the brightest being *Kafan.* Towards the end of his days he was coming close to socialism, which explains his presidentship of the first Progressive Writers' Conference in Calcutta in 1936. Prem Chand wrote both in Hindi and Urdu. He believed in Hindustani. He is the greatest modern prose writer in Hindi as well as in Urdu.

(5) Yashpal: *Dada Comrade* (plot involving Indian terrorist-politicals), and *Manushya Ki Rupa* (Man is Slave of Social Class).

(6) Bhagwati Charan Verma: *Tehre Mehre Raste* (Zig-zag Road), a story of political conflict with the Gandhian approach.

(7) Aggaye (Vatsayan): *Sekhar,* the evolution of an intellectual in the modern social setting; *Nadi Ke Dvip,* the story of a woman's quest for fulfilment.

(8) Jainendra: typical novels are *Suneeta,* conflict between sex and revolutionary ardour; *Tyagpatra* and *Parakh,* middle class life and its conflicts.

(9) Ila Chandra Joshi: *Sannyasi,* and *Pret aur Chhaya.* Both are influenced by Freud.

(10) Upenda Nath Ashk: *Girti Deewaren;* poverty and loss of values in post-war era.

(11) Amritlal Nagar: *Mahakal,* the theme is the famine and its social horrors; *Seth Banke Mal,* a satire on old feudal values.

(12) Dharmavir Bharati: *Suraj Ka Satwan Ghora* (Seventh horse of the Sun), political and social conflict (cross-section of a community).

Short stories of the following authors should yield valuable sociological conclusions:

Sudarshan and Kaushik are pioneers. Prem Chand again is indispensable. Yashpal, R. B. Benupuri, Amritlal Nagar, Amrit Rai, B. S. Upadhyaya, Pahari, Mahendra Asthana, Prakash Gupta, Prabhakar, Mrs. Chandra Kiran, Radhakrishna Prasad, Krishan Chander represent the new movement. The influence of Marxism is apparent, though the reactions vary. Vatsayan and Jainendra Kumar raise philosophical issues from the changing social content.

Among the poets the following should be considered:

Nirala, Dinkar, Vatsayan, Kidarnath Aggarwal, Bacchan (his later verses), Nemi Chand Jain, Nagarjun, Girja Kumar Mathur, and Bhawani P. Misra.

The poems of Sumitranandan Pant and Srimati Mahadevi Verma are not always related to social problems, yet it would be wrong to call them escapists.

There are very few playwrights in Hindi (their absence needs enquiry). But the radio has been a stimulus. The following dramatists require attention: Upendra Nath Ashk (*Adi Marg*), Jagdish C. Mathur (*Konark*), Amritlal Nagar (*Chakkardar Siriyan,* and *Gungi*), V. Prabhakar (*Jahan Daya Pap;* psycho-analytical). Prithiviraj, the famous actor and now a member of parliament, is helping the stage to grow. *Pathan, Ghaddar,* and *Deewar* are three of his famous plays.

Some interesting magazines are coming out. Their influence is greater than what is indicated by their circulation: *Naya Sahitya, Naya Samaj* (monthly), *Prateek* (monthly), *Hans, Nai Dhara, Alochana, Naya* (new) are significant. They contain articles, stories, poems by the writers mentioned above.

Among the critics the following are well-known:

Hazari Prasad Dvivedi, Nagendra, S. S. Chauhan, Prakash C. Gupta, Chandra Bali Singh, Namvar Singh, Vinay Sharma, Dev Raj, and Rambilas Sharma.

(c) *Urdu*

No significant modern social novel in Urdu is known to the author and the friends he consulted. It is worth enquiry. The second noteworthy point is that despite partition Urdu literature in west Pakistan and India are travelling the same road to social consciousness. Similarly, Bengali literature is still common to Bengal and eastern Pakistan. Six Muslims (another report says ten) of eastern Pakistan died in defence of Bengali language, which was their mothertongue. Barring the national note and a slight shift to Islamic symbols and words in Pakistani literature, not much difference exists between the Urdu literary tendencies of Pakistan and India. Probably, the social problems are the same in both. The third point is that some of the best Urdu writers were and are still Hindus. Besides Prem Chand, Krishan Chander, Akhtar Raipuri and Ashk write with equal felicity in Hindi and Urdu. It is not known how long this state will continue. The earlier tendency of Urdu becoming more Persianised and Hindi more Sanskritized is likely to be more pronounced. Meanwhile, however, Urdu writers of India are simplifying their language both for political and sociological reasons.

Urdu literature dealing with social problems is thus mainly confined to short stories, sketches and essays:

(1) Poets of the older generation, e.g., Hali and Iqbal were socially conscious. The national element was stronger in the former than in the latter. Iqbal wrote the famous national song, *Hindustan Hamara,* but his society was Islamic and the problems were human, metaphysical and cosmic. He was against injustice. Akbar Allahabadi, a lesser poet, was piquant in satire. The modern poets are led by Josh Mallihabadi, who is called the poet of the revolution. Other socially conscious poets are Ali Sardar Jafri, Mejaz, Saghar Nizami, Majrooh, Firaq, Anand Narayan Mulla (both Hindu), and Kaifi. Still younger ones are Jazbi, Rahi, Wamiq and Taban (some of them are pen-names). Among the Urdu poets of Pakistan, Faiz, Qusmi and Fyaz are prominent. Urdu poets are almost always progressive in their attitudes. Most of their progressivism is identical with Marxism. (Slightly less so for 'progressive' Hindi writers, one probable reason being their traditional resistances.)

(2) Prem Chand may be said to have set the pattern of modern Urdu short stories. The best writers are Krishan Chander (Hindu), Rajendra Singh Bedi (Sikh), Ismet Chaughtai, Manto, Kartar Singh Duggal (Sikh), A. A. Hussaini, K. A. Abbas, Raisa, S. Zaheer, Suhail, Qurret-ul-Ain, and Ramanand Sagar (Hindu). Urdu stories are effective, compact and delicate in their suggestion of social inequalities. Though they usually refer to Marxist ideology they are essentially humanistic. The conflict of Islamic faith with class consciousness has either not risen, or is defined out by Islam's essential social democracy.

(3) Urdu critics have become active in last two decades. The best known are Kalimuddin, Majnu, Firaq, A. A. Saroor, Ehtesham Hussain, Ali Sardar Jaffri, Abdul Alim, Abid Hussain, Abdulla and Ibadat Barrielvi (Pakistan).

(4) Urdu essayists convey the delicate flavour of the language and the sophistication of Indo-Islamic culture. Their satire is precious. Rashid A. Siddiqi, Kanihya Lal Kapoor (Hindu), A. Bokhari (Pakistan) have written essays full of wit and humour. S. Mujeeb and Abid Hussain write serious essays.

(5) Urdu drama, like Urdu novel, is undeveloped. Some one-act plays have been written by Upendar Nath Ashk, Rajendra Singh Bedi, Krishan Chander (all Hindus), Mujeeb, I. H. Qureishy, and Intisar Hussain. The social angle is prominent despite the form imposed by the radio.

17. *Social Changes and Intellectual Interest*

My only purpose here is to focus attention on certain basic issues and invite discussion. Far be it for me to suggest that my list of issues is exhaustive. After all, their selection is limited by the situational context of the selector's own experience.

The first issue is covered by the conjunction 'and' in the title of the theme. What is the relation between social changes and intellectual interest? Obviously, there is some relation. But unless we have a more precise idea of it than what exists we can neither take action, i.e., frame a policy, nor build up a theory of social action, general or specific. Sociology of knowledge may offer many valuable suggestions, but at present it does not go much beyond the statement of a tenuous connection between the weather of social change and the climate of intellectual opinion. But there are many types of social changes, each with an intensity and a field of its own, and interest is more than an opinion. In fact, there are many interests, though in the title only the singular is used. While it is true that there can be no opinion and no social change without a corresponding interest, the opinion has to undergo an arduous process of transformation to become an intellectual interest. On the other hand, the social interest may as well be as the particular interest of a certain class, either on the saddle or wanting to be on it, without being 'socialised.' Either class may then collect or hire verbalisers and scribblers to generalise the sectional interests on another plane.

In fact, there is no guarantee that one class will adopt only the general interests and no other. Interests are usually fabricated by the group in or on the way to power and passed on to other groups which are quiescent or decadent or to its allies nearby. Pressure-groups and lobbies are facts of democratic life and mould democratic public opinion. The presentation of the philosophy of fascism after the march on Rome and the capture of power is well known. The rest is noise and rape of the masses. Once it was called propaganda; now it has acquired the respectable name of communications.

If this be the inside story of the connection between social change and intellectual interest, that is, of the conjunction 'and,' our problem is to identify and classify social changes in the light of the dominant or the rival group interests and to unfold the procedure of the alliance between the verbalisers, the scribblers and the rationalisers, on the one hand, and the interest-holding groups, strata and classes, on the other. Then follow the problems of various means of communication, crude as radio blasts, flashing headlines, uniforms and flags, or subtle as theorising, symbolising, idealising and all the paraphernalia of the so-called 'intellectual' interests with which we are familiar. The importance of modern technology as the best means of speedy communication arises in this connection. It only serves other ends, and in the process crystallises them so that the sectional interests appear to be social, universal and eternal.

I am excluding the self-propagation of ideas. Faith may move mountains, but not even Cassirer can establish that ideas have moved a mound. Ideas can generate ideas among those who can hold them. There certainly is a history of ideas as such, though our theme is less abstract than that. After a degree of abstraction has been attained, ideas seem to acquire a sort of inner momentum of their own. Faraday to Einstein via Reimann, Minkowski, Lorentz and Planck is a continuous movement with its endogenous impulses; but I wonder if the extraordinary preoccupation with certain aspects of physics and physical nature in the twentieth century is governed solely by ideas. One need not go as far as Bernal in this matter by way of reaction, but his insistence on the close relation between social interests and intellectual interests is valuable. In any case, it need not be dismissed for its original sin of Marxism. It certainly poses problems to be empirically tested and analytically considered.

To put it in concrete illustrative Indian terms: we should find out how far Gandhiji's economic and social ideas have become the intellectual interest of the Indian economists, the Indian bureaucracy or other élite-groups. Simultaneously with it, one would like to know clearly how far the cotton textile factory interests, whose worship of Gandhiji was and is well known, do actively subscribe to his ideas on *khaddar*. On the other side, too, what is the social interest behind the mounting opinion that industrialisation involving larger investment in heavy industries is essential to planning, and which is the group that represents this interest? Once we have more or less precise ideas on these matters, we should be in a position to tackle the larger issue, viz., the connection between ideas and interest. I have a feeling that the intensive study of the social attitudes of groups in various strata will throw light on it.

In a sense, the connection indicated above is abstract, as all basic issues which are hidden are abstract to those who would not see them or to whom they would not be shown. In another sense, it is concrete, particularly, in the illustration given above from the field of economics. He who runs may sense that the flight from the fundamental questions which Gandhiji asked—and here lay his genius—is in some way related to the refinements of economic theory with which most of our academic economists are interested. In other words, the impact may often be negative or escapist. One may notice the same phenomenon in our culture enthusiasts. Not for them the stark, sub-human existence of the majority of our people, both in the villages and cities. The uncultured modes of living of the masses drive our culture-protagonists to the glorification of India's past and the eternal values of our traditions. The many forms of obscurantism including scientism, are interesting manifestations of negative impacts. I do not suggest that the process is conscious and deliberate. Apart from the interests involved in their perpetuation rationalised as ideologies or utopias forward or backward, the very process of the incidence of social change in intellectual interests is very complicated.

Marx himself was aware of the complexities of the relation and mentioned Greek art and literature. He marvelled at his own enjoyment of Greek drama centuries after it was composed, that is to say, at its survival as a source of joy despite drastic social changes[1]:

> Is Achilles conceivable at all in an era of powder and lead? Or for the matter the *Iliad* at all in these days of printing

[1] *Critique of Political Economy*. Engels gave a certain autonomy to law as well. Cf. Engels' letter to C. Schmidt, 27 October 1890.

press and press jacks? Do not song and legend and Muse necessarily lose their meaning in the age of the press? But the difficulty is not that Greek art and epic are connected with certain forms of social development but rather that they still give us aesthetic satisfaction today, that in a sense they act as a norm, as an unattainable paragon.

Taking the cue from the above serious exception one would like to know how far Gandhiji's major ideas have affected contemporary Indian thought, Indian painting, sculpture and music, to what extent his fundamental questions have vexed our modern thinkers and artists. The literature of the twenties and the thirties was to some extent influenced; but it was influenced by Marxism as well, and that too in a derivative way. Peasant and folk arts have also become popular of late, and they may be traced to Gandhism. But quite a good bit of them has an earlier ancestry. The fact of the matter is that we just do not know which intellectual interests connected with artistic creation and appreciation or popularity are Gandhian, pre-Gandhian, or just European intellectual interests, and to what extent. In other words, the sociology of art still remains a dark continent. Let us explore it a little and feel the problems even if we cannot formulate them in a manner that answers itself.

My first proposition is that there are many arts with varying degrees of abstraction catering for, or reflecting, the various levels of consciousness beginning from the phase when it is tied up with the tactile impressions to the rarefied one of audile images. My second proposition is that there are many types of social change differing in extension and intensity. Of course, all the arts are symbolic, because each art is a language. But there are different types and stages of symbolisation. Crafts have one, literature another, painting has a third, and music still another, in varying degrees of abstraction. Of course, they cannot be completely isolated from one another; *darbari kanada* cannot be divorced from the craftsmanship of the *veena*, or from the courtly life; nor can the frescoes of Ajanta and Bagh from the method of pounding and compounding pigments and the life-habits of Buddhist monks. Yet, in its full flowering, each art tends to have its own image—making and symbolisation. Now the question is in what way does a particular type of social change enter into the particular type of symbolisation and image-making? The question still remains unanswered even with the help of Marx and Jung. Consequently, the question of the connection between intellectual interest, ideas and images and symbols, is also to be probed.

I should like to exclude the further complication introduced by personality-structures, but I cannot, for the simple reason that at its passive worst the human personality is the medium through which this intimate process works. There can be no art without the artist, this we know; but for the present purpose we are thinking of the artist's intellectual interests and activities in the social context. The limitation is imposed by the subject matter of our discussion. Now it is obvious that if society furnishes the technical equipments and contents, social change should mean change in them also. This is borne out by history. What the culture-lag will be will depend upon the balance of power between two pressure-groups, the old with the sanction of traditions and the new with their élan.

In these last thirty years or so, the content of Bengali, Hindi and Urdu poetry is reported to have changed. Modern poetic topics are no longer wholly confined to romantic love and all that goes with it, viz., the obliging flora and fauna. Even Tagore wrote a poem on the waste-paper basket. Urban slums, railway engines, telegraph poles, village factions, black crows, factories, slums, strikes, prehistory, the unconscious, all have come in. The intrusion is more apparent in novels and stories. Modern folk-songs and folk-tales, which offer the greatest resistance to such things, refer to the *bideshiya* or *pardeshiya* leaving the village belle by train or aeroplane, and often to the national struggle. Modern Indian painting and modern Indian sculpture, when they are not derivative or nostalgic, are not above lifting a topic or two from the drab common life so long dismissed from the domain of art.

All this is truism. But the points to be noticed are these: (a) the change in content is more in one art than in another; (b) whatever changes are there are not equally reflected in the forms of the arts; and (c) such changes may or may not arise out of any genuine intellectual interest of the public. Thus, for example, the change is most apparent in literature, which is understandable, and least in domestic architecture, which is not understandable at all in these terms. Music, when it is not film music, has not undergone sea-change though the microphone has led to the restriction of the range and the volume of the human voice as well as of the time for invocation, known as *alap*. Some new attempts are being made at orchestration. But harmonisation is yet far away. Knowing the ease with which we have gulped the literary, the artistic, the political, the ideological, the philosophical ideas and institutions of the West without understanding their implications on social change, that is, without intellectual interest, one would have thought that harmonisation would be a mere gnat to swallow. But Indian music is still fighting a rear-ground action. I shall not speak about crafts. I shall wait for the completion of the Second Five Year Plan to see a marked change in the design of our household goods which are reported to have considerable employment potential and expected to check inflationary tendencies.

The next two points, the reflection in the forms of the arts as a result of changes in content brought about by social changes, and consequently by shifts in intellectual interests, are probably more interesting. Instances of new techniques bursting the old form are known, e.g., the keyboard making the tempered scale and harmonisation possible, the use of oil in the change-over to the perspective, ferro-concrete and new processes of welding in architecture. They were rare but are now becoming less rare in this century, thanks to the spread of modern technology and the easier access to its inventions which seem to be tumbling upon each other. These direct impacts, however, have to be translated into social attitudes before we can deal with them as intellectual interests operating as the background of artistic images, symbols and influences.

Scientific attitude, I think, should take the pride of place in the modern age. If it means 'mathematisation', then I am afraid it exercises little influence on modern art except probably remotely in certain refinements of modern music and architecture. On the other hand, if it means the habit of experimentation on the basis of minimum hypothesis and attested facts, then its connection with experimentation with new themes and new forms of art and literature appears to be close. Here, however, a doubt enters. How much of the anti-traditional love of experiments is due to social disruption and the consequent atomisation of the artist as an individual and how much of it is traceable to the spread of scientific attitude cannot be said with certainty.

Of course, it may be argued that it is the scientific attitude that has undermined the ground of social solidarity in absolute values and made for ethical relativity and the idea of patterns without direction, that it has been responsible for the loosening of bonds which had held society together and given a certain unity of space, time and action, in short, a classical order to all the arts, that by destroying faith in the given and the self-evident it has isolated the individual, made him lonely and set him on the search for the valid and the eternal. This line of argument would be plausible if we could forget that Descartes had come to his revelation 'I think, therefore I exist' standing before the old stove and not before the electric heater, that the ballad of the sad cafe may often be a paean to some modern hoodoo, that the search of the lonely creature may be as futile as that of Miss Gummidge or end up in the Anglo-Catholic church or a Trappist monastery, that the scientist, except when he is speaking in the Third Programme or writing a best-seller, is, in his laboratory, not interested in truth but only in the success of his experiment. It is not plausible, however. Therefore, this argument does not quite appeal to me.

A more plausible one could be that both the spread of the scientific attitude and the disintegration of the social order were in the ultimate analysis occasioned, (I would not say, determined or governed) by basic changes in the means and relations of production. If this is conceded without quarrelling about the word 'ultimate,' then the new attitudes may be said to only register the break up of feudal attitudes and the rise of capitalistic attitudes as described by Sombart in the wake of Marx. Be it noted that I am not assigning priorities.

Here arises one big problem: how far is the essence of the capitalist spirit, viz., rationalism with its concomitants of accounting, competition and acquisitiveness, that is, quantity for the sake of quantity, directly reflected in contemporary forms of poetry, sculpture, painting, etc.? Sombart thinks that it does penetrate into culture through strict adaptation of means to ends, that is functionalism and utilitarianism. For aught I know, functionalism has penetrated deeply only into architecture and films. We will speak of the films later on. In an indirect manner, however, capitalism and its suitable intellectual interests do affect culture through competitive advertisements, sales, serialisation, vulgarisation of taste, and certain bourgeois ideologies like 'cultural freedom.' These in their turn affect the art-forms and the subsuming attitudes of the consuming public

(Gasset's barbarians), who are the present-day patrons. So the process goes on in intricate and devious ways. All that I suggest here is that neither the scientific attitude nor the intellectual interests involved in capitalism *directly* affect the forms of art except in a few cases, and that in the long chain of indirect conditionings many counter-influences operate. Like Gaugin or Rimbaud one may run away from 'civilisation,' or one may live in the lonely crowd of Paris as an existentialist or a dadaist. By and large, this desperate situation has not yet arisen in India. But let us not lose hope. Our intellectuals of the cosmopolitan cities may yet seek refuge in the Andamans or the Lacadives or join the League of Frightened Philistines.

Scientific attitude may, however, indirectly mean for certain sections of non-scientists a critical attitude and a sense of facts or reality. These two meanings are reputed to be the undercurrents of a few art and literary movements in modern times. We all know of Leonardo's sketches in his notebook. Zola lived in a mine and collected millions of facts before he wrote *Germinal*. We have all heard of Flaubert's meticulous observation of facts. Pointillism or divisionism in painting started, at least, gained strength from a scrutiny of impressions in terms of the scientific theory of light and colours. There is no use in multiplying instances. Similarly, the attitude of non-acceptance of the given, be it the church or the state of the social order, unless it is tested by individual experience, informs many novels and poems. But, here again, many doubts arise. I would like to think that Dean Swift was not made the critical gnome that he was by his intellectual interests in science, that Karl Marx's devastating criticism was inspired by philosophy, that the literature of protest can trace its pedigree to the mystics and to the doctrines of love, which are certainly earlier than the habits of scepticism generated by science, and further that these sceptical habits do not often go beyond the laboratories or the workshops of scientists.

It is also my belief that the sense of facts is not always identical with the sense of reality, that it is the sense of reality rather than the sense of facts that makes for art vide the distinction between Balzac and Zola. I have also been told that science is not necessarily realistic, that it is essentially abstract and conceptual. I have also noticed different types of realism and social criticisms, one type of which is common in India, viz., romantic realism and idealistic criticism, and owe little or no account to science in any sense of the term. If these doubts are sensible, then I would like to know from you how they can be removed. Does it then mean that scientific attitude is tenuously related to artistic creation? Or does the ikon precede the idea?

Or shall we come to the conclusion that it is not scientific attitude that counts in art and literature, contemporary or otherwise, but just technology, that is to say, new means of communication reaching out quickly to a larger public who may or may not be interested in anything but entertainment, compensation or wish-fulfilment, projection, escape and sublimation, through no exercise of self-responsibility? But is anybody but a handful of backroom boys and some professors of sociology intellectually interested in technology? The public, the artists, the musicians, the writers, the craftsmen, so far as I know, are victims of technology, and the cleverer ones want to make the best of their situation. Of course, big machines have been the themes of poetry and painting. They are also reputed to have become symbols, though they are no more than images. It has also been held that the rhythm of the machines, including their designs, have entered into architecture. The latter is often patent, but the former is not. What relation does the sprung rhythm of Hopkins or the structurisation of Cezanne bear to the rhythm or the design of machines?

If anything, I should think that it is more Bergson's conception of time than the regular beat of the machines that has been responsible for the headache of contemporary artists in Europe. One would like to hear from those literary critics who have had sound training in philosophy if Proust's exercises in telescoping the past into the present, Joyce's inflation of the present, prime and pure existence into a huge balloon of experience, Virginia Wolf's stream with gushes and waves of consciousness, Eliot's preoccupation with temporal intersections and weavings, and the experiments of various authors with memory, stem out of Bergson or the conveyor-belt, or for the matter of that, from Einstein. Whatever the answer, here is an instance of intellectual interest in the philosophy of biology, psychology, anthropology and physics, which is much about all that Bergson and his followers may be said to have generated, having some connection with forms of contemporary art. The relation between psychoanalysis and surrealism in painting and its influence on a few novelists is well known. But my point is this: we do not quite know the mechanism of the influence operating in the artist's mind although the work of detection of influences has become a respectable vocation of art critics. The transmutation of intellectual interest into the process of artistic creation, what may be called personalisation, still remains a mystery. Can we throw light on it by case-studies? That seems to be the modest beginning of a scientific way.

There is one young art, however, into which quite a bit of science and a good deal of current intellectual interests have gone, I mean, the film. In this Film Age, the studio becomes a huge laboratory working in a team. The chemical and physical experiments apart, the spirit is that of a large laboratory rather than an artist's atelier. When each job is specified and specialised, the movement may be continuous, but the continuum is heterogenous. When the camera follows action and action is selected in typical scenes that move like a shuttle between the present and the past, then very little remains of the old plot, the old character, the old unities. What then is the philosophy of time of this new art form?

The following long quotation from A. Hauser's *The Social History of Art*[2] admirably sums up the position:

> The Bergsonian concept of time undergoes a new interpretation, an intensification and deflection. The accent is now on the simultaneity of the contents of consciousness, the immanence of the past in the present, the constant flowing together of the different periods of time, the amorphous fluidity of inner experience, the boundlessness of the stream of time by which the soul is borne along, the relativity of space and time, that is to say, the impossibility of differentiating the defining media in which the mind moves. In this new conception of time almost all the standards of the texture which form the stuff of modern art converge: the abandonment of the plot, the elimination of the hero, the relinquishing of psychology, the 'automatic' method of writing and, above all, the montage technique and the intermingling of temporal and spatial forms of the film. The new concept of time, whose basic element is simultaneity and whose nature consists in the specialisation of the temporal element, is expressed in no other genre so impressively as in this youngest art, which dates from the same period as Bergson's philosophy of time.

[2] Vol. II, p. 939.

On the basis of the complete agreement between film-techniques and the time-categories of modern art, Hauser describes the film as 'the most representative,' though 'qualitatively perhaps not the most fertile genre of contemporary art.' So far so good. But still I wonder if Griffith, Pudovkin or Eisenstein ever knew that Bergson's conception of time was being modified, intensified and deflected by them in their studios.

These are some of the problems which have vexed me for long. I claim that they are not purely personal problems. Let me conclude by entering my final doubt about this impact business: Why is science fiction so unscientific? Why is much of modern literature so unphilosophical in mood? Why is this pattern weaving in music, this design-centredness of abstract art so partially satisfying? Shall I conclude then that nature and art, knowledge and artistic creation are opposites, unmixable, incompatible, irreconcilable, and that the similarity between scientific thought and artistic process is at best a simile?

I would not like to come to that sad conclusion because whatever people may say, personality is still a whole and neither the artist nor the philosopher nor the scientist is a special type of creature, but everyman is an artist, a scientist and a philosopher at a certain time under certain conditions and opportunities. Or am I speaking only of India where, except in urban areas and among urban intellectuals, personality is not yet fragmented? So, allow me to feel that the master key to the theme is personality in its dialectical relation with group-attitudes and interests, both intellectual and otherwise.